M000169823

More Money, More Crime

More Money, More Crime

Prosperity and Rising Crime in Latin America

MARCELO BERGMAN

OXFORD
UNIVERSITY PRESS

OXFORD
UNIVERSITY PRESS

Oxford University Press is a department of the University of Oxford. It furthers
the University's objective of excellence in research, scholarship, and education
by publishing worldwide. Oxford is a registered trade mark of Oxford University
Press in the UK and certain other countries.

Published in the United States of America by Oxford University Press
198 Madison Avenue, New York, NY 10016, United States of America.

© Oxford University Press 2018

All rights reserved. No part of this publication may be reproduced, stored in
a retrieval system, or transmitted, in any form or by any means, without the
prior permission in writing of Oxford University Press, or as expressly permitted
by law, by license, or under terms agreed with the appropriate reproduction
rights organization. Inquiries concerning reproduction outside the scope of the
above should be sent to the Rights Department, Oxford University Press, at the
address above.

You must not circulate this work in any other form
and you must impose this same condition on any acquirer.

CIP data is on file at the Library of Congress
ISBN 978-0-19-060877-4

9 8 7 6 5 4 3 2 1

Printed by Sheridan Books, Inc., United States of America

Contents

Preface and Acknowledgements

THIS BOOK HAS matured over 15 years of research, observations, and data collection I began in 2002 when I arrived to Mexico after studying and working in US Universities. As I began to look at crime in Latin America, standard theories of crime from the north did not quite fit the Latin American scene, and traditional sociological explanations from the south came short of grasping the depth and scope of the emerging criminality in the region.

I decided to undertake the long and painstaking approach of collecting completely new data, to hear the voice of the offenders and the victims, to revise the quality of data governments produce, and to study the public agencies and organizations in as many countries as possible. The study of the crime problem in Latin American needs, first and foremost, good data. My goal has been, and still is, to start by collecting the best possible evidence to assess the extent of the crime problem in the region, and then attempt to respond to this rather simple question: Why is crime growing when Latin America is experiencing relatively good times? This book is the conclusion of this long journey.

Throughout these years, a large number scholars, organizations and public officers have helped me to critically reflect, analyze, and develop different parts of this research. To these students, specialists, and colleagues, I owe a big recognition. I will list here only those who helped me directly in the writing of this book, as I am sure I will leave hundreds that also contributed in many different ways.

I first want to express my gratitude to the two institutions that housed me during these years: CIDE in Mexico City and the Universidad Nacional de Tres de Febrero (UNTREF) in Argentina. Special recognition goes to Carlos Elizondo and Blanca Heredia at CIDE, and to Anibal Jozami and Martin Kaufmann at UNTREF, they have all provided the sustained support and trust I needed in order to undertake this project.

A very long list of scholars and colleagues has contributed to shape and refine the arguments of this book. I apologize for not listing them all. While in Mexico I received feedback from Arturo Arango, Luis Astorga, Elena Azaola, Rafael Fernandez de Castro, Gustavo Fondevila, Edna Jaime, Eduardo Guerrero, Ana Laura Magaloni, Layda Negrette, Gabriel Negretto, Luis Pasara, Rodolfo Sarsfield, Andreas Schedler, Guillermo Trejo, Carlos Vilalta and Guillermo Zepeda.

In Argentina, I benefitted from comments and contributions from Alberto Binder, Fernando Cafferata, Matias Dewey, Diego Fleitas, Hernán Flom, Alberto Fohrig, Sabina Frederick, Gabriel Kessler, Jaime Malamud, Carlos Rosenkrantz, Marcelo Sain, Catalina Smulovitz, Maximo Sozzo and Mariano Tomassi.

A long list of colleagues in the rest of Latin America has contributed in so many ways to sharpen, rectify or reflect on several of the ideas. Carlos Basombrio, Claudio Beato, Ignacio Cano, Gino Costa, Lucia Dammert, Hernando Gomez Buendía, Hugo Fruhling, Jose Luiz Ratton and Mauricio Villegas.

Many colleagues in the US and Europe have read parts or invited me to present my work in seminars and conferences. The conversations and comments from them have made the book better. My heartfelt gratitude to Desmond Arias, Cindy Arnson, John Bailey, Jose Miguel Cruz, Diane Davies, Manuel Eisner, Juan Carlos Garzon, Maximo Langer, Fiona Macauley, Vicky Murillo, Wil Pansters, Jenny Pierce, Peter Reuter, David Shirk, Wesley Skogan, Mark Ungar, Silvio Waisbord, and Laurence Whitehead.

Special recognition goes to four colleagues in the USA who provided invaluable guidance, particularly in data collection: James Lynch, Janet Lauritsen, Allan Beck, and Michael Rand. Also to colleagues and organizations in the region that have helped and facilitated the data collection: Ipsos in Costa Rica and Honduras, CESC in Santiago de Chile, the public defendant office in Peru, Jose de Jesus Filho and the Getulio Vargas foundation in Sao Paulo, Luis Amaya and Universidad Francisco Gavidia in El Salvador, and many Latin American officers at several organizations: Natalie Alvarado, Lina Marmolejo, Arnaldo Posadas, Andres Restrepo, Ana Maria San Juan, Rodrigo Serrano, Jorge Srur, and Karelia Villa.

This book includes original data from dozens of surveys I directed and that were funded by several foundation and organization. I particularly appreciate the support from the Hewlett Foundation, the MacArthur Foundation, Open Society, as well as the generous support of the Inter-American Development Bank (IADB), the United Nations Development Program for Latin America (UNDP), Comisión Andina de Fomento (CAF), the Woodrow Wilson Center for Scholars, and Organization of American States (OAS) security section. I thank UNDP, CAF and IADB for letting me use data from the surveys they have partially funded.

My gratitude goes to my research assistants and colleagues. At CELIV special thanks to Christian Arias, Diego Masello, Ana Safranoff, Antonella Tiravassi, Carolina Bologna, and Carolina Tripodi, and at CIDE to Adriana Villalon.

A special acknowledgment goes to James Cook at OUP for enthusiastically lead this project, and for the care that he took this book the best it could be. Five anonymous reviewers offered valuable input. I thank them for the feedback that helped me strengthen my argument. I also thank Emily McKenzie and the staff of OUP as well as Raj Suthan and the production team for the very professional assistance.

Very special thanks go to my sons, Martín, Adriel, and Eyal, who through the years have survived my "ups and downs" and were always on my side. Finally, I dedicate this volume to Monica, in so many ways, this is also her book. Her guidance, encouragement, trust, and critical support has made the development and completion of this project possible. She has been and still is my anchor, my mentor, and above all, my true love.

More Money, More Crime

1

Crime and Prosperity

A LATIN AMERICAN PARADOX

THE LATIN AMERICAN crime rate is now the highest in the world. While crime in Europe, the United States, and Asia is declining, homicides, thefts, and drug trafficking are reaching unprecedented levels in Mexico, Brazil, and Venezuela, as well as in Central America. Even traditionally low-crime nations such as Uruguay, Argentina, and Chile are in the midst of a crime wave that has resulted in social unrest and political turmoil. Fear of crime in Latin America is much higher than it was in the 1980s, and it now represents the primary social concern in most countries of the region (Dammert and Malone 2006; Kessler 2009). This outbreak of violence and fear has significant social, economic, and political implications that are transforming the social fabric and the daily lives of millions.

Even as crime has risen, Latin American nations have enjoyed a substantial economic expansion along with improvements in social indicators such as poverty and inequality (ECLAC 2016; UNDP 2015; Lustig et al. 2013; Lustig 2015). Most countries that emerged from dictatorships and civil wars in the 1980s have also succeeded in establishing new electoral democracies that have elicited greater citizen participation, higher trust in institutions, and more political transparency (O'Donnell 2004; Whitehead 2002; Hagopian and Mainwaring 2005; Mainwaring and Perez Liñan 2014). Despite these major economic and political gains, crime and violence have surged (UNDP 2013; CAF 2014; World Bank 2011). Governments and state institutions have been unable to mount effective law enforcement or vigorous criminal justice systems to address rising rates of criminal violence (Fruhling 2012; Brinks 2008; Beato 2012; Hinton 2006; Pasara 2014; Ungar 2011; Arias 2006, 2017; Lessing 2017). State legitimacy combined with economic development, major reductions in poverty and inequality, the availability of jobs, and overall prosperity were expected to improve public safety. Instead, the region has witnessed a steady deterioration in public security. Therein lies the Latin American paradox.

This book explains why crime has increased in all Latin American countries over the past twenty-five years, making this region the most crime-ridden and violent in the world. It also examines the social, economic, and political implications of this outbreak of violence. I posit a theory of rising crime, arguing that criminality has increased because it became a lucrative enterprise for many citizens, entrepreneurs, and public officials. These individuals have reaped the benefits of expanding demand for the illicit goods supplied by criminal networks. Diminished state capacities further reduced their systems' abilities to deter crime as police forces, courts, and prisons have been unable to adequately adjust to effective democratic governance. Increased criminal activity and the failure of institutions to contain it have created a vicious circle of high crime and weak state capabilities.

The research presented here documents crime patterns and trends in eighteen Latin American countries. It shows that crime is not static by any means; it is a dynamic and evolving trend throughout the region. This book presents three novel and very important contributions to the field. First, it shows that criminality is a regional problem rather than a problem for a few nations. Second, it shows that economic prosperity and weak law enforcement must be considered together to explain the upsurge of crime. Third, it provides a nuanced argument that accounts for different trajectories of violence and criminality in the countries of the region, transcending narrow economic, political, or legal explanations.

This introductory chapter lays out the foundations of the book. After a summary of the argument, it briefly reviews rising crime in the region, the disparate trajectories of different countries, and different interpretations of spiraling crime. It then turns to the toolkit that will be used throughout the book and that will serve as driving concepts for this study: the business of crime and the concepts of crime equilibria. It ends with brief remarks on the research method and data sources along with a short overview of the chapters to come.

Crime and Prosperity

Since the 1990s and into 2014, most Latin American countries enjoyed economic growth, reduced poverty, and lower inequality. As prosperity has grown, however, so also has the consumption of stolen goods, such as cars, cellular phones, and computers, the sale of illegal substances, production of illicit drugs, and smuggling. Car thefts, abductions, and human trafficking have all increased as well. Violent crimes such as homicides, robberies, and kidnapping have doubled in several countries and in a few cases, even tripled over a single decade. As fear of crime increased, citizens have searched for individual solutions such as the building of gated communities, relocation after displacement, and migration (Caldeira 2001; Dudley 2012; Carrillo 2009).

Crime has become a successful business that creates major money-making opportunities for criminal "entrepreneurs" who have no trouble recruiting low-income youth. Countless young people with dim prospects for social mobility have joined gangs and cartels as foot soldiers, and although hundreds of thousands have been killed and millions jailed, crime has not yet abated (Adams 2011; Auyero and Berti 2013; Kessler 2004; Misse 2006; Briceño Leon et al. 2012). Citizens have reacted by demanding an effective response from their governments, but with few results. Citizens' trust in the police has diminished; judges have been blamed for the "revolving door" syndrome; and governments have remained unable to produce effective responses to cartels and criminal organizations (Bagley and Rosen 2015; Garzon 2008; Lessing 2017; Villalobos 2014; Maihold and Jost 2014).

Prosperity has enhanced consumer demand. Some of the resold goods coming from theft and other illicit activities are channeled to secondary markets organized and supplied by illegal rackets. Outdated criminal justice systems have been unable to meet the challenge posed by these new profitable criminal enterprises. Poor law enforcement and the large profits from illegal activities combine to create a vicious cycle or a perverse equilibrium of high crime and an ineffective state. As organized crime has grown, governments have done little to promote sustainable upward mobility or to help law enforcement agencies become more prepared to deter criminality. In Latin America, prosperity has unintentionally fueled criminality.

What started with simple theft and low-scale trafficking has swelled into large secondary markets of stolen goods, extortion, kidnapping, human trafficking, and unprecedented homicide rates. This transition from the low crime equilibrium (LCE) that exists everywhere in the world to the consolidated high crime equilibrium (HCE) predominant in many Latin American nations is the result of the collapse of legal deterrence. This book analyzes both the development of crime as a business in the region and the inability of state agencies and officers to successfully contain it. Once HCE is established, it becomes extremely difficult to dismantle. This partially explains why many Latin American governments have failed to substantially reduce crime.

Although most countries have experienced similar trends of spiraling criminality, some have reached catastrophic rates of violence while others have managed to keep crime at moderate levels. Even among the countries that have witnessed a spike in crime, the intensity of violence and its speed of growth have differed from place to place. This book explains why the equilibrium between the money to be made from crime and the weakness of the criminal justice system has triggered a rapid rise in crime and a sharp intensity of violence in some countries, but only a moderate upswing in others. I conclude that when major opportunities for illegal profits appear, strong institutions and capable states are needed to neutralize the perverse effects of rising violent crime. "More Money, More Crime: Prosperity and Rising Crime in Latin America" explains why opportunities for illegal revenues have grown and why state effectiveness has, for the most part, lagged.

This book has a strong empirical foundation based on the best available data on the subject to prove the bold assertions it makes. Some of the data was either gathered especially for this work or is used here for the first time. It includes information from inmate surveys in six countries and fifteen victimization surveys that the author has directed, as well as other data sets collected to respond to the questions posed here. Although there is a vast amount of information, the arguments are presented in a simple way to help the reader grasp the concepts and the stories behind the data. I use this data to exemplify trends, to provide insight on the complexities of the problems, and to examine arguments from a human perspective.

Unlike crime in the United States and Europe (Rosenfeld and Messner 2009; Blumstein and Wallman 2006; Van Dyjk et al. 2005; Zimring 2007; Levitt 2004; Braga and Weisburd 2010), crime in Latin America has not subsided. Decades of economic prosperity might have created even greater tension in the social fabric. The region's recent history shows that economic growth does not improve public safety unless governments protect their citizens and promote genuine social inclusion.

The Explosion of Crime

Crime rates in Latin America are among the highest in the world. The homicide rate for the region in 2013 was 20.5 per 100,000, higher than that of Africa (12.5), Europe (3.0), Asia (2.9), and the United States (4.3) (UNODC 2014) One-third of homicides worldwide in 2015 happened in this region, which is inhabited by less than one-tenth of the world's population. In addition, the region has eight of the world's ten most violent countries (Amnesty International 2016). Although some countries suffer more than others, highly violent crime is endemic across the region.

Most countries have higher crimes rates today than they did two decades ago with homicide rates in the 2010s much higher than they were in the 1980s, despite year-to-year fluctuations.[1] Not only does Latin America have the highest violent crime rates in the world, these rates have been growing. In addition to homicides, other predatory crimes such as extortion, kidnapping, human trafficking, and aggravated assault have grown sharply over the last years.

The dramatic upsurge in homicides has been mirrored by rising rates of property crime. Homicides are understood as the best measure of criminality, though this must not obscure other simultaneous processes. Despite the lack of reliable data, it is clear that there has been an astonishing increase in property crime affecting hundreds of millions of people throughout the region every year. In one-third of Latin American households at least one person has been robbed over the last year; more than one million cars are stolen each year; and millions of cell phones, digital devices, and other personal belongings are stolen and sold on all-too-accessible secondary markets.

The rise in property crime is perhaps greater than the increase in violent crime. Although we lack credible information for the 1980s and 1990s (and for some countries, even for the 2000s), thefts have climbed significantly. From valuable personal items on the street to large-scale robberies of weapons, oil, and mining products, such as iron, gold and copper, the level of theft in the region demands an explanation as to its drivers.

The literature on criminality in Latin America does note that the region's homicide rate is the highest in the world but has neglected to address two important questions: Why have crime rates risen in Latin America while they have fallen in most of the world? Why has crime spiraled in most countries of the region? In addition, this literature has overlooked the significant increase in property crime that has had a con-siderable impact on the crime surge. Addressing these issues can provide insight on the regions' high murder rates and rise in violence. In this book, whenever possible, I attempt to present data on trends in violence, robberies, and illegal drug trafficking to show the distinctive nature of crime in the region. The overarching goal of my research is to explain what has happened in the region over the last twenty or thirty years to account for this upsurge in crime.

The Study of Crime in Latin America

In spite of the clear evidence of rising crime in the region, there is a sur-prising lack of general theories to account for it, although researchers from several disciplines have put forth different interpretations. Legal scholars, for example, have blamed the lack of fit between the old legal institutions and legal norms and the new patterns of criminality. Over the last three decades, law students have studied malfunctioning criminal justice systems (CJS) and proposed reforms to criminal procedure codes to improve their ability to address the crime threat.

Sociologists studying crime have focused on adverse social conditions: poverty, inequality, unemployment, and poor living environ-nments were thought of as conditions for breeding deviance. Evidence was generally poor for the region and hypotheses were rarely tested. Data was hard to come by and most studies have been based on ethnographies or other qualitative approaches.

Empirical research and scientific studies have only started to emerge in recent years. Influenced by schools of criminology in North America and Europe, researchers have begun to collect data (or use other available information) in an attempt to explain the high rates of crime (World Bank 2011; UNDP 2013). Scholars and experts from the field have discussed approaches such as strain, control, social disorganization, hot spots, de-terrence, and opportunities and choice (Briceño León 2008; Beltran and Salcedo Albarán 2003; Arias and Goldstein 2010; Sozzo 2014; Di Tella et al. 2010; Davis 2010). Their studies have provided insight into how criminality differs in cities or state/provinces (Koonings and Krujit 2015; Moncada 2016); the effect of urbanization and demographic trends

(Muggah 2012; Beato 2012; Escobar 2012); income inequality (Fajnzylber et al. 2002); the impact of gangs (Rodgers 2009; Cruz 2010; Bruneau et al. 2011); poor policing and ineffective courts (Azaola and Ruiz 2012; Arias and Ungar 2009; Cano 2012; Hinton 2006; Sabet 2012; Duce et al. 2009; Hammergren 1999; Fruhling 2009); failed incarceration policies (Antillano et al. 2016; Salla 2007; Bergman et al. 2014; Macaulay 2013); weak institutions (Snyder and Martinez Duran 2009; Yashar 2012; Bailey 2014; Cruz 2011); the political and social effect of victimization (Bateson 2012; Dammert 2012; Gaviria and Pages 2002); and many others. In spite of new and interesting results, this research has yet to provide a comprehensive account for the upswing in crime over the last two or three decades.

Poverty and income inequality have always been acute in the region. Unplanned urban developments and slums were very common in the 1970s and 1980s, yet the crime rate was only a fraction of its current level. Illegal drug trade has been high since the 1980s but until very recently only Colombia, and maybe Peru, have been seriously affected by crime stemming from illegal drugs. Broken communities and families, weak labor markets, drug trafficking, and poor law enforcement have all been found to correlate with rising criminality. Some studies have successfully identified these effects for single countries or cities, yet none of them present a general theory on the crime wave of the past decades.

In this book, I incorporate some of this front-line research and add new data to offer a general explanation for the rise in crime. My framework responds to such important questions as: Why do weak labor markets create more crime in certain contexts but appear to have few effects in others? Why do drugs and drug trafficking push homicides to very high levels only in some countries? Why do crime trends vary among cities with a similar urban makeup? Under what conditions can poverty and uneven income distribution further boost crime rates? In short, I present a general equilibrium model to make sense of disparate outcomes from otherwise similar or shared conditions.

This perspective accounts for several correlates of crime predominant in the region: the adverse social conditions of the underclass, rapid and unstructured urbanization, economic liberalization, weak law enforcement, corruption, and many others. I suggest a dynamic interplay of these and other causes to explain the triggering determinants of high crime. I claim that correlates of criminality can produce crime if they are triggered by social and economic conditions or are neutralized by constraining factors.

This interplay between incentives and constraints allows for multiple outcomes: stable or unstable equilibria of high or low criminality.

We will now turn to two features of crime in the region that have not received enough attention in the criminological literature of Latin America: the role of countries and the demand for crime.

The Role of Countries

Criminology research has overwhelmingly focused on the individuals who commit crimes, the offender who deviates. Most studies examine the conditions that make some individuals likely to embark upon criminal careers, and this has been the dominant paradigm within the discipline.[2] A second line of research has focused on the physical place and the characteristics of the acts of crimes, in other words, on the location and on the criminal events. The Chicago School focused on sites and locations within cities as criminogenic factors (Park et al. 1925; Shaw and McKay 1942). More recently research on rational choice, crime as opportunity, and the routine activities perspectives, (Cornish and Clarke 1987; Clarke 1997; Felson 1998; Weisburd et al. 2006), focuses on the places that enable criminal acts (the dark street block, the tavern, the street corner where drugs are sold, the "hot spot," etc.)

To summarize, research has traditionally centered on two dimensions, that is, the individual and his or her surrounding space (people and places). However, country is a significant third dimension that has received little attention in mainstream criminology. In the pages to come, I examine several national factors that help explain why under similar circumstances, there is a variance of possible outcomes. Of course, this perspective does not discredit decades of criminological research emphasizing state capacities (law enforcement) or correlates of crime (inequality, poverty, development, and so on). In this book, I introduce the "fixed" country effect as an additional dimension that has not received sufficient attention in the literature of the region.

History and local circumstances greatly affect people's concern about crime. For example, criminal violence in Colombia or Honduras cannot be explained by analyzing people and places alone. Thefts in Argentina and Venezuela are about more than diminished state capacities to deter crime, while the chaos produced by drug trafficking in Brazil or Mexico cannot only be explained by geography or chance. The criminogenic factors developed in the rich criminological literature play out differently in each national setting, yielding disparate outcomes. This book delves precisely into such outcomes.

The "Demand" for Crime

A second distinguishing feature of crime in Latin America, and perhaps its distinctive hallmark, is that over the last three decades, there has been a steady demand for the illicit goods that produced large illegal economies.[3] Overwhelmingly, the crime literature on "people and places" has focused on the "supply side" of criminality, on the individuals responsible for the crime and their surroundings. Yet very little attention has been given to the forces, interests, and incentives that crime has produced. This is somewhat puzzling given the large evidence and the number of studies underway.

Take, for example, the case of illegal drugs, typical of crimes where supply follows demand. Since many individuals want to use drugs and states prohibit them, a black market is born where certain individuals (manufacturers, dealers, bosses, and others) seize on the opportunity for profit. In Latin America, other illegal markets have also developed. Although some of these markets are historic, they have expanded significantly and the use of violence has increased since states have failed to contain them.

Illegal economies create criminal markets. A strong demand for cheap goods coupled with complacent authorities invites a perspective that not only focuses on the supply component of crime but also the dynamics created by the demand for illicit goods. This demand diminishes a state's ability to deter crime; leads to a rapid replacement of any offenders who are arrested; boosts violence when different criminal rackets compete with one another; creates more corruption; and so on. Subsequent chapters will provide additional perspectives to the study of crime from the demand side in order to better grasp the complexity of criminality in the region.

Toward a Perspective on Crime in Latin America

A distinctive feature of crime in Latin America is that it has affected all eighteen countries included in this study.[4] All have either a high crime rate that has persisted over time or have experienced an upward trend in criminality. However, the intensity of crime, its depth and extent varies significantly between countries or cities. For instance, the crime rates of both Chile and Venezuela have at least doubled since the early 1990s, yet there is a big difference between these two countries, as homicides in the latter country is at least twenty times higher. Similarly, Buenos Aires, Argentina and San Pedro Sula, Honduras experienced a noticeable spike in crime over the same period, yet the differences between these two cities are as astonishing as in the previous comparison. Although most Latin American countries share a similar trend of rising crime, the rates of intensity vary greatly. This begs for an explanation.

A general equilibrium approach allows for a flexible perspective to account for differences in trends and intensity of rising crime in the region, but the presence or absence of constraining variables has affected its growth rate and its intensity. The spread of crime as profitable business has created incentives for individuals or groups to get involved in illegal activities and to sometimes commit very violent acts. At the same time, variations in the quality of law enforcement have reduced or accelerated criminal activities. This general equilibrium is based on forces that accelerate crime and factors that restrain them, and this book analyzes these variables. Initial thresholds matter. Crime rates in Chile did not rise in the same way as they did in Venezuela, because in Chile the initial threshold of crime was very low and in Venezuela relatively high. As I will show in chapters 4–6, high thresholds of criminality put in motion epidemic mechanisms of crime contagion and spread that are hard to reverse. Once a country has reached an HCE, it takes an enormous amount of effort and resources to reverse course. Colombia is the typical example. Despite major investments in public security, major institutional reforms, the development of perhaps one of the best police departments in the region, and major investments in public security, this country still has one of the highest crime rates in the world.

The Business of Crime and Its Effects

Over the past three decades, crime in the region has thrived since becoming a profitable business.[5] Theft, the sale of black market goods, and drug trafficking have enriched criminal "entrepreneurs" who in turn employ hundreds of thousands—and perhaps millions—of people. The devastating effect of this growth has reduced states' ability to deter offenders from embarking on a criminal career, while also stimulating a diversification to other criminal activities. For example, the proliferation of weapons—an instrumental factor in the growth of crime—has led to a rise in the number of interpersonal crimes. Similarly, international drug trafficking has directly contributed to the growth of domestic drug markets.

The dramatic upswing in criminal behavior across the region can be seen in the rising trend in robberies and the trafficking of goods on illegal markets. I argue that the constant rise in homicide rates in many Latin American countries is a consequence of this phenomenon and can be mainly attributed to the rising number of acquisitive crimes and profit-driven felonies. As the crime business expands, violence increases, and the everyday life of residents is affected in myriad ways.

This poses several questions. Why has crime risen in this region and not in the rest of the world over the past thirty years? Why have certain countries in the region been more vulnerable to profit-driven crime than others? What explains the fact that among countries with similar contexts some have witnessed higher spikes in crime than others? Why have crimes that are not profit-driven proliferated more in certain countries than in others?

In this book, I propose a theoretical approach to address these questions. I argue that the growth of criminal activity, especially sudden growth in crime rates, reflects a breakdown of a social equilibrium. This collapse results in new opportunities that change the strategic decisions of new and existing players. In order to identify the conditions that lead to the breakdown of a social equilibrium, it is necessary to examine the social, economic, political, and cultural context in which crime occurs. A stable LCE shifts to a violent HCE at the point where the demand for illegal market goods is greater than the ability of local law enforcement to neutralize such demand, and organized crime grows.

Since the 1980s and 1990s, various factors have contributed to a rise in the demand for black market goods throughout the region. Institutions entrusted with protecting the legal economy were negligent about enforcement, and the authorities tolerated the black markets, or were unable to control them. The historic status quo in most Latin American countries—moderate deterrence and a modest quantity of illegal activities—began to wear thin. The illegal players who had once had a subordinate role in the economy began to expand their "business" following the debilitation of law enforcement institutions after the end of military rule. This is the starting point of this book: the social, economic, and political context in which crimes occur. The emphasis here, in other words, is on the crimes and not on the criminals, whose motives and actions are the focus of classic criminology.

Countries with high levels of criminality (Colombia, Guatemala, Mexico, and Venezuela) had unstable equilibria where violence spiraled out of control after a breakdown of the existing order. Countries with relatively low levels of crimes (Chile, Uruguay, and Peru) remained stable or the intensity of violence grew only slightly. What distinguishes the latter countries is that their law enforcement institutions had some capacity for deterrence. However, questions remain. Why did the equilibrium breakdown in certain countries and why were they more susceptible to vicious cycles of violence and high crime levels than others?

I argue that the rise in this illegal market business gradually generates a critical mass of individuals who are willing to get involved in crime. As long as the capacity of law enforcement and social institutions remains strong, LCE (i.e., few crimes or many property crimes but with modest violence rates) can usually be maintained. However, if the push for crime exceeds this capacity for law enforcement, the old equilibrium begins to crumble and violence and crime rise abruptly. There is normally a tipping point for the equilibrium; this can be caused by a rise in the "demand" for crime (e.g., drug trafficking or profits to be made on new criminal markets) or by the inability of law enforcement and social institutions to deter crime (e.g., weak states that subsequently collapse, institutions that are unable to adapt to new challenges, a dangerous rise in corruption, etc. see Levitsky and Murillo 2009). In summary, crime waves and HCE can be produced either by the overwhelming profits that acquisitive crime generates or by inadequate criminal justice institutional performance. Malfunctioning law enforcement must meet a rising demand for crime to reach a tipping point. Usually a new equilibrium emerges when there are changes in the status quo among preexisting forces, that is, the previously established crime equilibrium.

There are many examples to support this hypothesis, with Mexico being perhaps the most recent and notorious. Although Mexican law enforcement institutions have been corrupt and weak, they were able to adequately contain crime during the regime of the PRI (Institutional Revolutionary Party), the party that held power for seventy-one years. During the transition from Presidents Carlos Salinas and Ernest Zedillo (PRI) to President Vicente Fox, (PAN, National Action Party), the rise in street crime gradually exposed law enforcement's inability to guarantee public safety. At the same time, changes in the cocaine trafficking market and the tempting profits of this and other illegal drug markets led to a rise in crime that the old regime was unable to confront. In other words, as the drug trafficking business changed, criminals took advantage of the country's institutional weakness to destroy the pre-existing fragile balance, paving the way for the current wave of violence in some regions of that country.

A similar situation is found in Colombia where a historically weak state facing legacies of violence dealt relatively well with moderate levels of crime during the late 1960s and early 1970s. This delicate balance unraveled when the cocaine business—and later, the heroine business—began to put pressure on law enforcement agencies. Violence in Colombia exploded in the 1980s and grew dramatically in the 1990s.

Venezuela, and particularly its capital city of Caracas, also has spiraling crime rates but offers an example that is not directly tied to drug-trafficking. With a population of 30 million people, the country reported 7,000 homicides in 1999 and more than 20,000 in 2011. Notable here is the systemic collapse of law enforcement, which was unable to address even a "reasonable" number of street crimes due to other political processes, including the demise of the old regime in the 1990s and the decline in law enforcement capacities under the Chavez administration. Common theft, assaults, and even homicides arising from minor conflicts, grew exponentially because perpetrators were almost assured of impunity, which diluted the effect of deterrence—for a large number of Caracas residents, violence could be used to resolve everyday conflicts without repercussion. Violence spread among potential miscreants and pushed the country to a tipping point, not as a result of a sudden growth in the demand for crime but because of a collapse in enforcement.

Chile is at the other extreme. Its residents are known for upholding the law and its law enforcement officials are efficient and professional, and the country is characterized by compliance and low levels of crime. However, Chile has also suffered from a rise in crime, with more thefts and car robberies, as well as a domestic drug market that has doubled in size in a single decade. It is easy to understand why Chile has not followed the path of Colombia or Mexico, but less easy to understand why Santiago has not followed the path of Sao Paulo or Belo Horizonte, two Brazilian cities that, as happened in Santiago, have at least doubled the rates of robberies and drug consumption. (This book explores these types of questions.) Although crime has grown in Chile, violence has been contained, there is not a critical mass of actors who are working to subvert the existing balance (at least not for the time being), and no new tipping point has been reached. This can be attributed to several variables, including the strength of law enforcement and social institutions, which set a bar too high for most individuals to reach the decision that "crime pays."

Uruguay and Costa Rica each have LCE, though Costa Rica has not been able to close its borders to the path forged across Central America by drug traffickers, and pressure is growing and threatening its virtuous and stable balance characterized by low criminality and reasonably stable institutions. In Uruguay, street crime has grown but the threat of organized crime is low, and law enforcement institutions are still perceived as moderately effective.

Finally, it is useful to compare the cases of Honduras and El Salvador to Nicaragua, one of the poorest countries in the region. Like Honduras, El Salvador, and Guatemala, Nicaragua is on the main path of northbound drug shipments, and it has witnessed a significant rise in criminal violence (more than 10 homicides per 100,000 inhabitants). However, the homicide rate in Honduras is seven times higher and that of El Salvador and Guatemala is four or five times higher. Why hasn't Nicaragua collapsed in the face of the demand for crime the way its neighbors have? The answer would appear to be found in an LCE that so far has held its ground. Honduras and El Salvador rapidly gave in to the pressure of drug traffickers and *mara* gangs because their LCE was very fragile. In Nicaragua on the other hand, relatively low criminal violence and respected institutions sustained a virtuous equilibrium in one of the poorest countries in the region. Drug trafficking, though, could eventually undermine this equilibrium, making it difficult to predict this country's future (Rodgers 2007). However, like Costa Rica and Panama, Nicaragua has thus far demonstrated its ability to avoid the tipping point beyond which crime begins to mushroom.

This general perspective on crime equilibria leads to five working propositions. First, the crime equilibrium ex-ante is critical in the response of the system to a new threat. The study of the growth and strength of illegal markets cannot be isolated from the study of the institutional and social arrangement at the time the exogenous shock occurs. Balances can be weak, as in the case of Mexico under the PRI, but unless there is an important threat, they can hold crime at bay for decades. In other cases, robust equilibria can be undermined by the shock of a booming black market.[6]

Second, the breakdown of an equilibrium can be triggered either from growth in the demand for crime (Colombia) or from weakened enforcement (Venezuela)—there is no single cause, crime develops wherever opportunities and conditions are favorable. For example, a market for stolen goods such as cell phones can evolve where there is high demand for these products or when there is no effective enforcement tool to keep this market from developing. In both cases, the profit from stolen articles and the inability of law enforcement agencies to keep them from being stolen are both conditions that allow a stolen cell phone market to develop. Usually, demand for illegal goods grows where legal enforcement is weak, yet this is not always the case.

Third, any good with a high demand and restricted circulation (or a product that is banned altogether) has the potential to stress the existing equilibrium. Holland has the highest rate of bike theft in the world due to the sheer number of bikes in the country (Van Dijk et al. 2008, 71). However, the sale of stolen bikes is higher in Eastern Europe where control of this black market is more lax than in Holland. The greater the difference in cost between a legally purchased good and a stolen product, the more incentive there is to steal it. For example, in the United States, most used cell phones sell for very little, but not iPhones and iPads, which are often bought second hand; as a result, iPads (and most tablets) are more frequently stolen than cell phones. Both high demand for a banned product or a high cost for a legal good in high demand put pressure on LCE. This pressure, and the resulting illegal activity, can be neutralized with effective detection tools and criminal sanctions or through price policies such as tax breaks and import tariff cuts.

Fourth, violence is not always a part of black markets. All countries have markets for stolen goods, drugs, and other illegally traded goods. The level of violence is determined by the nature of the crime equilibrium. If the secondary markets for stolen goods are large or mature, there is a high level of theft, which is generally associated with growing levels of violence. In contrast, reduced demand for stolen goods generates a smaller supply (fewer thefts) and thus, less violence. However, state control over illegal markets is the most important factor in keeping violence in check (Naylor 2009). When state institutions such as the police keep crime under control for their own profit (as in Rio de Janeiro in the 1980s, Mexico under the PRI, and Buenos Aires province during the 1980s and 1990s), levels of violence remain relatively low. However, when police are no longer able to keep criminal gangs under control, violence spirals.

Fifth, levels of violence are also related to the subjective costs of joining illegal markets, and these costs are directly related to a state's deterrence power and ability to punish those found guilty of crimes. When the likelihood of detection and sanctions is high, markets tend to be more fragmented and violence tends to be low. This can be clearly seen in the drug markets in the United States and Western Europe, which remain relatively peaceful and without any dominant groups (a major drug cartel operating in Chicago or London would probably be quickly dismantled by law enforcement agencies). On the other hand, when deterrence is low, the business of crime is likely to become concentrated in fewer hands and the struggle between powerful groups will spur violence. Under HCE, organized crime tends to concentrate in fewer but more powerful groups and fights among syndicates can also trigger out-of-control violence.

This book argues that profit-driven crime has bolstered criminality in Latin America. Both penal law and the criminal justice systems of the region focus on deviants and those who violate the law, and have proven to be inadequate in addressing this new wave of crime. Little has been done to fight profit-driven crime through pricing policies, bank regulations, tax cuts, municipal licenses, and so on. Instead, the burden for dealing with crime has fallen on police, judges, and wardens, who have achieved modest results at best. Law enforcement agencies currently appear unable to address growing illegal economies. This is the current state of affairs.

The Notion of a Crime Equilibrium

In this work, I argue that crime environments matter since they create the conditions needed for crime to thrive and reduce the effectiveness of law enforcement. This section develops a central concept for this book: the idea of crime equilibria. I begin by introducing the idea and explaining its logic, and go on to develop important properties of crime equilibria. Chapter 6 provides a comprehensive description of HCEs.

Introductory Concepts

In its simplest form, in game theory, an equilibrium results from the strategic actions of two or more individuals who interact frequently (as in a game), producing an outcome that reflects the best strategy for each given the decisions that others have made. Very importantly, this creates the expectation that there is no better strategy, and thus generates incentives for players to keep playing the game in the same way as they have in previous iterations. Therefore, when everyone expects a particular outcome, this outcome will most likely be the equilibrium. If a game has only one equilibrium, that will be the outcome.

The concept of an equilibrium helps to frame the relationship between delinquents and authorities. When offenders believe that authorities will fail to detect them, crime is very likely to spread. Conversely, if most would-be delinquents believe that law enforcement agencies effectively target law-breakers, the crime-rate will, most likely, be low. Take corruption, for example. If offenders believe that they can escape arrest with a bribe and if police take bribes from offenders and then release them, the most likely outcome is persistent corruption and a stable equilibrium of high criminality. The type of equilibrium usually shapes the expectations and behaviors of players.

The crime equilibrium I develop in this book is not the typical equilibrium resulting from equally ranked players who voluntarily make decisions to cooperate with or defect from each other. I argue that many potential delinquents adopt a conditional strategy based on refraining from crime to the extent that they trust that other delinquents are being caught and punished. Therefore, for LCE there is no escape from the Hobbesian solution—that is, that a strong Leviathan will punish a large share of offenders.

A given crime equilibrium implies a large variation in the number of offenders in each country and denotes a relationship between offenders and law enforcers, where the latter prevent X amount of crimes but Y numbers of crimes are still committed.[7] This creates societies with low-crime environments or with high- and violent-crime ecologies. In the former, successful law enforcement agencies can target new offenders and imprison them in relatively high proportion, signaling to potential delinquents that they are likely to get caught and punished, and thus deterring many from embarking on a criminal career.

Nevertheless, a crime equilibrium transcends the proportion of offenders within society: more specifically, it characterizes the balance between the demand for crime and law enforcement's effectiveness at limiting criminal opportunities. Weak law enforcement can still produce an LCE to the extent that the opportunities for profiting from crime remain low. And a strong state might not suffice to deter crime if criminal opportunities abound. Multiple equilibria are thus possible.

Contagion

The framework of crime equilibria is extremely important for understanding why certain countries or cities rapidly shift from a low- to a high-crime environment. This is because a given crime equilibrium puts contagion mechanisms in motion. Contagion—the way in which would-be offenders make rational decisions to imitate the behavior of others—crucially explains how a critical mass of delinquents is formed and why changes in law enforcement rarely neutralize the powerful effects of imitation. In order to grasp its effects, let us start with an example.

Let us assume that in country A, the police solve half of all car thefts. Would-be offenders in country A would, therefore, have a likelihood of one in two of getting caught, and this high probability of capture would deter many potential carjackers. Now let us assume that the police in country B solve a quarter of such cases. The likelihood of arrest is now one in four, and the lower risks of apprehension are very likely to lead to higher crime rates. But, how much higher? I believe that this question has not been properly answered, because the effect of contagion has not been adequately addressed.

To keep crime low, countries A and B need to keep potential criminals on the fence rather than engaging in crime, but country A has a much easier task than country B. Let us assume that undecided, potential delinquents in country A will follow the likelihood of detection and only one in two would-be offenders will commit crimes, while the undecided in country B will opt for crime at the given rate of three out of four. If the level of enforcement is maintained, country A will keep the same crime rates from t_1 to t_2 (those arrested are replaced by newcomers at a replacement rate similar to the detection rate), while country B will experience a steady increase in its crime rate (33% growth from t_1 to t_2). However, due to the endogenous effect, at t_2 the odds of detection in country B would now drop (falling from 25 to 17 percent) and therefore would-be offenders will engage in crime at a much higher pace because the odds of arrest decrease substantially at t_2 (five out of six in this case). All things being equal, the contagion effect spurs crime very quickly and enforcement agencies have a hard time keeping crime at bay.[8]

In short, the dynamic evolution of contagion diminishes the enforcement capabilities of country B and an ever-greater number of law enforcement agents are needed to keep up with the endogenous increase of offenders. As enforcement diminishes only a strategy of overwhelming force can mitigate the spread of criminality.

Contagion, of course, spreads faster when there are greater opportunities to profit from crime. Market conditions, such as the difference in price between legal and illegal goods, the overall demand in comparison with supply of goods and services, and large gains from predatory behaviors, among others, affect a delinquent's decision to engage in criminal behavior. The individually perceived effectiveness of law enforcement agencies is weighed against the perceived gains from crime. Both effects are important.

Law Enforcement

Law enforcement effectiveness, as mentioned, is endogenous to the distribution of offenders. In societies with few offenders, enforcement is on average more effective, for at least two reasons: first, all things being equal, more resources can be allocated to detecting and punishing a smaller number of offenses. Second, and perhaps most importantly, the probability of contagion diminishes. Thus, the perception of effective enforcement fosters a virtuous equilibrium in public safety.

A central claim I make is that under LCE, deterrence is more effective and therefore a government's commitment to law enforcement becomes more credible. Enforcement is easier in LCE because strategies can be geared to convincing potential offenders that sanctions are highly probable. But under HCE, enforcement must first convince offenders that they are more likely to get caught and punished (while in truth, they are unlikely to get caught). Since there are so many offenders in HCE, the law enforcer is always working to catch up. In LCE, the enforcer's job is containment; under HCE, the enforcer must wage an all-out war to transform the status quo. Comparable enforcement measures lead to higher compliance when the enforcer can select targets more efficiently. In short, laws and regulations are perceived as unenforceable in HCE. Under LCE, conversely, enforcement enhances general deterrence and contributes to the image of an effective administration.

Once a country reaches HCE, the ability of law enforcement to gain control of crime dramatically diminishes. Colombia, Guatemala, El Salvador, Honduras, Venezuela, and recently some states of Mexico demonstrate the inability of law enforcement agencies to contain criminality and the adverse odds they face in attempting to reverse course once a critical mass of offenders have been established.

In sum, this analysis suggests several important consequences:

a) The lower the probability of detection in a given country, the faster the contagion. Impunity rates matter.
b) Failing to contain criminality at the onset of a crime wave will lead to rapid deterioration of public security. Once law enforcement begins to lag, LCE is challenged and the likelihood of containing criminality is jeopardized.
c) Given the speed of contagion, enforcement capacities need to increase just as rapidly to keep public security at its previous levels. This rarely occurs, because it is extremely costly.
d) Under HCE, potential offenders often multiply exponentially while law enforcement capacities rise at a much slower pace, even under the best-case scenario, and the gap between law enforcement and criminality continues to widen.

Critical Mass and Tipping Point

Very few outbreaks of violence produce HCE. Many countries and cities face challenges from criminality and control them while maintaining LCE. Why does one case turn extremely violent while others do not? First, countries that fall into HCE begin with high rates of crime. For instance, Chile and Uruguay are unlikely to fall into HCE because the equilibrium between criminality and law enforcement (supported by social policies and mores) is heavily tilted toward low criminality. Conversely, many areas in Brazil (particularly the northeast) could rapidly spin into out-of-control violence (if other conditions are met) since they already face instability. HCE usually evolves from an unstable equilibrium. The progression is from LCE to crime instability and only then to HCE.

An adaptation of the classic mechanism developed by Schelling (1978) on the critical mass that tips the point to HCE is very persuasive. LCE can turn into HCE when there is an accumulation of offenders who engage in crime because they perceive the odds of detection to be low and opportunity for crimes (such as drug trafficking, control of areas, and so on) are very high. In short, HCE might deteriorate very quickly, but it usually starts in an environment that is already suffering from high crime. Very often, a high homicide rate (at least 15 to 20 per 100,000), hundreds of extortions, and dozens of kidnappings, when accompanied by a high level of impunity, precede the rapid deterioration of an already fragile equilibrium. Once a tenuous equilibrium of high crime and poor law enforcement is challenged by new crime opportunities, it tips the balance towards a self-sustaining HCE.

The widening gap between crime and law enforcement capacities is typical and endogenous to HCE and explains the violent outbreak of high criminality in a span of only a few years in the region. Mexico slipped into high criminality in just three or four years, Venezuela in less than a decade, Honduras in less than seven years, and Colombia over the course of a decade (the 1980s). These countries had histories of entrenched violence (another variable studied in this book), but today HCE can be triggered at a surprisingly rapid pace.

Summary

Equilibria are understood as generally stable environments of high or low crime that signal to potential offenders whether to start a criminal career or refrain from doing so. Of course, other variables play a significant role (demand for illicit goods, the state of the economy, labor markets, the strength of the community, opportunities for crime, and so on), yet *ceteris paribus*, HCE establishes the conditions for the rapid spread of crime. Contagion and enforcement effectiveness are endogenous to the crime ecology and therefore have a large impact on the equilibria: they accelerate criminality in HCE and allow crime to be kept under control under LCE.

What Determines the Type of Equilibrium?

Several scholars have recently analyzed crime using similar frameworks. Bailey (2014) and Dudley (2016) have laid out a bimodal distribution or a "trap" where crime and enforcement capacities are in a stable status quo, which I refer to as equilibrium.

I argue that crime in the region is the outcome of two overarching processes analyzed in this book. The first is related to the opportunities for crime produced by high profits and the second, the capacity of regulatory agencies and law enforcement to keep offenders in check. These two processes together are responsible for the equilibrium in any given location.

The paradox of Latin America is that as the standard of living in the region rose, so did crime. With the proliferation of illegal drugs and stolen cars and other goods, some offenders got involved in extortion, kidnapping, human trafficking, and many other illegal businesses, producing more violence in the process. Law enforcement agencies either did not intervene or were mostly ineffective at the beginning; in some cases, they even became partners to criminals although in others they successfully fought against rackets.

The equilibrium perspective does not indicate the direction of causality. An upward trend in crime up might result from strong bottom-up pressures such as strong demand for illegal goods, including drugs, or from poor law enforcement that crumbles in the face of moderate pressure (for example, the case of the *maras* in Honduras). Once the equilibrium becomes unstable, it endogenously triggers other pressures that affect the nature of crime environments and put other mechanisms (contagion, the effectiveness of enforcement) into motion.

Despite the inability to determine the direction of causality, the merit of this approach is that it allows for a variance in outcomes. Take car theft as an example. The strong demand for used car parts derives from a large increase in car ownership over the last few decades that in turn created incentives for criminal organizations to supply these growing markets. Close to one million cars are stolen each year in Latin America and most end up dismantled for auto parts or sent overseas and sold. This booming market also exists in many other parts of the world, but its size differs significantly. Moreover, the level of violence exerted during carjacking also varies (very low in Chile, very high in Venezuela). In Brazil, hundreds of thousand vehicles are stolen each year, but proportionally to the number of vehicles owned, fewer cars are stolen than in neighboring Paraguay. Other considerations such as established marketing networks, the type of demand, corruption, political tolerance, and many others affect the level of theft and violence, which determines whether these crimes develop under LCE or HCE. In summary, the type of crime equilibrium varies according to the makeup of markets, politics, law enforcement capacities, and so on.

The types of pressures markets exert merits special attention. For example, all countries experience a domestic demand for gasoline, yet large quantities of gas are stolen from pipes and refineries to supply gas stations (at a fraction of the cost of legally acquired gasoline) in only a few countries (such as Mexico and Colombia). Why do such thefts occur very often in Colombia but only sporadically in Ecuador? Because existing rackets and distribution outlets in Colombia have made it hard for law enforcement agents to dismantle them, by using part of the proceeds of their booming stolen gasoline business to encourage corrupt police officers to take bribes and look the other way, and helping to consolidate these rackets in the process.[9] It is not just the demand for cheap gasoline that helps the HCE to develop, but a mature system of profit-making from selling goods in high demand along with a relatively mature criminal infrastructure.

In summary, high or low criminality results from several factors that produce a given equilibrium. Goods in high demand generate opportunities for offenders to supply such goods from illegal sources, thus creating illegal networks. This market demand becomes an important stressor for law enforcement capacities over a given period of time. To the extent that there is a sustained demand over time and law enforcement is already weak, crime as a business expands. In this process, new players got involved, violence increases in the absence of major consequences, and new businesses develop (extortion, kidnapping, trafficking, and the like). That is the nature of HCE.

On Violence and Crime Equilibria

The scale of violence is the great divide between LCE and HCE. Yet, in spite of low violence, there are two types of LCE: a) relatively low rates of criminality (such as Chile or Uruguay) and b) significant levels of property crime yet moderate rates of violence (Argentina and Peru). The rising trend of criminality notwithstanding, these LCE countries have avoided (at least thus far) the kind and magnitude of violent crimes typical in certain Mexican states—Colombia, Venezuela, and the Central American northern triangle.

In fact, what truly distinguishes HCE is the prevalence of highly predatory crimes. Not only are homicides rates notoriously higher in HCE, but the number of abductions, extortions, and large-scale robberies (such as in mining or oil), and kidnappings for ransom is also significant. On the other hand, these predatory crimes are very uncommon in LCE. Countries with large numbers of property crimes might face a serious deterioration in public security if law enforcement capacities are not capable of preventing their increase

In this book, I show that once a LCE unravels and rackets begin to emerge, a serious threat of crime diversification develops. In addition to drug smuggling and trafficking, gangs embark on other predatory and violent crimes for profit. The strategic use of extreme violence also correlates with a demise of deterrence, a rise in corruption, astonishing rates of impunity, and the consolidation of organized crime. This is rarely observed in LCE.

In short, some LCE countries might have above average numbers of property crimes, yet they avoid high rates of violence and the spillover effect into highly predatory crimes. The social fabric and some levels of effective deterrence prevent serious deterioration. Yet, this LCE may become unstable if crime opportunities remain and expand.

Implications

Several important implications of this approach provide a toolkit or useful concepts for the study of crime in the region. Here an initial set is listed, though several others will be noted throughout the book[10]:

Dual equilibria. There are multiple crime equilibria on a continuum from low to high levels of crime. Even HCE countries such as Venezuela or the Dominican Republic have significantly different rates of crime, as do LCE countries. Neighboring Argentina and Chile are both relatively low-crime countries, yet crime in Chile is nearly half that of its neighbor. I suggest the use of the dual-equilibria approach for two main reasons. First, it is a simpler concept to grasp and second, low- and high-crime equilibria are usually stable, whereas equilibria in the middle of the continuum are unstable and transitional. As we will see, the context in most countries can be defined as stable LCE or HCE.

Measurement. High or low crime is of course an abstract concept. Criminologists use rates of crime to measure a state of affairs that can then be compared with other units (cross-sectional) and across time for the same unit (longitudinal). In this context, high or low crimes are arbitrary constructs. For the purpose of analysis, I will use homicide rates as an initial measure of criminality and when data is available, I will use victimization rates as a proxy for property crime.[11] A rate of 10 homicides per 100,000 is used here, as this is the cutoff used by the World Health Organization (WHO) to determine whether homicides are epidemic in a country. For my analysis, any countries with less than 10 homicides per 100,000 are described as LCE; countries with rates between 10 to 20 are transitioning to instability; and countries with rates greater than 20 are in HCE.

Range. The geographical distribution of criminality shows that a given country has multiple regions, several with high crime and many others with low crime. Crime rates in northeastern Brazil are three to five times those of the southern Brazilian states. Mexican states along the Pacific (Guerrero, Michoacán, and Sinaloa) have ten times more crime than the eastern Atlantic states (Campeche and Yucatán). This uneven distribution of crime is also found in cities. In Rio de Janeiro, safe and crime-ridden areas exist side-by-side, just a few blocks apart as they do in Tijuana, Mexico, Bogota, Colombia, Ciudad del Este, Paraguay, and in many other cities. The concentration of crime in particular areas affects the type of equilibria. Given the uneven distribution of crime, the unit of analysis should be states or cities, but because of the lack of data, I use countries as the unit of analysis (see pages 31–32).

Stability. Crime equilibria are usually stable. Subsequent chapters will show that most countries settle on high or low levels and transitional states are unstable and subject to rapid change. Stability is a property of crime equilibria, yet evidence shows that moving from LCE to HCE is much more common than moving in the other direction. Only a handful of cities and a very few countries have successfully transitioned from HCE to LCE in less than fifteen years

Policies. One important merit of my approach is that it offers policy recommendations pertinent to each country or city's place on the equilibrium continuum. For example, countries or cities should be especially careful at the beginning of a crime wave and should significantly increase their enforcement capacities to avoid serious deterioration. In addition, different policies are required to bring crime under control in HCE than in LCE. Deterioration from LCE to HCE may occur relatively quickly, but restoring LCE can take years or even decades.

Crime Equilibrium: Profits, Organized Crime, and Politics

The bimodal concept of crime equilibria developed in this book is presented for the purpose of simplicity. No country lives purely under high or low criminality, since the heterogeneous distribution of crime and the longitudinal changes within countries or cities create a variety of crime equilibria. High or low equilibria are ideal-type models, because they tend to be stable and produce specific characteristics generally shared by countries with a specific crime environment. LCE and HCE differ markedly in the level of profits that rackets earn, in the type of criminal organizations that operate in those countries, in the type of engagement and connections between organized crime and politics, and in the efficacy of the criminal justice systems.

Crime is also affected by the level of development and the concentration of organized crime, by the involvement of politicians and political campaigns with criminal bosses, and by the deterrence ability of police and courts with regard to offenders and criminal networks. Under LCE, organized crime is weak and still developing; confronted by still-powerful police departments and courts, criminals make a profit but are held in check and rarely have the resources and profits to dictate policies. Crime bosses may contribute to political campaigns and may bribe officers, but they do not have entire departments of police or prosecutors on the payroll. Under HCE, the opposite is usually true.

Profits. Profits from illegal trade and crime obviously differ in different equilibria—adjusted for the size of the economy. In the world of illegal drugs, the participation of local rackets in their transshipment to high-income countries produces an extraordinary level of profits (see chapter 6). This creates pressure that undermines LCE and may tilt it to become HCE. Mexico is the obvious example of this, where organized crime overtook the leading role Colombians in the 1990s when Mexico became the main supplier of drugs to the United States. But the opportunity for large profits is not always a crime stressor. Peru and Bolivia, two of the three largest producers of cocaine, are LCE countries, not HCE. It is the opportunity for profits combined with particular politics, criminal justice institutions, and criminal rackets that produce HCE.

Profits for organized crime are largely determined by the type and aggregate demand for illegal goods, by competition within illicit markets, and by the difference in price between legal and illegal goods. For example, stolen cell phones are very common to every country in the region and are resold at well-known outlets. The selling price of a stolen mobile phone is determined as a fraction of the cost of a new, similar brand in legal outlets (usually between one-third and half of what new brands cost). Competition is intense among robbers, distributors, and sellers. It is relatively easy to steal a mobile phone in public places, there are a number of distributors that refurbish and readapt the phones, and there are literally thousands of individuals selling stolen cell phones at train stations, on public squares, and at many other outlets. This large fragmentation on the supply side of this business produces small profits for most players.[12] Conversely, the stolen car industry is much more profitable. New auto-parts are expensive and heavily taxed; the risk premium for robbers is high;[13] and dismantling cars for parts requires expertise, a strategic location, and cover up. Therefore, there are fewer players and profits are larger. Demand is steady and there is some concentration in this industry.

In short, the type of illegal business, the scope of opportunities, and the levels of fragmentation are decisive determinants of the profits generated by illegal trade. Under LCE, fragmentation is greater, the scope is smaller, and violence is reduced to a minimum.[14] Conversely, under HCE profits are larger and some level of concentration empowers rackets. More importantly, as will be seen throughout the book, crime diversifies, generating very large gains for criminal organizations. Illegal drugs, car theft, extortion, grand-scale theft (precious metals, gasoline), and human trafficking generate large revenues and present crime opportunities for organized units (small and large), which proliferate under HCE.

Organized crime. The business of crime requires organization. The scale of operations dictates the size of groups and their structure. Chapter 5 will provide an in-depth analysis of organized crime in the context of HCE. I argue that criminal organizations are usually small and interdependent units that cooperate or fight with one another for a share of the profits. Rather than big illegal firms, the business of crime resembles what Reuter (1985) defined as "disorganized crime," in which small units execute different tasks (theft, purchases, distribution, sales, money laundering, and so on), where each is autonomous and replaceable[15] and mostly operating as free market units. There is a misperception that powerful cartels are large corporations with thousands of people working for them. Rather, there are thousands of people in small independent units that interact for a fee, a share of the profit, or a cut of the goods traded or shipped.

Organized crime is well established under HCE and incipient under LCE. In HCE countries, several organizations have consolidated power, having established extensive networks with police, businesses, and politicians. These groups usually enjoy a short period of high visibility and hegemony until they are replaced by other groups, though the trade never disappears entirely. Some groups branch out to other businesses (for example, from illegal drug shipment to mining and oil theft rackets).

In LCE countries, groups are even more fluid, organizing for one or more deals and later disappearing, and their leaders are frequently engaged in legal enterprises, mixing them with some illegal businesses, making genuine efforts to cover up illicit trades.

Politics and crime. Only a handful of evidence-based studies have examined the role played by crime in supporting politicians and in particular, electoral campaigns, yet anecdotal evidence points to a fluid exchange between crime bosses and executive officers (Trejo and Ley 2016; Casas-Zamora 2013). This topic deserves a full research program that I unfortunately was unable to undertake in this study, though I do mention their importance in the following paragraphs.

The most noticeable aspect of the recent upsurge in crime is that most criminal activities have developed under the watchful eyes of the authorities. Most citizens in the region know where cell phones are refurbished or where stolen used car parts are resold in any major city of Latin America. No serious policy against money laundering has been implemented and very few people have been indicted for such crimes over the last few decades, despite the fact that billions of dollars from illicit trades circulate in the region. Governments seldom intervene in such cases and most illegal activities are tolerated in the region, as long as they do not produce unmanageable violence. However, the outbreak of large-scale violence occurs at a stage where governments have already lost their ability to regulate (in HCE). In short, authorities usually attempt to intervene when it is too late.

Why do governments tolerate certain levels of rising criminality? Two hypotheses might explain such tolerance: benefits and/or forbearance. Benefits are, of course, bribes and kickbacks paid by bosses and agents of the underworld to policemen, prosecutors, and/or politicians in return for the right to sell, trade, distribute stolen goods or manage illegal businesses, including stolen property. This is hardly new. Historically, leading rings in business rackets such as prostitution, gambling, and illegal alcohol have paid mayors, police chiefs, and even ministers kickbacks to turn a blind eye to their trade (see for example Astorga 2005; Caimari 2012; Picatto 2001). In the last two decades, major leaders of shadow markets in large cities, illegal drug dealers, and even cartel bosses have paid off mayors and police departments in Mexico, Colombia, and Venezuela. At a lower level, such practices also occur in Brazil, Argentina, Peru, and almost everywhere in Latin America.

Beyond the kickbacks, there is some disturbing evidence that governments have used money from the underworld to fund political apparatuses and electoral campaigns. Incumbents entrusted with granting licenses, police departments, and regulatory agencies, have used their discretionary power to tolerate illegal trade in exchange for illegal revenues channeled to different political purposes: from simple clientelism all the way to political campaigns.

Forbearance, a concept developed by Holland (2016), can also persuasively help to explain authorities' tolerance. Forbearance means that mayors, political bosses, and even ministers and presidents purposely bypass enforcement for the sake of other public benefits, or even more precisely, to avoid the perceived high costs of enforcing the law. Although this concept was developed for administrative violations, it can also be applied to crime tolerance because consumption of illegal goods brings benefits to incumbents. Latin American scholars can barely fathom the social and political costs for rulers of dismantling markets such as La Salada in Buenos Aires, Tepito in Mexico City, or the "cachinas" of La Victoria in Lima, or any others. In fact, since all major cities in the region have several shadow markets where illegal and stolen goods are resold with almost no auditing or control by authorities, there is a virtual green light for these operations. Why do authorities refrain from intervening?

Rulers opt not to intervene for several reasons, and not only because they may receive a kickback or funding to help them in the next election. They recognize that the cost of resistance will be very high, that these illicit markets are highly developed and that law enforcement agencies might be in collusion with the criminals. One additional and important consideration is the perceived benefits that these marketplaces and the stolen goods bring to consumers. Millions of Latin Americans buy drugs, stolen auto parts, digital devices, and even pirated films and stolen clothing in these outlets. Prices are only a fraction of the cost of new branded goods, and overall consumption therefore increases. In short, these shadow markets abet consumption, yielding political benefits for incumbents. So, it is perfectly rational for politicians to rely on forbearance for multiple reasons and in chapter 4, I will expand on this hypothesis.

In summary, illegal markets develop under the watchful eyes of authorities. The leverage of crime entrepreneurs under LCE is limited. Authorities tolerate low-scale criminality, particularly when violence remains under control. Conversely, under HCE, some territories within countries or specific trades and business are controlled by powerful bosses that either boast a strong bargaining position or directly challenge the authorities.

In the following chapters, I present initial evidence on the plausibility of the two-equilibria perspective. I do not fully test a theory but rather present a road map that attempts to unravel the rise in crime in Latin America over the last decades. Future research should analyze several of the following hypotheses with better data.

Data and Method
Sources and Data Collections

The empirical study of crime in Latin America is cumbersome, because data at the individual level is very difficult to collect. This book, however, is built on strong empirical foundations. In order to provide satisfactory answers to my research questions, I assembled a completely new database collected from the different projects detailed in the appendix, including four inmate surveys in Mexico and five inmate surveys in other countries (Argentina, Brazil, Chile, El Salvador, and Peru).[16] In these surveys, a sample of approximately one thousand randomly selected convicted inmates responded, in personal interviews, to more than two hundred questions targeted at gathering information on issues ranging from socio-demographics, patterns of personal involvement in criminality, due process of law, and prison conditions. Six thousand responses provide rich information on drugs and crime, the amount of profits made in property crime, corruption, recidivism, and many other topics.

I also use information from victimization surveys I directed, including eight in Mexico and one in Argentina, along with other surveys on which I worked, and initial evidence from two surveys of judicial file collections in Mexico and Argentina (of one thousand cases each), as well as other individual data from surveys. In addition, data from the LAPOP (Latin American Public Opinion Project) and Latino-barometer, from large organizations such as UNDP (United Nation Development Program), UNODC (United Nations Office for Drugs and Crimes), World Bank, and many others have been used. In short, I assembled data from multiple sources, both at the aggregate and individual level. I believe that this book is the first in the region to use such widespread data sources, the culmination of fifteen years of extensive research in the region.

Due to a lack of solid information, this book has both a descriptive and analytical goal. I present basic information on crime and citizen security from a regional perspective and for each country, and I offer a compelling argument to explain the current state of affairs.

The data contained in public records varies in quality between countries in the region and is not always validated or reliable. Unfortunately, most countries have devoted little effort to information gathering and processing. In addition, some countries have purposely kept analysts from accessing public security records—see appendix for several pitfalls in public data access in the region.

While most studies on crime and public security in Latin America focus on single countries and cities, this book attempts to explain a general trend of crime and the different intensities of rising crime within an overall regional pattern. By offering a comparative perspective, I attempt to identify variables that account for similar trajectories of criminality, as well as for different outcomes.

The evidence in the following chapters is presented very clearly in the form of graphs and tables. I forgo in-depth statistical analysis in favor of simplicity, fluidity, and a less-technical presentation. Only few simple multivariate models are included; readers who are not familiar with regression analyses can skip them without missing the core argument. The broad evidence is compelling and speaks for itself.

On Spatial Heterogeneity and Crime Equilibria.

Crime is highly concentrated. As chapter 2 will show, this is as true in Latin America as elsewhere. Most homicides and property crimes are heavily concentrated in a few cities or areas, while most regions have very few criminal events. Such uneven distribution of crime poses several challenges to the analytical tools developed in this book. Most of the data presented has been collected and reported at the national level, inhibiting an encompassing regional or city level comparison. This book will present comparative data at the local level whenever available, yet most information describes national trends.

The organizing principle of crime equilibria is still very useful for two main reasons. First, although criminal events are concentrated in given areas, the market dynamics of acquisitive crimes and the development of illegal markets transcend the local places where crime incidents occur. Second, criminal justice institutions are encompassing organizations that usually transcend local areas and in Latin America are better thought off as provincial or rather national organizations. In summary, despite the heavy concentration of crime incidents in blocks or circumscribed areas, their impact and/or possible containment are rather national than not.

Book Structure

The book is organized in three parts. In part I I describe the trends and magnitude of criminality and evaluate several hypotheses for the rise in crime in the region. Chapter 2 presents a comprehensive evaluation of violent and property crime trends in the region over the last twenty-five to thirty years for the eighteen countries of Latin America. It presents short and long time series for different countries and describes different type of crimes. This chapter discusses the merits of transcending homicide data to really assess the social transformations in the region and describes the book's dependent variable.

Chapter 3 discusses theories of criminology in light of the region's current crime wave by testing common assumptions of causes of criminality with data from the social, economic, and political realms and shows that there is only very weak evidence to support the claims that poverty, inequality, and lack of development explains crimes. This chapter shows the need to transcend these assertions and focus on the mechanisms that erode norms, the lack of social mobility, and the institutional weaknesses that result when larger opportunities for illegal profits arise. I contend that a complex process of multiple variables is better suited to explain the current situation in the region.

Part II studies the demand side of crime in Latin America. Chapter 4 begins to develop the core argument of the book. It shows that new secondary markets for stolen goods supplied to segments of societies willing to increase consumption emerged along with prosperity. After reviewing several of these markets—such as for cellular phones, digital goods, and firearms—this chapter exemplifies this trend with an understudied yet very important crime driven market: the car-theft industry.

Chapter 5 studies the impact of narcotics. Although this book transcends drugs and claims that crime is an encompassing industry that produces significant illegal profits, illicit drug production and trafficking are of course very important components of crime in the region. This chapter presents the debate on drug production, trafficking, commercialization, and consumption within the conceptual framework of this book and analyzes the effects of law enforcement strategies on the consolidation of cartels or the fragmentation of gangs, as well as the indirect effect of US drug policies.

Chapter 6 studies the HCE and provides an explanation on how, in most countries, crime for profit has evolved into very violent criminality, while also providing an overview of the organizations that specialize in different types of crimes. Special attention is drawn to the important spill-over effect this structure has in crimes such as extortion, kidnapping for ransom, and human trafficking, as well as the increasing level of violence they have produced. By tracking the trajectory of offenders as reported in inmate surveys, this chapter documents individual transitions from in-itial engagement in low crime to predatory "high-rent" criminality, and examines the importance of criminal groups in organizing criminality. An in-depth study of the case of Mexico that fell to HCE in a five-year span exemplifies the devastating effects of criminal diversification in weak states.

Part III examines Criminal Justice Systems (CJS). Chapter 7 focuses on the limited success of police in improving public safety, surveys different police structures and strategies to fight crime, and shows that in most countries law enforcement agencies have been unable to lead effective anti-crime programs. This chapter shows that police forces usually reacted slowly and erratically against rising crime, did not develop strong infor-mation systems to fight organized crime, and lacked the support of cit-izens due to police corruption and involvement with citizen repression under past dictatorships.

Chapter 8 studies courts and prosecutor´s offices and systematically analyzes one of the critical and understudied topics in the region: impu-nity. This chapter shows that the numerous penal reforms in the region have welcomed strong protections of rights but have relegated the devel-opment of effective prosecution and administration of justice to curtail criminality, weakening the CJS against stronger criminal organizations. This chapter uses information collected from six thousand inmates to doc-ument court and prosecutorial processes, from the "voice" of the indicted, and contrasts this information to the "official voice" of the courts of law.

Chapter 9 reviews the role of prisons in Latin America and the meager impact they have in containing crime and imposing deter-rence. Based on evidence from inmate surveys and from official records, this chapter shows the failure of rehabilitation, incapacitation, and of deterrence that backfire once the released inmates get back to the streets and crime. It analyzes the "substitution" effect, whereby offenders locked up in prisons are replaced by others in the criminal networks, so that incarceration barely makes any impact in the overall reduction of crime, particularly under an HCE. Original data depicts the poor state of prisons in the region, the link between inmates and "outside" crimes, the high rates of recidivism, and many other indicators of poor prison policies.

A concluding chapter summarizes the core argument of the book and presents guidelines to better address the challenges of criminality in Latin American nations. The Appendix provides details on the data.

PART I

Crime in Latin America, Trends and Magnitude

This first part begins by introducing and describing the dependent variable of this book: the rise in crime in Latin America. Data on region-wide criminality is presented in chapter 2 to portray changes in crime over the last three decades. Longitudinal information is used as much as possible to show that crime rates have grown, though not uniformly across countries. In addition, I assembled data, from different sources, on acquisitive, domestic, and highly predatory crimes to show the patterns and trends that are peculiar to Latin America.

Chapter 3 then expands on crime patterns in the region and analyzes correlates of crime. Rather than testing criminological theories, this chapter presents data and examines the association of crime with other social, economic, and political variables. Both chapters present new and rich evidence to prove that the crime wave in Latin America is large and that it begs for a comprehensive explanation.

2

Trends and Patterns in Latin American Criminality

Introduction

This chapter presents a comprehensive evaluation of trends in violent and property crime across the region over the last twenty-five to thirty years. It briefly assesses data-collection methodologies and discusses the merits of going beyond homicide numbers to assess the magnitude of the rise in crime in the region.

Latin America is one of the most violent regions in the world. It holds forty-seven of the world's most violent cities;[1] two-thirds of its countries exceed the World Health Organization (WHO) threshold for an epidemic of violence;[2] and victimization rates rank among the highest on the planet.[3]

While most regions in the world have seen a reduction in violent crime over the last two decades, Latin America has seen not only climbing rates of all crimes but also a rise in homicide rates, which is perhaps more puzzling. The homicide numbers are astonishing: close to 150,000 people are murdered in the region every year. Most remarkable, homicides are declining everywhere in the world but in Latin America (Table 2.1).

This puzzle is the topic of this book. During the last two decades, crime rates have been falling in Western Europe, the United States, Canada, and Oceania and even in sub-Saharan countries in Africa, while in Asia and the Far East homicide rates remain relatively low. In Eastern Europe and countries of the former Soviet Union, homicide rates surged after the fall of communism but began to decline in the mid-2000s. Only in Latin America and some African countries are homicides alarmingly high.

Table 2.1 Global homicide rates, 2000 and 2012

		Total homicides		Rate × 100,000		Change %
		2000	2012	2000	2012	2000–2012
Africa[a]		27,951	27,240	11.1	8.9	−19.8
Americas	USA-Canada	16,075	15,302	5.1	4.3	−15.7
	LATAM[e]	110,791	141,759	19.9	23.2	16.6
Asia[b]		106,623	94,161	4.6	3.5	−23.9
Europe[*,c]		9,703	6,084	2.6	1.3	−50.0
Oceania[d]		414	295	1.7	1.0	−41.2

[*] I exclude Russia and Ukraine to keep the focus on Latin America. These two countries have shown dramatic drops in the number of homicides. In 2000, Russia had over 41,000 homicides and Ukraine 3,800. In 2012, these numbers had declined to 13,120 and close to 2,200 respectively.

[a] Kenya, Malawi, Sierra Leone, Namibia, South Africa, Uganda, Algeria, Morocco, and Egypt.

[b] Countries excluded due to lack of data: Tajikistan, Turkmenistan, Uzbekistan, North Korea, South Korea, Brunei, Cambodia, Indonesia, Laos, East Timor, Afghanistan, Bhutan, Iran, Maldives, Sri Lanka, Armenia, Bahrain, Iran, Jordan, Kuwait, Lebanon, Oman, Qatar, Saudi Arabia, Turkey, and the United Arab Emirates. For some countries, such as India, China, and Japan, first available data was used from either 2002 or 2003. The most recent reporting year for most countries was 2012. When these numbers were not available, 2011 reports were substituted. In short, for some countries comparisons are for less than twelve years, but always at least nine years.

[c] Not included: Monaco, Luxemburg, Lichtenstein, San Marino, Kosovo, Montenegro, Malta, Andorra, Bosnia, Bulgaria, Russia, Ukraine, and Lithuania.

[d] Australia and New Zealand.

[e] Eighteen countries including the Dominican Republic. The first year reported for Bolivia was 2005. Data for Brazil is from Waiselfisz (2012).

Source: UNODC (2013) unless otherwise stated. Some countries were excluded because data were unavailable.

This chapter presents basic information on crime in Latin America: comprehensive data sets on crime trends collected for this book. Since data quality is very poor in many countries, different sources as well as varied types of information are presented to give the reader a general understanding of regional trends. Some countries have compiled decent information on major crimes since the 1990s while others have only recently started to collect such information. In a few countries victim surveys have been conducted for more than a decade, while others have none at all. For several countries data validity is problematic. Despite this, however, the evidence is overwhelming: the crime rate is very high and continues to rise.

This chapter is organized as follows: first, a brief discussion on the merits of studying crime in the region, focusing on changes over time;

second, a study of homicide and its characteristics; third, a study of the sharp rise in property crime; fourth, other crimes; fifth, the rising threat of illegal drugs.

A Brief Note on Trends and Data

A comparative analysis of homicides and property crimes represents a true challenge. The lack of single data sources and of shared criteria for categorization and validation of data makes the study of crime across countries difficult.[4] In the appendix I address several of these problems, describe the data used, and discuss the validity of the sources.

The study of crime trends has received plenty of attention in recent years (Goldberger and Rosenfeld 2008; Blumstein and Rosenfeld 2008; Eisner 2003). Trends are a more reliable measure of crime as a social problem since data from a longer time period avoids the pitfalls of occasional variations in crime rates that could be caused by special events or sudden changes in crime events. Moreover, information gathered over a period of time provides better assessments of criminality in a given country since errors in data collection and processing are usually systemic, and they depict trends more accurately.[5] Therefore, measurements taken over time can paradoxically reflect inaccurate crime rates but reliable trends.

Problems with data collection demand closer attention and better interpretation of the evidence. Countries with more efficient administrations produce richer statistics. However, these more developed countries usually have lower crime rates. Countries with severe criminality, on the other hand, have the poorest time-series data. Uruguay, Chile, and Costa Rica, for example, have longer and richer data sets than Guatemala, El Salvador, and Venezuela—and lower crime rates as well. Longer time series are usually found in countries with relatively low crime rates (the exceptions are Colombia and, recently, Mexico). In this book, I make an effort to provide country-specific measurements over time for many types of crime.

The reliability of trends is higher when time series are longer. Unfortunately, in Latin America data collection on criminality has been inconsistent over the last century. Moreover, in larger countries with federal systems, such as Argentina, Brazil, and Mexico, several states or provinces have not adhered to standard practices of data collection. Therefore, even in more advanced countries, the data quality at the subnational level is uneven.

In this chapter, I present data on different crimes from reliable sources, paying special attention to changes over time. I attempt to provide as much information as possible in order to assess not only what happened in the region recently but also to gauge changes from the 1980s and 1990s to the 2000s.

Homicide

Homicide is considered a good measure of criminality simply because it is the crime with the best available data.[6] Homicide rates are also sensitive to issues such as civil wars (Central America and Colombia), political repression (Southern Cone), and other factors that are not commonly associated with street crime.

The rates of intentional homicides are very high and they underscore the high violence and lethality in the region. As shown in Table 2.2, all countries in the region, except those of the Southern Cone as well as Peru and Costa Rica, have rising homicide rates currently higher than 10 per 100,000. Over the past decade and a half, fifteen out of eighteen nations had higher homicide rates than in the 1990s. With the exception of Colombia, declines in homicide rates have been quite modest while most increases have been significant.

Countries that emerged from severe internal conflicts in the late 1980s and 1990s (Colombia, Nicaragua, El Salvador, and Guatemala) had high rates of homicides. With the exception of Colombia—and a few years in El Salvador—homicide rates remain high in all of these countries. Nicaragua had higher rates during the 1980s (due to the conflict between the Sandinistas and Contra rebels), yet its rates had stabilized at relatively low levels until very recently. Conversely, countries such as Honduras, Venezuela, and the Dominican Republic have had high historic rates and suffered significant increases. Brazil and Mexico have large numbers of homicides but, due to their large populations, their rates are in the low and mid-20s. In summary, with the exception of Colombia, most countries since the 1990s either saw a significant spike in homicides or moderate increases.[7]

Several studies have underscored the high rates of homicide in the region (UNDP 2013; Igarape 2015; World Bank 2011). Here, I build on these studies to describe distinct patterns and of lethal crimes features: a) homicide rates have increased gradually over time; b) spatial heterogeneity

Table 2.2 Intentional homicide rates and rate of change, 1995–2012

Country	1995 (other years in parentheses)	2012 (other years in parentheses	Rate of change (%)
Argentina[a]	7.8	8.8 (13)	13
Bolivia	6.5 (05)	12.1	86
Brazil	25.5	26.7	5
Chile	3.1	3.8	22
Colombia	57.9	31.9	–50
Costa Rica	5.3	8.4	58
Ecuador	13.4	17.6 (10)	31
El Salvador	64.1 (99)	64.9 (10)	1
Guatemala	32.5	38.5	19
Honduras	42.1 (99)	91.0	116
Mexico	18.4	21.5	17
Nicaragua[b]	8.5	11.2	31
Panama	14.1	17.3	23
Paraguay[c]	12.0 (96)	11.5 (10)	–4
Peru	7.9 (98)	9.6	22
Dominican Republic	12.7	22.1	74
Uruguay	6.4 (00)	7.9	23
Venezuela	20.3	53.6	164

[a] From Ministry of Health data (APP).
[b] First measure, Nicaraguan National Police. Annual Report 2010, 15.
[c] First measure, counts reported by country to UNDP. Rate estimated by author.

Source: 1995 (or first measure) UNODC-CTS Homicides Statistics, except Guatemala, Panama, Paraguay, Peru, and Dominican Republic, UNDP (2013) annex (see Appendix; Brazil, Waiselfisz (2012, 18). 2012 (or last measure) UNODC Statistics. Homicides counts and rates https://data.unodc.org/#state:0.

reveals that homicides are not concentrated in chronically violent places but have spread to a number of cities and regions, a finding that requires new interpretations of the rising crime in Latin America; c) large increases in homicide under HCE usually occur over short time periods, confirming that tenuous equilibria are broken rapidly, producing a major escalation of violence; d) the recent increase in homicides is strongly correlated with urbanization, the proliferation of firearms, and the randomization of victims, which underscores the other distinct feature of crime in the region—the rise in property crime.

Homicide Trends

The current wave of criminality in Latin America began long before 1995. The initial surge probably dates back to the 1980s, perhaps even earlier. Little reliable information is available in the region for those years; only a few countries have data series dating back to the 1980s, and they are derived from different sources.[8] Figure 2.1 clearly depicts the dramatic rise in criminality that occurred in the region over the past 30 years.[9]

The countries shown in Figure 2.1 are among the most developed in the region and have systematic data collection by central agencies. Most have low or medium levels of violence (with the exception of Brazil, Colombia, and, recently, Mexico). The average rates of homicides in these

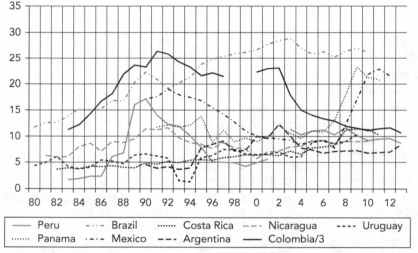

FIGURE 2.1 Homicide trends (per 100,000) for several countries for at least twenty years.

Note: The percentage of variation between the first year of observation and the last for each country is as follows: Argentina 86.6%; Brazil 123.9%; Colombia –12.1%; Costa Rica 159.6%; Mexico 23.2%; Nicaragua 43.6%; Panamá 81.0%; Peru 260.8%; Uruguay 88.2%.

Source: Author estimates; rates for Colombia are divided by three to fit the graph scale. Population rates from World Bank databases. Homicide data: Costa Rica, Poder Judicial. Departamento de Planificación, Sección de Estadística; Nicaragua, Anuarios Estadístico de la Policía Nacional; Panamá, División de Homicidios de la D.I.J-Policía Nacional; Uruguay, Observatorio Nacional Sobre Violencia y Criminalidad, varios informes [several reports]; Brasil, estimated from http://tabnet.datasus.gov.br/cgi/deftohtm.exe?idb2011/c09.def; Argentina, Ministry of Justice (http://www2.jus.gov.ar/politicacriminal/TotalPais2007_evol.pdf); Mexico, INEGI; Colombia, Beltrán and Salcedo Albaran (2003).

countries increased by 94.9 percent between the first and the last available measure, that is over a twenty-five- to thirty-year span.[10] While most nations had rates that were lower than or very close to ten in the 1980s or early 1990s, all had registered significant upsurges in violence several years later. Moreover, most countries have seen a sharp increase in a brief period of time (three to five years) rather than slow and steady growth. (A 30 to 40 percent increase over three to four years is generally considered a sharp rise in homicide rates.) This sharp upsurge is largely explained by the loss in states' deterrence capacity as well as social and economic transformations inherited from the legacies of the "lost decade" of the 1980s (see chapters 7 and 8 for further discussion).

Most of the studies from the region have failed to capture this rise in criminality because they are based on observations from only five to seven years. However, longer trend analysis shows that recent observations might constitute the tail end of the curve: most of the sharp increases in homicide rates occurred long before crime rates in the region improved (with the possible exception of late upsurges in Central America's Northern Triangle, Mexico, and Venezuela). The lack of good information for the 1980s and 1990s probably masked the fact that crime was on the rise long before official data and surveys on crime started to be systematically collected.

Latin American countries witnessed a twofold and in some cases even a threefold rise in crime beginning in the 1980s—as did the United States in the 1960s. But unlike the United States and Europe, where crime began to decline in the 1990s, this crime epidemic in Latin America has not ceased. Such scattered information points to a rising trend during the 1980s and 1990s, a leveling off in the early 2000s, and a recent upsurge in some countries.

Breakdown of the Crime Equilibria

Both Colombia's abrupt increase in homicides in the mid-1980s and Mexico's since 2008 have been tied to the rising violence of drug trafficking. Homicides doubled in these countries in a three- to five-year span. In addition, Argentina (in the early 1990s), Brazil (in the late 1980s and again in the late 1990s), Costa Rica and Panama (in the second half of the 2000s), and even Uruguay (recently) all suffered a significant increase in homicide rates over a short period. A similar trend is found with property crime: rather than a piecemeal increase in criminality, the spikes in many countries resemble a staircase, with sharp rises in criminal activity followed by stability until a new wave pushes crime up once again. Rarely do longer series show sustainable declines. Linear or curvilinear functions might not fit the observed data very well.

Table 2.3 shows that significant rises in homicide occurred in brief spans of three to six years in which murders doubled and even tripled, particularly under HCE.[11] As I will claim in the following chapters, a sudden sharp rise in criminality signals a breakdown of equilibria where the CJS fails to deter delinquents and the scope of crime expands rapidly, with a simultaneous spillover of certain criminal activities into others. For example, the notorious cases of Colombia in the late 1990s or Mexico over the last decade show that people associated with drug trafficking have ventured into extortion, kidnapping, and human trafficking, thus producing higher rates of criminality, including homicide. These offenders most likely realized that the police and other enforcement agencies lacked the capacity to contain criminality and therefore rapidly expanded into other lucrative criminal enterprises.

Heterogeneity

Spatial heterogeneity is a distinct feature of homicide, with homicides heavily concentrated in certain regions, towns, and even particular streets

Table 2.3 Rise in homicides for several countries over short periods

Country	First and last year	Initial rate	Last rate	Rate of change
Brazil	1982–1990	12.6	22.2	75%
Colombia	1983–1991	33.8	79.2	134%
Costa Rica	2004–2009	6.2	11.4	84%
El Salvador	2003–2009	36.4	70.9	95%
Honduras	2006–2012	46.2	91.0	183%
Mexico	2007–2011	7.6	22.8	200%
Panama	2004–2009	9.6	23.2	142%
Dominican Rep.	2001–2005	12.4	25.6	107%
Venezuela	1998–2003	19.1	44.2	131%

Source: Data from Figure 2.1 and UNODC (2014).

and blocks. The reasons why certain spaces are more vulnerable than others to crime is beyond the scope of this book.[12]

Aggregate national-level data mask the profound change in criminality at the sub-national levels. A recent study by UNDP (2013) confirms this pattern with data from different cities and regions for many LATAM countries. Brazil is usually cited as a good example of heterogeneous distribution of homicides (UNDP 2013; UNODC 2014).[13] Similarly, homicides in Mexico were concentrated in six of the country's thirty-two states;[14] 1 percent of municipalities had more than one hundred murders in a year, while 33 percent had none. Even so, in the midst of brutal civil strife, more than 80% of Mexico has remained relatively quiet. (Coscia and Rios 2012; Henle et al. 2015)

The uneven distribution of victimization observed by criminologists worldwide is also present in this region, where crime is highly concentrated (Table 2.4). Less emphasis, however, has been placed on the shifting pattern of such concentration. The classic claim of the Chicago School that physical places are the loci of criminal activities notwithstanding, Latin America over the last decades has had a "shifting concentration" of criminality.[15] The scattered data from the region suggest that crime has a dynamic spatial distribution that shifts as criminal opportunities appear.

Data for the largest cities in each Brazilian state over a ten-year span shows this shifting pattern. A national homicide average of 26.2 per 100,000 for both 2000 and 2010 masks this variance. For instance, from 2000 to 2010 the city of Sao Paulo saw its homicide rates drop fourfold, while some cities in the north and the northeast, such as Maceió, Salvador, Belem, and Fortaleza, have seen their homicide rates double during the same period.[16]

This wide variation is found throughout the region. In Argentina, the city of Rosario suffered a dramatic increase in homicide during a three-year span from 10 in 2010 to 22 in 2013.[17] The city of Medellin witnessed a dramatic upsurge in the 1980s. Ciudad Juarez in Mexico became one of the most violent cities in the world, going from less than 23 per 100,000 in 2007 to 269 per 100,000 in 2010 (300 homicides in 2007 and 3,500 killings in 2010)[18] in a spiral of violence closely related to drug trafficking. Yet certain cities have also experienced drastic shifts in crime that were not directly triggered by drugs, at least initially.[19] In San Pedro Sula, Honduras, homicide counts tripled in fourteen years (from 572 in 1997 to 1,747 in 2011).[20] The city of Caracas, Venezuela had

Table 2.4 Homicide rates in Brazilian cities, 2000 and 2010
(per 100,000 inhabitants)

City	State	2000	2010
Aracaju	Sergipe	39.9	42
Belem	Para	25.9	54.5
Belo Horizonte	Minas Gerais	34.8	34.9
Boa Vista	Rondonia	40.4	28.5
Brasilia	Distrito Federal	34.7	34.2
Campo Grande	Mato Grosso	39.3	21.7
Cuibá	Mato Grosso do Sul	69.5	40.1
Curitiba	Paraná	26.2	55.9
Florianopolis	Santa Catarina	10.2	22.8
Fortaleza	Ceara	28.2	45.9
Goinia	Goiás	28.6	39.8
João Pessoa	Paraíba	37.8	80.3
Macapá	Amapa	46.2	49
Maceió	Alagoas	45.1	109.9
Manaus	Amazonas	33	46.7
Natal	Rio Grande do Norte	10.4	32.3
Palmas	Tocantins	21.8	22.3
Porto Alegre	Rio Grande do Sul	39.2	36.8
Porto Velho	Roraima	61	49.7
Recife	Pernambuco	97.5	57.9
Rio Branco	Acre	36.4	25.9
Rio de Janeiro	Rio de Janeiro	56.6	24.3
Salvador	Bahia	12.9	55.5
São Luis	Maranhão	16.6	56.1
São Paulo	São Paulo	64.8	13
Terezina	Piauí	22.2	30.8
Vitória	Espírito Santo	79	67.1

Source: Waiselfisz, J. J. (2012).

less than 10 homicides per 100,000 in the early 1990s but exceeded 60 in 2005, while Quito had a rate of 9.87 in 1997 and 14.37 two years later.[21,22]

These examples of high criminality and very rapid and serious deterioration of public security require an explanation. In the following chapters, I will claim that this trend is due, at least in part, to two concurrent processes: 1) an important rise in the profits to be reaped from illegal activities and 2) the inability of law enforcement agencies to properly address these challenges. These are, of course, mutually reinforcing processes.

Firearms and Changing Homicide Patterns

Three distinctive characteristics of homicide have emerged over the last decades: 1) the increasing presence of firearms, 2) the shift from predominantly rural to urban locations (Escalante 2009), and 3) the increase in random victimization.

Rates of homicide by firearms in the region are the highest in the world. Guns are used in 28 percent of homicides in Asia and Africa, 10 percent of homicides in Oceania, and 13 percent of homicides in Europe. In the Americas, 66 percent of homicides are carried out with firearms (GSH 2013); this is supported by inmate surveys (Table 2.5). In the six countries in this study, firearms were the weapon of choice for homicide. And in the case of Mexico—the only case with repeated observations over a span of ten years—there has been a small increase in the use of firearms in homicides, from 39.2 percent in 2002 to 50.2 percent in 2013.

The wide use of firearms is associated with the relatively easy access to weapons and a lax enforcement of restrictions in most countries in the region (Small Arms Survey 2012). Moreover, there is a growing black market for firearms to commit other crimes (see chapters 3 and 4).

In general, homicides in Latin America are moving from rural settings to large cities. According to the inmate surveys—three out of every four homicides in the last decade were executed in urban settings. As in

Table 2.5 Homicides data from self reports: Use of firearms, location, and type of victims

	Argentina	Brazil	Chile	El Salvador	Mexico	Peru
Homicides committed with firearms (%)	67.8	61.3	61.7	76.2	46.2	62.5
% of homicides in cities[a]	83.2	81.5	85.8	51.6	72.7	68.1
% of random homicides	53.4	68.9	55.6	34.8	61.8	65.1

Source: Inmate Surveys.[a] Proportion of homicides in cities larger than 100,000 inhabitants.

other countries, the identity of victims is also changing as homicide is now more likely to occur during robberies, car thefts, drug trades, and other violent acquisitive crimes, with victims usually selected at random, rather than during conflicts among acquaintances, as it was tradition-ally perceived (Luckembill 1977). While in traditional and rural societies homicide resulted mostly from violent conflict between neighbors, family members, and known rivals, in modern urban settings homicides are mostly instrumental, the elimination of people in the process of obtaining a material gain.[23] For example, in Argentina during the 1990s the offender did not know the victim in 68 percent of homicide cases, and 64 percent of homicides were related to other property crimes (Bergman 2001).

Most homicides are tragic outcomes in the commission of other crimes (mostly for profit). The growth in homicides is largely correlated with the rise in property and for-profit crime, as well as the proliferation of firearms that in turn has facilitated the commission of property crimes. In summary, homicide rates have increased over the past thirty years, these rates are significantly above international levels, and, thus far, the level of violence has not subsided, although it might have reached a temporary plateau in the last few years. In the following chapters I present a set of hypotheses to make sense of these concurrent trends of rising violent and property or acquisitive crimes.

Property Crimes

Property crimes are the hallmark of criminality in the region in the past few decades, with an increase in theft the most noticeable feature of Latin American criminality. Although violence has grown significantly and has attracted media attention, property crime has been reported as very fre-quent and troublesome to most inhabitants of these countries. Measuring property crime in the region with the fragmented information available is challenging, and I use self-reports of crimes and countries' statistics to paint a picture of acquisitive crimes. This section starts with a look at victim data and then moves to official records and some longer trend anal-ysis. I then summarize the evidence.

Victim data. Thefts have become a major concern for people in the re-gion, and victim surveys, as table 2.6 shows, depicts the high prevalence of property crime.

Table 2.6 Personal theft victimization, 2014

Country	Personal theft victimization	Use of firearms in robbery	Other household member victimization	% of property crime where violence was used*
Argentina	18.0	6.1	23.9	43
Bolivia	22.1	4.6	31.0	35
Brazil	16.4	5.4	16.9	45
Chile	10.1	1.2	10.0	14
Colombia	19.6	6.6	22.4	52
Costa Rica	12.5	3.4	16.9	39
Dominican Republic	23.4	7.3	20.9	41
Ecuador	25.0	9.3	34.7	50
El Salvador	18.6	7.5	22.0	44
Guatemala	18.1	8.3	20.9	55
Mexico	23.6	6.1	24.9	36
Nicaragua	17.2	4.3	20.8	45
Panama	8.2	1.8	9.3	44
Paraguay	12.8	5.1	16.9	37
Peru	30.6	5.5	30.3	37
Uruguay	22.8	2.4	18.0	20
Venezuela	17.0	9.7	26.4	65

* Reported in UNDP (2013) chapter 3 for LAPOP 2012 survey.

Source: "The Americas Barometer," Latin American Public Opinion Project (LAPOP), www.LapopSurveys.org. Estimations based on responses to questions VIC1EXT, VIC2, and VIC Household, and calculations of positive responses for theft. For Argentina, Bolivia, Chile, Ecuador, Guatemala, and Venezuela, LAPOP data is for 2012. These questions were not asked or processed in these countries for the 2014 survey.

According to the LAPOP 2014 survey, the reported rate of theft is high. In most countries one out of six people has been robbed during the last year (second column), and one out of every five respondents reported that at least one member of their household was the victim of theft during the last year (fourth column). In addition, as mentioned earlier, the use of firearms in theft is also very noticeable: in most countries, almost half of all thefts involved the use of guns. The use of firearms appears to be low only in Chile, Uruguay, Costa Rica, and Argentina.[24] According to another study based on the same LAPOP survey (UNDP-annex 2013), 45 percent

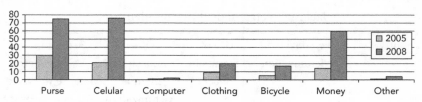

FIGURE 2.2 Personal theft: Selected items.
Source: Victimization Surveys, CIDE 2005–2008.

of thefts involved violence, ranging from 14 percent in Chile to 65 percent in Venezuela (fifth column).

A more detailed and longitudinally designed survey on victimization conducted in Mexico City and the state of Mexico between 2005 and 2008 coincidently captured the current wave of crime in Mexico and depicts the kinds of robberies thieves carry out.[25] As Figure 2.2 shows, crime has grown dramatically over a four-year span. The results show the percentage of households where at least one member of the household was the victim of certain crimes during the last year.[26] The most significant increase was in mugging and personal theft of such items as cellular phones, personal belongings, cash, computers, and so on.

Unfortunately, good data tracking property crime over an extended period of time are not available. Some countries have collected reports of thefts and robberies, although such data are scattered and at times very difficult to validate. There are very few longitudinal victimization surveys in Latin America. Despite several methodological limitations, a question included in the yearly Latinobarómeter survey—for most of the last twenty years—measures personal or household victimization. The overwhelming majority of victimizations have been various kinds of theft, which provides a proxy for property crime. Table 2.7 presents the percentage of validated respondents who reported that one member of the household was a victim of crime over the preceding year.

Latinobarómetro (and LAPOP) are general surveys that occasionally include two or three questions on personal experience with crime, but they are not true victimization surveys. However, since the same question has been asked many times over this period, changes in the rate of responses might indicate patterns of victimization. In short, these data are better used for depicting trends than for estimating actual crime rates.

Several important conclusions can be drawn from Table 2.7. First, rising crime is not limited to any single country, it is truly a regional problem. In most countries, the level of victimization has increased significantly

Table 2.7 Victimization rates for LATAM countries: Percentage (%) of affirmative responses

	1995 (other years in parentheses)	2001 (other years in parentheses)	2005 (other years in parentheses)	2010 (other years in parentheses)	2015	% change 1990s–2015
Argentina	27	46	42	42 (09)	47	74
Bolivia	28 (96)	45	44	41 (09)	43	54
Brazil	23	36	45	41 (09)	49	113
Chile	30	42	39	31	38	27
Colombia	38 (96)	34	37	34	44	16
C.R.	31(06)	31	44	36	39	26
Ecuador	36 (96)	36 (02)	34 (06)	36	39	8
El Salvador	52 (96)	36	34	70**	36	-31
Guatemala	60 (96)	41	40	38 (09)	40	-33
Honduras	28 (96)	36	32	34	37	32
Mexico	31	78 (04)	67	39	38	23
Nicaragua	33 (96)	41	37	30	31	-6
Panama	20 (96)	37	31	32	35	75
Paraguay	30	39	39	31	34	13
Peru	33	48 (04)	47	38 (09)	43	30
Dominican Republic	N/A	N/A	30	38	39	30a
Uruguay	16	30	39	32 (09)	41	156
Venezuela	43	48	48	39	49 (13)	14
Average	31	39	38	38	40	35

Notes: The first measure for Bolivia, Colombia, Ecuador, El Salvador, and Nicaragua was for 1996. The second measure for Mexico and Peru was for 2004.

a Rate of change between 2005 and 2015.

** This is an extremely high rate. This may not be an accurate measure.

The question asked was: Have you or any of your family members been assaulted, attacked, or the victim of a crime in the past twelve months? Note: Assault in Spanish is often interpreted as robbery rather than "attacked."

Source: Author estimates from latinobarometro.org.

over the past two decades, and the mean of self-reported victimization growth between the first and last observation is 35 percent. The rate of growth might be even higher, since over the past twenty years, the size of households shrunk in most countries of the region.[27] In addition, these rates probably do not reflect the true scope of crime, since the survey question might not adequately capture the scale of theft, mugging, or larceny.

Second, countries with relatively modest rates of victimization such as Argentina, Bolivia, Chile, Costa Rica, and Uruguay have seen a significant increase in personal crimes. While in 1995, the reported victimization rate was less than 25 percent for most countries, none had a rate lower than 30 percent by 2015 and most of these countries, in fact, had rates higher than 40 percent. In most of these countries, however, homicide rates remain under 10 per 100,000 and there are very few cases of extortions, kidnapping, or human trafficking, which are highly predatory crimes very common in HCE.

Third, reductions in victimization can only be seen in countries that were affected by civil wars and severe internal strife in the 1990s (Colombia, El Salvador, and Guatemala. For the rest of the countries, overall, the rates from circa 1995 are probably single observations from a continuous growth trend that began earlier and peaked in the 2005–2015 period.

In summary, similar survey data for all countries in the region show that victimization rates have been growing, that a large number of respondents or family members have been victimized, and that these rates probably occlude even more victimizations.

Official Records

While rates of theft have been decreasing or stagnating worldwide, in Latin America property crime has gone up. For the special report by the UNDP (2013), Latin American countries submitted data that confirms this trend of rising theft.[28] Table 2.8 uses data from that report as well as information from other sources to show rates at the beginning, the middle, and the end of the first decade of the twenty-first century. According to official records in each country, between 2005 and 2010 (or the closest year), the theft rate increased in all countries.[29]

Only one country had a significantly lower rate in 2010 compared to 2005. All others have either stagnant or rising theft rates. As was the case

Table 2.8 Thefts, mugging, and robbery (per 100,000) and percentage change

Country	Source	Circa 2000	Circa 2005	Circa 2010	Change 2000–2010(%)	Change 2005–2010(%)
Argentina[a]	UNDP	897.0	980.0	973.3	8.5	−0.7
Bolivia	UNDP	N/A	75.3	87.6	N/A	16.3
Brazil	OAS-2012	N/A	418.0	415.0	N/A	−0.7
Chile (armed robbery)	UNDP	N/A	727.1	1124.7	N/A	54.6
Colombia	OAS-2012	N/A	162.0	120.0	N/A	−25.9
Costa Rica	UNDP	658.3	876.4	975.1	48.1	11.3
Ecuador[b]	UNDP	N/A	N/A	657.3	N/A	N/A
El Salvador	UNDP	163.7	95.1	102.3	-41.7	7.5
Guatemala	UNDP	80	63	67.0	-16.3	6.4
Honduras	UNDP	N/A	N/A	133.4	N/A	N/A
Mexico	UNDP	519.2	496.3	688.3	32.6	38.7
Nicaragua	OAS-2012	351.0	392.0	488.0	39.0	24.5
Panama	UNDP	35.7	51.0	62.0	73.7	21.6
Paraguay	OAS-2012	71.0	43.0	394.0	454.9	816.3
Peru	UNDP	127.0	163.0	217.0	70.9	33.1
Dominican Republic	UNDP	N/A	104.4	210.9	N/A	102.0
Uruguay	OAS-2012	205.0	253.0	410.0	100.0	62.1
Venezuela	OAS-2012	145.0	103.0	106.0	-26.9	2.9

* The UNDP dedicated a great amount of effort to gathering information from countries. These data were last updated in November 2012. The OAS data were taken from the "Report on Citizen Security in the Americas 2012." For an explanation of these data collections see Appendix.
[a] The case of Argentina should be carefully analyzed since there are good reasons to suspect that data has been manipulated to deliberately show lower rates (see Fleitas 2015). I will develop this argument later.
[b] Robbery data estimated for 2012 based on the prosecutor's information for the period January–October 2012.
Source: UNDP and OAS-Alertamerica (see Appendix*).

with homicide, in Colombia property crime began to spiral upward in the late 1970s and peaked in the 1990s. For instance, the rate of *atracos* (robberies) was 38.5 per 100,000 in 1976 but had nearly doubled to 74.75 in 1995; car thefts for the same years went from 2,188 (1976) to 13,742 (1995); and there were 25 bank robberies in 1976 and 706 in 1995. Over the same period, homicide rates went from 27.8 per 100,000 in 1979 to

64.7 per 100,000 in 1995 (Beltran and Salcedo Albaran 2003). In summary, the trend in Colombia was similar to the other Latin American countries but began much earlier.

The magnitude of changes within each country shows that a rise in the amount of crime reported to the police denotes an increase in criminal activity. Most likely, rates are even higher since trust in authority has been decreasing in the region, which reduces the number of crimes reported. As with the trend in homicides, administrative data show an uptick of property crime in a relatively short time period.

Long-term trends. Data for longer-term trends in property crimes are even more difficult to collect. I was able to assemble time series for several countries over more than two decades, though they derive from different sources, using 1991 as the base year to track changes and compare rates. Figure 2.3 reveals a pattern often found in longer-term homicide trends: crime for the most part has been rising. There were short periods when crime remained stagnant or fell, however, over a longer period of time, crime went up markedly: the property crime rate has at least doubled in all of these countries.

The descriptive data (both the administrative records and self-reports) in this chapter paint a very clear picture: property crime has increased in most countries over the past several years. The richer data from the last few years (when countries and agencies began to collect more information more systematically) likely represent the tail end of an ascending curve that started two or perhaps three decades ago. Longer time series suggest that property crimes are two, three, or even four times higher today than in the early 1990s. Most Latin Americans have been the victims of property crimes over the past few years—often violent crimes. Thefts, sometimes carried out with violence, are the salient feature of public insecurity in the region.

The high rates of property crimes that are found in most countries of the region are of two different kinds: the highly predatory that include significant levels of violence (particularly high use of firearms), including homicides, and those where the level of violence remains under control. The criminal activity in several countries are considered LCE despite having relatively high and rising rates of property crime. What distinguishes Chile and Argentina from Mexico and Brazil is that the first two have illicit markets and high rates of personal victimization and theft yet the level of violence is contained, whereas in larger areas of the last two violence has not only spread out across the country but also occurs more often.

Rate of change with respect to base year = 1991

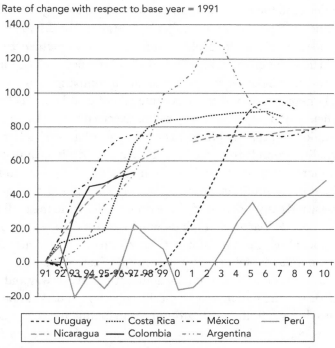

FIGURE 2.3 Property crime for several countries.

Rate of change with respect to base year, 1991.

Available property crimes series: Uruguay, thefts (hurtos); Nicaragua, violent thefts (Robo c/violencia); Costa Rica, thefts; Colombia, car thefts; Mexico, car thefts; Peru, car thefts; Argentina, property crimes (delitos contra la propiedad).

Source: Costa Rica, Sistema de Información sobre violencia y delito; Ministerio de Justicia; Mexico, AMIA, compañías de seguro; Argentina, SNIC, ministerio de Justicia; Uruguay, Ministerio del Interior, http://www.minterior.gub.ur/index.php/es/estadisticas; Colombia, Beltrán y Salcedo Albarán. *Revista Criminalidad Policía Nacional de Colombia 1976–1999*, 80–81; Nicaragua, Policía Nacional, Anuarios 1981–2010 (see country collections, appendix); Peru, UNDP 2013 (see country collections, appendix).

Other Crimes

Countries classify and count crimes according to their own legal definitions. However, criminal activities do not really derive from a legal rationale. For example, the murder of a woman by a family member and the murder of a woman during a robbery are both female homicides, but the motives behind the two crimes differ. Similarly, an occasional street larceny and a ring of car jackings are both classified as property crimes but differ greatly.

To understand the rise in criminal activity across the region, it is essential to define the type of criminality that is emerging. The driving forces behind the rise in crime are for-profit criminality and the emergence of illegal markets. Thus, the quantity of crimes tied to inter-personal conflict resolution between individuals is expected to fall in comparison to crimes that generate large gains. Also, as crime becomes a profitable business, "criminal entrepreneurs" and organized crime can be expected to take leading roles.

In addition to property crimes, Latin America has seen a large surge of criminality around drug production, drug trafficking, and the drug trade. In many countries there has also been an explosion of kidnapping and abduction for profit, extortion of various kinds, predation on public enterprises, and consolidation of crime rings dedicated to the theft of large amounts of goods that are in high demand and are then sold in different venues—including gasoline stolen from company pipes, merchandise and consumer goods stolen from trucks, and, of course, cars.

Official records and reports do not define crime in this way and none of the countries in the region systematically collect such data. Public crime records use legal definitions of extortion, kidnapping, the drug trade, and so on. One stolen trailer with consumer goods worth millions of dollars counts as one case, as does any petty theft in the city. Victimization surveys also do not adequately measure these crimes. To track the rise of such criminality, therefore, we must follow another imperfect strategy: using spotty information collected from organized groups in civil society, such as insurance companies, private security companies, chambers of commerce, and so on. Almost none of these data sets are longitudinally designed.

Abduction, Kidnapping, and Extortion

These predatory crimes have affected most countries of the region in the last decade: Table 2.9 summarizes basic but very incomplete information. The average number of abductions reported to the authorities in a given year is presented in the second column. The real magnitude of abductions is difficult to measure because these are highly underreported crimes. Fear of retaliation from kidnappers and a lack of trust in authorities lead many individuals to negotiate and/or resolve these cases on their own without official intervention.

Several questions in the LAPOP survey indirectly gauge household victimization of both kidnappings and extortions. Rates (per 1,000) of such victimizations are presented in columns 3 and 4, and suggest that

Table 2.9 **Average reported abduction and direct victimization through kidnapping and extortion***

	Average abductions reported annually 2006–2010	Kidnapping (per 1,000)	Extortion (per 1,000)	
		2012	2010	2012
Argentina	217	1.28	2.09	0.64
Bolivia	352[a]	0.83	4.71	12.23
Brazil	414[b]	1.31	7.58	8.69
Chile	191	1.34	2.68	2.24
Colombia	374	0.63	7.38	5.91
Costa Rica	8	1.33	1.33	
Ecuador		2.81	4.66	3.93
El Salvador	303	0.70	44.04	26.95
Guatemala	3631	2.09	17.71	15.47
Honduras	36		2.66	3.97
Mexico	649	3.93	43.31	39.96
Nicaragua			4.02	2.70
Panama	22		0.68	0.69
Paraguay	342		6.03	1.38
Peru	1408	0.56	8.70	20.23
Dominican Republic	43	0.66[c]	5.29	6.69
Uruguay		0.68	2.09	0.68
Venezuela		1.36	6.02	4.07

Empty cells denote no data available.

[a] For 2010, the data is preliminary.

[b] Crime counts refer to "extortion through kidnapping," not including Parana.

[c] Data for 2010 (no available results in these countries for 2012).

* Response to the question: "Thinking of the last crime you fell victim to, which of the following criminal acts best describes it?" Figures refer to the net percentage of population that fell victim to the mentioned crimes. Given the small percentages, rates were adjusted by 1000.

Source: Kidnapping average from UNDP 2013 except Colombia and Costa Rica from OAS 2012. Extortion rates are author estimates from LAPOP 2010 and 2012.

the numbers are very high, particularly for extortion. In some countries 3 to 4 percent of the population has been the victim of extortion. Many individuals probably know others who have been extorted, usually for ransom. In addition, another widespread pattern of abduction called "express kidnapping" has proliferated in most countries.[30]

Rates obtained from general surveys that only include two questions on crime can pose some validity concerns. Specially designed victimization surveys for Mexico, however, confirm these findings. For 2008, in the above-mentioned victimization survey for Mexico City, 1 out of every 200 households reported that a member of their household was the victim of an extortion in the last six months (Bergman and Sarsfield 2009). In addition, the largest victimization survey of Latin America, the 2012 ENVIPE of Mexico, estimates that there were 105,000 abductions—a staggering number indicating that 1 out of 1,000 Mexicans has been either abducted or threatened with abduction (Excelsior 2013).[31]

The most salient observation from Table 2.9 is that countries with high levels of extortion and kidnapping also have high rates of other crimes. For example, with the exception of Bolivia, all countries that have more than 10 extortions per 1,000 people have homicide rates greater than 10 per 100,000, and all countries (with the exception of Honduras) that have lower level of homicides (less than 10 per 100,000) also have a relatively small number of extortions. For sixteen countries (excluding Bolivia and Honduras) the correlation between homicides and extortions yields a coefficient of r=0.67. I hypothesize in this book that high crime equilibria produce the spread and contagion of highly predatory crimes, because law enforcement in these countries has either collapsed or has been seriously challenged.

Are extortion and kidnaping new or have they been widespread throughout the region for years or even decades? There is no good answer to this question because there are no data on the real magnitude of such crimes over the years. Again, Mexico sheds some light on the trends. A 2014 study assembled data on reported extortions and showed rates per 1,000 increasing from 0.9 in 1997 to 1.57 in 2002, 2.91 in 2006, 5.34 in 2010, and 6.79 in 2013. In short, in a seventeen-year span, extortion in Mexico grew sevenfold, though it is important to note that rates increased threefold from 1997 to 2006 before Calderon´s so-called war on drug even began.[32]

In summary, the scattered information available signals that there is a severe problem of kidnapping and extortion in the region, that the rates of these crimes are staggering, and these rates might be part of a longer trend that has been growing for several years. In particular, the rates are severe where other crimes are also very high, suggesting that HCE breeds predatory, for-profit criminality.

Other Organized Crime

Organized-crime research in Latin America has received significant attention in the last decade—as one of the most significant drivers of crime it deserves systematic study. Chapter 5 is fully dedicated to the most important profit-making crime, illegal drugs, while chapter 6 studies in depth the nature of organized crime in the region. Here, I briefly introduce other crimes that are executed by criminal organizations and then briefly introduce the study of narcotics and crime.

Large-scale thefts of tradable goods, some including high levels of violence, have grown, while several, new predatory crimes also have proliferated in the region: thefts of cash from bank-account holders after they leave the bank premises (*salideras/fleteo*), highway robberies of goods while being transported, and violent car thefts in which drivers are forced at gunpoint to give up their vehicles.[33] These crimes have been observed everywhere and are carried out by professional criminals and gang members whose parent organizations hold powerful firearms and use informants or guards to collect intelligence on potential victims so as to maximize yields from each crime. Profits from such robberies are relatively high and in many cases the tradable goods stolen are subsequently resold at fairs, stores, and through well-developed street vendor schemes. Highly predatory theft operates within fully developed networks with quasi-legal businesses feeding markets defined by many scholars as illicit (Holland 2016; Yashar 2012).

The magnitude of such criminal acts is far from negligible. Pemex, the Mexican oil company, reported in 2013 a loss of 750 million dollars, 39 percent higher than in 2011, from[34] gasoline sucked from oil ducts or stolen from trucks by armed delinquents and quickly resold to gas stations. In Colombia in 2002, stolen gasoline was tallied at an average of 7,270 barrels a day, equivalent to 3 percent of total daily gas demand, for a total loss of US$1.35 billion.[35] Many other countries have reported similar losses from these lucrative crimes.[36]

Highway thefts of trucks carrying merchandise are widespread in many countries, as discussed in chapter 4. Although the patterns vary, such crimes are usually perpetrated by members of well-organized groups who follow trucks carrying tradeable goods in response to information provided by informers. The criminals brandish weapons to stop a truck, leave the driver on the side of the road, and take the truck to a safe warehouse to unload the merchandise. The goods are sold later, mainly in shadow marketplaces: in most large cities of Latin America, there are several street markets where counterfeit goods are sold alongside such stolen merchandise.

Large-scale criminality appears to be expanding to new frontiers. In Colombia, for example, a booming illegal business transcends cocaine and has ventured into gold, the market for which has benefitted from rising international prices since 2008, and this switch has produced an increase in violence (Idrobo et al. 2014). Similarly in Peru, the largest gold exporter in LATAM, experts from the tax agency (SUNAT) estimate that 20 percent of gold exports come from illegal mining with a value of US$1.6 billion in 2013, part of which ends up in organized crime.[37] In Mexico, there are indications that cartels, such as the Zetas and Caballeros Templarios, are expanding into mining and metals through protection quotas charged to mining companies (many of them international) in the states of Michoacán, Tamaulipas, Chihuahua, Guerrero, and Morelos.[38] Similarly, there are many reports that organized crime is heavily involved in human trafficking, particularly migrant and sex smuggling into the United States. Profits are estimated, by some scholars, as amounting to several billion dollars per year (Ugarte et al. 2004; Hofmann 2015)[39]

It is almost impossible to prove whether this large-scale criminality has in fact been growing over the past decade, simply because there are no data for such activities for the 1980s or 1990s. However, the breadth of these criminal operations—rarely seen in low-crime societies—as well as the high estimated profits they produce indicate that very lucrative criminal businesses are growing in number as well as in size. Moreover, the scattered evidence I presented shows that the appropriation of goods offered in diverse market outlets are finding a strong demand supplied by large-scale criminal organizations. It appears that crime indeed pays.

Narcotics

A survey of criminality in Latin America cannot neglect one of the most lucrative enterprises in the region: the production, trade, and consumption of narcotics. Chapters 5 and 6 will develop an analytical framework for studying how drug trafficking impacts the overall rise of criminality in LATAM.

Here, I briefly review the extent to which the "narco-business" has grown in the region and highlight two noticeable, clear processes that have had a decisive impact on the rise of criminality: 1) the significant expansion of domestic markets, and 2) the increased flow of drugs throughout the region, and the diversification of drug routes in order to reach, major consumer countries. The growth in drug use and an increase in the seizure of drugs in most countries are used as proxies for the flow and magnitude of the drug business. Later chapters link these processes to the rise in crime in the region.

Consumption. Drug use has been rising in the region over the last decade, in particular among young people. Drug use is not itself considered a predatory crime: consumption trends are used to indirectly show the availability of drugs in domestic markets. Although there is no good data to empirically prove that the onset and the rise in drug use goes back to the 1980s and 1990s, this is presumed to be the case.[40]

The most widely used methodology to assess domestic demand for illegal drugs is prevalence rates obtained through surveys,[41] of which there are several that target populations for different drugs. Here I present data gathered from two target groups: general adult populations (usually ages sixteen to sixty-five), and high-school age students (usually fourteen to eighteen) (Table 2.10). I focus on two drugs: marijuana and cocaine (although synthetic drugs are becoming very important in the region, there are no reliable historic data on them). Surveys also measure use of legal substances such as alcohol and tobacco.[42]

I assembled prevalence estimates for many countries, using the first available public data on prevalence and the most recent I could find for each, to indicate the direction of change in prevalence rates. Most surveys follow standard methodologies supervised by the OAS (Organization of American States) observatory drug program (CICAD), though each country might have adjusted the surveys to its own national specifications. Interpretations of rates and comparisons should, therefore, be made with care.[43] These levels of consumption indicate that there is a domestic market for narcotics, particularly among the young.

Table 2.10 is intended to show changes in prevalence rates,[44] though comparisons between countries should be seen as indicative; prevalence rates for the United Sates are included to give an idea of the magnitude of each domestic market. The prevalence rates of a mature market such as the United States, shows that a few countries (Chile, Uruguay, Colombia, and, to some extent, Argentina and Brazil) have a medium-size market,

Table 2.10 Drug use in Latin America. First and last prevalence rates for groups and countries (Year rate in parenthesis)

	Marihuana (%)				Cocaine/Crack (%)			
	High School		Adults		High School		Adults	
	First	Last	First	Last	First	Last	First	Last
Argentina	3.5 (01)	10.4 (11)	1.9 (04)	4.2 (11)	1.0 (01)	2.7 (11)	0.3 (04)	0.9 (11)
Bolivia/a	2.0 (09)	3.4 (12)		1.7 (14)				
Brazil	6.3 (05)[b]	4.9 (10)	2.6 (05)[b]	2.6 (05)	1.8 (05)[b]	2.1 (11)	0.7 (05)[b]	0.7 (05)
Chile	14.8 (01)	30.6 (13)	4.0 (94)	7.1 (12)	3.2 (01)	3.6 (13)	0.9 (96)	0.9 (12)
Colombia/a	11.1 (09)	15.0 (12)	2.2 (08)[b]	3.7 (12)	1.7 (05)[b]	2.7 (11)	1.9 (04)[b]	1.0 (13)
Costa Rica	5.7 (06)	9.7 (12)	1.0 (06)[c]		1.2 (06)	0.8 (12)	0.4 (06)[c]	
Ecuador[a]	4.0 (09)	8.2 (12)			1.5 (08)[b]	1.0 (11)		
El Salvador	3.5 (08)[d]		0.4 (05)[c]			1.1 (08)[d]		0.4 (05)[c]
Guatemala	1.0 (04)[d]					0.5 (04)[d]		0.2 (05)[c]

Honduras			0.8 (05)[c]			1.0 (08)[d]		0.9 (05)[c]
Mexico	1.2 (08)[b]		1.0 (98)	1.4 (11)			0.5 (98)	0.5 (11)
Nicaragua[b]	2.2 (02)[b]		1.0 (06)[b]		2.3 (04)[b]		0.7 (06)[c]	
Panama		5.0 (08)			0.7 (05)[b]	1.5 (08)		
Paraguay[b]	3.0 (05)[b]	3.4 (12)	3.4 (03)[b]				0.4 (08)[b]	0.4 (08)
Peru	2.8 (05)		0.7 (98)	1.0 (10)	0.9 (07)	0.9 (12)	0.4 (98)	0.4 (10)
Dominican Republic	1.0 (08)[b]	1.0 (08)	0.5 (08)[b]		0.5 (08)[b]	0.5 (08)	0.2 (06)[b]	0.3 (10)
Uruguay	8.4 (02)	17.0 (14)	1.4 (01)	8.3 (11)	1.7 (03)	2.3 (14)	0.2 (01)	1.9 (11)
Venezuela			0.9 (05)[c]			0.3 (09)[d]		0.6 (05)[c]
USA	26.1 (01)	24.2 (13)	10.6 (02)	12.6 (12)	2.1 (91)	1.6 (13)	2.5 (02)	1.6 (12)

Empty cells denote no data available.

[a] For Bolivia, Colombia and Ecuador available data is for students at the university level; data was not available for high school students.

[b] OAS Observatory citizen security survey, Data Repository (Alertamérica, see Appendix. Indicators for illegal drug demand: General Population and school-age population. At http://www.oas.org/dsp/Observatorio/database/indicators.aspx?lang=en

[c] World Drug Report 2011. https://www.unodc.org/documents/data-and-analysis/WDR2011/StatAnnex-consumption.pdf

[d] World Drug Report 2011. https://www.unodc.org/documents/data-and-analysis/WDR2011/Youth_tables_complete_WDR2011.pdf

while the rest have very small overall demand. All countries seem to have room for this market to grow.

The most important conclusion to be drawn from Table 2.10 is that the number of drug users is rapidly growing in the region. Whereas drug use in the United States over these years has stagnated, in this region there has been a significant increase in prevalence rates, starting from a very low level, with an unmistakable upward trend in the number of users and presumably also of addicts and heavy users who create a steady demand for these substances. Moreover, the large proportion of young people who use drugs suggests the market will grow in the future—although evidence worldwide indicates that most drug users will desist in their thirties, a share of this cohort will continue to use drugs. In short, the larger cohorts of young users in Latin America predict larger domestic markets in the future.[45]

There is no simple reason why prevalence rates have been growing. Drug availability might not be the primary cause. For instance, Bolivia, Peru, and Colombia are the world's main producers of cocaine, but the drug's use in the northern Andes was low until the 1980s.[46] There are no theories or comprehensive explanation thus far to account for the rise in drug consumption over the past ten to fifteen years in the region.

I hypothesize that a small rise in drug use began in the late 1980s and early 1990s and then steadily increased at the turn of the century. Most domestic markets have not yet matured and others are no longer experiencing the vigorous growth they saw in the past (Bogota, Colombia; Santiago, Chile; Rio de Janeiro, Brazil). While there are no surveys from the 1980s or even the 1990s for most of the region, Mexico does have two national surveys from those decades, 1988 and 1998 (albeit with somewhat different methodologies), which track urban dwellers and their habits. For marihuana, the adult prevalence rates went from 3.0 percent in 1988 to 4.2 percent in 2008, and for cocaine from 0.2 percent to 2.4 percent. Clearly, Mexico did not have a domestic cocaine market in 1988 but did by 2008.[47] Scarce data for Chile also indicates a rise in the number of cocaine users among the general adult population, with prevalence rates doubling from 0.9 percent in 1996 to 1.8 percent in 2008.[48]

LATAM surveys provide little information on use frequency and quantities, unlike in the United States, making it hard to distinguish between occasional and heavy users in most countries and consequently to estimate market sizes. A recent study in Argentina (Bergman 2016) used a 2011 survey to classify 75 percent of cocaine users as heavy users and

25 percent as occasional—very similar rates to those reported for the United States (Rydell et al. 1996). The yearly domestic cocaine market in Argentina is ten to twelve metric tons per year, while the marihuana market is valued at U$175 million.[49]

In short, scattered measures of drug consumption are proof of a growing domestic market. Marihuana had an established market in the 1990s that has increased moderately. The domestic demand for cocaine has been steadily growing, albeit from very low thresholds.

Seizures. Over the past decades, illegal drugs have become widely available in the region. The increased domestic demand has been met with a growing supply, and, since many illegal drugs are produced in the region and exported to large lucrative markets in North America and Europe, the production and transshipment of drugs has increased the availability of cocaine, opiates, and cannabis in many countries. This large increase in illegal drug production, transshipments, and sales has also contributed to higher rates of crime and violence.

Large quantities of drugs move through the region. Only a fraction of these shipments is detected and seized by authorities. These seizures, however, provide a sense of the magnitude of the overall quantities of drugs produced and moved through the region.

Data collected from country reports to the UNODC on seizures of cocaine (salts, base, and paste) and marijuana herbs over forty years are presented in Table 2.11, with four observations for each country: 1980, 1990, 2000, and circa 2010. Again, the main goal is not to compare between countries but to trace the evolution of drug availability within each country. Although some single observations could be questioned and might not have been classified accurately (for example, a country may include in "marijuana herbs" other seizures of resin and plants, while another might include crack in this category or exclude crack from cocaine and its sub-products) the magnitude of seizures are very compelling and depict a significant and progressive rise in the drug supply.[50]

In addition, most of these figures are not adjusted to take into account drug purity, making it impossible to assess true changes in drug availability. It is highly likely that both THC and cocaine purity have changed over the years, but good information on this is not available. The information in Table 2.11 is, therefore, indicative but not precise.

Table 2.11 Seizures of marijuana herbs and cocaine-type drugs

	Marihuana Marijuana herbs (kg)				Cocaine/Crack Base, paste, and salts (kg)			
	1980	1990	2000	Circa 2010	1980	1990	2000	Circa 2010
Argentina	430	658	25,538	36,293	44	1,009	2,351	10,461[c]
Bolivia	4	15	3,740	4,373	400	12,400	5,600	26,892[a]
Brazil	88,503	9,561	159,073	155,071	92	3,017	5,516	24,059[a]
Chile	2,649	5,134	3,277	13,928[a]	75	236	2,076	8,350[a]
Colombia	743,813	653,322	75,173	255,000	2111	50,748	105,600	59,491[d]
Costa Rica	103	148	1,140	4,123[d]	N/A	6	5871	20,875[a]
Ecuador	101	498	3,079	4,605[b]	157	22.45	3,308	65,078[a]
El Salvador	N/A	85	455	87[d]	N/A	14	431	790[d]
Guatemala	70	1,300[f]	814[e]	4545	1	3,234	1,517	6,936[a]
Honduras	171	108	1,112	1,512	1	363	1,215	7,104
Mexico	69,873	594,778	2,050,402	2,313,115	29	49,879	23,195	21,631[a]
Nicaragua	N/A	683[f]	737	342[b]	N/A	762	961	9,800/a
Panama	989	106	3657	2,233[d]	54	4,001	7,401	52,429
Paraguay	5	4,861	199,282	309,836[b]	1	41f	96	600[a]
Peru	415	492	1,635	4,871	4,755	34,284	11,847	20,657[a]
Dominican Republic	N/A	498	1,526	1,300	N/A	2,588	1,313	8,600
Uruguay	N/A	6	805	1,967[b]	N/A	2	21	2,650[a]
Venezuela	370	6,4300	14,999	38,692	159	5,665	14,771	27,742[a]
USA	1,969,685	171,738	1,175,373[e]	1,692,943[d]	3,470	8,4831	99,700	121,819[a]
Total USA not included	907,496	1,336,553	2,546,444	3,152,677	7,879	170,494	193,090	374,145
change over decade %		47.2	90.5	23.8		2063.9	13.2	93.7

[a] 2009, [b] 2011, [c] 2012, [d] 2013, [e] 1999, [f] 1991.

Source: UNODC 2015. UNODC statistics/drug seizure report/seizures at https://data.unodc.org/; World Drug Report/Seizures.

Seizures of large quantities of drugs might be taken from traffic routes to large consumer markets or from vigorous domestic markets. Drugs are produced in both Mexico and Colombia and large seizures there are of drugs being shipped through their territory en route to other markets, while in the United States and Chile most drugs seized were designated for local consumption. It is estimated that authorities usually seize between 10 and 15 percent of all shipments, though no study has confirmed this claim. Most likely, certain countries are better at enforcing their laws and seize more drugs than others, but the information in Table 2.11 cannot indicate which of these nations are more effective at reducing supply.

The most clear and important conclusion to be drawn from Table 2.11 is the significant rise in drug seizures in every Latin American country, which indirectly proves the increasing availability of drugs. Although greater law enforcement resources might also explain the increased quantities of drugs seized, I claim that this has only a marginal effect. The amounts of drug seized are so large that they undoubtedly indicate that larger quantities of drugs are moving through every country of the region.

Several other obvious findings can also be derived from Table 2.11. There is a dramatic increase in drug circulation in the region. In the 1980s, Latin America had no significant domestic markets, thirty years later large quantities of both cannabis and cocaine sub-products circulate in all countries, with a particularly large increase in the 1990s, followed by further, steady increases throughout the region. However, there are important differences between countries, with producers or large transshipment nations—such as Peru, Colombia, Venezuela, and Mexico for cocaine and Paraguay, Mexico, and Colombia for cannabis—seizing significantly more drugs than the others. In the Southern Cone and in Brazil, there was an explosive rise in drug seizures in the 1990s and the beginning of the twenty-first century that can be explained in part by the steady growth of domestic demand. Central American nations also experienced a sharp increase in seizures, particularly since the turn of the century, as new routes were opened up to bring cocaine into the United States. Other countries, such as Argentina, Brazil, Venezuela, and several in Central America, are also used as corridors and gateways to export cocaine to Europe and East Asia, and a significant share of their seizures are, therefore, tied to international traffic rather than local consumption. This is not the case for marijuana.[51]

But the data presented in Table 2.11 does not answer the classic question of whether drug supply stimulates local demand. According to this hypothesis, new routes for drugs into the United States and Europe can help local markets develop because "movers" are usually paid in kind, creating new incentives for "pushing" sales domestically. However, marijuana, particularly in South America, does not leave the region for overseas markets, so the rise in marijuana seizures demonstrates that there is a genuine and growing appetite for this drug among new consumers. Most likely, increases in the seizures of drugs are attributed to both the development of new routes to reach mature overseas markets as well as rising domestic demand. These two are interrelated processes that, given the illegality of drug circulation, can produce more crime and violence.

Summary

Drugs have existed in this region for centuries, and cannabis and cocaine have been present for many decades. Yet, over the past twenty years, there has been a dramatic growth in both drug use and drug availability. This has created business opportunities for thousands and perhaps millions of people and has increased crime and violence in the region. The scattered data indicate that by the 1980s, illegal drugs were either just passing through (en route to the United States) or supplying very small domestic markets. Two decades later, quantities of illegal drugs have grown significantly, and by 2010 the number of users and the amount of drugs in circulation point to maturing domestic markets that still have room to grow. Criminal networks have developed to supply steady demand locally and overseas. Along with the drug trade, other criminal activities have intensified. Based on available information, I will contend in later chapters that: a) the rapid growth in domestic markets of narcotics has produced more violence and crime in many countries, and 2) stringent enforcement of drug trafficking has paradoxically forced traffickers to develop new routes, in turn producing crime in regions that were relatively crime free in the past.

Concluding Remarks

This chapter describes the dependent variable of my study: crime trends. There is little doubt that crime rates are very high and rising across Latin

America. Several studies have already documented this rise but few scholars have focused on the dynamic aspect of criminality in the region. The main claim of this book is that crime has been rising in all eighteen Latin American countries studied. While conclusions drawn from short term trends (three to five years) might be misleading because crime rates fluctuate, or because the data are poor for given years, when current rates are compared to the levels of crime in the 1980s or 1990s, the rise in crime is unmistakable. Even Colombia shows a similar trend, although the rise in crime there started earlier, in the late 1970s and 1980s. Both short and long data series were reviewed in this chapter to prove that levels of criminality are significantly higher today than three decades ago.

Through descriptive data I have shown that:

1) Crime is a regional issue rather than a problem for any single country, and so to explain rising crime trends, a theory that transcends single countries is needed.

2) Despite the overall trend, the intensity and scope of criminality varies between countries, which requires an analysis of domestic conditions to explain differences within countries.

3) From the scattered available data, it appears that the greatest increase has been in both property crime and for-profit crimes. Associated violence is probably a byproduct rather than the motive behind the development of markets for illicit goods.

4) There is clear evidence that many illegal activities have resulted in diversification into crimes such as extortion, abduction, and drug trafficking. Significant profits attract youth and many other players.

5) Countries with already high levels of crime and an additional significant increase over short periods witnessed a dramatic acceleration of criminality.

6) The growing presence of firearms is associated with rising crime.

7) Although crime is highly concentrated in urban settings, few researchers have focused on the shifting conditions of such concentration. In addition, the quality of data is poorer in rural areas, and there is still much to be learned about crime in rural settings. There is a need to explore whether the concentration of crime in several urban areas correlates with opportunities for crime.

The evidence presented in this chapter suggests the need for a general examination of the regional conditions that gave rise to this outburst of criminality, but without neglecting the subtle differences that resulted in different outcomes in each country. That is the challenge this study undertakes: how to explain differences in criminal activity in each country within a shared regional trend.

Few theories explain criminality from a regional perspective. Most explanations derive from a long tradition in criminological studies that isolate the variables that affect crime. Given the vast differences between Latin American countries and the variance in social, economic, and political conditions in the region, I present a general framework rather than a full theory of rising crime in Latin America, searching for a model or general perspective that identifies a set of components to answer the questions just presented. This is the task of this book. In the next chapter, I start by reviewing covariates and general models of crime and examining how well they fit the Latin American context.

3

Why Has Crime Risen in Latin America?

Introduction

Winston Churchill allegedly characterized Russia as ". . . a riddle, wrapped in a mystery, inside an enigma." Crime could be similarly defined. After more than a century of frontline research, and with thousands of papers and books written on the topic, many questions still remain: Why is it that among societies with similar characteristics, some have higher crime rates than others? Under what circumstances will people resort to violence?

In spite of its enigmatic nature, crime is better understood today than it was twenty or fifty years ago. Theories on the causes of delinquency and violence have been empirically tested, and we have a better understanding of crime traits, crime waves, and the role played by institutions of social control in containing criminality. Yet, this enhanced understanding of crime comes mainly from developed countries and provides little insight into the developing world, which is where most reported crimes occur. In particular, very little is known about crime trends and the causes of criminality in Latin America. There are still major controversies in the region about the role played by macro-variables such as poverty, inequality, unemployment, and ethnic cleavages or demographic patterns, among many others. Few studies have examined the effect that changes in family structure, school attendance, community organizations, addictions, and many other variables have on criminal behavior in the region. And of course, very little is known in Latin America about the precise effect of crime triggers such as drugs and firearms.

This chapter is organized around covariates of crime. I do not discuss the merits of different theories but instead identify key variables that correlate with crime and assess whether they fit into the regional context. Rather than delving into theories such as strain, control, social disorganization, and crime as opportunity, I focus here on covariates such as labor markets, family structures, income inequality, guns, and drugs, and so on, while providing descriptive data to ascertain their association with crime in the region.[1] In summary, this chapter uses laymen's terms to present the variables most commonly associated with criminality and determine whether they fit into the Latin American context. By doing so, I briefly evaluate how different crime theories might explain crime patterns in the region.

Initial Notes on the Study of Crime

After introductory remarks on the study of crime, I will question the framework of deviance as a paradigm for the study of crime in Latin America and then offer a succinct review of current approaches to the study of crime in the region. Next, I present a summary of extant research in criminology on trends in homicides in order to isolate possible predictors for the current crime waves in LATAM. Introductory notes on property crimes will lay out the ground for the focus of this chapter, the covariates of crime in Latin America.

What Has Caused Latin America's Rise in Crime?

In this book, I call for a comprehensive explanation on the rise in crime in Latin America. Recent studies in the region have failed to address the nuances of sudden or slow increases of crime over the past two decades; in particular, they do not properly account for the differences in crime intensity, rises in the magnitude of crimes, or variations in the type of criminality. The dual-equilibria approach partially addresses several of these questions.

Traditional schools of criminology have their origins in deviance theories. Although many scholars have argued that both environment and social context affect the choices delinquents make, their theories focus on individuals who deviate from dictated norms and put less emphasis on the social processes that breed such criminality. In addition, they mostly underestimate the rationality of offenders in the sense that this rationality serves only for immediate gratification (control theory), peer recognition, and the pursuit of immediate gains (social disorganization theory), to overcome social adversity (strain theory), and so on. Many criminological theories assume a normal world where crime is an abnormal behavior that serves as an adaptation strategy for some individuals during adverse conditions.

But what happens when crime is perceived as a legitimate vehicle of social adaptation? What happens when illicit and criminal activity exceeds 20 percent of a country's Gross Domestic Product (GDP)? Is an individual who works for and profits from a car theft ring a true deviant? Do the small drug dealers across the Americas—who number in the millions—qualify as criminal offenders who cannot overcome a social pathology?

I argue that the rising crime problem in Latin America should be analyzed from a broader sociological and economic perspective because it is inadequately explained by classical criminological theory, though I will draw on the rich criminological scholarship in order to explain many aspects of this trend. My central argument, however, relates to the macro-level social, political, and economic changes in the region that have caused a dramatic upsurge in delinquency. Instead of merely discussing the shortcomings of criminal justice systems, I examine other variables to explain why criminality has skyrocketed. I do not assume that offenders are undeterred deviants. Instead, I believe they are rational individuals who were recruited into the ranks and files of thriving industries. I do not challenge criminological theory, but instead refocus the analysis on what I believe is a critical social problem in the region.

The Perspective from Latin America

In recent years, scholars in the region have begun searching for the causes of the current wave of criminality. The study of crime and deviance in Latin America has been historically dominated by legal scholars, and criminology was taught at law schools. Most studies focused on dogmatic debates and criminal law, while there were few empirical and quantitative studies before the 1990s. This has changed recently as scholars from the social sciences, both in Latin American universities and in research centers around the world, began to pay attention to the severe deterioration in public safety in the region. Drawing on different disciplines (anthropology, sociology, political science, and economics, among others) a new line of evidence-based research began to emerge. As it is impossible to review the hundreds of papers and books published over the past two decades, I will briefly summarize the most salient explanations that derive from traits of this literature.

Weak state institutions. Many studies have pointed to a deficiency in judicial, correctional, and police institutions as the critical factor that explains the rise in crime—some of the contributions to this topic are reviewed in the final three chapters of this book. Most scholars (Fruhling 2009; Azaola 2008; de Lima et al. 2014; Sain 2008; Carrion 2002; Hinton 2006; Ungar 2011; Bailey and Dammert 2005) have focused on the severe malfunctioning of corrupt institutions (such as the police) which have been unable to meet the new challenges presented by rising crime.

Legal structure and justice reforms. Several scholars from law schools in the region have adopted a critical perspective on traditional criminal legal procedure and conducted empirical studies on judicial institutions in order to advance major justice reforms. Led by the Santiago-based think tank Centro de Estudios de Justicia de las Américas (CEJA), Chile, Colombia, and Argentina have pioneered legal reforms and studies for judicial underperformance (Pasara 2014; Riego and Duce 2009; Binder 2004; Zepeda 2004).

Community breakdown and urban settings. Influenced by currents in the United States, scholars in the region have studied the serious deterioration of community as a root cause of criminality. Slums and deprived neighborhoods in large metropolitan areas have received special attention and several empirical studies were completed. Works by Beato (2012), Goldstein and Arias (2010), Muggah (2012), Gaviria and Pages (2002), and Krujit and Koonings (2007), as well as other anthropological studies (e.g., Auyero and Berti [2013], Davis [2007], Caldeira [2001]) exemplify this emerging and eclectic line of research.

The political-economy perspective. Over the last few years, a literature has emerged focusing on the particular institutional make-up of political organizations and their readiness to address the heretofore severe mismanagement of security issues. Moncada (2016), Magaloni et al. (2016), Yashar (2012), Bailey (2014), Snyder and Duran-Martinez (2009), Trejo and Ley (2016), and many others have made new and important contributions to elucidate the underperformance of administrative and political institutions by focusing on the interaction between governments, formal institutions, and organized crime.

The classic sociological perspective. A large number of works have examined the effect of major social changes that took place in the region over the last three decades. Urbanization, industrialization, migration, poverty, and many classic sociological topics have been analyzed in the context of high criminality. The transition to democracy and in particular, the significant social changes resulting from neoliberal reforms in the 1990s are two important topics emphasized in recent works (Misse 2006; Kessler 2004; Briceño-León 2008; Krujit and Koonings 1999; McIlwaine and Moser 2003).

Organized crime and drugs. Some have focused on the enormous illegal drug trade and the impact of organized crime, which has itself evolved over the past two decades, studying the disruption caused by drugs and the emergence of cartels and other complex, business-oriented criminal organizations with a violent modus operandi. This has been particularly relevant in Colombia and Mexico (Garzon 2010; Guerrero 2011; Escalante 2009; Tokatlian 2010; Bagley 2009) and also in Brazil and Central America (Arnson et al. 2014; Lessing 2017; Mazzitelli 2012).

Conflict. There is a growing corpus of literature on Central American gangs (*maras*) and their connections with two broad processes that have severely exacerbated criminality in this region: the legacies of civil wars and conflicts of the 1980s and 1990s, and the out-migration from the United States of young Central Americans back to El Salvador, Guatemala, and Honduras (Bruneau et al. 2011; Wolf 2013; Cruz 2010). The legacies of armed conflict and their effect on crime have also been felt in Colombia (Llorente et al. 2002; Krujit and Koonings 1999; Arnson et al. 2014) and to a lesser extent, in Peru.

An economic analysis of crime. Economics scholars have recently developed a new research agenda based on the rational choice perspective in crime, in particular, using the deterrence framework, the interplay between an individual's motivations to commit crime and Latin American institutional capacities to respond to such offenses, along with analyses of broader determinants of crime (Di Tella et al. 2012; CAF 2014; Mejia and Restrepo 2016; Thoumi 2003).

While there are myriad perspectives on criminality in Latin America, there is no dominant paradigm to explain its rise in crime. Moreover, there is no comprehensive theory or overall perspective that answers the question: Why has criminality reached such high levels (and is continuing to rise) in the region as opposed to everywhere else?

Rising Homicide Rates

What are the determinants of homicide? What lessons can be drawn from the criminological literature to understand current, regional homicide trends? As we saw in chapter 2, homicide rates for most countries in Latin America have increased since the 1980s and 1990s. Longer and more reliable trends exist for homicides simply because it is the crime most commonly reported with somewhat reliable data over extended periods. Here, I briefly summarize findings from studies on homicide trends that can shed light on the debates on new waves of crime in the region.

Several studies worldwide have identified key variables that at least correlate with large-scale homicide variations. In a review of risk factors for high homicide rates, LaFree (1999) made six generalizations. He found that economic inequality was the most consistent significant predictor and identified a negative relationship between homicide and economic development. The study found no support for the hypothesis that urbanization, unemployment rates, and demographic structure are associated with homicide rates.

A thorough literature review by Trent and Pridemore (2012) grouped homicide predictors into five bundles that are similar to those developed by LaFree (1999). These are: development and industrialization, deprivation, urbanism, population structure, and social and cultural heterogeneity. The authors have not reach any "definite generalizations" on the strength of theoretical perspectives (2012, 133), and they did not find clear support for the effects of urbanization and population structure on homicide. However, two variables did have an effect on homicide: development and deprivation (child poverty and inequality). Yet the overall picture remains inconsistent.

Nivette (2011) has conducted a meta-analysis and provides a statistical summary for predictors that have been used in extant research, and the average effects (as measured by the standardized mean effect size correlation coefficients M_r) found across the studies. The variables identified as having a positive association with homicide rates included income inequality, family structure, female work occupation, and ethnic cleavages.[2] On the other hand, social welfare, ethnic homogeneity, and development had negative associations with homicides.[3] These associations reveal that some variables covary with homicides, though no definite causal effects could be identified.

Rosenfeld and Messner (1991) separately analyzed data for thirty-two societies to examine whether modern covariates of homicide can be replicated for pre-state societies. The authors included a range of potential covariates related to social inequality, social disorganization, and social development. They concluded that none of the available measures of social inequality were related to homicide, though they did find five macro-level risk factors that covaried with levels of homicides. Rates were found to be lower in societies with intense political oppression, a predominance of larger settlements, high total population, some degree of separate centralized political authority, and a differentiated military organization (such as a standing army). Interestingly, the authors believe that violence is suppressed more effectively in societies that have formalized conflict-resolution mechanisms, greater centralized formal authority, and formal coercive mechanisms. In short, they are in line with the assumption, stated first by Hobbes, that effective state structures reduce interpersonal violence (Pinker 2011).

Most of these studies use similar constructs rather than exploring new theoretical and empirical possibilities. Eisner (2013) examines studies that, in addition to identifying classical predictors of crime, analyze the link between variation in homicide rates and measures of state functioning such as governance indicators, corruption, and variables that reveal levels of state legitimacy (Neumayer, 2005; Eisner and Nivette 2014). The previously ignored state-functioning variable could prove relevant when addressing variations in intra-societal violence.

In summary, analysis of longer processes and of several societies jointly either does not show a strong effect of inequality, poverty, urbanization, and community structure on homicides, or produces inconclusive results. Extant research appears to indicate that, in general, the reduction of interpersonal violence covaries with the development of some sort of legitimate central authority.

Property Crime

Longer trends for property crime are harder to find, and only a handful of studies examine the causes behind the spike in thefts, larcenies, and fraud. This raises several problems when attempting to unravel the Latin American riddle: What accounts for the widespread and consistent increase in thefts in the region?

Variables associated with state functioning, should not be overlooked. The efficacy of police and courts (or the lack thereof) could either encourage or deter crime, particularly property crime. Corruption and state legitimacy are key factors that can motivate or deter potential offenders from engaging in criminal behavior. The precise weight of these variables within the explanatory models can be debated, yet there is little doubt of their significant role in the rising crime trend throughout the region (UNDP 2013). Acquisitive crimes appear to be correlated with inflation and other socio-economic trends (Rosenfeld and Levin 2016). Unfortunately, due to a lack of data, it is impossible to conduct time-series analysis to evaluate sweeping trends in the region. I will show, however, that for the past two decades, there is no strong evidence that deprivation and/or development correlates with a rise in property crime.

Accounting for the Rise: Covariates of Crime

Over the past three decades, scholars, experts, and laymen have stressed different explanations for Latin America's rise in crime, all anchored in common assumptions and popular discourses that have been rarely tested. Here I pose a simple question: If crime has risen in every nation of Latin America, what factors common to all countries can explain this increase? I list eight potential variables associated with the rise in crime in the region, and I present data to empirically evaluate the impact of each of them, that is, how they covariate with violent and property crime in Latin America.

Inequality

Many studies have shown that countries with wider gaps in income distribution tend to also exhibit higher rates of crime (Fajnzylber et al. 2002; World Bank 2011; Kessler 2014).[4] Some studies rely on homicide data while others use different measures of property or total crime rates. However, there is no conclusive evidence that sweeping inequality indeed breeds criminality. To fill the empirical gap, a large body of literature relies on strain theory (or some other theoretical approach) to explain why differences in income can produce larger cohorts of delinquents.

In order to avoid a Type I error—incorrectly accepting a hypothesis—the causal effect of inequality on crime requires solid proof that has yet to be produced. There appears to be a degree of association in some models, but this might be caused by other variables, omitted from the model, that are hard to identify and/or control. Most studies use cross-sectional designs and data that do not adequately control for social or economic changes that could have produced crime waves. Longitudinal or time-series data within countries could shed light on this problem.

For example in 1977, Colombia with a Gini coefficient of 0.51, suffered 2,851 car thefts; ten years later, although the Gini coefficient had decreased to 0.45, 3,654 cars were stolen (Beltran and Salcedo 2007). In 1997, the Gini coefficient had risen to 0.49 while the number of stolen cars skyrocketed to 15,653.[5] In short, while the Gini coefficient has experienced moderate fluctuations throughout the time period, crime rates rose only moderately from 1977 until 1987 but then increased dramatically (by close to 500 percent) in the following decade.

Table 3.1 presents the Gini coefficient and crime data for eighteen countries in the first decade of the twenty-first century along with Person r

Table 3.1 Crime and inequality (2000–2010)

	Gini Coefficient (avg. annual)	Thefts: Pearson R	Homicides: Pearson R
Arg	0.48	−0.10	0.18
Bol	0.54	−0.57	−0.81
Bra	0.55	0.22	0.66
Chi	0.52	N/A[a]	N/A[a]
Col	0.56	0.61	0.21
CR	0.49	0.02	−0.08
Ecu	0.51	0.95	−0.11
El Sal	0.46	−0.56	−0.88
Gua	0.54	0.05	−0.23
Hon	0.56	N/A	−0.84
Mex	0.48	−0.24	−0.02
Nic	0.43	N/A	0.16
Pan	0.54	−0.88	−0.81
Par	0.52	−0.55	0.81
Per	0.49	−0.40	−0.83
Dom	0.49	−0.25	−0.46
Uru	0.45	−0.06	−0.19
Ven	0.50	0.20	−0.12

[a] Chile has only three pair observations since it only reports on the Gini coefficient every three years.

Source: Author calculations based on theft rates × 100,000 reported by OAS alertamerica.org; Homicide rates from sources of Table 2.2, and Gini coefficient from the World Bank (WDI 2015).

correlations for both measures when there are at least four pair observations per country throughout the decade. A high positive coefficient indicates a strong association between crime and income distribution. For property crime, only Ecuador and Colombia show such strong results, while all others have moderate and non-statistically significant associations or a negative association, implying that while income distribution improved in each country, theft also increased.[6] For homicides, with the exception of Brazil, Chile, and Paraguay, the Gini coefficient is not associated with homicide trends in LATAM countries. These stylized facts show that reducing the income distribution gap has no apparent effect on crime in the region. As most countries experienced a reduction of inequality, they also witnessed a spike in delinquency, particularly in property crime.

Despite improvements during this decade, inequality in LATAM remains very high. I claim in the following chapters that unequal societies with limited vehicles for genuine social mobilization are prone to producing new generations of criminal entrepreneurs who seize on crime opportunities and supply cheap labor for illicit markets on the rise.

Growth

It is generally assumed in Latin America that stagnation has produced more criminality due to the erosion of economic opportunities, particularly for the underprivileged. The consequences of the so-called "lost decade" of the 1980s and the neo-liberal period of the 1990s have been perceived as highly criminogenic. The next sections will delve into the effects of unemployment and poverty on crime. First, I briefly present data on GDP and homicide in the region to evaluate the effect of growth (or lack thereof) on crime.

Figure 3.1 depicts the yearly rate of growth GDP per capita over a period (usually ten to fifteen years) for each country and the yearly variation in the homicide rate during the same years. I used available data for each country for the period of high economic growth— the 1990s and, especially, the first decade of the twenty-first century. This graph evaluates the rates of change for the eighteen countries under study and clearly shows a high correlation between GDP and homicide. Moreover, most countries are close to the fitted regression line indicating that a strong association between changes in homicides and changes in economic growth is quite likely, albeit in the opposite predicted direction: the higher the country GDP

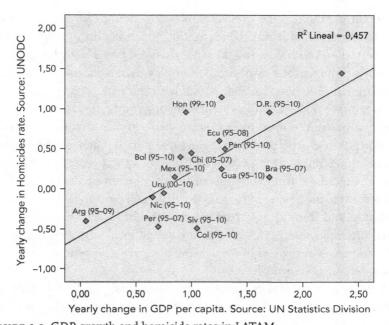

FIGURE 3.1 GDP growth and homicide rates in LATAM.

Source: Author elaboration using data from WDI (2015), homicide rates presented in chapter 2, and homicide data from UNODC (2014).

per capita growth, the higher the rise in homicides.[7] Data for property crimes is unfortunately not available for the 1990s for most countries, but a simple correlation between thefts and the GDP per capita of each country for 2009 shows an R correlation of 0.41, indicating that there is also a positive association between property crime and GDP per capita.[8] In short, the initial evidence suggests that crime in the region covaries with growth but in an unexpected direction. It appears that in Latin America, prosperity correlates positively with crime.

Unemployment

Crime is also associated with unemployment. Many studies have surveyed the relationship between the job market and crime, mostly noting that the quality of jobs, particularly entry-level positions for relatively underprivileged young males, negatively correlates with levels of crime (Freeman 1995, 1996; Grogger 1995; Piehl 1998; Levitt 2001). The weaker the job market, the higher the crime rate. Again, tests are mostly cross-sectional and do not fit very well with time-series data.

In Latin America, the explosion of youth unemployment has indeed affected the levels of crime.[9] Liberalization policies in the 1990s had an adverse effect on youth entering the labor markets, particularly for unskilled or poorly trained urban teenagers. Unemployment rates among the young have dramatically risen in cities throughout the region (Bergman 2002). In Argentina, male unemployment rates for youth ages 15–24 increased from 11.4 percent in 1990 to 23.6 percent in 1999. In Brazil, it rose from 8.7 percent to 18.4 percent during the same period. Unemployment went from 17.0 percent to 22.8 percent in Chile; from 15.3 percent to 32.0 percent in Colombia; from 9.8 percent to 14.8 percent in Costa Rica; from 11.2 percent to 20.0 percent in Ecuador; from 14.3 percent to 17.3 percent in Paraguay; and from 19.9 percent to 22.2 percent in Venezuela.[10] In summary, unemployment rates among the young expanded significantly: in most countries by the end of the decade, close to 20 percent of males aged 15–24 were unemployed.[11]

Studies of work and crime offer important insights on this problem. Offenders typically hold jobs while they commit property crimes, yet these tend to be low-quality jobs that pay poorly. Fagan and Freeman (1999) called this a "double up"—when youngsters work and commit crimes sequentially or concurrently. This pendular movement between illicit activities and informal jobs results from limited job opportunities and a predominance of low-paid jobs. However, once youngsters take a step toward crime, the path back to "regular jobs" narrows (Hagan 1993; Sampson and Laub 2005) since work skills erode with time and a criminal record becomes a stigma.

Weakening job markets during the 1990s in Latin America appear to have affected both the opportunities and the income of unskilled youngsters. Studies based on inmate surveys have found that offenders in the region have "doubled up." (Bergman 2013; UNDP 2013) Most offenders began their criminal activities in their teens and had faced difficulties on the job market, often working low-quality and poorly paid jobs on the informal market. Other qualitative studies (Kessler 2004; Misse 2006) also describe the effect of deteriorating job-market conditions on teenagers.

This macro-level association fails to explain why some youngsters turn to criminal careers while the overwhelming majority do not, nor why the existence of a large cohort of youngsters facing low-quality jobs is not a predictor of a crime-ridden society. For example, in countries such as Brazil or Colombia weakening labor markets appear to strongly correlate with crime rates, while in others such as Chile and Costa Rica similarly weakening labor markets appear to have little effect on crime. In short, although a large cohort of youngsters facing a challenging job market may indeed be a risk factor for a rising crime rate, this does not on its own explain a crime surge. Other variables or trigger effects are needed to explain the variation in numbers of criminals and crime rates between different countries with similar contexts. Moreover, no single causal effect has been identified for a surging crime rate, though a simple association between labor markets for youngsters and crime might omit other causal factors. I stress the need to account for the new income opportunities for youngsters that illicit secondary markets create. The demand for illegally marketed goods matters as growing markets for illegal goods and poor state capacities to deter potential offenders has allowed "crime as work" to prosper.

Poverty and Crime

A widely shared misconception in Latin America asserts that poverty has contributed to the rise in violent victimization. Both extreme and moderate poverty are high in most countries of the region, though most criminologists do not support the hypothesis that higher poverty leads to higher crime. The question of whether poverty generates more crime depends on several other variables.

Initial evidence from Latin America does not uphold the poverty–crime association either: from the 1990s until around 2010 most LATAM countries experienced a drop in poverty rates, while crime rates increased in most countries (Table 3.2).

Over the last decade, several factors (such as prosperity arising from the commodity boom and conditional cash transfer programs) contributed to a sizeable reduction in the number of individuals living under the poverty line (Lustig et al. 2013). Even if methodologies differ from country to country, the within-country variation over the years becomes a reliable measure. There is no doubt that a reduction of poverty rates has been one of the major success stories in the region over the last two decades. Why, then, has crime continued to rise?

Poverty in itself does not breed criminality; it must be combined with other variables. Countries with higher poverty rates are more likely to exhibit higher degrees of violence (World Bank 2011). Nevertheless, most poor individuals do not commit felonies and having larger cohorts of people growing up in poor conditions in a country does not inevitably

Table 3.2 Poverty in eighteen Latin American countries (Percentage of people living in poverty)

Country (first and last year of time series)	Extreme poverty		Moderate poverty	
Argentina	N/A	N/A	N/A	N/A
Bolivia (97–11)	18.6	8.1	33.6	15.5
Brazil (90–13)	9.7	3.1	23.5	7.6
Chile (90–13)	4.4	1.0	14.9	2.5
Colombia (91–13)	9.8	3.3	24.9	11.8
Costa Rica (90–13)	4.8	3.1	10.7	6.9
Ecuador (00–13)	12.8	3.7	29.5	11.7
El Salvador (95–13)	9.1	3.5	24.0	14.9
Guatemala (89–06)	18.5	11.3	35.5	25.5
Honduras (90–10)	31.5	22.8	50.2	39.1
Mexico (89–12)	5.9	4.2	18.7	12.7
Nicaragua (93–09)	24.3	11.7	41.9	26.1
Panama (01–13)	9.0	5.3	17.7	10.1
Paraguay (99–13)	14.1	7.1	29.1	16.6
Peru (97–13)	10.1	1.3	20.7	8.1
Dominican Republic (02–13)	8.8	7.6	20.9	17.7
Uruguay (07–13)	0.6	0.2	5.1	1.5
Venezuela (90–12)	5.0	2.7	15.7	9.1
Latin America weighted average (97–13)	7.7	3.9	19.8	10.6

Source: Cepalstat (2015). Poverty rates are as reported on the website http://interwp. cepal.org/cepalstat/WEB_CEPALSTAT/Portada.asp?idioma=e.

lead to a higher crime rate. Criminologists have shown that the poor who commit crimes are motivated by other factors such as weak self-control, deteriorated urban environments, the tensions between their aspirations and their material conditions, and the poor deterrence capacities of formal and informal social control, among others.

Community Breakdown

Societies experiencing rapid transformations have in some cases also experienced breakdowns in social cohesion, a loss in trust of traditional authority, and a higher vulnerability to crime. Cities that have shown rapid growth over the past decades in Latin America, Africa and several countries of East Asia also exhibit high crime rates. The Latin American landscape shows that poor and rapidly growing neighborhoods and towns with low social cohesion and deteriorated infrastructure have been hotbeds of delinquency and more recently, of violent domestic drug markets (Beato 2012, Muggah 2012). Slums in their many forms—*favelas, villas, barrios*— and emerging marginalized towns on the outskirts of booming cities are also plagued by chronic violence. Yet, many new and growing urban developments have not succumbed to widespread criminality and instead have proved capable of containing it. Under what conditions do rapid urbanization and deteriorating conditions spur criminal violence?

Crime in the region is higher in urban areas. In Latin America, according to LAPOP (Latin American Public Opinion Program) surveys, three out of four crime victims live in cities. Several metropolitan areas with significant population increases have experienced considerable crime rates. Many cities, such as Recife and Fortaleza, Brazil; certain US–Mexico border towns, such as Tijuana and Ciudad Juarez; and cities that benefitted from the commodity boom and attracted new residents such as Rosario, Argentina and Santa Cruz, Bolivia, have experienced rapid population growth without a parallel increase in community organization or infrastructure. All have also witnessed above-average rises in homicides, thefts, and drug-related crimes. However, theories must account for counterfactuals, and not every city in Latin America that experienced rapid growth saw an equivalent rise in crime. In large metropolises such as San Pablo, Brazil and Bogota, Colombia, crime actually fell. Chronically crime-ridden cities such as Rio de Janeiro, Brazil and Medellin, Colombia did not experience a spike in homicides or violent crime over the past decade. Buenos Aires, Santiago (Chile), and Mexico City saw modest rises in criminality despite the fact that they have sprawling and disadvantaged suburban areas. Urbanization and poor infrastructure do not immediately produce upswings in crime, yet in some cases the pace of growth has been found to covary with criminality.[12]

Why do some cities avoid surges in urban violence while others do not? From the early work of the Chicago school (Park et al. 1925; Shaw and MacKay 1942) to the recent work of Sampson (2013), scholars have looked at social disorganization within cities and communities to identify crime triggers. Briefly, these theories claim that rapid urbanization, densely populated slums, and weak formal authorities and institutions stimulate gang activities, the retreat of individuals from community engagement, a lack of formal supervision of youth, and many other conditions that neutralize the mechanisms of social control which are instrumental for reducing crime and violence.

Table 3.3 summarizes features of urban development trends in the region, to assess the effect of urbanization on crime. The first columns show

Table 3.3 Share of urban population in cities with over 20,000 and 100,000 inhabitants and rate of change of the two largest metropolitan areas in the 1970s and 1990s

Country	20,000 + pop.		100,000+ pop.		Metropolitan areas	Growth of largest cities (%)	
	1990	2000	1990	2000		1970–1980	1990–2000
Argentina	74.9	76.6	61.8	62.3	Greater Buenos Aires	1.6	0.6
					Greater Córdoba	2.2	1.1
Bolivia	49.6	54.4	41.3	44.9	La Paz[a]	2.8	2.6
					Santa Cruz[a]	6.6	5.1
Brazil	58.9	64.6	45.6	49.6	San Pablo	4.6	0.8
					Rio de Janeiro	2.5	0.6
Chile	72.5	76.9	60.8	63.6	Santiago	3.4	1.3
					Valparaiso	1.8	0.8
Colombia	59.2	65.0	49.3	53.9	Bogota	3.0	2.7
					Medellin	2.4	2.7
Costa Rica	N/A	49.2	N/A	33.9	San Jose	3.6	3.3
					Heredia	4.2	5.4
Ecuador	48.0	54.3	36.4	44.2	Guayaquil	4.6	2.8
					Quito	4.3	2.2
El Salvador	35.5	44.0	28.0	29.9	San Salvador	3.3	0.2
					Santa Ana	1.7	1.6
Guatemala	23.7	30.7	19.0	20.2	Guatemala	1.8	3.6
					Quetzaltemango	2.1	3.3

Honduras	N/A	32.5	N/A	24.3	Tegucigalpa	4.8	2.7
					San Pedro Sula	4.1	4.3
Mexico	57.1	60.5	47.5	50.2	Mexico City	4.3	1.5
					Guadalajara	4.0	2.0
Nicaragua	41.0	41.4	22.7	21.9	Managua	3.4	1.3
					Leon	3.4	1.2
Panama	47.0	57.3	36.3	51.2	Panama City	3.0	3.6
					Colon	0.4	3.3
Paraguay	39.0	44.8	31.6	35.3	Asuncion	3.3	3.1
					Ciudad del Este	19.4	5.1
Peru	56.8	62.1	48.0	53.5	Lima	3.7	2.0
					Arequipa	4.2	1.8
Dominican Republic	45.2	52.6	32.2	41.4	Santo Domingo	6.1	3.2
					Santiago de los Caballeros	4.7	3.6
Uruguay	74.3	72.0	50.3	47.4	Montevideo	0.7	-0.4
					Salto	0.8	0.8
Venezuela	71.7	74.3	59.5	61.6	Caracas	1.9	0.3
					Maracaibo	3.2	2.8

[a] Data for the metropolitan cities of Bolivia is unavailable for the 1970s, so data from the 1980s was used.

Source: Cepalstat (2015) http://interwp.cepal.org/sisgen/ConsultaIntegrada.asp?idIndicador=269&idioma=e.

the share of city dwellers in each country. Two statistics are presented: the percentage of people living in cities with more than 20,000 residents and those in cities with a population in excess of 100,000. The last columns present the growth rate for the two largest cities in each country for both 1970–1980 and for 1990–2000.

The data indicate several features of Latin America's urbanization process. First, most people in the region live in cities. Despite important variation among countries, between half and three-quarters of Latin Americans are city dwellers. A small share of the population lives in small towns (with a population between 20,000 and 100,000), but most live in large cities.

Second, this table also confirms an important feature of recent Latin American development: countries that industrialized earlier have a larger share of inhabitants living in big cities. The data indicate that urban growth continued at a rapid pace during the 1990s.

Third, large metropolitan areas continue to grow. With the exception of Montevideo, thirty-five large cities in the region grew and more importantly, the pace of growth for the largest cities was slower in the 1990s than in the 1970s.[13] This was true not only in countries which industrialized earlier (Argentina, Brazil, Mexico) but also in Peru, Ecuador, and the Dominican Republic. Some cities have witnessed dramatic growth recently (such as San Pedro Sula, Honduras; Guatemala City; Colon, Panama) but the vast majority have actually witnessed slower growth in the last decade. In summary, while more Latin Americans are living in urban settings, mostly in large cities, the pace of metropolitan growth has slowed over the last decades.

Although cities grew rapidly in the 1970s (and even earlier), the significant rise in crime didn't start until the 1990s or even the 2000s. Why didn't crime increase dramatically in the 1970s or 1980s? Several cases are illustrative. San Pablo had its biggest growth spurt in the 1960s and 1970s, but crime did not peak until the late 1990s and early 2000s, when the city's growth began to flag. Similarly, Rio de Janeiro saw an upswing in criminality in the late 1990s, during a period of modest urban growth. Cities in Argentina and Mexico did not develop high crime rates when their metropolises expanded significantly in the 1960s and 1970s—crime rose in the late 1990s and early 2000s when city growth became sluggish. In summary, rapid urbanization might have impacted crime only as a lag effect, but this hypothesis must be tested.

None of the theories of social disorganization and weak institutional capacities claim that rapid urbanization produces crime. The type of urban setting, the density, and the quality of city growth all impact the mechanisms of social control that affect criminality. In Latin America, slums existed for decades without resulting in the upswing in violent crimes that the region experienced over the past decade. It appears that community breakdown and weak institutionalism cannot be attributed only to large and unplanned urban sprawl; other factors as yet unaccounted might be at work. I hypothesize that large, new illegal markets have fostered the social conditions that breeded criminality. Crime opportunities and weakening deterrence have undermined social control and accelerated community breakdown in many large new cities across the region. The growth of illegal economies created criminal opportunities for residents of slums and other neighborhoods, making these communities more vulnerable to crime.

Another perspective on crime and cities stresses that crime is highly concentrated. Moreover, as noted in chapter 2, a spatial heterogeneity of criminal activity shows that crime is often concentrated in areas as small as a few city blocks. This "hot spot" perspective (Weisburd et al. 2012) is linked to the crime as opportunity theory (Felson 2002; Braga and Clarke 2014). According to this perspective, offenders are considered rational predators looking for opportunities to commit crimes and remain undetected. Therefore, crime is more likely to occur when formal supervision is poor and the circulation of people and goods is high. Large cities and certain neighborhoods are prone to becoming hot spots of crime.

Several recent studies in the region (Garcia et al. 2013; Tudela et al. 2012; Jaitman and Ajzenman 2016) have followed this line of research, showing that crime indeed tends to be concentrated in a few spots within large cities. There are some methodological concerns[14] and an important question has yet to be answered: Why is crime more intense in certain areas. Moreover, the concentration of criminal activity does not itself reveal why crime finds certain niches or why other similar cities or locations are targets. Policing of hot spots has been found to displace crime and reduce felonies. Yet many risk-prone areas do not become crime ridden. It appears that the socio-spatial features of poor neighborhoods affect their vulnerability to urban violence, though additional factors must also be considered to fully explain the development of a crime hot spot.

In summary, urbanization and community breakdown are associated with crime in the region; however, it remains unclear which factors trigger criminality in some communities but not in others.

Demographic Trends

Extant research in criminology has long established that age and gender are critical variables in offenders' propensity to commit crimes. Males commit more crime than women, and youth aged fifteen to thirty are also more likely to resort to criminal activity—young adults find other options when they begin to develop mature relations, establish families, find permanent jobs, and so on.[15] Therefore, ceteris paribus, the larger the cohorts of youngsters in a country or region, the more crimes can be expected there.[16]

Demographic trends, therefore, play a significant role in criminality. Rates of births and longer lives alter the relative composition of cohorts, and large migration waves affect also the cohort sizes since migrants are usually young people in search of jobs. For instance, crime rates in Western Europe have dropped over the past decades partly because people are living longer and birth rates are lower, producing smaller cohorts of young people susceptible to crime. Conversely, in the United States, the sharp increase in criminality during the 1960s and 1970s has been partly attributed to the large post-World-War II baby boomers who reached adolescence and young adulthood in the late 1960s (Blumstein et al. 2007; O´Brien and Stockard 2002). Research has also identified the direct effects of demographic trends on society, economy, and crime cycles.

How does demographic trend affect criminality in LATAM? This subject has not received enough attention in the region (for exceptions see Soares and Naritomi 2010; Bergman 2001). Fertility rates, the age of mothers upon the birth of their first child, large waves of migrations, longer life expectancy, and other factors have altered the compositions of cohorts across Latin America in different ways. For instance, Uruguay has a very small cohort of young people[17] and also a relatively low crime rate. Conversely, during the 1990s and 2000s, Honduras and El Salvador received a great number of young people expelled from the United States, many of whom were recruited by local gangs, thus contributing to rising crime.

From the evolution of size cohorts of young people we can draw at least three observations that merit close attention (Table 3.4). First, countries with larger cohorts tend to have higher crime rates. By the year 2000,

Table 3.4 Cohort size of males ages 15–24 as a percentage of the total population*

	1965	1970	1975	1980	1985	1990	1995	2000	2005	2010
Arg	8.45	8.73	8.72	8.12	7.97	8.15	8.83	8.95	8.57	8.41
Bol	9.62	9.49	9.75	9.92	9.85	9.85	10.04	10.19	10.10	9.93
Bra	9.10	9.70	10.15	10.29	10.09	9.84	9.91	10.03	9.60	8.65
Chi	9.07	9.46	10.03	10.49	10.46	9.80	8.77	8.28	8.46	8.45
Col	9.17	10.00	10.67	11.08	11.20	10.40	9.77	9.90	9.73	9.31
C.R.	9.61	9.63	10.15	11.03	10.64	9.28	8.78	9.22	9.52	9.23
Ecu	8.91	9.47	10.10	10.20	10.34	10.32	10.08	9.83	9.78	9.62
El Sal	9.08	9.42	9.62	9.58	9.62	9.88	9.78	9.51	9.67	10.28
Hon	8.98	9.34	9.79	9.99	10.13	10.05	10.04	10.26	10.53	10.83
Guate	9.64	10.05	9.78	9.41	9.37	9.59	9.92	10.20	10.17	10.29
Mex	8.98	9.26	9.79	9.83	10.13	10.88	11.04	10.25	9.68	9.55
Nic	8.77	9.51	10.59	10.26	9.74	9.86	10.44	11.00	11.16	10.71
Pan	9.47	9.63	9.98	10.33	10.53	10.50	10.21	9.69	9.25	8.84
Par	9.10	9.83	10.31	10.30	10.23	9.71	9.57	10.14	10.57	10.55
Per	9.11	9.42	9.65	9.96	10.34	10.30	10.26	10.06	9.92	9.72
D.R.	8.33	9.14	10.06	10.55	10.50	10.19	9.87	9.79	9.73	9.55
Uru	7.84	7.89	7.91	8.01	7.76	7.93	8.38	8.04	7.59	7.78
Ven	9.36	9.58	10.16	10.74	10.77	10.30	9.93	9.94	9.87	9.39

* I selected the composite of this cohort because nearly all evidence shows that this group has the largest share of potential offenders.

Source: Author elaboration from Cepalstat (2015). Population, by age group and gender, Demographic-Population Indicators. www.eclac.org.

for example, those countries with a population share lower than 9 percent such as Chile, Argentina, and Uruguay had relatively low rates of crime, while those with more than 10 percent of young males such as Guatemala, Honduras and Nicaragua had higher crime rates. This trend is not a causal explanation, because there are few exceptions, including Paraguay and Bolivia.

Second, as the data in Table 3.4 indicate, most countries in the region share a demographic pattern. Cohorts of young males began rising even before the 1960s, peaked in the late 1980s and 1990s, and then began a slow but steady decline. Countries differ by a few years or a decade with regards to the onset of growth and decline, yet the pattern appears to be similar across the region. Two broad processes explain these demographic trends: a decrease in fertility rates in Latin America since the middle of the 20th century and longer life expectancy, which diminishes the percentage of youth in the total population.

Third, although differences between highest and lowest cohort size are just 2 percent of the total population, this difference proves important. For instance, young males represented 9.26 percent of the Mexican population in 1970, while twenty-five years later they accounted for 11.04 percent—an almost 20 percent rise in the number of youngsters competing for jobs and resources. Even small variations, therefore, can have great implications.

The most intriguing conclusion we can draw from Table 3.4 is that the peak in the relative size of young male cohorts preceded the peak in criminality for every country by close to a decade. For example cohorts of young males were greatest in the 1980s in Chile, Peru, the Dominican Republic, and Venezuela and crime there peaked ten or fifteen years later. Other countries, such as Argentina and Brazil, had both larger crime rates in the year 2000 and relatively large cohorts a few years earlier. All countries, however, had smaller cohorts in the 1960s and 1970s than they did a decade or two later, when crime began to climb.

A plausible hypothesis suggests that demographic trends might have a lagged and/or a cumulative effect on crime: there is not a linear function between cohort sizes and crime rates but rather a "triggering" effect that could potentially initiate a crime trend. Table 3.4 has one underlined observation per country that signals a moment very close to the peak of the young male cohort. This coincides with the onset of the crime rise in each country. Returning to Mexico, its large crime wave occurred in the late 2000s, with crime rates triple those of the mid-1990s, yet the observable important spike in criminality in Mexico began in the mid-1990s (this is particularly so for property crime). Similarly, Colombia had a peak in criminality in the mid-1990s and in the 2000s, but its high-crime trend began in the mid-1980s. In almost every country, a large young male cohort correlates with an upward crime trend. The only exceptions are Costa Rica and Chile.

I hypothesize that larger young-male cohorts are a stressor that might trigger an increase in criminality. Whether or not a crime wave develops will depend on many other important factors, such as state capacities, economic cycles, and other demographic variables, as well as other crime triggers such as availability of drugs and firearms, and of course, access to illegal economies. Therefore, I claim that relative size cohort should be understood as an intervening variable that might accelerate or slow down criminality in the region.

Control Theory: Families and Households

Transformations in family structure in Latin American and their impact on crime have received little attention (for solid contributions see Villarreal and da Silva 2006; Adams 2016). Despite controversies, an established line of research in criminology emphasizes the close association between social upbringing and delinquency. Control theory (Gottfredson and Hirschi 1990) and several of its variants have identified that poor early childhood supervision and a lack of effective control of youngsters increase the likelihood of risky behaviors, including crime. Adult supervision and engagement in child rearing all the way through adolescence are considered covariates with individual crime propensity.

Researchers in Latin America have been skeptical of this finding. Scholars have seen this approach as conservative, as it diverts the attention from macro factors such as social and economic variables, corruption, repression, and/or poorly performing state institutions. This section briefly reviews how these neglected micro-social changes could have indirectly triggered crime in the region.

Family structure. Along with rapid urbanization, families and household structures have dramatically changed over the past decades in Latin America. Fertility rates have dropped, the average age of first-time mothers has risen, and household size has shrunk. Despite differences from country to country, trends are similar throughout the region.[18].

In addition to these well-documented transformations, other processes might have led vulnerable populations into crime, particularly the social conditions in which children were raised. The involvement of extended families in children's lives diminished, single-headed household increased, women joined the workforce in greater numbers, and social protection programs decreased since the 1990s, inadvertently putting more youngsters at risk of engaging in violence and crime. A large number of offenders in the region share similar characteristics: they grew up in an at-risk environment and unstructured household where high at-risk behavior has gone unchecked.

Very few scholars have paid attention to these and other transformations. A UNDP study reports that despite a drop in the adolescent fertility rate in Latin America and the Caribbean from 86 per 1000 young women in the 1970s to 75 per 1000 in the 1990s, the region still remains only second to Africa in adolescent fertility (UNDP 2013, 25). Moreover, countries in the region with homicide rates above 20 per 100,000 also have high adolescent fertility rates (see Cepalstat 2015).[19]

Child-rearing patterns have also changed in the region. In the early 1990s, an average of 21.1 percent of Latin American children ages 0–14 lived in households headed by single mothers, and this share had risen to 27.1 percent by around 2005.[20] Twelve countries witnessed more than a 7 percent increase among children living in female-headed single parent households over a ten- to fifteen-year span. Nearly all of these children live in poverty and face adverse social and economic conditions. However, the overwhelming majority of youngsters that are raised in extremely poor, single-parent households do not resort to crime. In this section I hypothesize that the larger these cohorts are, the more likely it is that a number of minors will engage in criminality. A correlation between the percentage of children living in single-mother households in seven countries (those with full data) around 2005 and the homicide rates in these same countries eight to ten years later yield a statistically significant R coefficient of .42, suggesting that these two variables might covary.

Rapid changes in family structure and job markets during the 1990s had devastating implications for the poor. Disadvantaged mothers who worked in the informal economy and lacked effective support in child rearing were particularly vulnerable, and those living on the marginalized outskirts of growing cities were especially hard hit (Alves da Silva 2014). The extended family structure that had been an instrumental part of child rearing in rural areas has weakened in the newly emerging urban settings. Grandmothers—who in the past had babysat while Mom was at work—also began working in informal markets and free daycare and other programs were not available to mothers. Schools deteriorated rapidly during the 1990s and early 2000s, and many children lacked the parental and institutional supervision at an early age that control theory has deemed instrumental for fostering self-control. These processes may have produced an adverse impact among several youngster who engaged in at-risk behavior.

To lend support for these assertions, fine micro-level analysis is needed; however, I am unaware of any longitudinal studies in the region that have tested these hypotheses. Data from the inmate surveys lend support to the plausibility of control theory. Approximately 20 percent of the inmates reported that they had never met one of their birth parents (usually, and overwhelmingly, their father). More than 35 percent of these offenders left home before turning fifteen, in many cases due to abuse or lack of attachment to the family. One out of four inmates did not finish elementary school, and 85 percent never completed high school.[21]

Using the inmate study for Argentina, I have estimated the impact of social upbringing on offenders who are inclined to commit violent crimes and likely to become repeat offenders. Given the wide distribution of type of offenders in prisons, repeat offenders and violent delinquents are rough proxies for predatory crimes and long criminal careers.[22] This model estimates the impact on prison inmates of variables such as home violence during childhood, one-parent or two-parent households, home abandonment at an early age, substance abuse, and access to firearms by parents or close family members (brothers and other family members living in the same household).[23]

Among inmates who grew up in non-crime environment, 76 percent were non-violent offenders, while among those that did grow up in an environment prone to crime, 62 percent were violent and /or repeat offenders. Nearly 75 percent of those who did not have access to guns were first-time and moderate offenders, whereas 59 percent of those who grew up around guns were more serious delinquents. In addition, 63 percent of inmates that grew up in environments where alcohol and drugs was very much present committed serious crime.[24]

Results from a logistic regression that tests the likelihood of an inmate being repeat offender and being convicted for violent crimes in Argentina are presented in Table 3.5.

Table 3.5 Parameters for logistic regression for repeat convictions

Variables	B	Exp (B)
Crime environment	1.26[a]	3.538
Familiarity with drugs	0.58	1.662
Education	−0.72	0.484
Familiarity with firearms	1.19	3.314
Constant	−2.36	0.094

[a] 0.001 −2Log Likelihood 1214.061 Cox and Snell R square: 17.6, Nagelkerke R square: 23.5.

Source: Inmate survey Argentina (2013).

Inmates in Argentine prisons were more likely to recidivate and commit more serious crimes if they grew up in a crime-ridden environment and suffered from a poor upbringing (leaving home at very young age, having one or two parents in prison, lacking parental supervision at a certain period while growing up, and/or growing up with firearms in the house or easy access to guns). Based on this model, if these conditions are met, an offender is more than three times as likely to engage in more serious and persistent criminal behavior than in less frequent and non-violent crimes. These variables appear to have even more power to predict future criminality than other commonly used variables, such as level of education and drugs.

This estimation for Argentina provides indirect support for the theory that upbringing has an impact on the criminal careers of certain offenders. Regression analysis cannot ascertain the true impact these variables have on propensity to commit crimes, due to the absence of a non-delinquent control group. This evidence only shows that poor child rearing might have lasting consequences for very risky criminal behavior in some individuals.

Drivers and Triggers

Alcohol, firearms, and drugs are three important triggers of criminality. Both alcohol and drugs suppress self-control and can motivate people under their influence to undertake risky behaviors, including criminal acts. Firearms, on the other hand, facilitate crime for those motivated to commit them. The profits associated with the illicit drug trade, particularly drug trafficking, provide large incentives for some to earn a living by trading in these illegal substances.

Following is an overview of the effect of these crime triggers in the Latin American context, surveying the central propositions in the literature and evaluating the merits of these assertions for the countries being studied. As we will see, these triggers do impact on crime. The real challenge is to identify the mechanisms by which these triggers have been involved in crime waves since the 1980s and 1990s and determine to what extent the presence of alcohol, drugs, and firearms has increased in the region and contributed to the rise in crime.

Alcohol. Alcohol is legal everywhere in the region, therefore the alcohol–crime connection is only relevant when alcohol is present before crimes are committed. Alcohol is believed to play a role in certain domestic violence episodes, street crimes, and other disputes (Dingwal 2006). The inmate surveys appear to confirm that offenders were often under the influence of alcohol when committing crimes. One out of three offenders acknowledged having consumed alcohol or drugs at least six hours before the alleged offense was committed. Most admitted that alcohol was the predominant substance and the true scope of alcohol use before crime is probably underreported. For instance, in the United States more than 40 percent of detainees admitted using alcohol at the time they committed their offenses (Greenfeld 1998).

Until very recently, the number of crimes perpetrated under the influence of alcohol was higher than the number of crimes committed under the influence of all other drugs combined, presumably because alcohol is inexpensive and widely available. While hard-drug users in Latin America make up no more than 10 percent of the adult population, more people use alcohol. Between 2004 and 2008, the rate of adult alcohol use over the previous thirty days was reported as 37 percent for Bolivia and Ecuador, 38 percent for Brazil, 34 percent for Colombia, 49 percent for Chile, 34 percent for Peru, and 45 percent for Paraguay. In contrast, in the United States this rate was 54 percent and in Canada 77 percent.[25] Among high-school students, rates are either higher (46 percent Argentina, 44 percent Brazil, 50 percent Colombia, 52 percent Uruguay) or at similar levels (27 percent Bolivia, 35 percent Ecuador, 40 percent Paraguay).[26] Although most users do not abuse alcohol, the number of intoxicated individuals have become a social and health problem in most countries of the region.

The association between alcohol outlet density and violence, on the one hand, and the availability and accessibility of alcohol on the other has become a predictor of violence and crime around establishments selling alcohol. In addition to the individual-level factors influencing alcohol use and criminal behavior, sociological research in the United States and Europe have looked into neighborhood-level mechanisms, such as the physical features of the urban landscape, poverty levels, and social organizational features that either affect the rate of alcohol use or the risk of victimization (Alaniz, et al., 2000; Gorman, et al., 2001; Scribner et al., 1999; Gouvis et al. 2008). This line of research sheds light on a critical question for Latin America: Has the greater availability of alcohol, particularly in the context of weak social-organization structures, affected the increase in violent crimes such as assault, homicide, and domestic violence?

Alcohol consumption has a long history in the region, raising a few questions: What has changed recently? Are the rates of use and abuse higher? Has the easier availability and greater affordability of alcohol indeed increased levels of intoxication? Unfortunately, few studies have empirically tested the connection between alcohol and crime in the region. The inmate surveys show that alcohol use was present among 47 percent of those convicted for thefts, 21 percent of offenders who had committed homicide, 15 percent of those who engaged in drug crimes, and 18 percent of those who committed rape. As in other latitudes, alcohol use appears to be a component of some violent crimes as well as petty crimes and theft.

The effect of variation across time cannot be properly assessed without longitudinal studies. The four waves of inmate surveys in Mexico dating from 2002 to 2013 yielded no statistical difference in the rate of alcohol consumption before crimes were committed. Approximately one-third of the inmates in each wave who were arrested within two years before taking the survey reported using alcohol six hours before committing their crimes. But these studies do not prove that the growing number of offenders derives from greater alcohol consumption rates.

The inmate surveys, however, do provide evidence that prevalence of alcohol in one's social background increases at-risk behavior, though they do not support arguments on the effect of alcohol availability on rising crime. First, close to 35 percent of the inmate population reported that alcohol abuse was very common in the household in which they grew up. Growing up in households where at least one family member abuses alcohol increases the likelihood of committing violent and predatory crimes as opposed to other crimes. Second, it does not appear that the density of alcohol outlets triggered more crime, since alcohol is widely available across the region (there were no prohibition laws, and regulation of access to alcohol among minors has been always weak). The upsurge in the consumption of alcohol is tied to an overall trend of rising demand due to other social processes.

In summary, the scattered data indicate that alcohol use and abuse has been rising in the region and across the world, but the connection between high consumption and rising crime trends remains unclear. There is no evidence to prove that the rapid increase of criminality since the 1990s is related to higher levels of alcohol abuse. First, there is a long tradition of drinking in the region. Second, the percentage of people who are arrested while intoxicated is similar in this region to that of other regions. Third, no studies to date have proven that alcohol availability in the region is linked to crime.

Illegal drugs. Are drug use and the drug trade responsible for the rise in crime in the region? Researchers have paid significant attention to the way in which illegal drugs have contributed to violence in many countries of Latin America, and chapters 5 and 6 analyze the role played by organized crime and the effect that the drug trade has had primarily on HCE. The large worldwide demand for the illegal drugs produced in the region has generated a plethora of violent and illegal enterprises that have intensified crime significantly. In this section I briefly discuss the effect of drug use and abuse on criminality in Latin America.

Illegal drugs can affect street crimes in at least two different ways: a) some individuals under the influence of powerful substances might be inclined to rob or assault others because drugs lower inhibitors and self-control mechanisms; b) youngsters in search of illegal means might feel motivated to rob or assault others in order to acquire money for drugs. According to earlier theories of crime, these two paths to criminality are predominant among youngsters living in poverty and poorly organized communities. As the irruption of illegal substances penetrated disadvantaged neighborhoods, some residents became addicts. These individuals then served the drug trade either by selling or pushing drugs or by helping drugs dealers; or, they resort to petty theft for the money they need to buy illegal drugs.

Unlike alcohol, which has always been available and used in the region, the widespread consumption of illegal drugs is relatively new. Heroin and cocaine have been produced for decades in Mexico, Peru, and Bolivia, yet no significant level of domestic demand was noted until the 1990s. Moderate levels of use for marihuana, in contrast, were reported for decades, but its consumption has surged over the last twenty years.[27] The extent of drug use indicates that some domestic markets remained small, particularly in the 1990s. For instance, rates of heroin use are minimal in Latin America.[28] MDMA (also known as ecstasy) is relatively new. And last year prevalence rates for cocaine in most countries did not exceed 1 percent of the adult population, while for marijuana rates fluctuated between 2 and 7 percent. In summary, drug use has been rising since the 1990s and 2000s but prevalence rates, except for pockets of high demand, remain moderate. They were definitely small when crime rates began to climb in the 1990s.

Drug users are indeed prone to engage in delinquent behavior. Many petty crimes in Latin American metropolises are carried out by young people who need money to buy drugs, but also to support themselves and their families. Chapters 5 and 9 will show that drug abuse is associated with violent crimes; some inmates report that they have used drugs just before committing the crime that led to their arrest. Large numbers of users might breed higher crime rates, though it is impossible to test this assertion without a control group. A large number of drug users cannot independently explain the process that triggered the current rise in crime because this wave preceded the drug epidemic. The rates of drug use in the region did not reach moderate levels until about five years ago, and drug users are mostly marijuana smokers who tend to be the least involved in criminal behavior.

Drugs, however, were a major trigger of violent crime as it relates to drug trafficking, a subject to be analyzed in later chapters.

Firearms. There has been a great debate, both in the United States and in Latin America, on the connection between guns and crime. Advocates of legal gun ownership claim that guns protect people and could deter delinquents from robbing or assaulting potential victims (Lott 2010) and that outlawing gun ownership may actually serve the "outlaws" who can still gain access to illegal weapons and use them to commit crimes. On the other hand, prohibition advocates assert that restricted access to firearms drastically reduces people's ability to engage in crime. Guns kill people, and therefore, severely restricted use diminishes fatalities. (Zimring 1991; Cook and Moore 1995)

For criminologists, the firearms debate revolves around issues of instrumentality and availability. Do guns—and easy availability of firearms—produce more crimes and more fatal outcomes and if so, to what extent? The evidence appears to suggest that guns do indeed make violent encounters more lethal (Siegel et al. 2013). They can also lead to more thefts and other crimes, because they give the offender the power to intimidate others and gain control of a violent encounter (Ayres and Donohue 2003). Victims might then choose not to fight back against assailants, reducing fatal outcomes. However, it is hard to isolate the instrumentality of weapons as an independent causal effect on criminality.

The availability of firearms is linked to instrumentality. Research has shown that guns at home increase the likelihood of suicides, homicides, and domestic violence (Kellerman et al. 1993). Easier access to weapons for would-be delinquents might accelerate their involvement in street crime (Ayres and Donohue 2003), and the overall supply of firearms can turn simple disputes into murders (Cook and Moore 1995).

There are two critical questions on the role of firearms has played in Latin American crime. First, have weapons become more available, and if so, to what extent can they account for spiraling criminality since the 1990s? Second, how can weapons be isolated as an independent causal effect of criminality? In other words, if more weapons are available to would-be delinquents, can this explain an upsurge in crime? These questions merit comprehensive research. Here, I provide an overview on the impact of firearms on crime in the region.

Firearms account for a large proportion of homicides in the region. As shown in chapter 2 while 42 percent of murders worldwide are attributed to gunshots, in Latin America that rate exceeds 65 percent (Small Arms Survey 2012). According to different estimates, more than 50 million firearms are in the hands of individuals and most are illegally owned (Stohl and Tuttle 2008).[29] The annual cost of small guns, parts, and ammunition in the region is estimated at eight billion dollars per year (Simone 2013).

There are various sources of weapons. Some are "leftovers" from armed conflicts in Central America and Colombia, while others are stolen from the police and armed forces. Most arms were originally produced in the United States and smuggled into the region or were produced by Brazil's arms industry. Semiautomatic assault weapons and other firearms are sold in Texas gun shows to smugglers who subsequently arm organized crime gangs in Mexico and Central America at an estimated rate of two thousand weapons per day (Simone 2013).[30] In short, the available evidence indicates that there is a wide supply of both small firearms and assault weapons in the region, supplied by different sources (Fleitas 2016). States have limited capacities to regulate legal ownership, and black markets offering everything from handguns to assault weapons have proliferated in the region.

The inmate surveys lend support to the argument that easy access to firearms increases crime. An average of 60 percent of the inmates in all six countries had a firearm or had contact with weapons since adolescence.[31] When asked whether they had ever held a gun before turning fifteen, 20 percent said they had,[32] and close to 50 percent had access to guns before turning eighteen. In addition, a thriving black market for weapons reveals that law enforcement officers have turned a blind eye to crime networks: for inmates who reported having guns, 48 percent said they acquired the weapons from friends or from the police.[33] In short, the data indicate that it is relatively easy to access weapons in Latin America.

The data also confirm that guns are instrumental in the commission of crimes. According to a UNDP (2013) report in 2010, 78,439 homicides were committed using firearms in fourteen countries of the region.[34] Firearms were involved in 47 percent of all homicides in Uruguay, rising to 82 percent in Colombia. Nearly, two out of every three homicides results from the use of firearms. Guns are also widely used in robberies. According to the survey conducted by LAPOP, one out of three victims of theft reported that the thief had a weapon (reported by UNDP 2013). This should be seen as a baseline. Among inmates, 41 percent reported having carried a weapon when they committed the crime, and among these, 25 percent admitted having used it. In summary, the use of firearms in crime appears to be widespread and has "helped" offenders in the commission of felonies.

Despite the instrumentality and the wide accessibility of weapons in the region, there is still no firm evidence that firearms have triggered the current crime wave. How new is this process? Are more guns producing more crime, or is the drive to commit crime sending miscreants out to search for firearms? Despite the strong association between crime and weapons, causality remains unclear. Some countries with significant accessibility to firearms, such as Argentina, Chile, or Paraguay, have relatively low levels of criminality, whereas the wide availability of firearms in Brazil or Mexico has contributed to spiraling violence. Although the precise connection between weapons and crime in Latin America still needs to be determined, three conclusions can be drawn from the evidence available: violent encounters have become more lethal; guns have helped delinquents to commit other crimes; and greater accessibility has allowed delinquents to acquire guns.

Summing up. Drugs, alcohol, and firearms have contributed to spiraling crime in the region. However, it is unclear whether these are independent causes that spurred current crime waves, or whether they merely augmented and intensified crime that derives from other unknown factors. Alcohol has been present in the region for many decades, if not for centuries, and widely accessed in different affordable versions. The widespread consumption and sale of hard drugs is relatively new but began to be noticeable several years (if not decades) after the crime waves began. Finally, the evidence appears to indicate that more guns indeed produced more crime, yet the presence of arsenals and many weapons in a region marred by bloody armed conflict (from the Mexican Revolution to the civil wars in Central America) have produced black markets of firearms going back over a century.

It is unlikely that these drivers triggered the current crime wave, although they have accelerated criminality, particularly under HCE. Countries that faced large crime waves and have weak regulation capacities were unable to deter offenders from engaging in at-risk behavior. The presence of drugs and firearms in HCE countries has dramatically increased violent crimes.

Crime predictors in LATAM: A Summary

When crime began to spiral in Latin America, no comprehensive theories were advanced to account for this dramatic development. Scholars and law enforcement officials from the region relied on fragments of classical theories on crime developed in Europe and the United States and adjusted them to the Latin American environment. Others looked to dysfunctional and obsolete criminal justice systems. Still others examined the effects of single variables such as drugs, firearms, unemployment, inequality, and so on.

Interpretations of the heightening of crime have recently emerged, though research continues to be marked by a lack of comprehensive theories. Despite the important steps taken over the past decade, there is no clear vision in the region as to what is really happening. This chapter has presented different perspectives and explanations of rising crime in light of available evidence. Here, I summarize several leading hypotheses or simple explanations developed in the region to account for the rise in crime and briefly assess their merits:

a) H1. *Crime has grown worldwide.* The available data do not support this theory. In the same period, as shown in chapter 2, only a few countries in Eastern Europe and sub-Saharan Africa have witnessed similar spikes in crime. In a few countries of Eastern Asia, crime has risen only moderately; there has been no increase in crime in the Middle East, moderate or null growth in Western Europe, and significant decreases in crime in Canada and the United States. In other words, there is no evidence of an upsurge in crime worldwide.

b) H2. *Neoliberalism.* Nearly all of the LATAM countries have experienced the effects of the so-called "Washington consensus" in the 1990s, a decade in which social exclusion, unemployment, and inequality all rose, creating an environment for crime to flourish. Although this question merits further research, the evidence indicates that these factors alone are not sufficient to explain the hike in crime. Social exclusion and inequality were just as severe in the 1960s and 1970s, though robbery and violent crime were far below the rates they have reached over the past few decades. However, as I will show in the next three chapters, these processes developed in a way that did in fact have an important impact on crime; I refer to these as predisposing factors.

c) H3. *The firearm market.* The evidence indicates that homicide and robbery rates are associated with the proliferation of guns. What remains unclear is whether this results from a rise in the demand for firearms or from their widespread availability. In other words, it is difficult to determine causality. There is evidence that a greater number of weapons does not produce more crime. In the United States, there has been an important drop in crime but sustained growth in the number of firearms held by civilians, with more than 200 million firearms in circulation in that country. Weapons would instead appear to be a factor that facilitates crime but does not cause it.

d) H4. *Cultural changes.* Scholars have argued that Latin America has experienced a major cultural shift in the past decades, especially among youth, who ultimately are involved in the vast majority of crimes. Other indirect factors include changes in the legal culture, a reduced influence of religion, changes in family structure and in sexual practices, and so on. Naturally, cultural shifts are broad and difficult to identify. In chapter 4, I will argue that the effects of changes in spending patterns and consumerism have sparked tensions that have led to an increase in criminal activity.

e) H5. *Drugs.* Undoubtedly, the trafficking and sale of drugs, especially cocaine, has contributed to spiraling violence across the region. At the same time, drug markets are not necessarily associated
   with spikes in violence, as can be seen in Europe, Canada, and many
   countries of Latin America. In order for this variable to be linked to
   the intensification in crime across the region, it would have had to
   affect all Latin America. In at least half of the countries, criminal activity surged before drug trafficking and consumption became widespread. Therefore, drugs appear to be more of a contributing factor,
   albeit a significant one, but not a true cause.

f) H6. *Transitions to democracy.* For a region that suffered from the
   arbitrary and cruel governments headed by military dictators or
   that had withstood civil wars, it is difficult to acknowledge that
   the growth of both regular and organized crime coincided with
   the processes of democratic transitions and peace accords. There
   is no exact correlation, but it is evident that these occurred simul-
   taneously. However, I argue that it is not the transition per se but
   the processes that the transitions set up that indirectly reduced
   the dissuasive capacity of states in the region. In summary, the
   return of democracy contains what I consider an important but
   overlooked variable: the weakening of states and of their deterrence capacity.

g) H7. *Uncontrolled urbanization.* A long tradition in criminology has
   held that rapid urban growth with insufficient urban planning,
   overcrowding, and urban concentration (high population density,
   limited access to public services, a deterioration of family and cultural networks) has contributed to a rise in criminal activity. The
   import substitution industrialization (ISI) process from the 1950s
   to 1980s enhanced the growth in LATAM of *barrios, favelas, colonias,*
   and *villas.* In these marginal areas, there has been limited access to
   state support and criminal networks found fertile ground to recruit
   potential delinquents. However, in countries like Argentina, Brazil,
   and Mexico, this urban development preceded the actual growth in
   crime, as the outbreak of underpriviledged neighborhoods in these
   countries dates back to the 1950s, 1960s, and 1970s. In other words,
   disorderly urban growth is associated with high levels of criminal activity, but cannot be considered a direct cause.

h) H8. *Breakdown of the social structure.* Several indicators highlight severe problems in education, job markets, and family structures. This

chapter has shown that some of them in fact covary with rising crime. However, the evidence is not strong enough to consider these variables as causal effects. I claim it is better to speak of a rupture of established social equilibrium than to identify poverty, unemployment, and inequality as causal factors in rising crime.

i) H9. *Demographic transformations.* These variables have received little attention, but initial data indicate that demographic patterns, such as size of cohorts, household structures, and trends in migration, correlate with criminality to some extent. There is a need for further research to gauge the precise effect.

The lack of a compelling theory for LATAM's rise of violence and thefts support the enigmatic character of crime. This chapter has provided an overview of standard explanations of criminality along with initial evidence to test the plausibility of different perspectives. The next chapters will integrate several of these variables into a comprehensive approach to the different trajectories of rising crime in Latin America. I will show that the development of illicit markets for the consumption of illegal goods in the midst of relative prosperity put pressure on weak and failing enforcement institutions, yielding different crime equilibria.

PART II

The Business of Crime and the Spread of Illegal Markets

This second part begins to unpack the central argument of this book. Chapter 4 is devoted to the growth of property crimes that facilitated the development of illegal secondary markets. It shows that a rising demand for cheap stolen goods fed the emergence of networks that profited from the business opportunities provided by trading such goods. Chapter 5 is devoted to the largest of the illegal markets: narcotics. It explains how the domestic and the international illegal drug markets have affected many countries of the region. Chapter 6 studies countries with HCEs, in search for an understanding of why their societies developed into highly dysfunctional and violent environments.

Overall, this part calls the attention of the reader into an understudied topic of criminality in Latin America: the rise in property crime and the overall businesses of crime that transcends narcotics have together created jobs and business opportunities for millions and have shaped daily lives in many Latin American cities. The appetite for cheap and illegal goods has been a stressor for the crime equilibria in the region.

4

Profits and Opportunities

THE GROWTH OF ILLEGAL MARKETS AND CRIME

Why, we must ask, have urban violent crime rates increased substantially during the past decade when the conditions that are supposed to cause violent crime have not worsened—have, indeed, generally improved?

—REPORT OF THE US NATIONAL COMMISSION ON THE CAUSES AND PREVENTION OF VIOLENCE (1969: XXXVII)

IN THIS BOOK I show that a sharp increase in the demand for consumer goods has in turn stimulated a growth in secondary markets.[1] Crime in Latin America has risen in part to meet such demand by creating vigorous markets in stolen and illicit goods, supplied by networks of criminal rings, which function for the most part as "normal markets." The weak institutions of the criminal justice system have either failed or been very ineffectual in their capacity to deter crime. As a result, new equilibrium of high crime and low deterrence has emerged, creating incentives for many citizens to join criminal networks and profit from new criminal enterprises.

Markets of stolen and illicit goods exist everywhere; this is by no means a new Latin American phenomenon. Most countries have a history of illegal trade, stolen products, counterfeiting, and smuggling, which penetrated legal markets in tradable goods (Malone and Malone Rowe 2013; Andreas 2013). But the contemporary emergence of new markets, which drive up crime, is distinguished by its scope. The supply of stolen products and the rise in consumption of illegal goods have generated large markets. Prosperity in the region has enhanced consumption of these goods for a growing number of new consumers who are able to satisfy their appetite for consumption only if prices are low. Crime has risen rapidly in part because of strong demand for goods, on the one hand, and weak state institutions on the other, which enabled new "entrepreneurs" to organize the supply of these goods to meet a growing demand. Once crime reached a tipping point, violent and predatory crimes (homicide, kidnapping, extortion) rose to unprecedented levels.

In this and the following two chapters I analyze the emergence of markets where criminality has thrived and the role played in those markets by organized crime. In chapters 7, 8, and 9 I turn to the study of the deterrent capabilities of the criminal justice institutions. I contend that these two broad components (criminal markets and justice institutions) operate in equilibrium. The stability of the equilibrium depends on each country´s specific conditions. Overall, as demand for illegal goods produces significant rents to be distributed among new elites and powerful groups, state institutions designed to neutralize illegality will require higher capacities. To the extent that they are unable to obstruct the consolidation of these markets, crime organizes and imposes even higher challenges to state institutions, changing the crime equilibrium. That has been the tragic outcome for many nations in Latin America.

This chapter examines the rise in consumption of illegal goods in the region, beginning with a discussion of consumer trends, and showing that in most countries of the region, these have had a dramatic increase in consumption since the 1990s. Using available data for several countries, I claim that a rise in private consumption was widespread at most income levels and has been most noticeable among low-income households. I then turn to a sociological interpretation of the rise of consumerism in the region. Next, I examine rates of victimization in order to assess the magnitude of this initial stage in the development of illegal markets and prove that the extent and type of victimizations fuel illegal markets, although high levels of violence are unevenly distributed in the region and emerge only occasionally. Although this rise in consumption does not by itself explain the rise in crime, the correlation between crime and rising consumption across income levels invites an analysis of the emergence of secondary markets that will be further developed later in this chapter. Pains are taken to provide a thorough understanding of the magnitude of crimes that have forged secondary markets. Finally, the chapter documents trends that have not been systematically examined in previous works, using various different sources of data on goods such as cell phones, appliances, and firearms, and an in depth study of car thefts, using a typical case to exemplify how illegal markets for stolen cars operate. The chapter concludes by putting together these findings within the conceptual framework of crime equilibria.

The Rise in Consumerism

In many countries of the region, crime did not increase significantly during the so-called lost decade of the 1980s.[2] A sharp upsurge in crime, however, erupted precisely during the 1990s, a decade known as the neoliberal period. Crime began to rise before the Mexico´s 1995 economic crisis that spilled over throughout the region, and it intensified after the crisis. In short, crime had moderate increases in the 1980s but a new wave rose abruptly in the 1990s, correlating with periods of economic expansion.

A second and sharper wave of criminality occurred in the middle years of the first decade of this century, during the peak of the commodity boom. The data in chapter 2 have shown that economic expansion was followed by remarkable increases in criminality, particularly in property crime. Of course, this process has been far from uniform. However, and this is the core argument presented here, against the prediction of several criminological theories, more prosperity and plenty of jobs have not produced the anticipated reduction in crime. This chapter addresses this puzzle.

Growth and Consumption Trends in Latin America

The GDP and other economic indicators for the years 1991–2010 show significant improvements. Table 4.1 shows the growth in GDP per capita for each country in the region over several time periods. GDP grew moderately in the 1960s and 1970s, stagnated or decreased during the 1980s, and in most cases had an important growth surge during the 1990s and a vigorous expansion in the first decade of the twenty-first century.[3]

Private consumption (Table 4.2) increased at a much higher rate than GDP from the 1990s on, proving that a large share of economic growth in the region was tied to a remarkable rise in households expenditures on goods and services. Especially after the low performance in the lost decade of the 1980s, GDP growth and personal consumption rebounded vigorously. Even in historical perspective, the improvement in household consumption was significant: Table 4.2 shows that the spike in consumption in the years 1991–2010 has been remarkable. Brazil is a good example.

Table 4.1 Percentage change in GDP per capita

Country	1961–1980	1981–1990	1991–2000	2001–2010
Argentina	38	−20	24	20[a]
Bolivia	19	−18	13	22
Brazil	28	2	10	28
Chile	34	19	50	29
Colombia	66	15	8	28
Costa Rica	85	03	30	30
Dominican R.	10	0	52	45
Ecuador	67	−02	−03	22
El Salvador	N/A	−05	38	14
Guatemala	73	−13	17	9
Honduras	51	−5	8	22
Mexico	99	−8	15	7
Nicaragua	05	−33	16	16
Panama	70	−14	24	56
Paraguay	121	6	0	20
Peru	31	−30	23	56
Uruguay	33	−7	27	37
Venezuela	08	−14	−7	13

[a] For Argentina the right-hand column refers to the period 2001–2006. No reliable data have been reported by that country since 2007.

Source: Author's calculations from GDP per capita converted to 2005 dollars from World Development Indicators, http://databank.worldbank.org/data/home.aspx, accessed March 14, 2014.

While in the 1980s GDP per capita stagnated, during the 1990s it expanded by 10 percent, and over the next decade almost tripled (to 28 percent). Average household expenditure grew at an even faster pace, with negative growth in the 1980s replaced by vigorous increases of 16.5 percent and 30 percent in the next two decades. Most countries in the region report similar patterns of growth.

Growth in consumption was spread across different segments of income, but it was most noticeable in the last decade among low-income groups. Unfortunately, the historical data do not allow a breakdown of household or personal expenditures over extended periods for different social strata; however, there are data on personal income. Since for lower income deciles it is safe to assume that most of the income is used for personal or household consumption, the trends and changes among lower

Table 4.2 Percentage change in household expenditure per capita

Country	1980–1990	1991–2000	2001–2010
Argentina	N/A	8.1[a]	13.9[a]
Bolivia	−13.1	11.8	−2.4
Brazil	−9.4	16.5	30.0
Canada	15.2	18.8	22.6
Chile	4.4	64.8	43.0
Colombia	4.6	5.2	23.4
Costa Rica	−5.0	24.9	21.8
Dominican Republic	4.2	49.3	59.8
El Salvador	−1.7	45.5	15.7
Ecuador	−2.0	−4.9	31.5
El Salvador	−1.7	45.5	15.7
Guatemala	−11.8	17.2	11.9
Honduras	−6.3	5.7	27.6
Mexico	−2.2	25.7	11.7
Nicaragua	−54.9	24.4	26.1
Panama	16.9	38.9	33.6
Peru	−24.2	16.9	44.6
Paraguay	N/A	−8.0	27.1
Uruguay	−8.0	41.9	30.0
United States	28.6	29.1	10.3
Venezuela, RB	−13.4	−10.8	44.6
Latin America & Caribbean	−5.5	18.2	23.5

[a] For Argentina, data for the 1990s is from the period 1993–2000 and for the 2000s from 2001–2006.

Source: Author elaboration based on World Development Indicators processed from household final consumption expenditure, converted to 2005 dollars, http://databank.worldbank.org/data/home.aspx, accessed March 16, 2014.

deciles of income indirectly reflect changes in the magnitude of consumption for these social groups. The data suggest that they have driven up overall demand.

To measure changes in income by deciles, I converted incomes to 2012 prices and calculated the rate of change between first and last year of available data based on household surveys for every country for the 1990s (Table 4.3) and the following decade (Table 4.4).

The data on income from these household surveys show that increases for lower and middle income groups were impressive and most likely translated

Table 4.3 Percentage change in personal income by deciles during the 1990s

Country	Period	Decile									
		1	2	3	4	5	6	7	8	9	10
Argentina	1992–1999	−40.2	−28.0	−23.9	−21.1	−16.6	−14.9	−12.8	−10.4	−7.7	−3.4
Brazil	1995–1999	−5.6	−1.8	−1.6	−2.2	−2.1	−2.3	−3	−3.1	0	0
Chile	1992–1998	15.4	21.9	24.4	27.6	28.6	28.7	29.3	32.5	36.7	30.2
Costa Rica	1992–1999	48.0	31.0	28.2	28.4	27.9	28.7	29.5	32.6	38.4	45.3
Dominican R.	1996–2000	−1.3	2.3	2.9	3.5	4.4	8.8	12.5	15.0	16.8	32.4
Ecuador	1995–1999	120.5	23.7	4	−6.8	−10.8	−12.7	−13.5	−13.4	−12.8	4
Honduras	1991–1999	−37.9	3.2	19.3	28.2	32.9	38.1	42.9	46.9	51.5	44.8
Mexico	1994–1998	−26.9	−23.9	−19.7	−17.7	−17.2	−17.2	−17.8	−19.0	−18.5	−23.9
Nicaragua	1993–1998	132.0	63.2	48.1	38.1	31.7	28.6	21.7	16.6	13.7	18.4
Panama	1991–1999	231.0	108.0	59.1	42.1	35.1	33.3	30.5	26.9	27.7	33.0
Paraguay	1995–1999	19.7	16.0	14.6	11.0	6.0	4.6	2.5	2.5	2.6	−10.8
Peru	1997–1999	−6.8	−8.4	−8.0	−10.2	−11.7	−10.4	−10.6	−8.7	−5.8	6.1
Uruguay	1992–1998	−11.3	−9.5	−4.0	−0.3	2.3	4.4	7.4	10.7	14.5	15.6
Venezuela	1992–1999	−44.2	−38.1	−35.0	−32.3	−30.4	−28.4	−26.6	−24.3	−22.0	−12.2

No data is available for this period for Colombia, Guatemala, or El Salvador.

Source: Author estimation from data provided by SEDLAC (2013).

Table 4.4 Percentage change in personal income by deciles, 2000–2012

Country	Period	Decile									
		1	2	3	4	5	6	7	8	9	10
Argentina	2000–2012	125.1	86.4	75.6	68.0	62.2	54.2	48.6	38.8	27.8	8.7
Brazil	2001–2012	159.4	108.7	95.5	86.0	78.9	72.3	61.4	50.9	38.3	26.6
Chile	2000–2011	59.9	50.6	47.8	43.8	38.6	33.9	31.1	28.8	25.4	15.4
Colombia	2001–2012	267.8	109.9	86.8	84.9	86.7	89.5	88.6	88.3	83.0	56.4
Costa Rica	2000–2012	127.6	75.9	66.3	64.5	66.0	64.9	64.9	70.2	79.5	81.8
Dominican R.	2001–2011	10.7	6.3	1.4	-1.4	-3.4	-5.4	-3.8	-6.1	-10.5	-13.9
Ecuador	2003–2012	122.2	87.8	78.6	74.1	69.2	65.8	59.8	55.2	45.7	12.9
El Salvador	2004–2012	79.3	32.3	19.1	14.8	11.5	7.2	2.2	-1.2	-4.5	-7.2
Guatemala	2000–2011	1.0	-8.9	-11.5	-13.3	-14.0	-14.6	-14.6	-15.1	-17.6	-23.2
Honduras	2001–2011	1.2	1.6	0.1	-1.5	-1.7	-1.5	-3.8	-2.9	0.3	18.3
Mexico	2000–2012	55.8	38.1	27.9	25.1	22.8	17.6	15.5	14.0	10.2	1.1
Nicaragua	2001–2009	92.5	48.8	37.7	32.8	26.6	21.5	16.4	9.7	-0.4	-28.7
Panama	2000–2012	537.7	122.2	87.4	73.7	66.1	59.5	52.7	46.2	40.6	33.9
Paraguay	2001–2011	39.0	31.2	31.9	29.1	28.3	27.3	25.6	23.6	18.8	15.2
Peru	2000–2012	121.9	110.0	105.3	99.1	95.1	87.5	81.5	74.9	66.1	47.5
Uruguay	2000–2012	15.4	13.8	11.3	8.6	7.7	7.6	7.5	5.7	2.7	-6.5
Venezuela	2000–2006	47.1	42.1	40.3	38.6	36.0	34.2	34.0	32.5	31.7	34.8

Source: Author estimation based on data provided by SEDLAC (2013).

into a spike in private consumption. Income inequality increased in some countries during the 1990s and had decreased moderately in the following decade, showing that lower income groups had larger percentage increases than higher income groups.[4] Personal consumption, however, has been consistently higher throughout this period.

In short, aggregate data point to a steady rise in economic growth since the 1990s, rising overall consumption in all countries, and a steady improvement in particular by lower income groups in some nations since the 1990s and for most countries especially during the first decade of the twenty-first century. As shown in chapter 2, this process correlated with a significant rise in crime. I will claim later in the rising demand section of this chapter that this growth in consumption has partly fueled the development of secondary markets in illicit goods.

Why the Appetite for Consumerism?

Rising consumption does not necessarily imply higher criminality. In this chapter I argue that the higher demand for cheap goods created incentives for the establishment of supply chains that specialized in stolen or illicit products. It is first a demand-driven market that has enabled illegal markets to emerge and consolidate.

Over the last few decades a large literature on the expansion of consumerism in the region has shown that this process coalesced with the incorporation of new segments into a "consumer society."[5] In a penetrating essay, García Canclini (2001) has proposed a parallel between consumerism and citizenship, arguing that to a large extent the incorporation of new citizens into the re-democratized Latin America has enabled new paths of integration for the individual's social participation precisely through the formation of personal identities associated with people as consumers rather than as political and community members. Identities are defined mainly by what is being consumed, rather than any other social affiliation, and therefore community belonging is determined greatly by access to the world of brands, fashion, and so on.

The significant change brought by mass consumption introduced many structural and symbolic effects that are beyond the scope of this book (see Bourdieu 1984, 1999; Bauman 2007).[6] Clearly, the "democratization" of consumption has been noticeable on every street corner of the region. Consumption for the vast majority of inhabitants was limited to the attainment of basic needs, particularly food and housing. In the twenty-first century, an overwhelming majority of Latin Americans devote their resources and time to clothing brands, fashion styles, and entertainment. Basic needs remain a central concern for some segments of societies, particularly in rural areas, but for a large majority of the population, identities are shaped by full participation in consumerism. In practical terms this means that people believe they have the right to access goods that allow them full recognition by others.

This process is not unique to Latin America. The rise in consumption for different deciles of income has been noticeable everywhere, particularly in East Asia, sub-Saharan Africa, and Eastern Europe. Illegal markets have also developed in these regions, and some degree of violence has also ensued. What distinguishes Latin America is the scope and the extent of illegal markets and the poor law enforcement capacities to dismantle emerging new rackets.

Rising consumption also brought political benefits to new democratic governments. The wide support for the 1990s market reforms, particularly among disadvantaged sectors, is partly explained by the availability of less expensive but quality goods due to globalization, the liberalization of trade, and the reduction of tariffs, all of which facilitated higher private consumption (Baker 2009). Cheaper goods legally imported from East Asia, in addition to the counterfeit and stolen goods that inundated the marketplaces, were snapped up by eager citizens driven by consumer interests that shaped new identities.

The profound change in the region's patterns of consumption during the past decades created business opportunities for new entrepreneurs. New patterns of mass consumption have enhanced the development of secondary markets, patronized in particular by low-income groups. Today in Latin America every city has at least one major locus of makeshift stores where stolen or counterfeit products are widely and openly traded. Illicit products are sold in large marketplaces under the watchful eye of the authorities.[7]

Rising Demand

There are many illegal products in great demand. Narcotics are of course the most coveted and profitable of these goods, but other large markets have developed to meet rising demands. As will be shown in the car theft section later in this chapter, markets in stolen automobiles and auto parts have increased significantly over the recent decades. Markets in electronic goods such as computers, and lately cell phones, PDAs, and other digital products, have likewise grown. Today every inhabitant of any Latin American city knows where these goods are sold at lower prices. Most citizens also know the dubious origin of the products. Many of them are refurbished goods that, through a process that began in a theft, and through an established chain of commercialization, reach well-known outlets where demand is high.

These secondary markets exist everywhere, even in the most developed countries. Chains of stolen and tradable goods can be found in the streets of Chicago, London, Berlin, and so on. Illegal economies are hardly new. What distinguishes Latin America is that authorities generally react late and erratically, usually when these markets are already consolidated and the cost of intervention is perceived to be high. The inability of weak governments to react promptly to the establishment of these outlets and chains of commercialization allowed a growth in these markets. The move to an equilibrium of higher crime and low law enforcement in the region has been fueled by rising consumer demand and erratic government intervention.

The size of these markets is hard to estimate. Drugs of course represent a large share, but the extent of other markets is impressive. For example, it is assumed that close to a million cars are stolen each year in Latin America. Between 10 and 15 percent of cell phones are stolen each year in the region, and several million Latin Americans are victims of the theft of some electronic or digital equipment every year.

Historically, there were many markets for illegal goods. The two most notorious and high-demand illicit services were prostitution and gambling. To varying degrees, these markets thrived, and many times with the complaisance and partnership of the police and public authorities. But other markets of goods in high-demand have also thrived. For example, under ISI (Import Substitution Industrialization) and other periods of tariff barriers, the contraband traffic in coveted goods has been considerable. In most countries of the region, customs administrations failed to seal borders, allowing consumer goods to reach markets (and many corrupt customs officers to become rich in the process), particularly luxury goods and such widely consumed products as alcohol and tobacco. However, the smuggling of these goods very rarely involved violence and theft.[8] What distinguishes today´s black markets is that many of the tradable goods have been stolen from ordinary citizens. In sum, an increasing demand for goods that are stolen in robberies and through other illegal activities has greatly contributed to the rise of crime in the region.

Secondary Markets and Crime

Following a description of illegal secondary markets and the way in which stolen goods, often "return" as tradable products to the marketplace, I will briefly introduce the various ways these markets are organized and make some annotated remarks on the use of violence, which will be further developed in the following chapters.

From Personal Victimization to Markets of Goods

In urban Latin America, many youngsters have experienced or witnessed the theft of their cell phones. Many others have had their bikes and even their tennis shoes forcibly taken. In other cases, females in particular have had their purses grabbed by motorcyclists who leave the scene in a hurry. Anecdotal evidence abounds. Almost everyone has a close relative who has experienced one of these types of mugging. Secondary markets begin with such widespread individual victimization.

Survey data support this assertion. Approximately 22 percent of people in Latin America experienced some sort of victimization within the last twelve months, mostly these types of robberies. Other surveys confirm such trends. A longitudinal survey for the federal district and the state of Mexico showed that small thefts (defined as less than US$100 in value) were experienced by 10 percent of the population during the last six months. The percentage of households in which at least one member aged fifteen or older has been victimized by a theft valued at more than US$100 increased from 13 percent of households in 2005 to 22 percent in 2008.[9]

A recent nationwide survey in Mexico, with more than 90,000 respondents (ENVIPE—Encuesta Nacional de Victimizacion y Percepcion sobre Seguridad Publica 2016) produced similar results. This survey found that the rate of robbery in the street or on public transportation for people aged fifteen and older was 8,570 per 100,000 in 2011, rising to 10,037 per 100,000 in 2012, and 11,903 per 100,000 in 2014, a 39%

increase in just three years. Extrapolating these rates to the total population would yield more than 10 million thefts per year—presumably small
scale, such as cell phones, money, purses, and personal items. Significant
rates were also found for other items. For example, this survey found that
partial or total car thefts were reported by 4,083 (2011) and 4,886 (2014)
per 100,000 inhabitants, with 2,231 (2011) and 2,656 (2012) burglaries per
100,000 inhabitants.

A large 2007 victimization survey (with 23,000 respondents) in
Buenos Aires found that 26 percent had been victimized in the past twelve
months.[10] Just 3.6 percent of the respondents were victims of kidnapping,
sex crimes, or physical aggression, while 22.4 percent were victims of
some type of theft. Half of these were victims of nonviolent theft, while
the other half had their cars or personal belongings in their cars stolen,
or were victims of burglary or robbery of some scale, including the use
of violence. In short, most of the victimizations were thefts; half could be
considered minor and the other half serious. In approximately 60 percent
of these cases some violence occurred.

Victimization surveys in Chile also depict a similar trend. In 2013,
according to Chile's official yearly urban victimization survey (ENUSC—
Encuesta Nacional Urbana de Victimizacion), 24.8 percent of households
had at least one member who had been the victim of a crime. The overwhelming majority suffered property crime (larceny 7.8 percent, burglary
4.2 percent, theft with violence or intimidation 3.9 percent, and other
types of theft 5.3 percent).[11] Chile, however, is one of the few countries in
the region in which personal victimization did not rise between 2007 and
2013. As will be shown in chapters 7, 8, and 9, effective deterrence indeed
plays a role.

Surveys in Colombia also reveal the prominent role of property crimes.
The 2013 presidential victimization survey shows that 18.5 percent of
people fifteen years or older reported being victimized in the last twelve
months. Fewer than 3 percent reported fights or other non-property crime.
The rest suffered personal, household, or car thefts. In close to 40 percent
of these cases some sort of violence was used.[12]

These and other victimization surveys depict a clear trend throughout
the region: The extent of theft is very large, from cell phones to luxury cars.
Approximately half the thefts were of items of relatively small value, while
the other half were of items valued at 100$ and up.[13] Some of these thefts
are of course opportunities that thieves take in order to acquire goods they
covet or money to spend. In economic terms these thefts are considered

transfers of belongings, and their market effects are neutral. Although there are no good measures, I estimate that these make up a relatively small share of total thefts. The overwhelming majority of thefts are of goods that are not kept by the offenders but rather are resold in public venues.

Stolen items probably represent a very minor fraction of all tradable goods, but even if they stand at 1 percent of GDP, the incentives are significant enough to attract youngsters who participate in property crimes, as well as "entrepreneurs," organizers, and a large number of workers. Although the starting points of these markets are criminal acts, their nature quickly changes. At the commercialization stage these markets are already run by legitimate businesses, staffed by decent employees, and driven by honest consumers. Only at the initial stage do crime rings recruit potential delinquents from a large pool of marginalized citizens in exchange for relatively low pay. Just a few of these delinquents become leaders of successful criminal operations.

Several scholars have made initial inroads into the study of the organization of such markets (Naim 2006; Salcedo Albarán and Garay Salamanca 2016; Soares and Chimeli 2017). An in-depth examination is outside the scope of this book.[14] However, it is important to describe, even if only briefly, how the supply of these stolen goods is organized. There are two types of systems for the supply of illegal goods: the organization scheme and the individual initiative. In the first, a criminal organization, large or small, becomes a vertically integrated operation, and as a single organization recruits people to steal goods, arranges the refurbishing or "recycling" of these goods, and sells them to established outlets. Such organizations might control the whole process or just part of it. The second system is a true market atomization, in which some people steal and exchange their booty for cash in known locations. The goods are then resold to other agents and finally reach the outlets. This system constitutes a safer mechanism for large entrepreneurs, because it distances them from the first illegal and sometimes violent stage in the illicit chain. The cost of illegalities in terms of risks of apprehension and arrest, even when they are relatively small in Latin America, is paid ultimately by the thieves. This second, atomized structure is the more commonly found in the region.

The atomized nature of this type of criminality is clearly different from the mafia type of organized crime (Reuter 1985) and has been very well adapted to the Latin American consumer boom of recent years. It allows wide participation by many individuals in perfectly honest jobs that are not identified as part of an illegal chain of trade. Authorities avoid the dismantling of makeshift outlets, they look the other way when secondary markets in high-demand goods grow (as is the case with cell phones and clothing), and they are tolerant of dubious schemes of commercialization, because the "democratization of consumption" brings immediate political and administrative benefits that outlast long-term costs.[15]

In sum, economic growth and the increase in individual consumption has created opportunities for illegal markets to prosper. The large scale of victimization has produced a large quantity of goods that return "refurbished" to the marketplace. The atomized structure has developed into a true market wherein the first criminal stage is structurally disconnected from the subsequent, somewhat legal chain of commercialization.

Why Cheap Stolen and Illicit Goods?

The trade in illicit goods has expanded worldwide. Economic growth driven by individual consumption creates opportunities for both legal and illegal suppliers. The secondary markets develop when illegal suppliers succeed in establishing outlets for the commercialization of such goods and law enforcement agencies fail to neutralize them. When powerful trade organizations pressure authorities to neutralize the counterfeit or stolen products, the scope of these markets will be small.[16] On the other hand, when established industries profit from illegal secondary markets, they are unlikely to force governments to make strong efforts to curtail illegal industries. In short, strong governments, law enforcement agencies, and private sectors, can reduce the scope and violence of these illegal economies. In Latin America, adjusting for wide variance between countries, these neutralizing factors have been relatively weak.

Markets where highly desired cheaper goods are traded, whether of legal or illegal origin, will naturally thrive. From this perspective, high demand for cheaper and illicit goods has a natural market explanation. If stolen or illegal goods can be "produced" and sold at lower cost than the same goods sold in a legal venue, this price difference will naturally generate higher demand for the illegal "brands." The thriving markets in illegal goods are largely explained by the low cost of these products vis-à-vis the steady demand.

The usually lower cost of stolen goods is due to a combination of factors: ineffective deterrence; a large "supply" of delinquents, which lowers the cost of potential thieves;[17] and the relatively high cost of legal goods. In contrast, where law enforcement is effective, where starting pay for low-skilled workers is relatively high, and where taxes are low, the price differential between legal goods and the same goods of illegal origin will be small, reducing the incentive for individuals to participate in illegal markets. In short, deterrence, labor markets, and taxes do make a difference.

Although they are very important, administrative and economic factors alone do not explain the demand for illicit goods. Several other factors, such as informal labor markets, corruption, and political and cultural variables contribute to peoples' consent to these illegalities. First, in many of these countries informal labor markets constitute at least a third of the labor force.[18] Second, corruption is important because many illegal markets are either run or at least tolerated by police and other officials in exchange for a share of the profits.[19] Third, politics also matters. Governments seldom want to intervene and disband illegal outlets because, in the short run, they are perceived as a win-win situation, where voters enjoy low prices and suppliers give kickbacks to local patrons and other brokers (*punteros politicos* in a classic populist trap, short-term benefits trump long-term drawbacks). Fourth, and very importantly, a culture of violent dispute resolution and weak social order permeates regular transactions, lending legitimacy to black or illicit markets and other spheres of daily life where government authority is absent.[20]

In sum, economic, political, and cultural variables have also contributed to the development of secondary illegal markets. Although in this book I focus the attention on the under-studied dynamic of secondary markets and poor deterrence, these other variables have greatly contributed to fueling crime in the region. Before turning to the functioning of secondary markets, I will make some brief comments on violence and diversification of crime that will be further developed in chapter 5.

Violence and Branching Out

Illegal markets are not inherently violent. In fact, a large literature has shown that participants in illegal markets prefer to avoid violence, because it is costly and produces inefficiencies (Gambetta 1996; Varese 2011, 2012; Kalyvas 2006; Szabo de Carvalho et al. 2013). The threat of violence is necessary because there is no legal recourse for parties to enforce contracts; therefore, it is rational to rely at times on extreme acts. But all things being equal, individuals in illegal markets will refrain from violence, particularly at the middle and upper level of operations, leaving it limited to street conflicts of retailers, or the initial stage of mugging and robbing.[21]

Nevertheless, violence often erupts, particularly when markets are not well established. In order to take advantage of new opportunities, some people in pursuit of profits might attempt to settle disputes violently. I claim that there are two patterns of criminal violence in the region. The first is associated with a share of the pie—the violence among groups vying for a market share of profitable goods (an obvious example is the drug market). The second, and to some extent related pattern, is associated with the development of new areas of criminality—for example, the kidnapping and extortion "businesses" that have rapidly grown during the last decade.

Violence is usually associated with new opportunities for larger profits. For example, an organized cell that worked for a large DTO (Drug Traffic Organization) might have control of a territory, contacts within the police, and officers on its payroll. Its "infrastructure" would allow this cell to venture into the profitable extortion business. A challenge from competitors of the DTO might produce an escalation of violence. In other words, once criminal rings reach a threshold level of operation, they can branch out into other criminal businesses. This happens because delinquents anticipate the low capacity of police to enforce the law and deterrence fails. When states have strong enforcement capacities, as in most developed countries, kidnapping for ransom and extortion are very rare events.

In 2012, according to nongovernmental organization (NGO) reports and official records,[22] three of the world's top five countries in kidnapping for ransom were Mexico, Colombia, and Venezuela. In Mexico, the lion's share of kidnappings is concentrated in ten states (Chihuahua, Coahuila, Michoacán, Morelos, Guerrero, Veracruz, Durango, Sinaloa, Tamaulipas, and Jalisco). In Venezuela, while in the early 1990s there was an average of 25 kidnappings reported per year, during the period 2005–2009 kidnappings averaged 320 per year (Rujano 2012). In El Salvador, 90 percent of small businesses regularly pay extortion fees (Villalobos 2014).

In sum, while homicide statistics fluctuated during the last two decades, violent robberies, car thefts, extortions, and abductions have grown steadily. Predatory crimes and extreme violence in the region have been climbing. Not only is violence up, but crimes are more often random. Thirty years ago, most homicides occurred among acquaintances. People who avoided cantinas, land disputes, and drug trade areas could feel safe.

Crime changed when it became an integrated part of a market chain. Now that anyone can be a victim of extortion, robbery, or car theft, the level of anxiety has risen.

Illegal Secondary Markets

Latin American criminology scholarship is concentrated overwhelmingly on homicides and illegal drugs and so has overlooked property crimes, which have also led to an increase in violence. Here, I illustrate some of the concepts analyzed thus far, summarizing the markets in cell phones, digital devices, and firearms, and offering some notes on other less common but greatly profitable stolen goods. In the following section, I present an in-depth analysis of car theft, a market with a very significant volume of trade.

These markets, as mentioned, are not entirely illegal. While they originate in illegal acts, the stolen goods very quickly enter legal venues of commercialization. For example, "refurbished" laptops or tablets that might once have been stolen are retailed in perfectly legal stores. Appliances and other goods stolen in burglaries are sold to pawn-shops. These are doubly illegal goods in that their resale not only originated in crime but also is not taxed.

Cell Phones

Over the last few years cell phones have become a much-demanded commodity. The industry is very dynamic, and innovation has increased the consumer´s appetite for an array of devices. The most important profits in the industry belong to Internet and phone service providers, who are constantly looking to increase the number of subscribers and therefore, have no intrinsic interest in ascertaining a phone's origin. If government does not regulate these large companies in order to curtail the illegal use of cell phones, these firms might probably ignore the problem and look the other way.

Cell phones stolen and diverted to the secondary market are a perfect example of the argument presented in this chapter. Stolen products reach customers who can then buy high-demand goods at much lower prices. This market in stolen goods has two effects: On the one hand, industry expansion based on innovation benefits from high turnover of devices. High-end customers take advantage of their victimization and purchase the latest versions, while low-end customers can afford relatively good products at a reduced price. On the other hand, phone service providers expand their customer base and boost their profits. In sum, crime supports the expansion of this dynamic industry in times of prosperity.

Most phones are naturally replaced to keep up with rapid innovation. However, there is a stratified demand, from simple phone services to integration of multiple digital devices. Muggers and thieves look for high-end goods that have a large demand and retail value, but there is also a small market for "old" brands. Thieves might target victims with high-end phones, but often they simply grab a victim's purse, money, jewelry, and of course phone. They know where to resell the equipment at an already set market price.

There is scant data from official sources on cell phone theft; most estimates derive from self-reports (survey respondents) and from studies conducted by mobile communication companies. The number of victims that reported their phones stolen is very high. A study in Argentina estimated that 2.2 million phones were stolen in 2012, since 16 percent of individuals who contracted for new services said they were doing so following the theft of their old phone.[23] In Peru, a 2007 study estimated that at least 13 percent of cell phones offered in the marketplace were stolen.[24]

Victimization surveys support these estimates of the extent of cellphone theft. Mexico's metropolitan survey showed that 70 percent of small property crime (see note 9) involved cell phones and 7 percent of survey respondents said they had been victims of such crimes within the previous six months. A much larger victimization survey of 95,000 Mexicans in 2012 did not include questions on thefts of specific items, but out of the twenty-seven million victimizations reported, at least 2 percent were thought to include the theft of cell phones. When people were asked in a small Tijuana survey whether their cell phone had ever been stolen, 37 percent answered affirmatively.[25] In México City, according to official records, 156,000 phones were stolen in 2012. Indeed, the entire region has been plagued by cell-phone theft: Ecuador suffered 216,000 thefts, Brazil more than two million, and Peru close to one million. In Chile in 2010, 340,000 cell phones were reported as stolen.[26]

In Bogotá, Colombia, according to one study, more than 1,600 phones are stolen every day—an average of one phone per minute—meaning that there are more than 620,000 such thefts per year in a city of 6.7 million inhabitants.[27] This estimate is consistent with other studies, suggesting that there are 9,500 cell-phone thefts per 100,000 inhabitants.[28] Nationwide, a DANE survey of twenty cities in Colombia suggested that 1.2 million people had their phones stolen in 2012.[29]

The patterns are similar in Central America. Data from Guatemala police reports for 2012 counted 122,000 cases of cell-phone theft. Since many cases are never reported to the authorities, the total number is probably much higher. Other reports estimated that for the last trimester of 2011, an average of 30 cell phones were stolen per hour in Guatemala alone.[30] Cell-phone theft is clearly rampant in this country and the government has been forced to legislate harsh punishment for people involved in the resale of stolen cell phones, with penalties of up to fifteen years imprisonment.

Overall, given these figures from different studies and self-reports, every year between 7 and 10 percent of Latin Americans are victims of cell-phone theft. Since the population of the eighteen countries under study was 590 million in 2013, it can be estimated that at least 40 million cell phones were stolen that year. Although not every phone is refurbished and diverted to secondary markets, a conservative estimate of 50 percent re-use at US$20 per unit yields a market of US$400 million. Given the size of this market, it can be concluded that there is a strong demand that produces significant profits, and more importantly, that thousands of people, mostly youngsters, who specialize in street robberies are recruited into this market to make a living and to see this street crime as real work.

Other Digital Devices

There is much less reliable information on markets in electronics. However, most people in urban Latin America are aware of the danger of leaving laptops or video devices unattended. Many individuals in the region avoid even using them in public places. Usually these items are stolen in a mugging or in a burglary or theft from a car in which they were left. Laptops, MP3 players, digital cameras, and tablets are rarely sold in open spaces close to busy transportation hubs but rather in specialty stores.

The number of thefts, as Table 4.5 shows, can be estimated from the Mexican ENVIPE victimization surveys that asked respondents what type of objects were stolen. Thefts in the category "electronic equipment" were almost triple those of household appliances.

Table 4.5 Thefts of appliances and electronic equipment

	2011	2012	2013
Home appliances	286,333	347,172	318,460
Electronic equipment	982,526	1,048,853	896,223

Source: ENVIPE microdata and projections for the years 2011, 2012, and 2013.

Small Arms

Guns and other weapons have been the subject of many studies in the region (Dreyfus et al. 2011; Fleitas 2010). Most of these works relate to the lethal role firearms play in crimes and their correlation with murder rates. Others studies relate to the illegal importation into Mexico of weapons legally purchased in the United States (McDougal et al. 2013; Dube et al. 2013; Chicoine 2011). Here I provide a brief overview of another understudied topic: the black market of firearms.

Guns are of course instrumental in the commission of many crimes, particularly robberies and homicides. In the vast majority of cases, delinquents report easy access to firearms. For instance, in Brazil it is estimated that there are 17.6 million handguns in private hands, 57 percent of them illicit (Dreyfuss et al. 2011). Mexicans who can access the US firearms market directly or through smugglers have purchased more than $100 million worth of weapons in legal retail stores in the southern states of the United States and smuggled them into the Mexican market during the period 2010–2012 (McDougal et al. 2013). Most of these weapons are believed to have been channeled to DTOs.

A more direct approach to measuring access to firearms is through survey self-reports. Table 4.6 presents data on inmates' access to weapons prior to incarceration. As mentioned in chapter 3, 25 percent of the inmates who had guns used them before they were fourteen years old, further evidence of the easy access to guns in the region.

Most inmates had a history of access to firearms, and more than half of those who reported having guns were not worried about the police knowing they had such weapons. Several inmates said they had stolen firearms in the past, though one out of six inmates had bought a gun six months before being arrested for the crime for which they were incarcerated, and among these, on average, one-third purchased their guns from licensed dealers.

This evidence indicates that in recent years guns could be easily accessed and indirectly denotes a large black market in guns. Although no

Table 4.6 Inmates' access to firearms prior to arrest

	Argentina	Brazil	Chile	El Salvador	Mexico	Peru
Ever had a gun	80.5	70.5	75.7	49.8	42.3	39.7
Worried about police detecting gun[a]	40.0	54.7	35.3	44.2	28.9	40.6
Ever stole a gun[a]	51.2	19.9	48.7	18.4	10.7	24.7
Got first gun by purchase[a]	30.0	45.3	19.4	22.0	28.5	15.1
Got first gun by theft[a]	12.0	6.8	32.2	4.7	3.6	9.6
Got first gun from a friend[a]	37.0	26.1	27.4	36	26.9	21.8
Bought a gun six months before arrest[a]	19.6	19.7	11.4	14.2	12.6	13.0
Bought from a licensed dealer[b]	17.7	35.2	14.5	24.4	32.7	42.1
Valid N	1175	751	789	1135	1212	1185

[a] Percentage of those who reported ever having a gun.
[b] Percentage of those who bought a gun six months before arrest.
Source: Inmate Surveys 2013.

time-series survey for inmates is yet available, very likely the easy and relatively cheap access to guns has contributed to rising criminality in these countries.[31] This has led not only to more property losses but also to more injuries and deaths.

The total value of the guns black-market is probably not very high, but the illicit trade is important for the way in which it facilitates other crimes. Acquisition of low-cost firearms, or access to guns through family or friends, empowers offenders to commit felonies. The returns from property crimes easily covers the cost of handguns. To the extent that the penalty for carrying guns is not high (low deterrence), cheap and easy access to firearms raises criminality.

Less Conventional Thefts

Theft of other "less conventional" goods has developed significantly over the years. In Colombia, as mentioned in chapter two Ecopetrol reported that in 2002, the amount of gasoline theft was very large,[32] and although the authorities subsequently reported a drastic reduction, the scope of losses appears to be significant.[33] One estimate for that year surpasses $200 million, just for Colombia.[34] In Mexico, as mentioned, the estimated value of gasoline stolen from pipelines, stations, and transportation system would amount to close to US$635 million for 2013.[35] Although no similar data are available for other countries, it is well known that gasoline extraction from pipelines and theft from tank trucks are common events in many countries of region. The stolen gasoline finds its way to established gas stations whose owners and licensed operators purchase it at a reduced price and mix it with legally acquired gas, boosting their profits.

Operations of this size and type of robberies for the purpose of reselling stolen goods are rarely found in developed countries. For example, in Latin America there is a widespread phenomenon known as truckjacking or "asphalt piracy." Trucks transporting legal goods are followed and intercepted and their drivers then threatened at gunpoint and left on the roadside while the thieves drive the trucks to makeshift depots. The goods are unloaded and the trucks are abandoned far from the crime scenes, all in just a few hours.

The size of these thefts is considerable. According to the Argentine organization in charge with preventing truck robberies, between 2009 and 2012 an average of 135 full truckloads per month were stolen, 83 percent of them between six in the morning and six in the evening—that is, in broad daylight—and 89 percent in the city and province of Buenos Aires.[36] Although the report does not put a value on the stolen goods, most of them were highly tradable: 31 percent food items; 20 percent toiletries; 11 percent medicines; 11 percent sneakers and shoes; and 8 percent electronics items. These reported robberies are from large firms mainly in Buenos Aires and surrounding areas. The total number of truck robberies is likely much higher.

Information from other countries signals a similar process. In Chile, where law enforcement is among the stringest in the region, approximately one hundred large truckloads of goods were stolen and never recovered in 2013, according to the police. Each truck held goods in the range of $25,000 to $100,000.[37] In Mexico, particularly after the upsurge in violence since 2008, criminal groups linked to DTOs have also diversified into truck robbery. Although no data have been released by the authorities, the chamber of cargo transportation indicated that truck robberies increased by an average of 30 percent over the last few years, and in 2012 they increased by 38 percent. As in Argentina, these trucks were loaded mostly with highly tradable goods: food, clothing, medicines, and tennis shoes.[38]

As a share of GDP, the size of these robberies is not great. However, they are very profitable for the gangs and individuals that carry them out. More importantly, it appears that the magnitude of these thefts is rising, signaling that there is a growing demand for these stolen goods.

Important questions remain unanswered: Why is this happening in the region? How new are these schemes? Are these large-scale thefts localized or a widespread phenomenon? I claim first that although theft, corruption, and illegal markets are not new in the region, the extent and scope of such operations has become very noticeable since the 1990s, precisely the years when criminality started to climb significantly. Second, the development of these large-scale robberies and the resale of illicit products in established secondary markets is a widespread regional phenomenon, rather than isolated or local. Third, as the demand for consumer goods rises, criminal networks emerge to exploit the profits these markets generate.

Car Theft

Car thefts are the consummate example of organized criminality. Some people steal a car for a fleeting pleasure (joyriding). Some steal cars in order to commit other crimes, such as kidnapping or bank robbery, that are part of a larger organized crime scheme. But for the most part cars are stolen by criminal rings to meet two demands: one from overseas, especially for high-end cars and 4x4s, the other to meet the demand of the domestic auto-parts sector, for which cars are dismantled in "chop shops" and their parts sold in secondary markets. In short, the motives for car theft include joyriding, prolonged personal use, export (via smuggling and fake documentation), and "chopping."

In Western Europe and the United States, the majority of car thefts are by and for joyriding youths[39] and most are quickly recovered by the police (Clarke 2002). In addition, in OECD countries cars are usually stolen from parking facilities or the car owners' premises when the owners are not present. In contrast, in Latin America most cars are stolen for profit by organized crime groups, and many of them are stolen from their owners while driving, and who are aggressively threatened by armed criminals.[40]

Meeting the demand for stolen cars or for auto parts requires at least a modest organization.[41] Certain individuals steal the vehicles, others disassemble them, others market their parts to specialized stores, and still others manage the finances and security of these operations. The organizations that steal cars to sell overseas (usually luxury cars) must hire people to drive the cars, to bribe security and custom agents, to fake the paperwork, and so on.

Car-theft operations are based on the existence of at least two components: a market and an organization. If the cost of such an operation is low enough to undersell legal goods, there will be room for profit and for illegal activity. However, if the cost associated with apprehension and incarceration is high, returns on these illicit goods become lower and so the ability to forge effective criminal groups is reduced.[42] In short, all things being equal, when countries have poor and lenient enforcement of their penal laws, the cost of illicit trade diminishes and illegal markets grow.

Trends and Scope

Economic growth does not trigger more crime unless other conditions, among them weak deterrence, are met. The fact that there is a growing car ownership – *parque automotor*—does not necessarily produce more thefts to meet the demand for auto parts. Data from the United States and other countries refute the hypothesis that car thefts are epidemic everywhere. As shown in Figure 4.1, the rate of cars stolen in the United States has been declining for decades. In 2010, the rate of car thefts was only 25 percent of the rate in 1993. In Europe, the available data (see Table 4.7) show that most countries have declining or stagnant rates of car theft. Eastern Europe countries had an increase in the 1990s after the fall of the Berlin Wall, but once central governments regained authority, rates began to decline. Over the last few years even Eastern Europe has seen a significant decline in auto thefts.

For an international perspective on car thefts, Table 4.7 presents rates of auto-thefts per 100,000 inhabitants for many countries in Europe, Asia, and Oceania that provided data to the United Nations for at least four years between 2003 and 2010.[43] Only 7 countries out of 48 had modest increases in thefts between these two observations, while the other 41 countries saw drops, many of them very noticeable.

In contrast, as Table 4.8 shows, car thefts in Latin America had a very different trend during the same years, following a different trajectory.

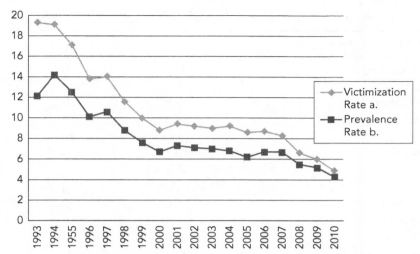

FIGURE 4.1 US car thefts (adjusted victimization and prevalence rate per 1,000).
a. Number of victimizations per 1,000 households that occurred during the year.
b. Number of households per 1,000 that experienced at least one victimization during the year.
Source: From Lauritsen and Rezey (2013) Bureau of Justice Statistics, National Crime Victimization Survey, 1993–2010, Appendix Table 16.

Car theft in the region is rising while rates in the rest of the world are declining. These data, however, describe a recent trend (the last decade or so) and cannot properly test the effect of long-term prosperity on crime. Some countries, fortunately, do have data sets for a longer period.

There are three sources of data for stolen vehicles. The first is reports to police or other official agencies. Excluding homicide, car theft is probably the best reported crime, since car owners usually need a police report for insurance claims. But many car owners, particularly those who own old and small cars, do not carry insurance.[44] A second source, victimization surveys, provides reliable indirect evidence on victims of car thefts. The third measure is statistics for insured vehicles tracked by car insurance umbrella organizations. Figure 4.2 for Mexico presents data on both stolen insured vehicles and those that were finally recovered.

Over a ten-year span the number of stolen insured cars grew by 60 percent. Fewer than 40 percent of these vehicles were recovered. However, since at least one-third of car thefts are never reported to the police,[45] it is safe to conclude that well over half of all stolen cars are never found, and

Table 4.7 Car thefts around the world (per 100,000 inhabitants)

Country/territory	2003	2010
Hong Kong	33.7	13.4
Japan	50.9	76.9
Thailand	30.5[a]	27.7
Bahrain	112.0	104.0[b]
Cyprus	155.9[a]	199.0[c]
Israel	526.8[a]	362.3[b]
Turkey	38.4	25.4[b]
Belarus	18.0	14.9[c]
Bulgaria	113.5	52.5
Czech Republic	248.4	141.5[c]
Hungary	123.6	67.3
Poland	142.1	43.2
Romania	5.1	13.8[c]
Russian Federation	35.9	33.3
Slovakia	97.9	69.3[c]
Ukraine	14.7	9.4
Denmark	440.4	338.1[c]
Estonia	34.0	64.9
Finland	420.7	207.8
Iceland	132.9	150.5[c]
Ireland	307.7	255.3
Latvia	158.5	64.0
Lithuania	203.7	62.0
Norway	441.6	222.4
Sweden	752.1	373.2
United Kingdom (England and Wales)	552.8	192.3
United Kingdom (Northern Ireland)	361.2	156.9
United Kingdom (Scotland)	352.8	166.9
Albania	22.5[a]	19.6
Bosnia and Herzegovina	61.4[a]	43.3
Croatia	52.5	35.6
Greece	52.8	242.9
Italy	382.9	326.3
Malta	219.1	89.3
Montenegro	12.4	13.5[b]
Portugal	286.0	190.2
Serbia	37.7[a]	33.3
Slovenia	34.2	26.3
Spain	281.5[a]	142.5
Austria	134.7	61.4
Belgium	319.1	184.6

Table 4.7 Continued

Country/territory	2003	2010
France	427.1	333.0[c]
Germany	133.2	101.4
Liechtenstein	64.7	8.3
Netherlands	167.5	129.2
Switzerland *	967.7	103.9
Australia *	495.5	245.8
New Zealand	579.4	457.7

[a] 2005; [b] 2008; [c] 2009.

Source: UNODC 2012.

Table 4.8 Car theft in Latin America (per 100,000 inhabitants)

Country	Source	Circa 2006	Circa 2010	percent Change
Argentina	UNODC	85.0	156 (2008)	83.5
Bolivia	PNUD	34.1	39.4 (2010)	15.5
Brazil	PNUD	80.3	76.5[b] (2009)	−4.7
Chile	PNUD	33.0	61.0 (2011)	84.8
Colombia	UNODC	45.0	47.0 (2009)	4.4
Costa Rica	UNODC	118.0	133.2 (2009)	12.9
Ecuador[a] (2003)	UNODC	43.0	52.0 (2006)	20.9
El Salvador	PNUD	25.9	17.6 (2011)	−32.0
Guatemala	PNUD	25.0	23.0 (2010)	−8.0
Honduras	N/A			
Mexico	PNUD	136.1	200.7 (2011)	47.5
Nicaragua	UNODC	136.0	180.0 (2009)	32.4
Panama	UNODC	19.0	28.0 (2009)	47.4
Paraguay	PNUD	12.6	20.2 (2010)	60.3
Peru	PNUD	613.0	695 (2010)	13.4
Dominican R.	N/A			
Uruguay	PNUD	127.8	197.5 (2010)	54.3
Venezuela	N/A			

Empty cells denote no data available.

** Some experts suggest that the rate should have the total number of cars as a denominator, and indeed this would be a better comparative measure, but unfortunately such data is not available for many of these countries and/or for multiple years, so rates per 100,000 inhabitants represent the best available equivalent.

[a] No information is available for Ecuador at UNODC for these years.

[b] The rate for the last observation in Brazil does not include the car thefts in the states of Minas Gerais, Santa Catarina, and others.

Source: Compiled by UNDP (2013) based on countries' official records.

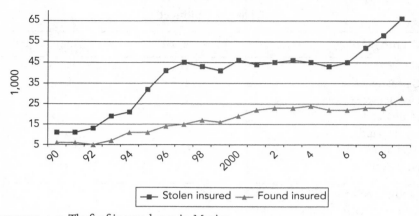

FIGURE 4.2 Theft of insured cars in Mexico.
Source: Estadísticas históricas de Mexico. Cuadro 21. 20. www.inegi.gob.mx.

most likely are channeled to the illegal market. At a conservative estimate, the value of Mexico's black market is greater than US$300 million per year.[46]

The most appalling figures on the extent of car theft in Mexico have been provided by its large national victimization survey (ENVIPE). In 2011, according to this survey, 604,000 vehicles were stolen, and more than 2.5 million car owners reported theft of parts of their automobile or of items left in the car, such a car stereo, GPS, or other belongings.[47]

Two broad conclusions can be derived from Mexico's data: First, the extent of car theft is very large and the number of unrecovered vehicles is significant. More importantly, this is not a one-year problem but a long trend that indicates the existence of an established industry. Twenty-year data sets show very clearly that there is a strong and sustained growth of car thefts over the last two decades.

Scattered data from judicial and police sources in Peru and Colombia allow the measurement of long-term patterns of car theft in these countries, and likewise signal a rising trend (Fig. 4.3). Colombia had a sevenfold rise in car theft during the peak years of the drug cartels' confrontation with the central government, and police data show a fourfold rise between 1990 and 2002, while in Peru the number of vehicles stolen at least doubled from 2000 to 2009. These cases show—and I will return to this point in other chapters—that a rise in crime does not correlate with economic crisis. They rather point to an association between rising crime and times of economic growth. The large number of these thefts creates larger profits. For instance, for 2009 the Colombian police estimated

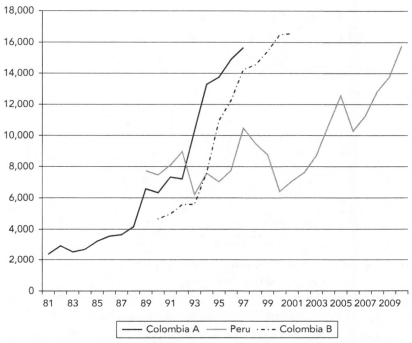

FIGURE 4.3 Car theft in Peru and Colombia.

Source: Colombia A: Beltrán y Salcedo Albarán (2003, 29), data extracted from Revista Criminalidad. National Police of Colombia Perú: Ministerio del Interior de Perú (2013). Colombia B: Data from Hurtos de Automotores by the *Policía Nacional, Revista Criminalidad.* Reported in Pablo Casas et al. (2005, 159).

that the total value of car thefts there was 251,236 million pesos (approximately US$125 million), with motorcycle thefts valued at an additional 46,352 million pesos (US$23 million).[48]

The information for Argentina is cumbersome, but it depicts an interesting pattern. There are no good official reports on car thefts, but insurance companies provide useful data.[49] From 2007 until 2011 these sources tallied a yearly average of 55,000 stolen cars that were never recovered,[50] while theft from vehicles, including musical equipment, GPSs, and personal belongings, doubled from 80,000 in 2007 to 164,000 in 2011.[51] Data for a longer period from a smaller sample of the largest fourteen insurance companies, which account for approximately 60 percent of the car insurance market, shows a similar pattern (Fig. 4.4). These tallies are also consistent with partial official records reported by the Organization of American States (OAS), according to which, 52,500 vehicles were stolen

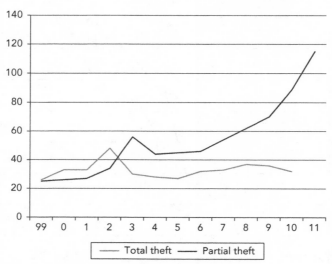

FIGURE 4.4 Car thefts and thefts from cars in Argentina.
Source: Author elaboration based on CESVI (2014).

in 2003, 62,000 in 2008.[52] Finally, estimates based on other umbrella insurance companies' reports of stolen vehicles rose by 37 percent between 2004 and 2011.[53] Approximately half of the vehicles were stolen by delinquents using firearms, another rising trend.[54]

Although data for longer time spans were difficult to assemble for other countries, those that traditionally had the lowest crime rates in the region show a similar trend. Chile had a threefold increase in car thefts in just six years, rising from 11,991 cases in 2005 to 34,448 in 2011,[55] and in Uruguay data for just the three years 2007 to 2009 show that car theft increased over this period by 14.6 percent.[56]

Based on these figures, it is possible to calculate that every year approximately one million cars are stolen in Latin America. Most of them are never recovered. This makes car theft an "industry" worth at least $3–4 billion a year. Despite the scattered nature of the data, it is clear that most countries have witnessed a large increase in car thefts since the 1990s.

Assessment

Is this black market in stolen vehicle driven by a flourishing supply or by a strong demand? This is a difficult question to answer. The data indicate that a higher supply is being met by a strong demand. In other words, as an increasing number of cars are stolen, the "industry" is finding a market for them. I argue that this is a demand-driven market, in part because used auto parts have not become cheaper, pointing to a sustainable demand. In short, some people steal because others are eager to buy these goods. Particularly for stolen auto parts, this is a mature market that has reached equilibrium and has trimmed transaction costs.

Two critical questions must be answered: first, why there is an increasing demand for stolen goods, and second, why suppliers can develop and organize these markets under the surveillance of law enforcement agencies.

Secondary auto-parts markets developed due to a large increase in vehicle ownership. For countries such as Brazil, Mexico, and Argentina, the number of new vehicles increased by at least 50 percent throughout the 1990s. This growth has been explained by investment in new technologies that reduced prices while economies enjoyed a period of expansion. Individuals from the lower middle class as well as the unionized working class were able to afford small vehicles because prices were lower and credit became available.[57] The rise in purchases of new cars also created a large used-car market for first-time car owners. This too has been a demand-driven market. The price differential—the ratio of a used car's price to the price of the same model when new—shrank or held steady. In short, as prices of new cars came down, prices of used cars did not significantly decline and in some cases even increased, suggesting that there has been a high demand for these used models.

Black-market auto parts are crucial for this segment of consumers. Low-income car owners have limited resources to purchase new auto parts. As car ownership grows, so does the market for stolen vehicles. In principle, the growing demand for cheaper replacement parts could be met by a drastic reduction in the manufacturer´s prices and/or a reduction in taxes and transaction costs. Neither of these occurred. The prices have not significantly came down, and the ensuing black market has followed the expansion of the total vehicle ownership.

Shortages in supply can also augment crime. Policies that restrict imports or that heavily tax certain goods such as necessary replacement parts for vehicles might generate a sudden rise in thefts that are sometimes carried out with extreme violence. For instance, during a tire shortage in Argentina in 2012 an estimated 70 percent of auto parts stolen were tires, and prices on the black market increased by more than 200 percent.[58] The case of motorcycles in Venezuela also illustrates this point. In 2003, in part to alleviate traffic in the city of Caracas, the government allowed imports of cheap motorcycles from China. Given the country´s limited access to foreign currency, in 2006 the government reversed course and severely restricted imports. However, the many motorcycles already on the road required replacement parts that were not available in the marketplace. Soon the number of motorcycle thefts began to climb, with many motorcyclists robbed at gunpoint, including some that were killed at the scene. For example, during the first five months of 2009 the authorities in Caracas registered more than 2,200 motorcycle robberies, and the actual number is believed to be much higher. Police reported that in those robberies there were 71 homicides of motorcycle owners who resisted the thieves.[59]

In sum, the stabilization of credit together with new technologies that lowered car prices produced a larger new-car market as well as a healthy used-car market for new consumers with limited resources. A larger and older car ownership (*parque automotor*) demanded cheaper parts that were obtained from stolen vehicles. "Crime entrepreneurs" seized the opportunity and were able to meet this rising demand. Car thefts are lower and trending downward in other parts of the world that also had a significant growth of vehicle ownership. In Latin America a particularly perverse combination is observed. Times of relative prosperity and rising consumption have been met by weak state institutions. The opportunities for high profits on high-demand goods have enhanced the consolidation of illegal markets that at times became very violent.

Summing Up: Prosperity and Crime

Studies in criminology have long signaled the correlation between periods of economic expansion and property crime.[60] Prosperity usually provides greater returns on criminal activity because there are more opportunities and targets. In this chapter I have argued that the economic expansion in Latin America over the last twenty-five years has been at least moderately associated with rising criminality. The strong increase of consumerism has driven the consolidation of secondary markets in illicit goods, many of them originating in blatant theft of the desired goods.

Economic expansion, however, does not automatically translate into higher criminality, particularly violent crime. As shown with the case of carjacking, many countries in Europe and Asia have benefited from strong markets and at the same time reduced crime. The rise in criminality depends also on other factors after controlling for the economic expansion effect. Two necessary and interrelated conditions that affect the development of criminal networks: weak institutional law enforcement and the nature of perverse equilibria. Chapters 7, 8, and 9, will delve into the poor deterrence capabilities of states in the region. In the final paragraphs of this chapter I summarize how the escalation of crime creates a critical mass of criminality, reaching a tipping point beyond which the crime equilibrium is very difficult to reverse.

Illegal economies have at least two stages: the initial developing phase, and the established mature phase. When a market has matured and diversified, it is very difficult to crack it down and reverse its course. For example, once there is a strong demand for drugs, attacking the problem from the supply side yields very poor results, particularly when demand is relatively inelastic. Conversely, when demand for certain goods is elastic, effective deterrence increases the costs of illegal goods and demand consequently adjusts. In short, the effects of deterrence in mature illegal markets depend greatly on the elasticity of price and supply. All things being equal, when there is a strong demand for illegal goods, the most effective way to reduce crime is by a combination of strong deterrence and shrinking price differentials between similar legal and illegal good; in short, a combination of state and markets.[61] At this stage, when the demand for illegal goods is strong, as is shown in other chapters, state enforcement might fail due to the scale of the market, the number of players already involved, and the venues already established. This is also a self-sustaining perverse equilibrium: when illegal markets are already established, buyers look to purchase goods in these venues, mimicking the behavior of others who purchased goods at lower prices, and thus naturally sustain demand.

State enforcement (deterrence) has a better probability of success at the developing stage of illegal markets when channels of commercialization are not yet established, consumers do not know exactly where to buy the desired goods, suppliers have not gained a strong foothold in the marketplace, and so demand is not yet very strong. In short, not only is dismantling an incipient criminal network easier at the outset, but it has a strong endogenous effect because it limits the expansion of demand for illegal goods.

In this chapter I have shown that several secondary illegal markets appear to be mature. The extent of theft suggests that a large volume of stolen goods find their way to commercial outlets. This signals that demand is strong and, more importantly, it has not abated over the years. As I have shown, the trends in property crime have clearly been upward in the last decade.

In sum, the makeup of secondary illicit markets in Latin America points to the existence of a perverse equilibrium of high crime.

I argue in this book that states in Latin America have reacted late and erratically to the development of secondary markets. Not only governments did not curtail their early initial development, they even have taken a permissive approach to the commercialization of illegal goods, in part because the authorities—mainly the police and some high-ranking officials—extracted kickbacks from these ventures. However, and inadvertently, these policies create endogenously a strong and sometimes inelastic demand for illegal goods, to a point where the effect of deterrence naturally diminishes. In short, by reacting late and erratically, states have created their own "iron cage" that has curtailed their deterrent effect.[62]

Chapter 5 analyzes the organization of the supply side of criminality by reviewing the operation of a very important "industry," the illegal drug market, and the Drug Traffic Organizations.

5

Drug Business and Crime

ONE KILOGRAM OF coffee ready for export at a Colombian farm gate costs approximately three dollars. This kilogram of coffee is retailed in New York for twelve dollars. One kilogram of high purity cocaine in Colombia ready for overseas shipment costs US$1,600. The cost of that same kilogram fractioned for street sale in Chicago or Los Angeles skyrockets to US$150,000. While the value added from production to retail of a legal commodity such as coffee increases threefold, this illegal drug is marked up almost a hundred times.

This astonishing profit is the driving force behind this lucrative illegal market, which recruits thousands of individuals, many of whom are willing to risk their lives for a good income—the truck drivers, the security guards, the street dealers, the money launderers, and so on. The profits, which are unevenly divided according to power distribution, hierarchies, and strategic market decisions, can also create incentives for violence.

This chapter studies the drug trade, the most profitable of all illicit markets. I analyze this industry within the broader framework of the book, which examines the effects these markets have on crime and how states respond. I claim that because of these dramatic profit rates, it is nearly impossible for law enforcement agencies to dissuade players from engaging in illegal activities. In fact, there is a perverse endogenous effect, because effective law enforcement produces a rise in prices and thus greater profits for illegal drug producers, carriers, and dealers, creating even more incentive for risk takers to engage in drug trafficking and production. More importantly, an in-depth examination of the business aspects of trafficking, the structural organization of the illegal drug industry, and the enforcement capacities of state agencies will explain why large or small organizations rise, under what circumstances violence can erupt, and how the type of equilibriums that are established affect states and their capacities.

In this chapter, I argue that drug markets can be violent or relatively calm. The sizeable earnings that motivate some individuals to deal drugs do not necessarily translate into lethality. Violence results from other variables at play, such as the overall earnings of the industry, the region-strategic location, the type of pre-existing criminal networks, the fragmentation or concentration of the industry, the timing and strength of law enforcement intervention, among others, which combine to produce different equilibria of crime and violence

This chapter begins with an overview of the production, consumption, and trafficking of drugs in the region to provide introductory notes on the magnitude and characteristics of the industry. I then analyze the structure of illegal drug markets, the organization of gangs, and the so-called cartels. Next, I analyze the conditions under which violence might erupt and identify some variables in the drug trade that may produce lethal outcomes. Following that, I review the emerging domestic markets for illegal drugs in Latin America and individual propensities to join illegal markets by examining the profiles of people who produce, transport, or sell drugs. The final part of the chapter frames my findings within the overall theoretical approach of this book and studies the implication of illegal drug markets within the type of equilibriums established, presenting a set of testable hypotheses on when the illegal drug trade could propel more violence and crime.

Production, Consumption, and Drug Trafficking

Over the past decade, hundreds of articles and books have been written on drug production and trafficking, mainly focusing on Mexico, Colombia, and Brazil (Mejia and Restrepo 2013; Lessing 2013; Thoumi 2003; Astorga 2005; Gootemberg 2009; Tokatlian 2009; Bruce 2012; WOLA and TNI 2011; Maihold and Jost 2014). They describe different aspects of the drug trade, with the vast majority concentrating on the violence and the operation of DTOs. In this chapter and the next, I analyze the business side of the drug trade and examine its effect on crime and violence in the region.

The production, trafficking, and sale of drugs are forbidden, and they constitute a crime.[1] Moreover, since illegal drug transactions generate profits that are never reported to authorities, individuals do not pay taxes on them, which constitute another violation of the law. In the whole illegal supply chain, there are numerous breaches of the law, from environmental violations to money laundering.

Crimes, however, do not necessarily produce violence. Little attention has been paid to the link between the drug trade and criminal violence, and the effect of one upon the other remains unclear (MacCoun and Reuter 2001). For example, according to the World Drug Report, every year in Western Europe at least 4,000,000 people use cocaine, 1,500,000 consume heroin, and 22,000,000 use cannabis (WDR 2011), yet there are very few drug-related homicides registered. Conversely, in Brazil, where the level of consumption is lower, thousands of homicides in 2013 were "drug-related." Clearly, other variables trigger violence, and this chapter will examine some of them.

The Latin American "drug problem" is qualitatively different from the drug problem in the United States and Europe. Latin America has been predominantly a producer and supplier of drugs, while the United States and Europe are mostly consumers. Illegal drug use in the region has been relatively modest, though this has begun to change over the last years. Cannabis growers have emerged, particularly in the United States,[2] while consumption of hard drugs has grown dramatically in many Latin American cities. Following is an overview of the most salient phases of the drug industry, providing the reader with data and some general considerations of the "drug problem" in Latin America.

Illegal drugs are defined here as narcotics whose sale is forbidden by law. Note that in some cases these narcotics might not be illegal for consumption (countries such as Portugal, the Netherlands, Uruguay, and others do not penalize the consumption of some substances). There are hundreds of different drugs on the markets, but I concentrate on four large "families": cannabis (marihuana and hashish), opiates (heroin), cocaine (coke paste, crack, and cocaine hydrochloride), and synthetics (amphetamines, meth, ecstasy).

The illegal drug industry can be conveniently divided into three stages: production, trafficking, and consumption. While Latin American countries have predominantly been centers for the production and trafficking of several drugs, consumption has been rising since the 1980s, not only in producer countries such as Mexico and Colombia, but also in non-producer nations such as Brazil, Chile, and Argentina. The rise in drug use in Latin America is tied to patterns of consumption among emerging cohorts as well as broader social and cultural processes. Consumption and growing rates of prevalence, particularly among youngsters, has become a social problem. In short, Latin America has a production and transshipment drug challenge, and has been facing a larger problem of drug use and abuse for twenty years.

Before analyzing the business of drug crimes and its effects on violence in the region, this section provides basic descriptive information on trends and characteristics of the illegal drug industry, beginning with the production of illegal drugs in Latin America

Cannabis. Historically, Mexico and Paraguay have been the largest producers of marihuana, although lately production has expanded to other countries, such as Bolivia, Brazil, and Colombia, as well as others. Marihuana is produced from a plant that is relatively easy to grow, where soils and climate are favorable. Over the last decade there has also been a significant rise in hydroponic marihuana production that does not require soil and is generally considered of much higher quality than outdoor-grown plants. The lion's share of the marihuana consumed in the United States until the year 2000 was produced in Mexico, while cannabis in Europe came predominantly from the Middle East and northern Africa. Since the turn of the century, however, hydroponic growers in states along the Mexican border (California, New Mexico, etc.) have taken a large chunk of the domestic marihuana market away from Mexican dealers, and recently, the legalization of cannabis in Colorado, the state of Washington, and California have boosted production in those states.

Opiates. Among these four illegal drug families, heroin has the lowest production share in the region. It has been mostly produced in northwestern Mexico and smuggled into the United States (as we will see, heroin use in the region is very low). During the 1990s, Colombia also became a heroin producer. But, more than 90 percent of the world's heroin is produced in Asia, and LATAM has a small share of the world's heroin market. Over the last decade, a renewed rising demand in the United States has stimulated increased production of different types of opioids in Mexico, particularly in the states of Michoacán and Guerrero.

Cocaine. This is the most lucrative of Latin America's illegal drugs. Refined cocaine and its derivatives are produced from the coca leaves that grow in the Central Andes (mainly Bolivia and Peru, its point of origin). The plant was successfully transplanted to Colombia, which became the world's number one producer during the 1990s (more recently, Peru has become the largest producer).[3] Several less expensive, smokable forms of cocaine have been developed under different names such as crack, *bazuko*, and *paco*. These drugs are developed from cocaine paste (an early stage in the processing of cocaine from the coca leaves), or from the "leftovers" of drug production which are mixed with other chemicals, creating highly toxic and cheap drugs.

Designer or synthetic drugs. A long list of narcotics and stimulants are produced from chemicals processed in small labs across the region. These include amphetamines, methamphetamine, ecstasy, and crystals, among others. They are all produced from the combination of widely available chemicals such as ephedrine, phenyl-2-propoanone, safrole oil, and many others. The key element in the production of these drugs is access to a large quantity of precursors. Worldwide, the demand for these drugs has risen sharply over the last decade, with an estimated 35 million users per year (WDR 2014). Although these substances can be processed anywhere, many Latin American nations have become large producers due to lax government controls, allowing these drug manufacturers to acquire and stock large quantities of chemicals.[4] In addition, penalties for such clandestine labs in the United States and Europe are severe, creating bigger incentives for illegal drug producers and traffickers to move them to labs in countries where law enforcement is lenient.

Table 5.1 shows the scale of drug production for poppy (heroin) and cocaine and provides data on seizures of synthetic drugs and cannabis herb. Seizures do not reveal the actual levels of production of given drugs, but are indicative of each country's ability to enforce drug laws. However, due to lack of reliable information, comparisons are merely approximate to the size of the market. More importantly, the last column in the table shows the share the entire region has in the production and/or seizures of the listed drugs.

The reader should approach this data with caution[5] as the statistics on production and trafficking are based on sketchy and incomplete information. Production is usually estimated from aerial and satellite images of cultivated areas of poppy, marihuana, or coca leaves; from drug seizures; and from assumptions based on demand for the drugs. Despite the patchy data, a clear trend emerges. First, Peru, Bolivia, and Colombia are the world's producers of coca, but some cheap derivatives of these drugs are also concocted in homemade labs in large cities of Brazil, Argentina, Mexico, and many other countries to serve their respective domestic markets.

Table 5.1 Production and seizure of various drugs in Latin America and the United States

		Arg	Bol	Bra	Col	Mex	Par	Peru	United States	World %
Cocaine	Area (ha)		30,900		68,000			59,900		100%
	Potential (metric tons)		113		450			302		100%
Poppy and Opium	Area (ha)				356	19,500				10.1%
	Potential (metric tons)				9	425				5.5%
ATS Seizure	Amphetamine (metric tons)				0.02	6.1			7.7	21%
	Ecstasy (metric tons)	37.0		7.6	6.3	1.1			3,411	71%
Cannabis	herb seizures (number)	92	26	131	208	2,105	84	2	2,049	80%

Empty cells denote no data available.

Source: Author elaboration based on WDR (2011).

Second, the production of poppy and heroin in the region is relatively small, though it appears that during the past decade production has been rising.[6]

Third, the marihuana market is continuously shifting. Marihuana is the most widely consumed illegal drug and there are many large areas of production in the region. The permitting of its medical use and the subsequent further legalization in some US states has increased production for this large market.

Fourth, law enforcement data suggest that there has been a significant rise in the production of synthetic drugs. Argentina, Brazil, and Mexico, large countries with developed chemical industries, import from the Far East large quantities of chemical precursors to produce a wide variety of these drugs. It appears that this market is experiencing a vigorous rise.[7]

Trafficking and Commercialization

Prohibition affects the way illegal drugs are transported, smuggled, and retailed on the market. I call these stages trafficking and commercialization. Most illegal drugs are produced in remote areas, at a safe distance from large consumer centers, and then shipped along various routes to the consumer markets. Drugs need to cross borders, traffickers are continuously developing routes to guarantee supply, and carriers must develop sophisticated logistics to avoid detection and confiscation. As will be shown later, this stage has led to the emergence and consolidation of powerful DTOs. The key player in the drug business, as Saviano (2013) stresses, is not the producer but the distributor. The Mexican–US border has become the most notorious route for illegal drugs in the world where traffickers have specialized in smuggling drugs.[8] These reach the US market through many venues, such as short flights by small private airplanes, small vessels, tunnels carved beneath the border, hidden drugs inside commercial trucks that cross the border daily, and many others.[9] Other maritime and air routes have been used to reach overseas markets. Spain is considered the main gateway for cocaine entering Europe. Data on shipment seizures, collected recently from Argentina, Venezuela, Brazil, and Mexico, suggest that these are the ports of departure for the cocaine to Europe (WDR 2014). Most illegal drugs flow from producer to consumer countries and reach faraway regions in an integrated global market. If there is a demand, any drug can reach any market.

Shipments of drugs are usually fractioned and relatively small. This is a very important and somewhat overlooked feature of the drug trade that derives from the high cost of seizures, whereby the impounding of a ton of cocaine, for instance, can mean losses for drug traffickers in excess of thirty million dollars. This is why drugs are trafficked in small loads. Shipments vary in size from small quantities carried or ingested by mules (who suffer severe health risks) to loads of several kilograms of refined cocaine. But the overwhelming majority of shipments that cross the American and European borders weigh less than 100 kg.[10] The high risk of seizure at the border (estimated at between 10 and 20 percent[11]) has led to sophisticated shipment logistics for border crossing.

The transportation of cocaine or heroin differs from that of marihuana. The latter is more bulky and its cost per gram is much lower. Therefore, very small shipments of cannabis are rare, while small loads of cocaine and heroin, carried by individuals, are very common. Large DTOs develop sophisticated schemes for smuggling loads of 10 to 50 kg at a time (hidden in cars and cargo containers, passed through tunnels). Mid-level suppliers, in turn, might smuggle 1 or 2 kg of cocaine on individual flights or by land. The successful smuggling of a drug shipment makes for hefty individual profits and can create strong incentives for small scale traffickers.

Strong enforcement at borders has a direct impact on pricing as well as on the logistics, structure, and organization of the illegal drug business. The booming demand for illegal drugs has led to the rise of "drug entrepreneurs" who have seized on the opportunities for large profits. The so-called war on drugs has paradoxically produced a new cadre of entrepreneurs in the region who have mastered transportation and shipping in order to get consumers the illegal substances they demand while making major profits.

Consumption

The consumption of illegal drugs in Latin America has been low.[12] Since the 1990s, however, rates have risen, in some cases quite dramatically. There are at least two hypotheses to explain this growth in domestic markets of illegal drugs: a) the greater accessibility of illegal drugs and b) a genuine new demand for drugs from new urban cohorts. In short, this growth can be explained from a supply-side and from a demand-side perspective. The first hypothesis suggests that this rise in drug use derives from drug availability in the marketplace because of trafficking (OEA 2013; WDR 2011). As routes for drug shipments began to make their way through countries and regions of Latin America, DTOs paid servicemen and organizations in kind, which they in turn converted into cash by pushing domestic sales. Many have claimed that this is a supply-driven market (UNODC),[13] although no empirical studies have tested these hypotheses for Latin America. The rising demand could also derive from shifts in consumer trends of new cohorts, in which case, supply chains then developed to provide drugs to new markets. Most drug users in the region live in large cities and are socialized in environments that promote alcohol and drug consumption. An alternative testable hypothesis is that a cultural change among urban youngsters in LATAM has probably driven the rise in demand and therefore the development of the supply chains. It is beyond the scope of this book to examine illegal-drug consumer patterns in Latin America, though there is no doubt that use of a variety of drugs in the region has increased over the last two decades.

Methods for obtaining statistics on consumer markets of illegal drugs are mostly imperfect and, as mentioned in Chapter 2, are based on population surveys containing questions on patterns of consumption and using data from hospitals, prisons, and other institutions that provide information for targeted groups. Surveys are usually conducted with different methodologies and therefore comparisons should be made with caution. In addition, some surveys in the region do not discriminate between recreational or occasional consumers, and between regular users or drug addicts, making it difficult to estimate the size of the drug market and the level of consumption. For most countries, data is based on two types of surveys: a) general population and b) adolescents and students. Table 2.10 in chapter 2 track changes in drug use for two drugs. 5.2 presents here rates of consumption for several drugs in a number of countries over the past year relying on similar methodology.

Several conclusions can be drawn from this data. First, most Latin American countries have a sizable number of consumers; however, it appears that most are occasional and recreational drug users. This data does not allow us to estimate the size of the domestic markets.[14] Second, despite the upward trend, rates are relatively low for most countries except for most drugs in Argentina, Chile, Brazil, Uruguay, and for single drugs in others. Third, the scattered data also signal a more troublesome trend among low-income users: the proliferation of cheap cocaine derivatives that exacerbate the health hazards associated with drug use (OEA-CICAD 2011). WDR (2014, 36) estimates that in South America, the number of cocaine drug users (mainly smoking various forms such as crack, *paco*, and bazuko) went from 2 million in 2005 to 3.35 million in 2012.

Table 5.2 **Illegal drug consumption (%)**

Country	Marihuana	Cocaine	Heroine	Ecstasy
	Prevalence rates for the general population (12–65)			
Argentina	3.75 (2010)[c]	0.81 (2010)[a]	0.09 (2010)[a]	0.05 (2010)[a]
Bolivia	4.50 (2007)[b]	0.65 (2007)[a]	0.60 (2007)[a]	0.10 (2007)[b]
Brazil	8.80 (2011)[a]	0.71 (2011)[a]	0.50 (2005)[a]	0.16 (2010)[a]
Chile	7.10 (2012)[c]	1.10 (2012)[c]	0.29 (2010)[a]	0.01 (2010)[a]
Colombia	2.27 (2008)[b]	0.81 (2008)[a]	0.02 (2008)	0.28 (2008)[b]
Costa Rica	2.60 (2010)[a]	1.00 (2010)[a]	0.60 (2010)[a]	0.15 (2006)[a]
Ecuador	0.70 (2007)[b]	0.25 (2007)[a]	0.11 (2007)[a]	0.20 (2007)[a]
El Salvador	0.35 (2008)[c]	0.24 (2008)[c]	0.01 (2008)[c]	0.01 (2008)[c]
Guatemala	4.80 (2005)[a]	0.21 (2005)[a]	0.20 (2007)[a]	0.08 (2005)[a]
Haiti	0.70 (2009)[b]	0.87 (2005)	0.20 (2006)[a]	0.56 (2005)[a]
Honduras	1.06 (2005)[b]	0.12 (2005)[b]	0.15 (2005)[a]	0.08 (2005)[a]
Mexico	1.20 (2011)[a]	0.50 (2011)[a]	0.38 (2011)[a]	0.04 (2011)[a]
Nicaragua	1.06 (2006)[b]	0.69 (2006)[a]	0.02 (2006)[a]	0.01 (2006)[a]
Panama	3.60 (2003)[a]	1.20 (2003)[a]	0.20 (2007)[a]	0.40 (2003)[a]
Paraguay	1.60 (2005)[a]	0.44 (2008)[b]	0.03 (2003)[a]	0.09 (2005)
Peru	1.00 (2010)[c]	0.67 (2010)[a]	0.18 (2005)[a]	0.05 (2010)[c]
Dominican Republic	0.31 (2008)[a]	0.30 (2008)[a]	0.07 (2008)[a]	0.05 (2008)[a]
Uruguay	8.30 (2011)[a]	2.10 (2011)[a]	0.18 (2011)[a]	0.20 (2011)[a]
Venezuela	1.66 (2011)[a]	0.64 (2011)[a]	0.03 (2011)[a]	0.12 (2011)[a]

Sources: [a] UNODC; [b] CICAD; [c] official sources for Latin American countries. Data are from the most recent year available (in parentheses).

In short, Latin America is on a path from being a region of drug producers and trafficking to being a region that also has growing domestic markets. This has had an important effect on crime.

Price, Profits, and the Structure of Illegal Trade

The high profits to be made from illegal drugs trade can be explained by a simple market mechanism: these are goods in high demand among a large customer base ready to spend a good deal of money. Becker et al. (2004) and many of their followers have claimed that the demand for illegal drugs is relatively inelastic (i.e., that demand does not shrink initially when price rises). This in theory produces large profits for traffickers because there will always be buyers. But this is an oversimplification. Demand is somewhat elastic because market access for drugs is not easy as it is for other legal goods, and competition among suppliers (from DTOs to street dealers) can lead to violence. In addition, switching between drugs and the emergence of assorted types of synthetic drugs, as well as overwhelming use of cocaine derivatives such as crack by low income users, denote that elasticity does play a role in the drugs trade.

Many factors drive up profits, in particular strong demand versus limited supply, strong enforcement at the transshipment or at the street level, and the level of competition among suppliers. I argue that stringent law enforcement in countries where consumption is very high (the United States and Western Europe), results in a considerable price increase in drugs, and provides even more incentives for production and trafficking. Those who are eliminated from the illegal drug industry (physically or through market mechanisms) are easily replaced by a large army of newcomers. Drawn by the very attractive incomes that can be derived from trafficking and dealing, these individuals are willing to risk imprisonment and even their own lives.

The way individuals and organizations operate in the illegal drug trade in Latin America has received little attention in spite of the major impact they have on the drug business structure.[15] Figure 5.1 shows the different

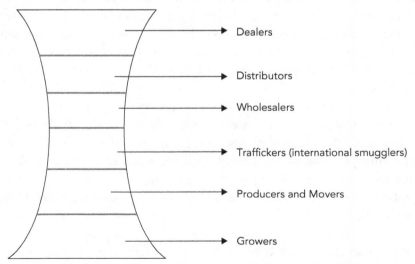

FIGURE 5.1 The drug industry: production, trafficking, and commercialization.

players and roles in the drug industry, with the growers and farmers on one end and the street vendors and dealers on the other. At these stages, the structure of the business is highly atomized due to its illegal nature. There are no known large landowners that produce marihuana or coca leaves, nor large retailers of illegal drugs. Given the high cost of sanctions, the atomized structure is economically more efficient, and it allows growers and street dealers who have been apprehended to be quickly replaced.

Growers and dealers outnumber producers and sellers. Producers or processors, depending on the type of drug, buy the raw material from growers and then make the drugs in makeshift laboratories. In some cases, particularly with cocaine, large DTOs can control the final stage, although oftentimes cartels purchase the illegal drug from local producers.[16] On the other end, distributors link cartels with street dealers. They usually control a town or a large section of a city and have their own network of street dealers. Sometimes large organizations control city distribution, although DTOs often sell the drugs to independent distributors instead in order to reduce their risks.

In the middle are the traffickers, smugglers, and large wholesalers. They are the critical links, because they bring the drugs to consumers by moving them from production to retail. There are few players at this stage, which is very important to note. Only a large and sophisticated organization can transport and smuggle drugs across borders and have the financial depth to absorb occasional seizures. In sum, a large number of individuals "work" in the drug business. There are hundreds of thousands of growers and dealers in the cocaine supply chain, hundreds of players at the intermediate level, and only a handful of groups that transship, smuggle, and to a lesser extent wholesale the drugs. These latter are the powerful DTOs, which handle the riskier and more profitable part of the business.[17]

This structure results in a very uneven distribution of profits. Table 5.3 presents a typical price structure for a kilogram of cocaine.[18] Adjusting for purity, the highest rates of profits are at the retail level; however, as shown in Figure 5.1, these profits are divided among tens or even hundreds of thousands of street dealers. On the other end, at the production level, profits are very small and also divided among many poor farmers.[19] Hefty profits are being made at the mid-level of the trade, the transshipment from Latin American countries to wholesalers in Europe or the United States. Traffickers make between 20 and 25 percent of the final retailed price; however, these profits are divided among few organizations. Two

Table 5.3 Cocaine price structure

Stage	Price (US$)
Base production	$900 (per kg cocaine paste in Colombia)
Final production at origin	$1,700 (per kg pure cocaine in Colombia)
Wholesale price in Miami or Dallas	$21,000 (85%–90% pure, per kg)
Intermediate price in Philadelphia or Chicago	$31,500 (75% pure, average per kg)
Retail price in Philadelphia or Chicago	$105,000 (65% pure, average per gram)

Source: Author elaboration from Reuter and Caulkins (2011) and Narcotics News (http://www.narcoticnews.com/Cocaine/Prices/USA/Cocaine_Prices_USA.htm).

factors explain why there are only a handful of players in the trafficking business: a) stringent law enforcement along the borders of large consumer countries and b) the degree of specialization and deep financing required to successfully smuggle illegal drugs. The limited market competition for smugglers has allowed strong DTOs to emerge in Latin America.

While the retail price of one gram of pure cocaine in a US city averages US$150 and approximately €150 in Amsterdam or Paris (RAND 2014; UNODC 2011), in Latin America, the price of one gram of high purity cocaine ranges between US$30 and US$50. This extreme variation in international prices merits an explanation. It can be attributed to three aspects of the market in Latin America: first, supply is larger, demand is somewhat lower, and the cost of labor is much lower.[20] Second, transportation and smuggling to penetrate markets abroad is expensive. Third, the risk premium associated with lenient law enforcement in Latin America reduces the final cost of drugs—while the average sentence for drug trafficking in the United States is sixty months, in six Latin American countries it is forty-four months.[21] The likelihood of detection, the severity of sanctions, and the possibility of bribing a way out of the criminal justice system in Latin America, makes the cost of drug trafficking in the region much lower (this is discussed further in chapters 7, 8, and 9).

The lion's share of drug trafficking into Europe or the United States is borne by large DTOs whose carriers must get past several border and customs controls before the drugs reach the marketplaces. Just as they must ensure that thieves or rival gangs don't get their hands on the stash, they must elude or bribe politicians, policemen, or state agents in the region.

In addition, they must keep shipments off the radar of US military and enforcement agents who patrol the sea, air, and land of so-called drug corridors (Valdés 2013). Once drugs reach the US border they are usually fractioned to prevent a single confiscation of a large amount at a crossing point. Smugglers make multiple shipments and use different and very creative methods to reach the United States and Europe.[22] Although a good number of shipments are detected and seized, the vast majority cross the border and reach warehouses for further distribution.

Little attention has been paid to this simple logic of the drug business, which has significantly impacted the region. Stringent US law enforcement has empowered and strengthened organizations that are capable of eluding control and smuggling drugs, making the few players involved extremely rich and violent. Given the somewhat inelastic demand for drugs, such strong enforcement has paradoxically created incentives for risk takers to engage in these lucrative enterprises. For example, if the enforcement at the US border were as lenient as it is in Latin America, the price of drugs in the US would probably be much lower, as would the profits for DTOs. Between 2001 and 2008 the number of police patrolmen in the United States doubled,[23] while interdiction in Colombia and drug corridors increased (Castillo et al. 2014; Valdés 2013). Therefore, cocaine prices (and profits) went up significantly (NDIC 2010), with smuggling into the US market increasingly concentrated among a select group of outlaws.[24]

Strong interdictions in the "North" have produced another overlooked effect: more crime in the "South." Since traffickers and producers know that a large share of drugs will never reach the retail market, they are overproduced, exacerbating the conditions that breed criminality at this stage. For example, the world consumer market for cocaine is 500 metric tons per year, but production is estimated at 750 tons (WDR 2014). Such overproduction breeds more violence in Colombia among factions and guerrillas and worsens environmental conditions for farmers, among other impacts.

Rigorous enforcement increases profits for smugglers. Let us assume that 1 kg of cocaine purchased in Colombia costs US$2,000 and after it is smuggled into the US it wholesales for approximately US$26,000. The logistics of transshipment is expensive and frequent drug seizures impose heavy costs on the organizations.[25] Given the risks, it is reasonable to assume a 25 percent profit margin, that is US$6,000 for every kilogram of cocaine that reaches the United States. American demand for cocaine has been approximately 300 tons per year. By this estimation DTOs make the lion's share of US$1.8 billion in gross profits by just getting cocaine to the United States.

Enforcement leads the drug trade to be concentrated among relatively few groups. These groups are at times challenged by new ones, particularly when powerful bosses are captured or organizations are disbanded. New, smaller organizations that are capable of handling large quantities of drugs rapidly acquire firepower, earmark more money for paying off law enforcement, and ultimately collect large profits. Consequently, true competition among DTOs to reduce prices and profits is actually hampered by the strong US enforcement that indirectly and perhaps unintentionally favors concentration and specialization. The recent history of drug trafficking (Astorga 2005; Thoumi 1994) shows that the flow of heroin and marihuana from Mexico into the United States was dominated by very few organizations linked to Felix Gallardo and Sinaloa barons in the 1970s and 1980s. The large cocaine transshipments into the United States in the 1980s and early 1990s were led by two powerful Colombian cartels (Medellin and Cali), and the heroin, cocaine, and synthetic drugs trade since the mid-1990s was handed by shifting coalitions of seven or eight Mexican organizations (Sinaloa, Golfo, Zetas, Juarez, Tijuana, la Familia, and others). Inner conflicts as well as government interventions have broken up some large groups into smaller, specialized, but still powerful organizations that are led by lieutenants of older, large organizations in Colombia, Mexico, and other countries. As a result, specialized, highly profitable, and very deadly gangs have emerged to replace large drug trafficking oligopolies and have contributed to the escalation of crime and violence in several countries.

Drug Trafficking and the Emergence of Violence

The use of violence is seldom a good business decision because it carries costs and risks that entrepreneurs usually prefer to avoid (Schelling 1980; Tilly 2003; Gambetta 2010). Violence, however, can become a rational alternative for those who want to change a status quo. In the drug business, violence is ultimately a mechanism of dispute resolution for achieving a rational goal.

Most of the literature on violence has focused on the transshipment and trafficking of drugs (CAF 2014; Valdés 2013; Maihold and Jost 2014). The recent Mexican war on drugs and the extreme violence in Colombia during the 1990s and the 2000s reveal the levels of violence that the drug trade can produce. Some scholars argue that the driver for violence is market size, which generates incentives for groups to fight for sizable profits (Mejia and Restrepo 2013; CAF 2014). I claim, however, that other variables should not be overlooked. For example, large profits are made at the retail level in the United States and Europe where violence is low. Even in Latin America, profits alone cannot account for the magnitude of violence. For instance, San Pablo in Brazil is three times the size of Rio de Janeiro, but has half Rio's homicide rate. Rosario, Argentina, is one-fifth the size of metropolitan Buenos Aires, yet it has three to four times more drug-related homicides. Even if the argument is made solely for the production and transshipment stage, it cannot apply in Peru and Bolivia, which are major cocaine producers, or in Paraguay's marihuana trade, where violence is relatively low. Other conditions have made Colombia much more violent than Peru and Bolivia. This chapter points out the variables that can trigger high levels of violence, with special emphasis on the growth of domestic drug markets.

The link between violence and illegal drugs remains unclear.[26] Most transactions are conducted peacefully, but violence can erupt over the control of outlets, routes, and distribution when rival groups fight for market share. Conversely, when control over transportation, distribution, and sales is clearly established, the evidence shows that violence decreases significantly. Three conditions must be in place for violence to emerge in the drug trade: a) the lack of viable mechanisms to resolve conflicts between groups, b) unstable drug markets, and c) poor law enforcement. As Arias (2017) argues, micro-level armed regimes formed in urban areas affect local governance to the degree gangs consolidate and synchronize among them. DTOs ability to reach such consolidation affects the nature of the market and its level of violence.

First, drugs are illegal and thus courts of law and other legal institutions cannot resolve conflicts delers or traffickers. In the drug trade, hierarchical and dominant organizations establish clear territories and responsibilities, usually diminishing the loci of violence between agents. Leading organizations such as the PCC in San Pablo keeps violence under control (Nunes Dias 2013).[27] Conversely, when the structure of the drug trade is highly atomized with no dominant player, several groups might resort to violence in order to control a territory. In Rio de Janeiro, for example, several powerful groups compete for sales. The lack of a single leading drug organization creates incentives for fights over market share.

Second, unstable markets can increase violence because dealers can rush to control routes and outlets to extract even larger profits. Emerging markets where demand is growing rapidly might serve as an invitation to a turf war. This is what happened in major US cities in the 1980s and early 1990s when changes in the crack/drug markets elicited violence. According to several theories of 1990s crime reduction in America, once the turf war settled, homicides and other crimes began to decline (Blumstein and Rosenfeld 1998; Blumstein and Wallman 2005; Levitt 2004). In Latin America, the growth of domestic markets in large cities (Northeastern Brazil, Caracas, Buenos Aires, Rosario, Santiago de Chile, and Mexico City, among others) correlates with a rise in violence since the mid-1990s.

Third, violence erupts when law enforcement fails. When deterrence is low vis-à-vis profits and market growth, the incentives to fight for turf rises. In this chapter and in chapters 7, 8, and 9, I analyze the effects of a breakdown in equilibrium (Kleiman 2009). I claim that violence erupts when the perceived cost of its use is very low. In Latin America, police and courts are very ineffective, and therefore gangs and individuals do not perceive that the cost of engaging in violence is high.

Enforcement agencies, however, can impact the level of violence. Usually the success of stringent policies shapes the drug business, in what has been called the balloon effect (Drucker 1998; Laffiteau 2011; Bagley 2012), producing at times more violence. When in the mid-1990s the Peruvian government began to shoot down planes full of coca paste on their way to Colombia, it produced higher violence in the neighboring country (Angrist and Kugler 2008). The success of Colombian interdiction policies under the Uribe administration has shifted part of the drug processing and trafficking industry into Ecuador, Venezuela, and Central America, where violence has escalated (Castillo, Mejia, and Restrepo 2013). However, not every enforcement in response to shifts in drug trafficking has produced more violence. Despite some crackdown efforts by its authorities, Paraguay has produced more and more marihuana in the past decade without a significant increase in violence, and as mentioned, Peru has dramatically increased its production of cocaine while drug-related violence remains stable. Hefty profits can be stressors to the given equilibrium but other conditions are necessary to trigger violence in the drug business.

The three conditions mentioned above—the structure of the market, the rising demand for drugs, and poor and erratic law enforcement—are not mutually exclusive. They are generally intertwined and are more continuous than dichotomous variables. For example, the more atomized the supply, the greater the demand for drugs; and the lower the enforcement capacities of states, the greater the potential for infighting among groups for routes and turf.

Drug-related violence in Latin America is on the rise. In addition to violent conflicts among large DTOs, smaller drug suppliers fight over the right to produce and sell. Three midsized cities epitomize this general trend: Fortaleza in Brazil, Rosario in Argentina, and Acapulco in Mexico. Over the past few decades, Fortaleza in northeast Brazil has received a large number of migrants from rural areas, who flocked to the city in search of industrial and service jobs. Poor urban planning and inadequate infrastructure have produced shantytowns where drug consumption has proliferated. The rate of drug-related homicide rose dramatically accounting for the lion's share of violent deaths in the city, increasing from 20 per 100,000 in 1998 to 45.7 per 100,000 in 2010 (see Waiselfiesz 2014, chapters 4 and 5). Similar patterns can be found in many other northeastern Brazil cities such as Recife, Natal, and Bahia.

The violence in Rosario, 300 km north of Buenos Aires and the third largest city of Argentina, has puzzled many observers. A relatively quiet city with a population of more than one million, Rosario has recently benefitted from the boom in soybean exports shipped from its ports, allowing the city to rebound after decades of economic stagnation. Along its outskirts, drug trafficking has grown over the past years, with more than two hundred homicides believed to be drug related in 2013. Several accounts of police officers and their ties to drug barons, as well as an attack to the house of Santa Fe's governor are testimony of the escalating violence in this otherwise calm city.[28]

Acapulco, a traditional tourist town in the southwestern Mexican state of Guerrero, has recently become a focal point of extreme violence. The number of homicides for the state of Guerrero climbed from 766 in 2007 to 2,646 in 2012.[29] A large share of these homicides occurred in Acapulco where gangs battled for the right to distribute drugs in the growing domestic market, including the tourist corridor.[30] Although Guerrero (2014) has argued that homicides have decreased slightly, in 2013 more than 500 executions were reported in Acapulco. Drug use also appears to be on the rise in the shantytowns on the city's outskirts.

The stories of these three cities resemble those of many others in the region. High demand for relatively cheap drugs produces a market that is supplied by small and mid-level groups that easily recruit underpriviledged youngsters willing to push sales or protect business for meagre incomes. As Levitt and Venkatesh (2000) have shown, these low-level workers in the drug business do not earn very much initially but they hope to climb the ladder of their organizations and make larger profits. The use of extreme violence appears to establish one's reputation within the groups. A unique study based on more than two hundred interviews done by the *Observatorio de las favelas* (Carvalho and Soares 2013) shows that foot soldiers in Rio de Janeiro begin working in drug retail networks as street informants and security soldiers at very young age (13–15): 67 percent of youngsters aged 16–18 years old who work in these drug retail networks come from unstructured families, and earn less than the minimum wage. Follow-up interviews two years later found that 19 percent of these youngsters had been murdered (for a similar United States study see Bourgois 2003).

The rise in criminal violence in the region can partly be explained by the surge in the domestic demand for drugs, which created opportunities for profits. However, not all drug deals are violent. The last section of this chapter will show that the violence generated by domestic markets results from unregulated competition among groups in search of a market share. The regulation or control of crime can be handled by the police, by other authorities, by a dominant organization, or even within the drug gangs themselves.

Domestic Drug Markets

Who are the individuals that transport and deal drugs? What are their expectations? What is the real level of income? How much violence do they exert? Here I present original data that sheds light on these questions for the first time. Using responses from the inmate surveys, I claim that drug dealing is widespread, providing a good source of income for hundreds of thousands of individuals. Most importantly, I show that most transactions are non-violent.

Inmates serving time for drug-related crimes were asked to respond to several questions on their drug dealing. Offenders in drug related crimes are usually dealers, manufacturers, carriers, or leaders of the drug trade.[31] Approximately 15% (more than nine hundred) of the inmates interviewed took the survey, and their responses portray a clear picture of drug offenders and the type of activities they undertake.[32] These individuals provide a very good perspective on the domestic drug business activity.

Table 5.4 shows that the two most important drugs on the market are marihuana and crack-cocaine. More than 90 percent of the inmates convicted for drug-related crimes were indicted for dealing one of these two drugs. Surprisingly, few people were prosecuted for dealing synthetic drugs, a rapidly growing market.[33] Additionally, individuals appear to specialize. Respondents rarely acknowledged dealing or trafficking multiple drugs.

The criminal justice systems target both street dealers and carriers. Dealers probably outnumber carriers[34] so it is safe to assume that police and customs allocate more resources to arresting offenders responsible for drug transportation. Very few respondents acknowledged having both sold and moved drugs. Lastly, approximately 10 to 15 percent of convicted offenders in drug-related crimes admitted that an authority (mostly the police) participated in the alleged crime, mainly by receiving kickbacks or by providing some sort of protection.

More than 50 percent of convicted inmates admitted that they had carried out a similar drug transaction during the last year prior to detention.[35] Most of these respondents reported being indicted for similar drug offenses several times in the past. Table 5.5 shows that the most common motivation for engaging in drug-related transactions was economic. As Table 5.7 shows, these inmates tended to abandon other jobs and had

Table 5.4 Drug dealing by inmates in six countries (% sentenced)

Drug	Argentina	Brazil	Chile	El Salvador	Mexico	Peru
Marihuana	47.40	40.50	29.40	68.60	42.20	8.70
Inhalants	1.00	2.60	0.00	0.00	1.10	0.50
Cocaine paste/ cocaine/crack	50.80	53.40	69.80	26.80	51.40	84.20
Synthetics	0.50	2.30	0.80	0.30	2.10	0.90
Other	0.20	0.50	0.00	2.80	1.10	5.40
Heroin	0.00	0.70	0.00	1.40	2.10	0.50
N	111	314	133	82	24	240

Source: Inmate Surveys 2013.

Table 5.5 Reason for selling or moving drugs (%)

	Argentina	Brazil	Chile	El Salvador	Mexico	Peru
To pay for personal consumption	10.1	14.9	13.5	1.8	19.2	16.4
Was not earning an income	15.6	34.4	26.8	8.7	80.8	28.7
Because there was a lot of money to be earned	50.1	38.1	42.1	6.9	0	48.6
Other people asked him to	2.9	1.2	5.1	2.2	0	4.8
To help his/her family	7	6.5	0	0	0	0
For excitement	5.8	4	0	0	0	0
Other	0	0	8.4	3.3	0	15.1
Doesn't know/ didn't respond	7.9	0.9	4.2	77.2	0	0
N	104	223	135	80	25	61

Source: Inmate Surveys 2013.

some level of education compared to other offenders—dealing drugs appears to be a good source of income. The data clearly show that only a very minor share of drug addicts (14 percent for the entire sample) dealt drugs in order to earn enough for personal consumption.[36]

The growth of domestic markets for illegal drugs provided many youngsters with a good source of income. Table 5.6 presents self-reports of incomes for the six countries in the study, but it is safe to assume that similar trends can be found in the other countries. These comparative data show the scope of earnings for drug offenders in the region for the first time. The first row indicates the monetary amount of the offense which inmates were sentenced for; the second is the value of the drugs that the individuals generally sold or carried during a month; and the third averages the profits they made monthly. I present means and medians since a few number of very large traffickers in the sample skew the results.

Table 5.6 Earnings from drug dealing (in US$)

Survey question	Argentina		Brazil		Chile		El Salvador		Mexico		Peru	
	Mean	Median	Mean	Median	Mean	Median	Mean	Median	Mean	Median	Mean	Median
What was the value of the illegal drugs whose you were convicted for?	1.273	39.43	343	40.23	40.97	3.51	1.163	17	138	274	266	360
What was the approximate value of illegal drugs you have transported/sold in a month?	1.273	176.5	32.91	6.44	75.08	5.27	2.110	64	26.2	15.14	499	360
How much profit did you made from that drug dealing?	637	23.61	12.63	2.15	20.37	2.11	491	23	1.711	1.514	206	360
N		104		223		135		80		25		253

Source: Inmate Surveys 2013.

Table 5.7 Profile of offender groups by type of crime committed

	Drug-related Crime	Theft	Homicides	Sex crimes	Other
Percent of inmates who attended secondary school	68.8	59.8	55.0	49.4	68.2
Percent of inmates who had jobs one month before arrest	71.2	84.0	75.2	93.8	84.4
Percent who left home before turning 15 years of age	30.1	44.8	37.2	28.5	38.4
Average income over last month activity (legal and illegal, in US$)	670.4	497.1	427.3	481.93	348.25

Source: Inmate Surveys.

Several initial findings stand out. First, given the amounts of the transactions, most inmates imprisoned for drug-related crimes worked on domestic markets or did menial support work for larger trades. Less than 10 percent of those surveyed reported transactions worth US$10,000 or more. Second, by Latin American standards, and given the skills and job history of these inmates, the income level of drug-related offenses was reasonably good. As the majority of respondents acknowledged (see Table 5.5), they dealt drugs because of the income they could earn. Very few sold or carried drugs to have the means to finance personal addictions. Third, the profit margin (monthly transactions compared to profits) is quite large. We can assume that most of these inmates were individual "entrepreneurs" (dealers and carriers); though they had ties to larger organizations, they were not on their payroll. Fourth, more females are involved in drug-related offenses than in other crimes. While less than 5 percent of the general prison population are women, they represent 16 percent of drug offenders. For both young and older mothers, particularly in poor neighborhoods, working as drug carriers or running "kiosks" from their own homes has become a viable source of income.

Who are the people that work in these drug-related transactions for the domestic markets? The surveys provide some insight. First, most individuals incarcerated for drug offences have a slightly higher level of education than other inmates. While the percentage of inmates that attended secondary education was 55 percent for homicides, 48 percent for sex crimes, and 59 percent for theft, it was 69 percent for drug-related crimes. Second, education correlates with profits. The Pearson r coefficient between years of schooling and profits is 0.45 and statistically significant at p = 0.01 for the entire sample.

Third, compared to others, most inmates in jail for drug-related offenses come from relatively low-crime environments. I drafted a scale based on questions related to households where individuals were raised and the neighborhood they lived in. The data show that individuals who were arrested for drug-related crimes came from relatively safer settings.[37] Differences in scale points compared to inmates who committed other crimes were significant at p = 0.01. Fourth, most drug offenders have had jobs previously, but they reported earning a much lower income in these other jobs. On average, drug-related-crime offenders earned much more than any other offenders, came from lower-crime environments, and were less likely to have left their homes as teenagers. In addition, those involved in the drug trade were better educated and had opted to forgo "real" jobs because they were making more money from drugs.

In summary, a large number of people in the region rely on the illegal drug industry for their income. Expanding domestic markets provide earnings for millions of youngsters and women. Individuals are loosely connected to the organizations that supply the drugs, and they earn a higher income than they would in other jobs available to them. As stressed in this chapter, the retail and courier stage of the drug industry is relatively autonomous, as large cartels forfeit profits in exchange for lower legal liability.[38] The data from the inmate surveys show that the domestic drug industry attracts slightly more educated people, and probably more entrepreneur-oriented offenders.

Despite the economic opportunities the drug trade and sales provides, it is worth noting that financial advantages are not the only motivations for youngsters to join the illegal drugs trade. A search for respect, meaning, and "career opportunities" serves as an important motivation, particularly for youngsters, to join gangs and delinquent networks (Burgois 2010; Carvalho and Soares 2013). While here I have focused on economic opportunities, other drivers are important and are discussed in chapters 3, 4, and 6 of this book.

Drugs, Violence, and the Crime Equilibrium

Illegal drugs profits and markets can certainly generate more criminality and violence. However, causality is far from unidirectional. In fact, other factors play crucial roles in making the illegal drugs trade highly violent. In addition to earnings and market structure other variables are important, such as regional strategic location, levels of fragmentation of supply chains, pre-existing criminal networks, time of reaction of initial enforcement, and many others.

Here, I elaborate on the impact illegal drugs have on crime in the region, and analyze the effects on large-scale violence when the equilibrium breaks down. To illustrate the arguments, I begin with four brief case studies (in Mexico, Argentina, Brazil, and Chile), and then summarize the conditions in which high crime and violence can erupt.

Mexico. Since the days of prohibition, the state of Tamaulipas in Northeast Mexico has been a launch pad for smuggling and other illegal activities, because of its strategic location and easy access to the central and eastern United States, as well as its four large points of entry to eastern Texas. In the late 1980s, the high demand for cocaine and the difficulties the Colombian cartels faced when it came to smuggling their goods into the US made the old *pistolero* gangs with local connections and political protection into the ideal partners for the Colombian kingpins. In the 1990s, the new, local Gulf cartel grew dramatically. Profits skyrocketed and leaders began to rely on more "professional" protection. Gunmen were recruited from the Mexican and Guatemalan armies (the Zetas and the Kaibiles) and despite power struggles among the leadership, lieutenants and other agents diversified the operations into other lucrative enterprises. The Mexican government occasionally intervened to arrest or kill leaders (Garcia Abregú, Osiel Cardenas, Heriberto Lazcano, Miguel Angel Treviño) but the main corridor for drugs and profits remained active. Tamaulipas became one of the most crimes-ridden states and has one of the largest homicide rate (32 per 100,000 in 2013). Similar stories with different local nuances are found in Ciudad Juarez, Chihuahua, Tijuana, Baja California, and other places.

Tamaulipas moved from a LCE in the 1980s to an HCE in the 2000s because of the high profit from the drug trade. It was never a state of law and order with effective institutions. In fact, the state was a hotbed of corruption. Yet crime remained low because local patrons, the party elite, and the leaders of security forces had a basic agreement with gang leaders that established clear boundaries.[39] Crime bosses garnered illegal incomes from crimes, sharing a portion with politicians and security authorities, who were in turn permissive with low-level criminality. However, this permissiveness was contingent on violence being contained. Drugs, however, changed the basic structure of incentives, as profits skyrocketed. The United States applied pressure to limit drug trafficking, and the Mexican government began to intervene. In addition, Tamaulipas's strategic location was coveted by other syndicates, particularly the Sinaloa cartel, which has been searching for years for low-cost routes to reach the lucrative central and eastern regions of the United States.[40]

Border regions and strategic location are more vulnerable to heavy drug trade and the subverting of LCEs. Control of routes is pivotal for the business (drug smuggling) and generates incentives for traffickers to devote significant resources to secure such a key pillar of the enterprise. However, not every border town or state will easily fall into an HCE. For example, Canada has a very long and busy border with the United States, in which large amounts of illegal drugs are consumed, yet there are very few reports of drug smuggling and crime along this border. Russia, meanwhile, has become the one of the main corridor along which heroin moves into Europe, but drug-related crimes are relatively contained. Routes and profits can become stressors for LCEs, but other conditions are necessary for high criminality to develop.

Argentina. Since the 1990s, Argentina's role in the illegal drug industry has grown. The domestic market has expanded, and according to reports and data from seizures, the country has also become a launching pad for large shipments of cocaine to Europe, especially because of the high movement of people to and commerce with Spain, now the main port of entry for cocaine into Europe. Yet unlike Brazil and despite a few isolated episodes of violence, Argentina maintains a low level of drug-related violence. Most of the cocaine for domestic or international transshipment arrives from Bolivia and Peru where the scale of violence is also low. The Bolivia–Argentina border is long and very porous, as are the smuggling routes from Paraguay into Argentina which have been developed over decades for many other goods besides drugs. Air radar controls are dysfunctional and small airplanes easily make border crossings without detection. There is a ceaseless supply of mules and other small carriers from Bolivia and Peru, and enforcement at borders has been traditionally poor and corrupted. Despite some confiscations in the northern provinces of Salta and Formosa, most of the drugs are believed to easily reach distribution centers in Buenos Aires and Rosario.

Despite the presumed large quantity of drugs crossing its borders, Argentina has relatively low levels of violence because profits are much smaller there than those in Tamaulipas: enforcement at borders is light and security authorities, albeit through corrupt and at times illegal practices, have controlled illegal activities until very recently. More importantly, even as drugs flow, there is only scattered evidence of typical gang crime diversifications, such as extortions, kidnappings, and the like. It remains to be seen whether larger profits will subvert this tenuous equilibrium. Argentina's low crime environment is under stress and might become unstable.

Brazil. While some of the domestic markets are very violent others remain relatively calm. As shown in previous section, drug-related violence has grown in midsized cities in the region. Large metropolitan areas with established law enforcement institutions faced different outcomes from drug-related activities. Throughout the twentieth century, Rio de Janeiro has been a large city with substantial rates of criminality. Its topography and large networks of criminal groups made some *favelas* hotbeds of crime (Misse 2007). When the crack cocaine epidemic erupted in the late 1980s and 1990s, violence exploded. Homicide rates rose from 20 per 100,000 in the early 1980s to 65 per 100,000 in 1997. The following decade witnessed a slow but steady decline in violence until 2008, when the rate had fallen to 32 homicides per 100,000. The much-publicized Rio de Janeiro program UPP (Cano 2012; Hendee 2013) has been moderately successful in reducing violence in the most renowned *favelas*.[41] The drug trade controlled by gangs in these shantytowns appeared to have moved to other areas, particularly the even more marginalized outskirt of the city such as *baixada de fluminense*.[42] But, homicide rates in Rio (24) are still double those of San Pablo.

Rio de Janeiro is a city with a long history of criminality. Rates of crime were historically among the highest in Brazil, and several social and economic factors have been mentioned as facilitators. Many gangs and groups battled for the control of profits that were orchestrated from the most populated *favelas* (Arias 2006). The crack cocaine epidemic added a new level of violence to the dispute for the control of domestic markets. Several renowned gangs (Comando Vermelho, Amigos dos Amigos, Terceiro Comando Puro) disputed turf and sizable profits, while law enforcement agents were either absent from these neighborhoods or partners in crime.[43] The drop in homicides began when markets stabilized (as had occurred in the 1990s in the large US cities) and when local and federal authorities made a significant effort to regain control. The above mentioned UPPs achieved only moderate and transitory results after a major effort and an outlay of significant resources. Only strong enforcement was able to contain the out-of-control violence that resulted from the atomization of criminal groups and years of policy neglect. These effects were transitory as crime erupted again after 2016.

Chile. Domestic drug markets do not produce violence if other conditions are not met. The metropolitan area of Santiago de Chile is not as large as Rio de Janeiro. Its geography does not provide any natural sanctuary for gangs, nor has the level of drug addiction or the number of consumers grown significantly in recent years. However, this city of close to seven million has the highest rate of drug consumption in Chile, which in turn has among the highest rate in Latin America (see Table 5.2). For instance, in 2008, the prevalence rates of cocaine and marihuana were similar to those of the United States. Although Chile is a small market, drug dealers sell large quantities and profits are attractive enough to produce battles and clashes for market share. Yet this metropolitan area has a homicide rate of 3.9, the lowest for large cities in Latin America.

In the 1960s and 1970s dealers in Chile were key players in the regional cocaine traffic before their places was overtaken by the Colombian drug kingpins in the early 1980s (Gootenberg 2009). A set of repressive raids by the Pinochet government reduced the leading role Chilean traffickers once had, precisely when the demand for cocaine in the United States began to rise. Yet, even when Chile had an important role in the cocaine business, violence was low.

Chile is known to have the strictest law enforcement agencies in Latin America. Still, cocaine and other drugs are successfully smuggled across its northern borders with Bolivia and Peru, and they safely make the 2,000-km journey to Santiago. The data on drug seizures are scant for such large prevalence rates (see Tables 5.1 and 5.3). A hard-core network of drug distributors and dealers successfully elude police and "push" sales in various areas and neighborhoods, catering to both rich and poor. Yet violence is relatively low. There is no known dominant cartel or organization that leads or controls the drug business. Conflicts appeared to be limited to individuals, and *carabineros* (Chile's police) and other agencies rapidly intervene when conflicts between parties do escalate.

Chile has avoided high criminality because police targeted drug dealers that resort to violence. In the absence of large drug organizations, the supply of drugs is fragmented with no major organization disputing others, and violence is contained between individuals who are easily identified and targeted by law enforcement agencies. In short, as in many cities of the United States, a relatively large domestic drug market operates without any major organized groups, and Santiago is relatively calm.[44]

Summary

In this book, I differentiate between high and low equilibriums of criminality. LCEs exist in most places and is characterized by a low homicide rates, some violent but contained conflict resolution, and power struggles that are resolved by less violent means (bargaining, exchanges, informal agreements, and so on). Under HCE, violence gets out of control. I argue that sometimes the profit that illegal drugs generate can weaken LCE, creating strong incentives for individuals and groups to fight for these large gains. In doing so, they enable criminals to "branch out" into other criminal activities (see chapter 6).

Earnings, however, do not necessarily break down LCE. High profits are stressors that test the strength of the other factors necessary to keep high criminality from emerging. Here, I have presented four cases that examine the threat of drug markets and large profits and show very different outcomes. It is beyond the scope of this book to describe the many variants of illegal drug markets as stressors of equilibriums, but these examples reveal several of the conditions that can make drugs a trigger for high criminality. The following are several potential stressors that can turn low crime into high crime:

Earnings and opportunity costs. To the extent that profits skyrocket, the stress on LCE will be very high. This factor is obvious, but nevertheless very important to keep in mind. For example, all things being equal, cocaine and heroin generate more violence than marihuana, because they are more lucrative drugs.

Strategic location. This is another obvious but very important variable. Areas that are strategic for drug routes or centers of large consumption are at high risk. For instance, the Venezuelan and Central American corridors have been impacted by higher violence in the last decade precisely because they became new routes for drug trafficking into the United States and Europe.

Pre-existing networks of criminality. This appears to be a very important variable. The cases of Tamaulipas and Rio de Janeiro show that criminal organizations provide the initial infrastructure for drug operations to emerge and grow rapidly. In a similar vein, routes for cocaine through Central America were developed by families and local criminal networks established in Honduras and Guatemala that provided the Zetas and the Sinaloa cartels with the infrastructure to transport drugs through their territories (UNODC 2012).

Fragmentation or hegemonic control. All things being equal, fragmentation in illegal drug supply (both traffic and retail) brings a larger potential for conflicts that might escalate into violence. However, atomized fragmentation very rarely produces extreme violence (as in the retail street markets in the United States and Europe). It is fragmentation among competing midsized or large-scale organizations that poses a threat to the equilibrium, as in Colombia and Mexico.

Strong initial enforcement. A late reaction to the growth of an illegal market can be deadly. This is an understudied and very critical variable. Once networks of criminality are developed and contagion mechanisms reproduce illegal activities (see chapter 1), the deterrence capacity of law enforcement dramatically diminishes. The moderate levels of violence in Chile show that initial police enforcement limits the extent of the market and more importantly, deters the deadly process of criminal diversification. It is uncertain what direction Argentina will take, since its law enforcement is not exerting tight controls as in Chile, but nonetheless police and courts still have high leverage.

Under LCE, law enforcement agencies can successfully control individuals and criminal organizations. When the "threat" of high profits and strategic location become stressors, LCE can be self-sustained to the extent that networks of criminality remain atomized and relatively nonviolent (i.e., they solve inner conflicts by non-violent means). Once crime networks are established, violent armies are forged, and hefty profits flow, it becomes difficult to maintain an LCE.

The nature of the equilibrium explains variations in outcomes. Despite sharing similar traffic routes, Nicaragua has much lower crime rates than neighboring Honduras and El Salvador largely because law enforcement agencies did not allow the use of violence and strived to keep strong organizations from developing. Most likely drugs flow steadily through Nicaragua, but violence is contained. In Honduras, as chapter 6 will show, precisely the opposite has occurred. Lack of action during the initial stage of route development created strong incentives for the Zetas and other groups to control the territory. Even with the current support of the US army and navy, drugs still flow and violence is very high. This is because, as explained in chapter 1, once an HCE takes root it becomes extremely difficult to reverse.

In summary, the earnings that illegal drugs produce, particularly due to restricted markets and strong enforcement by the United States and European states, create large opportunities for profits. Illegal drugs become a stressor for an LCE because they mobilize individuals and organizations to enter and spar for these profits. Once a critical mass of drug traffickers and dealers exists, contagion mechanisms accelerate, as many people and groups rush to enter the highly profitable business. A tipping point is reached and the equilibrium shifts. If several competing groups come together and do not find ways to settle disputes, and when law enforcement reacts late and erratically, the conditions for high violence mature. In short, illegal drugs might create incentives for high rates of violence, but other conditions are necessary to trigger an HCE. The following chapters examine several of these conditions.

6

Organized Crime and High Crime Equilibrium

NICARAGUA AND HONDURAS are neighboring countries with a long history of conflicts. Both are small and poor, and both are strategically located along the Central American corridor by which drugs are smuggled northward from South America. In 2013, Nicaragua's homicide rate was 12 per 100,000 while that of Honduras was 80 per 100,000. But, while the former has avoided high crime equilibrium (HCE), crime in the latter has spun out of control. Similar structural conditions have yielded totally different outcomes.

This chapter studies HCE. It analyzes countries or cities where crime has exploded, where it appears that nothing works, where criminal organizations seemingly do business at will. In a vast area, comprising the northern triangle of Central America (Guatemala, El Salvador, and Honduras) along with Colombia, Venezuela, some regions in Brazil, and more recently, large areas of Mexico, a criminality that is qualitatively much different than the crime observed in the rest of the region has developed. Although crime in these countries, given crime's spatial heterogeneity, is heavily concentrated in special zones or cities, while other areas are under low crime equilibrium (LCE).

Why does criminality spin out of control in countries that maintained LCE in the past? What are the distinctive features of high crime common to all these cases? How likely is it for countries or regions to switch course and reduce such high rates of criminality? In this chapter, I claim that HCE results from spiraling criminal activities run by organized crime and a near collapse of state deterrence. When criminal organizations run their core business with impunity, they quickly diversify their criminal activities to other highly profitable criminal endeavors. This diversification produces crimes such as human trafficking, extortion, kidnapping, and the like, terrorizing populations and generating competition among gangs for the high profits associated with such endeavors.

HCE is defined by high homicide rates, by intense fear of crime among local residents, by organized cells turning profits for crimes, and by a near collapse of state law enforcement agencies which are incapable of solving even a small fraction of the crimes. In the final concluding chapter 10, I will delve into policy recommendations that can help countries avoid falling into the trap of HCE; however, this chapter explains why most countries face extremely difficult challenges in trying to move from HCE back to LCE.

This chapter has two parts. The first examines the patterns and factors that explain the nature of HCE. First, I develop the analytical tools that allow us to grasp the perverse nature of HCE and the social mechanisms that generate it: contagion, diffusion, and branching out. I then identify several variables that are usually present in these environments such as organized criminality, violence and brutality, and partnerships between law enforcers and criminals. Finally, I present examples of crimes under an HCE in Latin America. In the second part, this toolkit is used in an in-depth analysis of one country that has recently gone from LCE to HCE: Mexico.

High Crime Equilibrium

This chapter offers an explanation as to how crime for profit has created very violent criminal environments in many countries. HCE erupts when two processes intersect: 1) major opportunities for illegal profits emerge, and 2) social or political capabilities to contain criminal entrepreneurs are limited. Both conditions are necessary and mutually reinforcing. They are better depicted as equilibria because no single variable determines any other, they evolve together.[1]

The difference between HCE and LCE is not merely a question of degree; they reflect completely different environments which produce disparate social dynamics. Here, I analyze the salient features of high criminality and signal critical junctures or turning points that can trigger the shift toward HCE. Special attention is drawn to the mechanisms that promote an adverse equilibrium and the prospects for reversal. I show the important spillover effect this structure has on crimes such as extortion, ransom kidnappings, human trafficking, and the increasing level of violence they have produced.

Analytical Perspective

There is a qualitative distinction between societies with high and low crime. Rather than conceiving of criminality as a continuous variable, a better analytical grasp can be obtained by studying the type of equilibrium in each country. If country A has a homicide rate of 30 per 100,000, it should not be simply perceived as three times more violent than country B with a rate of 10 per 100,000. In fact, country A has a severe crime problem and faces adverse odds when it comes to reversing that. The equilibrium approach is more useful because under HCE, violence becomes embedded. Once very high rates of criminality reach a certain threshold, they completely transform a country's social institutions.[2]

Contagion. In chapter 1, I explained the adverse effects of contagion and diffusion of crime and how HCE triggers (endogenously) several mechanisms that rapidly increase the severity of crime. Venezuela is a good case in point. In the late 1990s, this country already had high rates of criminality, particularly in the city of Caracas. According to the *Observatorio Nacional de Violencia*, in 1998 the country homicide rate was 20 per 100,000 (4,550 cases)[3] while in 2011, this had increased threefold to 67 per 100,000 (19,459 cases) (Briceño-Leon et al. 2012, 59–61). Kidnapping in the state of Zulia increased even more dramatically from 41 reported cases in 1999 to 589 ten years later (Rujano 2012; Briceño-Leon et al. 2012, 218). For the country as a whole, the number of kidnappings reported to the police rose from 113 in 2001 to 1,168 in 2011 (ONC 2014, 35). Such an astonishing rise in abductions, rarely seen under LCE, is typical of HCE.

HCE sets the conditions that allow criminality to explode. Gangs and organized crime engage in criminal activities that generate sizable profits with very low probabilities of arrest or punishment. Individuals hear about the high rates of impunity and about what criminals are earning, which generates high incentives for criminal careers. This very important mechanism, contagion, occurs at a much higher rate under HCE, because at the structural level law enforcement is increasingly unable to detect or punish offenders. For example, in Venezuela, while the police made 118 arrests for every 100 homicides in 1998 (5,017 total arrests), in 2008 there were just

9 arrests per 100 homicides (1,357 arrests) (Briceño-Leon et al. 2012, 137). This impunity is staggering.

In a low-crime environment, law enforcement is in a stable equilibrium with criminality. For example, a certain number of police officers suffices to make enough arrests for deterrence to be effective. Would-be offenders know that the probability of detection and punishment is relatively high, which keeps many of them from committing crimes for fear of punishment. Conversely in HCE, enforcement capacities severely lag criminality, diffusion is faster, and impunity creates incentives for would-be delinquents to join the ranks of organized crime. The business of crime thrives and authorities find it difficult to contain contagion. Public security deteriorates rapidly, as the mechanisms at work in HCE reproduce fast.

New Income Opportunities

Chapter 5 showed that the state of Tamaulipas in Mexico and the country of Honduras had low crime and poor law enforcement until a substantial opportunity for crime arose and destabilized this tenuous equilibrium.[4] I call these threats "criminal business opportunities," because they usually represent major, if illegal, economic opportunities. New drug-related businesses, secondary markets for goods, human trafficking, and ransom kidnapping, among other crimes, suddenly become sources of coveted earnings for individuals and gangs.

Why do these threats produce HCE in some countries while they are neutralized in others? One reason is state capacities—the ability of states to deliver public goods, in this case security. The example of a particular type of bank robbery is illustrative. In many countries, thieves have developed a new method of bank robbery in which delinquents target bank customers who cash large checks from tellers or withdraw large amounts of cash from personal accounts. A teller, or another bank "customer" who is watching from the line, identifies a possible victim and notifies other members of the gang who are waiting outside to follow the customer by car or motorcycle once he or she leaves the bank. The customer is intercepted and robbed a few blocks away, in a place where no police are in sight.[5] Banks claim no liability since thefts are committed off their premises.[6] This type of theft, rarely seen in Europe or the United States, has become very common in the region, particularly in Mexico and Argentina. In Mexico, there is no official data but thousands of cases each year are reported in the news,[7] and in Argentina the banking association has estimated that close to 10,000 people fell victim to crimes such as these in 2010.[8]

A well-known case of a young pregnant woman who was shot and subsequently lost her unborn child produced an uproar in Argentina, forcing the state to implement a set of regulations that has put an end to such robberies. Banks were required to install security cameras, allowing police to follow up on several cases that occurred shortly after the incident involving the pregnant woman. These and other measures eliminated most of these account-holder robberies, known in Argentina as *salideras*. Under LCE, the state is able to impose strict protection measures, assign responsibilities, and ultimately solve important cases. Through increased crime deterrence, bank robberies have been reduced in Argentina, but they remain widespread in Mexico and many other countries in the region.

In sum, the tipping point into HCE requires two simultaneous processes: a) an already shaken equilibrium of high criminality and poor law enforcement, and b) new opportunities for hefty earnings. This is why new markets for illegal drugs can pose such a threat and become lethal where LCE is already shaken. Countries with low criminality and strong state capacities are capable, at least initially, of neutralizing the challenges of major new illegal incomes and of organized crime.

Salient Features of HCE

Here I briefly describe four salient features of HCE: brutality, organized crime, law enforcement partnership with crime, and low institutional legitimacy.[9]

Violence and Brutality

The scale and scope of violence under HCE is very high. Most crimes, even those undertaken exclusively for profit, might involve lethal violence, and there is large number of hit men, *sicarios*, who are willing to kill victims for a few hundred dollars.

Central America's Northern Triangle has been a hotbed of brutal killings. During the civil wars of the 1980s, paramilitaries engaged in *muerte ejemplar* (deaths that set an example or sent out a warning) involving torture, dismemberment, beheading, hanging, and the public exhibition of mutilated bodies. These and other brutal executions have also been seen in Mexico and Colombia. It is said that Mexicans "learned" terror techniques from Guatemala's *Kaibiles*, who were recruited by Mexican

DTOs (Villalobos 2014). In contrast, there are few cases of brutal killings under LCE.

Brutality under HCE is used to intimidate opponents and ensure compliance, to subdue adversaries and silence witnesses, and to achieve discipline within the organizations (this is in line with the concept of instrumentality developed by Eisner [2013]).[10] Brutal deaths are used to send messages, either to the public at large or within an organization. Such killings have also become a rite of passage for new gang members, with youngsters occasionally obliged to carry them out to show their loyalty (Aguilar Camin 2015). In most cases, DTOs use brutality to intimidate and obtain desired outcomes such as the withdrawal of opponents from the field or the refusal of witnesses to testify.

Extreme violence has also been seen in highly polarized civil wars and armed struggles in such places as the Balkans, the Middle East, and sub-Saharan Africa, usually related to ethnic, religious, and/or political conflicts. In Latin America, however, the main driver has been conflicts over profits, with violence not an outburst of deep resentment (though resentment can be present) but a rational tool employed to pursue organizational goals. Such extreme violence is distinctive of equilibrium where the social fabric is severely damaged and where law enforcement as well as other social institutions malfunction.

Organized Crime

In this book I claim that crime arose in Latin America in response to a whole range of industries that exploited illegal business opportunities. To take advantage of these niches, criminals organized to make profits and develop new markets. The scale of criminality in the region would not be possible without organized crime.

This type of criminality has been associated with well-established organizations like the mafia and drug cartels. However, the emergence of organized crime in Latin America is closely related to the development of small and medium-sized organizations that came into being to make money and supply illicit goods. Organized crime is defined here as ". . . loosely affiliated networks of criminals who coalesce around certain criminal opportunities" (Finckenauer 2005, 65–66). For the most part, these organizations pursue profits by exploiting illegal trades for economic gains. They are characterized by some structure and continuity (organized crimes are rarely "one-shot" businesses); they threaten and use violence; and they rely on corruption to neutralize law enforcement agents.

Although they are involved in illegal enterprises, some groups also run legitimate businesses.

As Finckenauer (2005, 67) states "The predominant forms of organized crimes exist to provide goods and services that are illegal, regulated, or in short supply. It is the presence of one or more of these limiting conditions and a desire by a large enough segment of society for the particular goods and services that make their provision a profitable business."[11] Chapters 4 and 5 showed how new economic conditions in the 1990s led entrepreneurs in the region to supply goods and services to impoverished but nonetheless voracious new consumers who demanded the products that illegal channels could deliver at competitive prices. Low costs were possible because the premium for engaging in illegal and criminal activity was very low. Technological change, international commerce, and the expansion of credit increased the demand of new consumers for coveted goods. Paradoxically, this economic change and prosperity created new markets for organized crime.

Corruption and Law Enforcement

Crime rises exponentially under HCE because in most cases, law enforcement agents are heavily involved with gangs, serving as partners of crime, lending protection, and/or covering up their crimes.

The infamous 2014 incident in Ayotzinapa, Mexico, where forty-three university students were detained by local police and handed over to a gang of *sicarios* to be executed and their bodies secreted became a vivid example of partnerships between state agencies and organized crime. This case is not a rarity. Under HCE, police and other agencies often cooperate with organized crime for at least three reasons: profit sharing, fear of reprisals, and sheer incapacity.

There is a need to distinguish between police corruption and actual collusion with organized crime. Worldwide, most police departments have just a few corrupt officers who receive kickbacks to turn a blind eye to prostitution, gambling, or other illegal businesses.[12] Even in LCE, some systemic police corruption may occur with top ranking officers or politicians receiving kickbacks in exchange for providing protection for illegal activities. What distinguishes corruption or police malfunctioning in HCE is that police departments collude with organized crime to the extent that serving criminals becomes their main priority. For instance, as shown in chapter 5, in the case of Tamaulipas, police prioritized working with and protecting the corrupted political elite of the PRI during the 1980s while gangs took second place. In the past few years, they have switched allegiances to serve first the DTOs.

Under HCE, many law enforcer agencies lose their autonomy. By prioritizing the mafias, state capacities become so diminished that political elites have limited capabilities to restore the rule of law using agencies such as the local police and the judiciary. When the central government seeks to regain control, it usually does not trust these institutions and must entirely rebuild them or bring in new forces such as the army or federal police. Colombia and Mexico chose these strategies with varying rates of success.

Two important implications follow. In the short term, precarious law enforcement is unable to deter criminals. Consequently, a greater number of various crimes occur (including typical street and interpersonal crimes) because mechanisms for traditional conflict resolution are hard to replace (Escalante 2011). In the long term, the deep mistrust of citizens hampers the rebuilding of the state's capacities. Only very intense (and hard to sustain) political effort can produce tangible results (as seen in Colombia and Chihuahua, Mexico).

Chapter 7 will show that most Latin Americans believe that police partner with criminals. I argue here that there is a qualitative difference in such involvement under LCE or HCE. Under LCE, police keep the upper hand and are capable of dismantling illegal operations at the request of political leadership at any time (this also happened in Mexico during the PRI administrations). Under HCE, police lose their capacity to regain control and they serve organized crime rather than the public.

Mistrust and Lost Legitimacy

The citizens of countries that have embarked upon a path of high criminality also show high degrees of mistrust in government. This covariate has been found in many studies that examined waves of crime and high rates of homicides (LaFree 1998; Roth et al. 2011; Eisner 2003; Rosenfeld 2011; Nivette 2011). As Bateson (2012) claims for Latin America, victims of crime can be more politically active, yet this might actually translate into less trust and further loss in the legitimacy of law enforcement agencies. Individuals living in regions with very high criminality are often cynical, they may organize but are doubtful that the state will deliver justice or work for the benefit of citizens.

Public opinion indicates that such mistrust is widespread throughout the region. However, citizens in countries such as Chile, Uruguay, and Costa Rica have the highest level of trust in government, while Colombians, Venezuelans, Guatemalans, and Mexicans are extremely distrustful of their respective institutions. Low legitimacy and HCE correlate. I hypothesize that this mistrust facilitates the rapid downfall of countries into HCE because low legitimacy facilitates high criminality.

Latin America poses a conundrum because crime exploded after transitions to democracy. If legitimate state structures and political integration produce less crime, the expectation of more inclusive democracies should have yielded more peaceful societies, yet exactly the opposite has occurred. Possible explanations for this include the incomplete nature of democratic transitions (O´Donnell et al. 2011; Bergman and Whitehead 2009) and, as I claim throughout this book, feeble state capacities to face the challenges produced by relative prosperity.

Predatory Crimes under HCE

Kidnapping and abductions are typical and very serious crimes generally run by organized crime. Abductions are conducted by groups with well-defined tasks, such as leaders, planners, informants, apprehenders, security guards, negotiators, police officers, and at times, money launderers.

It is difficult to assemble robust comparative data on kidnappings. Most victims refuse to report the incident to the police. Prevalence rates are also biased by state capacities: countries such as Chile and Argentina show high reporting rates because authorities are more successful at solving cases, while Mexico and Guatemala are not. However, according to Control Risk, a global consultancy firm that analyzes security risks worldwide, Mexico, Venezuela and Colombia are among the top nine countries in the world with the highest rates of kidnappings.[13]

Data from the inmate surveys show that in Mexico and El Salvador prison populations include relatively large numbers of inmates convicted for kidnapping (Table 6.1).[14] Extrapolating to the total prison population, at least 10,000 inmates are serving time for kidnapping. In addition, close to 97 percent of inmates reported that they did not carry out the abductions alone; they were part of "joint" initiatives.

The data indicate that police officers partnered with kidnappers. While in Chile and Argentina there are no reported police partnerships in such predatory crime, in Mexico, Brazil, and to some extent Peru, policemen

Table 6.1 **Kidnappings and extortions**

	Argentina	Mexico	Peru	El Salvador	Brazil	Chile
Inmates convicted of kidnapping (%)	1.9	9.6	1.7	4.0	1.9	1.4
Inmates who report police participation in abduction (%)	0	13.5	8.1	N/A	11.0	0
Mean value of ransom[a] (US$)	54,839 (105,933)	253,242 (1,396,276)	3,882 (5,788)	2,053 (2,122)	39,021 (45,551)	86,058 (26,252)
Mean value of extortion[a] (US$))	420(121)	45(44)	9,911 (21,276)	333 (1,290)	131,720 (236,578)	N/A

Values for ransoms were converted to US dollars at the time of conviction. Standard deviations are in parentheses.
[a] Question: "How much money did the authorities claim you obtained from the kidnapping (or extortion)?"
Source: Inmate Surveys 2013.

are commonly involved in abductions.[15] It is extremely unlikely that a country or region with LCE will witness heavy police involvement in such severe predatory crimes.

Most kidnappings were carried out for ransom. The survey data shows that the ransom amounts vary greatly. Chile is the only country with low variance yet it also has the lowest rate of convicted kidnappers in its prisons. As these data are from inmate surveys, they do not include unobserved cases of offenders who avoided detection. Ransoms range from a few hundred to hundreds of thousands of dollars,[16] and the ransom data show that there are different types of organizations involved, ranging from low-end groups looking for a quick turnaround and relatively meager returns to more sophisticated gangs seeking high-level earnings.[17]

According to the surveys, kidnapping is on the rise. Inmate surveys from Mexico, conducted since 2002, also show a continuous rise in the number of offenders. The proportion of kidnappers within the already swelling prison population has been noticeable, rising from 11.7 percent in 2002 to 14.8 percent in 2006 and 21.9 percent in 2013.

Extortion has also run rampant in recent years, ranging from calls falsely indicating that a family member has been abducted and demanding ransom, to mafia-style protection fees for businesses. Survey data show that although there are no cases in Chile and few in Argentina, extortion amounts vary greatly with significant variance in the other countries. In El Salvador, 18 percent of inmates serve time for extorting others, and extortion has become a common income source for gangs, known as *maras*, engaging in illegal activities.

Human trafficking is also a very serious and highly underreported crime. In Guatemala, for example, 434 people were rescued from traffickers by the authorities in 2011 (the figure was 319 for 2012). Yet according to official and NGO estimates, the actual number of human beings trafficked was close to 13,000 for 2011, and 9,500 in 2012, with sexual exploitation (including of children) making up 74 percent of cases.[18] In Peru, between 2011 and 2013, 2,324 people were rescued.[19] Between 2004 and 2011, Guatemala had 1,851 reported cases and El Salvador 460, while Costa Rica and Nicaragua had only 64 and 127 cases, respectively, (UNDP 2013). Human trafficking is more likely to occur under HCE.

Other highly predatory crimes are deeply rooted in the region. As discussed in chapter 4, car theft, particularly carjacking, is very common, with especially high rates in Mexico, Colombia, and Venezuela,[20] and as shown in chapter 2, homicide rates in some countries are among the highest in the world. In HCE, most of these homicides follow other profit-seeking crimes such as drug sales, vehicle thefts, extortion, and protection rackets.

In summary, crimes for profits are run by organized criminal groups and are more likely to exist and quickly disseminate in countries with HCE.

HCE Case Study: Mexico

Between 2007 and 2015, 80,000 people were killed in Mexico and 34,000 more disappeared and are presumed dead. Hundreds of thousands—perhaps millions—have abandoned their homes or have been uprooted, while millions of Mexicans have been directly touched by the so-called war on drugs. Thousands of people were kidnapped for ransom, hundreds of thousands have fallen victim to extortion, and an unknown number of individuals were trafficked. This ongoing tragedy has taken shape in just a short period.

Several theories have been propounded to account for this severe deterioration of public security in Mexico. Most emphasize two processes: 1) the war between drug syndicates, which has produced more deaths and injuries than direct confrontations with the security forces (Hope 2013; Valdés 2013; Castillo et al. 2012; Longmire 2013); and 2) the Calderon administration's attacks against the cartels since 2007, which has led to the emergence of new groups and cartels that have exacerbated the violence (Guerrero 2011; Osorio 2014; Rios 2013; Calderon et al. 2015). Other scholars have suggested that the dismantling of corrupt but often effective police forces eliminated traditional patterns of conflict resolution, which have since been replaced by violence (Escalante 2011). Researchers have also paid particular attention to ineffective political response at the federal and subnational level (Trejo and Ley 2016). Other hypotheses point to efforts to control territory as the catalyst for violence. In particular, these theories suggest that the violent takeovers of other syndicates by the ruthless leaders of the Zetas in the east and the Sinaloa Federation in the west have produced a level of bloodshed never seen before. I will not dispute these or other theories, but in the following pages I will pose several questions showing that they fail to provide a comprehensive response. I will then present a road map that adds another dimension, one which has not been sufficiently studied before now.

Most hypotheses on violence in Mexico are based on a questionable assumption: Mexico was perceived to be on the way to modern, low-level criminality when illegal drug traffic began to grow. I will show that this is a typical type I error, that is, a "false positive," because incomplete data has been used to draw a faulty conclusion. Mexico had a severe crime problem before the so-called war on drugs began, and was unable to withstand the challenge of the drug stressor. A country already pushed to the edge of LCE plummeted rapidly into HCE.

As I stress throughout this book, HCE is rarely seen throughout an entire country. Since crime is by nature spatially heterogeneous, countries can have both HCE and LCE regions. In fact, like Brazil and Venezuela, most of Mexico's states continue to live under LCE. Yet certain regions, particularly in the north and west, have been overrun by criminal syndicates. Once deterrence diminished, syndicates branched out and diversified their criminal operations, causing further deterioration of public security and law enforcement. Some states (Michoacan, Guerrero,

Sinaloa, Tamaulipas, and Coahuila) have vast areas with no functional
state institutions or where state officials collude with criminals. In
short, major criminality in Mexico goes beyond struggles for plazas and
trafficking routes to encompass predatory crimes committed by rings that
are only loosely linked to drug syndicates. A theory of HCE is better suited
to explaining this breakdown of public security.

Breakdown in Public Security

Homicide rates are indicative of the way public security began to collapse
in Mexico in 2008: in just four years, homicides tripled to 23 per 100,000,
following a steady reduction in the homicide rate since the 1990s, and also
since the years following the Mexican Revolution of the 1930s (Figure 6.1).
In December 2006, Felipe Calderon was inaugurated as president, and
2008 is considered the year an all-out war began between DTOs for the
control of plazas and trafficking routes.[21]

Most homicides however, cannot be directly attributed to DTO
executions. According to a special report by the Justice in Mexico Project
(Heinle et al. 2014), for the period 2008–2012, the number of organized-
crime-style homicides tallied by three different sources represented approximately 30–50 percent of the total number of homicides recorded by
the Mexican office of statistics, INEGI (for SNSP there were 51.1 percent,

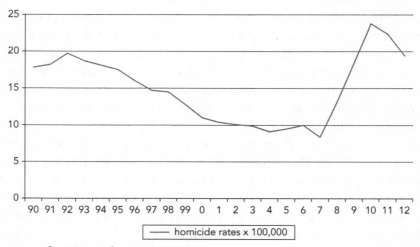

FIGURE 6.1 Homicide rates in Mexico.
Source: INEGI 2014.

Table 6.2 Homicide rates (per 100,000) and number of homicides in several Mexican states, 2010 and 2012

State	2010	2012
Baja California	47 (1,528)	17 (581)
Coahuila	16 (449)	41 (1,160)
Chihuahua	182 (6,407)	77 (2,772)
Chiapas	4 (199)	8 (390)
DF	12 (1,077)	12 (1,086)
Guanajuato	8 (445)	12 (684)
Guerrero	45 (1,555)	76 (2,646)
Jalisco	14 (1,072)	20 (1,560)
Mexico	14 (2,111)	18 (2,907)
Michoacan	16 (723)	18 (827)
Sinaloa	85 (2,423)	48 (1,395)
Tamaulipas	28 (965)	46 (1,561)
Veracruz	6 (461)	13 (1,019)
Yucatan	2 (34)	2 (41)

Source: INEGI (2014), http://www.inegi.org.mx/inegi/contenidos/espanol/prensa/ Boletines/Boletin/Comunicados/Especiales/2014/julio/comunica3.pdf or www. inegi.org.mx (total number of homicides in parentheses).

for the newspaper Milenio 39.5 percent, and for the newspaper *Reforma*, 34.9 percent).[22]

Even the rapid increase in homicide rates (see Table 6.2) does not fully capture the drastic changes within regions. The sheer number of homicides in a two-year period (2010–2012) show that organized crime shifted targets according to business opportunities. During this period, states bordering the United States (with the exception of Tamaulipas and Coahuila) saw a decrease in total homicides, as homicides in general "moved" southward (to Guerrero, Jalisco, Michoacán, and the state of Mexico). Although DTOs had established traffic routes in the northwest, violence there did not abate.

In Mexico, some regions remain relatively calm while others have extreme levels of criminal violence.[23] Yucatan and Chiapas, for example, have very low homicide rates, while Chihuahua, Guerrero, and Sinaloa have rates resembling the death rates in a civil war. Such uneven geographical distribution is typical of the spatial heterogeneity of crime incidence. I argue that it is as important to analyze the speed of change and deterioration in public security under different types of crime equilibria. Under LCE, shifts in homicide rates of 2 or 3 homicides per 100,000 in a two-year span are extremely unlikely; however, they are typical under HCE. Of Mexico's thirty-two states, sixteen experienced shifts of more than 4 homicides per 100,000 between 2010 and 2012. These sixteen states were all under HCE in 2010 or 2012 (a rate of at least 15 homicides per 100,000 is considered bordering on HCE). In contrast, among the thirteen states that had a rate of 12 or fewer homicides per 100,000 in one of these years, only three experienced shifts higher than 4 homicides per 100,000.[24] In sum, HCE usually produces drastic changes in criminality, while under LCE rates remain stable because the mechanisms of diffusion and diversification of criminal activity are much more contained.[25]

Crime and Violence in Mexico

Mexico has rarely seen peaceful conflict resolution. In fact, it has a long history of high criminality.[26] In the first decades of the twentieth century, the death toll of the Mexican Revolution exceeded one million people (though not all due to direct confrontation and violence). Since the end of the revolution, and based on a data set assembled by Picatto (2003), a clear trend emerged, with crime gradually subsiding from the 1940s until

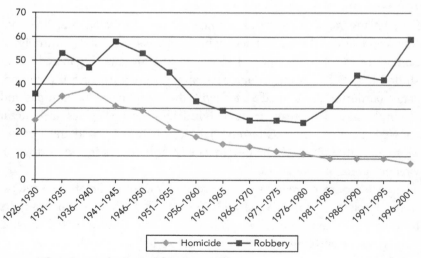

FIGURE 6.2 Accused criminals (per 100,000).

Source: Author elaboration based on Picatto 2003, Table 34.

the late 1970s. At that point, although homicide continued its downward trend, property crime rose significantly (Figure 6.2).

The sustained reduction of homicides led scholars to the erroneous conclusion that overall crime was diminishing. In fact, improvement in medicine and health care access, the temporary drop in access to firearms after the revolution, and the dwindling numbers of interpersonal conflicts together reduced the homicide rate. But, robberies and other crimes for profit gradually rose starting in the early 1980s.

The total number of crimes reported to authorities (which are mostly property crimes) depict a very different trend than the number of homicides shown in Figure 6.2, although the data are less than perfect. While homicides dropped by 47 percent between 1990 and 2006, the rate of reported crime over the same period increased by 50 percent (Fig. 6.3).

There are legitimate concerns regarding reported crime data (particularly property crime), and therefore the homicide rates are considered more trustworthy. Nevertheless, there is no cause to doubt that these trends are real. The rise in property crimes can be considered valid because there is no particular reason to suspect an increased reporting rate that would bias the trend. Car theft is a highly reported crime, and as Figure 4.2 shows the number of vehicles stolen in Mexico has increased (by more than 400 percent) between 1990 and 2006.

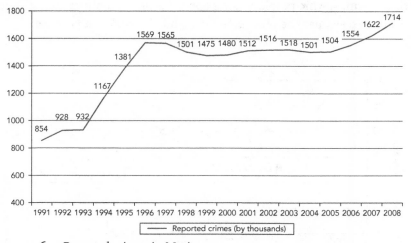

FIGURE 6.3 Reported crimes in Mexico.
Source: CIDAC, http://www.cidac.org/vnm/pdf/pdf/IncidenciaDelictivaViolencia2009.pdf (México).

No series of victim surveys covers this entire period. However, a longitudinal study conducted from 2005 to 2008 for the state of Mexico and Mexico City (with eight waves every six months) also shows an upswing in crime that began before 2008 and the supposed onset of the war on drugs, including 20 to 24 percent of households reporting that at least one member had fallen victim to a serious property crime in the six months prior to the survey (Fig. 6.4).[27]

In summary, the assumption that Mexico was on the path to low criminality until the 2008 drug war erupted must be challenged. Different data sources show that a severe predatory and property crime rates have been increasing at least since the 1980s and particularly the 1990s. Crime in Mexico has been endemic, because of social cleavages and economic deterioration, and because law enforcement lagged, and deterrence was poor. Once would-be delinquents realized that state officials and law enforcers were ineffective, large criminal enterprises sprung up and crime raged out of control.

Drugs and Violence

HCE develop when stressors challenge weak LCE. In the first chapter I emphasized that this stressor may result from a demand side, or more bluntly from crime opportunities, or from a supply side, that is, the existence of well-established criminal networks, such as the mafia or other criminal rings, which exploit rising opportunities. In both cases, weak deterrence accelerates the process of HCE and also makes it possible.

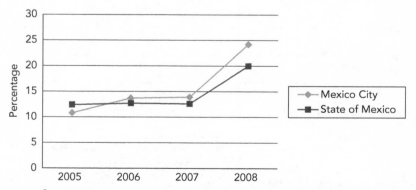

FIGURE 6.4 Serious property crime in Mexico State and Mexico City.
Source: Bergman and Sarsfield (2009).

Illegal drugs in Mexico became a major stressor that triggered extreme violence and have contributed to creating the conditions for more criminality, first by neutralizing very poor law enforcement capacities, and second by allowing offenders to branch out into other crimes. Here, I briefly review the violence triggered by drug-related crimes—the fight for plazas and traffic routes.[28] The next section addresses the diversification of criminal activities.

Two very important questions have yet to be properly answered in Mexico: Who is fighting whom, and why are they fighting? Most accounts describe large DTOs sparring with one another presumably for the right to ship and sell illegal drugs. According to this version of events, ten or twenty leaders of large syndicates targeted other groups in order to take over their territories or to avenge other killings. In some cases authorities that confronted and eliminated gang leaders produced spinoffs and new organizations that sparked more violence, at least initially. I argue that the narrative is much more complex. Only a portion of executions is related to the shipment of drugs into the United States. Most of the violence is associated with the control of territories for a whole range of lucrative activities, with domestic and international drug markets representing an unknown percentage of these earnings. There are large, medium, and even small organizations that specialize in violence. HCE is distinguished by this type of illegal, for-profit industry.

By most accounts, the lion's share of violence results from confrontations between armed groups. A database that tracked journalist reports of nineteen newspapers in Mexico from 2000 to 2010 (Osorio 2014) shows that most violent events are executions, abductions, or other violent encounters between groups or individuals allegedly linked to DTOs. More than 80 percent of the newspaper reports make no mention of the direct participation of any of the armed forces (the federal police, army, navy, or local police),[29] though, according to the same source, by 2010 approximately 20 percent of violent encounters were initiated by a federal force or were in response to attacks. The data clearly show that there were episodes of violent events since at least 2003, with a clear surge in 2005, a drop in 2006, and yet another increase in 2007. In addition, while there was a noticeable increase of violence especially after 2008, the number of drug and asset seizures remained stable or even decreased over the same periods (Osorio 2014, 35, panel A and B).

This aggregated information does not allow to precisely analyze the nature or the characteristics of the people involved or the reasons behind each episode. The headlines "fighting for territory" or "for plazas" do not clearly explain why one group (or individual) decides to attack another. What does "territory" mean? It might be the right to control drug shipments. It might be the right to buy heroin or marihuana from farm producers. Or it might be the right to carry out extortions in a given area. For example, the powerful and deadly Zetas are not known to be heavily involved in trafficking drugs into the United States (Grayson 2012, Mazzitelli 2012)—these shipments were handled by the "gulf cartel." The main income for the Zetas, and for many others DTOs in Michoacán and Guerrero, is believed to come from other profit-making enterprises—abduction, extortion, protection services, gasoline robbery, human trafficking, and so on.

Groups or individuals probably fight one another for different reasons, but so far official records do not present a clear picture. This typical shortcoming in terms of the data collection and analysis of HCE results from a lack of criminal investigation policies, which will be examined in chapter 8. A Human Right Watch report (2011) has estimated that less than 10 percent of the homicides and "disappearances" that currently occur in Mexico are ever investigated. This implies that in the majority of cases, questions such as what really happened and why people were killed, abducted, or kidnapped are never asked or answered. In many cases, the authorities are not even able to ascertain the victim's identity.[30]

The lack of criminal investigation does not allow us to truly understand the patterns and trends of DTO violence, and many questions remain unanswered: Are *sicarios* (hitmen) committing murder at the behest of high-up cartel bosses? Are abductions and kidnappings part of a larger ring operation or simply initiatives of small groups linked to larger DTOs? What ransoms are being demanded? Who decides who to target with violence? Are DTOs corporations with an army, or just a group of syndicates that hire gunmen and other logistical workers to run their operations? The available public data do not provide even this simple information, probably because the authorities have been unable to compile it (see chapter 7 for the link between information and state ability to deter). Despite the lack of good data, I will raise several questions that challenge the idea that most of the violence occurring in Mexico is caused by ten or twenty cartel leaders fighting for control of the illegal drug market. Furthermore, I claim that violence has more to do with the collapse of deterrence, which has produced opportunities for gangs and organizations loosely connected to DTOs to profit from various markets, that even include government public spending projects (Trejo 2014).

I hypothesize that deaths, injuries, extortions, kidnappings, and other crimes are conducted by a plethora of gangs and individuals linked to criminal organizations, which in some cases operate independently, or under the watchful and approving eye of cartel leaders. Several indicators and data from the business side of drug trafficking initially support this claim. I will show that: a) the market for extortion and abduction is very small compared to that for the shipment of drugs into the United States, and therefore it would not be rational for powerful drug barons to have strong incentives in order to get into those businesses; and b) the growth of the domestic drugs market is too small to justify such a dramatic increase in violence.

First, the "market" for extortion and kidnapping represents an insignificant share of the illegal drugs smuggled into the United States. Why would a large DTO devote energy to and engage in a time-consuming "industry" that represents only a very small fraction of their core business? Of course, business diversification makes sense if it does not involve additional risk, but despite poor deterrence, kidnapping and extortion (especially of well-known or rich people) are nonetheless risky enterprises. According to journalist accounts, ransom for a mid-range kidnapping can yield US$10,000.[31] There are costs involved in kidnappings, such as bribing the authorities, feeding and sheltering the victim, paying everyone in the ring their cut, and so on. Let us assume that the net profit for an average kidnapping is US$5,000. In turn, let us assume that one kilogram of cocaine purchased in Colombia costs US$2,000 and wholesales for approximately US$26,000 in the United States (see chapter 5). The logistics of drug shipment and seizures are pricy.[32] Given the risks, as mentioned, it is reasonable to assume a 25 percent profit margin, of US$6,000 dollars for every kilogram of cocaine smuggled into the United States. DTOs successfully smuggle at east two hundred tons of cocaine every year, making approximately US$1.2 billion in profits. How many people need to be kidnapped for an average ransom of US$5,000 to yield a reasonable profit for these organizations? Based on these rough estimates, 25,000 people would have to be kidnapped each year for an average ransom of US$10,000 just to make abductions worth 10 percent of the cocaine smuggling business.

This estimate includes earnings only from cocaine, not from marihuana, synthetic drugs, or heroin. When profits from the entire illegal drug business are included, the kidnapping of 25,000 people per year represents less than 3 percent of the gross profits of DTOs. This simple estimate shows that it does not make sense for big drug leaders to orchestrate such operations. Although some of the drug prices and ransom estimates could be questioned, the overall picture should remain clear: once the numbers are examined, the extortion and kidnapping business is clearly too small for the top six or eight DTOs to directly engage in these enterprises. Of course, cartel leaders are involved in some "strategic" extortions and other illegal activities (especially those that yield large profits), but the lion's share of these activities is probably run by other units that I will call scavengers.

Most likely, small or mid-sized organizations, those which find it difficult to access the lucrative smuggling business, engage in human trafficking, extortion, and kidnapping. Although there are not enough data to support this assertion, it appears logical to assume that once an organization carves a niche in the drug smuggling business, there are few incentives to diversify into much less lucrative and much more costly activities. In short, it is in the interest of those who do not have access to the larger pie of illegal drugs shipment to develop these "side businesses."

The Zetas appeared to be such an organization, since they have not developed the rich network of drug smuggling into the United States and have an atomized organizational structure (Mazzitelli 2012; Salcedo-Albaran and Garay-Salamanca 2016) that creates strong incentives for regional cells to control territories for different illicit activities. La Familia in Michoacán, Guerreros Unidos in Guerrero, El cartel del Milenio in Jalisco, have similar structures, although the scale of their organizations varies.

In summary, the cohesive and disciplined organizations that make high profits from the transshipment of drugs into the United States have lower incentives to engage in costly fights over the profits of Mexico's domestic market. That being said, it is important to note that the loosely connected gangs hired by powerful bosses for "special assignments" are naturally inclined to engage in any number of violent acts that have not been specifically ordered by the DTOs.

Domestic Markets

A second source of violence, many claim, is the growing retail market for illegal drugs within Mexico. As demand for cocaine and synthetic drugs grows, cartels fight for the right to control the lucrative plazas. I claim that although the fight for corners and retail venues should be credited with a share of violence, it is unlikely that large cartels are directly responsible. More likely, mid-level organizations and street gangs battle for the right to sell these drugs.

The magnitude of the Mexican retail market for drugs can be estimated from the Mexican survey on drug use and addiction (Encuesta Nacional de Adicciones) that provides prevalence estimates for different drugs and for different years. From 2002 until 2008, the percentage of urban adults age 12–65 who reported having used an illegal drug increased from 4.6 percent to 5.2 percent (ENA 2008, 41).[33] Marihuana and cocaine are the most commonly used drugs. Marihuana users increased from 3.5 percent to 4.2 percent of the population, and cocaine use doubled from 1.2 percent to 2.4 percent. Crack also increased from almost negligible consumption in 2002 (0.2 percent) to 0.7 percent in 2008, and similar increases can be seen for synthetic drugs. However, these are measures that track consumption over a lifetime. The prevalence of last year's use is considered more suitable for tracking markets trends.

Figure 6.5 depicts prevalence trends for four illegal drugs. It is noteworthy that consumption of heroin and inhalants has remained the same, marihuana has seen small increases and cocaine use initially increased since its introduction in Mexico in the late 1980s and early 1990s, but then remained steady from 1998 until 2011.

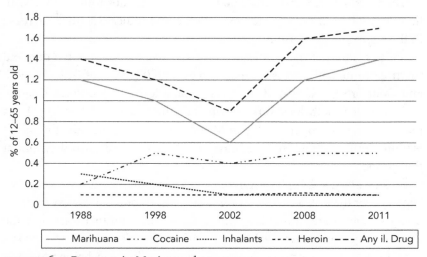

FIGURE 6.5 Drug use in Mexican urban areas.

Source: Author elaboration based on data from the Mexican survey on drug use and addictions (ENA 2011, 25–28).

Use of drugs within the past month provides a more accurate assessment of drug abuse. In 2008, 0.9 percent of the sample (approximately 675,000 of Mexicans) reported using at least one of these illegal drugs within the past month (mostly marihuana).[34]

The domestic market of illegal drugs in Mexico is relatively small. Just 1 percent of 15–65 year olds admitted to having used marihuana over the last year, 0.4 percent cocaine, and 0.2 percent amphetamines. These rates are among the lowest in the world, particularly given the wide availability of these drugs in Mexico. Most countries in Europe have significantly higher rates.[35]

One of the main pitfalls of these surveys is that they fail to target two large segments of users that bear the lion's share of the demand: drug addicts living on the street, who are not easily included in samples of students or households, and prison populations, which account for a relatively large share of heavy users. Fortunately, we do have some rough estimates on drug use in prisons from four inmate surveys in Mexico. According to these data, the number of substance users in prison has remained steady, at 19 percent in 2002 and 17 percent in 2013 (CIDE 2014, 74).[36] Half of these respondents reported using drugs, the other half alcohol. A relatively lax corrections policy has created a drug market inside prison, normally supplied by visitors (family) and gangs. Marihuana is the most frequently reported drug while reports of cocaine, heroin, and synthetic drugs are substantially lower.[37] In short, rates remain steady, although the rise in the inmate population could indicate a small increase in the aggregate drug use in prisons.

Finally, although no studies on tourists have been done, the demand for drugs among visitors is estimated to be high (the state of Quintana Roo and Guerrero house two of the most visited tourist attractions, Cancun and Acapulco, both locations known for a high demand for drugs). As tourism has not grown notably in Mexico over the last decade, though, it is unlikely that the tourist drug demand has risen significantly throughout this period.

In summary, although the domestic markets for illicit drug have grown slightly over the last decade, they remain relatively small. It is very unlikely that a sizable share of the drug war is associated with turf wars over the right to sell in such a relatively small market. In addition, marihuana production in Mexico has probably shrunk, as so much is now being produced in the United States (see chapter 5). Heroin production in Mexico to serve the US market is believed to be on the rise. This evidence suggests that the growth of the domestic market has been negligible and seems unlikely to have produced such extreme violence. The explanation for such high criminality should be sought in the eruption of numerous illegal profit-seeking enterprises run by violent gangs following the collapse of deterrence.

Other Predatory Crimes

Drug activity has robust effects on violent crime that are independent of other disorganization indicators (Martínez et al. 2008; Baumer et al. 1998; Ousey and Lee 2002). Homicide is not the only crime that has grown. Extortion, kidnapping, and violent theft have also increased dramatically, while they still remain seriously underreported crimes.[38]

The number of kidnappings reported to police has risen consistently over the last decade,[39] as has extortion which began to increase before homicides did in 2008 (see Table 6.3).

Table 6.3 Kidnapping and extortion trends
in Mexico (total reported events)

Year	Kidnapping	Extortion
2001	595	1,337
2002	623	1,636
2003	751	1,910
2004	795	2,416
2005	653	2,979
2006	707	3,157
2007	934	3,123
2008	1,620	4,869
2009	2,404	6,332
2010	2,593	6,113
2011	3,237	4,594
2012	3,351	7,284
2013	3,382	8,196

Source: "Cifras de homicidio doloso, secuestro, extorsión y robo de vehículos 1997–2014." SESNSP SEGOB.

Since 2011 (the first year with somewhat trustworthy data at the municipal level), the number of municipalities with at least one case of reported kidnapping has risen from 293 in 2011 to 349 in 2013. In 2013, 31 municipalities had ten events or more per year, and 67 percent of all reported kidnappings occurred in just six states (Guerrero, Michoacán, Estado de Mexico, Tamaulipas, Morelos, and Veracruz). Only one of these states, Tamaulipas, is a US border state. As mentioned in chapter 5, while in the 1990s there were almost no kidnappings or abductions (0.15 per 100,000) in Tamaulipas, in 2013 this climbed to 6.10 (ONC 2014). The high number of kidnapping has also been captured in urban victimization surveys (ENVIPE), with 114,000 reported in 2010, 98,000 in 2011, and 105,000 in 2012.[40]

The kidnapping of migrants, particularly from Central America, merits special mention. It is known that Mexico has become a transit country for Central Americans trying to reach the United States. Many organizations, particularly the Zetas, have seized on the opportunity to kidnap migrants, steal their property, demand ransoms from their families, and even enslave them or recruit them to commit crimes. The number of migrants who pass through Mexico and fall victim to these organizations is unknown. A study (ONC 2014, 114) reports that, according to information from Mexico's Federal Police, 71,000 abducted foreigners were rescued by the police between 2007 and 2014. Assuming many cases go unreported, the real number of migrants abducted is probably much higher. This is another source of income for organized crime, and it is likely that some of these illegal proceeds are shared with police and migration authorities.

Kidnapping and trust in the police are closely intertwined. Using data from ENVIPE (Mexican Victimization Survey) and reported crimes in different states, one study (ONC 2014) finds a 0.49 correlation between the percentage of people who do not trust the municipal police and the reported kidnapping rate, and a 0.41 Pearson r between the rate of no trust in detective units and the known rate of kidnappings. Lack of trust in the police reduces the likelihood that crime will be reported (see chapter 7), therfore, it can be safely assumed that the kidnapping rate is probably much higher, and the real coefficients probably stronger. Similarly, there is a positive 0.26 Pearson r between perceived police corruption and reports of kidnapping, signaling that corruption is indeed associated with high levels of kidnapping (ONC 2014, 86).

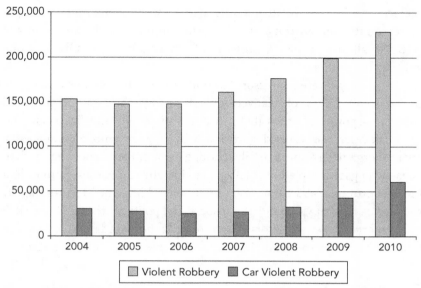

FIGURE 6.6 Violent robberies.

Kidnapping, extortions, and violent car robberies are usually carried out by organizations that enjoy certain levels of impunity, a typical feature of HCE. As shown in Table 6.3 and Figure 6.6 kidnapping, extortions, and violent car robberies in Mexico have increased dramatically over the first decade of the twenty-first century, revealing the serious threat of high crime environments. Notice that these "industries" were already large and growing rapidly even before the outbreak of extreme violence in 2008, when these predatory crimes have skyrocketed. Under HCE, well-oiled organizations that specialize in predatory profit-making industries proliferate.

Summary

Until the 1970s, drugs in Mexico were produced for shipment to the United States by several independent bosses. In the 1970s and early 1980s, the leading Sinaloa traffickers took control of drug trafficking under the complacent eye of the corrupt PRI government. That monopoly broke up in the late 1980s, producing several DTOs and infighting throughout the 1990s and 2000s. The erosion of the Colombian cartels, the relative success of the Uribe government during the 2005–2008 interdictions, and stronger enforcement by the US border patrol[41] have increased the profitability of cocaine and the money to be made by

Mexican traffickers. Meth markets also grew, and Mexican traffickers seized on this opportunity, increasing the production and shipments of ATS. For all these reasons, gangs and traffickers have been battling one another for profits.

Illegal drugs were a stressor that undermined the tenuous and fragile previous equilibrium of relatively low criminality. The overwhelming and corrupting power of drugs (both in terms of money and firearms), and the weak deterrence exerted, particularly by local law enforcement agents, enabled organized crime to easily recruit gang members. These gangs then began to engage in a plethora of illegal but lucrative industries, from violent thefts to extortion, abduction, and human trafficking. The Mexican tragedy transcends the drug problem; it is a social and political crisis because HCE only emerges when stressors take root. In other words, social violence erupts where deep social and institutional problems remain unresolved.

Concluding Remarks

This chapter focused on countries that have fallen into HCE; countries where deterrence has completely collapsed over extensive areas and crime has spread very rapidly. Contagion, critical mass, the tipping point (Schelling 1978) and the emergence of new opportunities are several social mechanisms that help explain the eruption of HCE.

The conceptual framework of HCE vis-à-vis LCE is very useful because violence should not be studied as a continuous variable. Its relationship to enforcement is not linear; instead, it resembles an exponential function in which crime gets out of control and enforcement instruments cease to be effective—the typical array of instruments of policing and administration of justice are fruitless, and impunity grows endogenously. Therefore, as chapter 10 will show, the corrective measures for HCE are different than those for LCE.

Although each country has its own unique structure, HCE emerges from a similar pattern. This also explains why certain areas of a given country are targeted for operations by organized crime and not the entire nation. These are areas with some previous history of corruption and/or violence where some criminal organizations have operated for years under the complacent of authorities (Astorga 2005). Then a major stressor, the opportunity for hefty profits, challenges the previously off-balance equilibrium. Law enforcement deterrence begins to crumble, and new gangs and criminal enterprises spread like wildfire. The stressor can be different in each country, but serious deterioration in public security progresses in a similar way. Organized crime evolves from the consolidation of new illegal market opportunities against a sudden deterioration of weak law enforcement agencies that cannot adequately adapt to new stressors.

The downfall into HCE involves six steps. Within a country, *geographical heterogeneity* allows organized crime to target weak spots as bases of operation. *Unstable intermediate crime equilibrium* precedes the vulnerability of regions. Then a *major stressor* unravels the equilibrium, followed by an *accelerated pace* of public security deterioration and *diversification* into many predatory and highly violent crimes. Finally, *poor state capacities* fail to regain control with standard methods of law enforcement.

Using Mexico as an example, this chapter has shown that although drug barons and cartels have produced their own, large share of violence, the diversification of criminal activity and the fact that criminal networks have "branched out" into new violent crimes has had deadly consequences. Recently, property crime has increased and gangs specializing in for-profit crime have mushroomed; as a result, several states have been unable to crackdown on crime. The stressors brought by the drug trade and the large corrupting profits it has generated have nullified institutional law enforcement capacities. In addition, impunity has endogenously increased, deterrence has been diluted, and new deadly gangs have emerged. These account for a large share of the violence and crime under HCE.

PART III

The Criminal Justice System and Deterrence

The following three chapters are about the three pillars of the criminal justice system in Latin America: the police, courts, and prisons. This is far from a thorough discussion. I review and select several topics for each chapter to ascertain how they have affected state capacities to deter crime.

As emphasized throughout this book, countries that fall into the HCE trap have very weak capacity to investigate, convict, and imprison crime bosses and are rarely capable of disbanding criminal ring operations. The most salient characteristic of HCE is the collapse of deterrence due to the ineffectiveness of police, courts, and prisons. Some countries might still have relatively high rates of property crimes (Peru, Nicaragua, and even Argentina), yet highly predatory crimes (homicides, abductions, extortions, and the like) remain relatively under control, precisely because state capacities are moderately effective in containing them.

These last three chapters study the abilities of state capacities to neutralize the damaging effect of unstable crime equilibria. Each chapter first overviews salient indicators of performance of these three pillars of the criminal justice systems and then analyzes in depth salient characteristics of these institutions as they impact the ability to control crime: information and investigative capacities for the police, impunity for courts, and incapacitation for prisons. Under HCE these basic performance are deficient, partly because, endogenously, the scale of the problems vastly exceeds the state's capacity to control crime.

A high level of corruption that fuels violence and crime is a distinct feature of HCE. Corruption allows rackets to consolidate power, further diminishing state capacities and eliciting the demand side of crime. The following chapters analyze levels of corruption within the police, the courts, and the prisons in the region, signaling a clear difference between nations. Although most LCE countries in the region have not performed very well and have large pockets of corruption, they have been able at least to exert moderate pressure on criminal rings, they still are capable of running police departments, courts, and prisons—or perhaps, have not been challenged by a serious stressor. Therefore, they avoided the high rates of predatory crimes so common under HCE.

7

The Police in Latin America

Introduction

Police departments in the region have mostly failed to enhance public safety. Crime has grown, fear of crime has risen, and citizens do not trust their officers. The following pages study the limited success of law enforcement deterrence in the region, underscoring two variables that correlate with rising criminality: a) the failure to incorporate modern, large-scale policing techniques, particularly the misuse of information and intelligence, and b) the failure of police to adjust to new standards after transitions to democracies, undermining bonds of trust between police and citizens.

The police in Latin America have recently been the focus of numerous studies (Ungar 2011; Sabet 2012; Brinks 2007; Hinton 2006; Huggins 1998; Seri 2013; Dammert 2014; Fruhling 2012). This chapter analyzes the role of police in fighting crime in the region. It argues that police capacity to reduce public insecurity is contingent on the scope and breadth of existing levels of crime. Law enforcement deters crime when the threat of criminality is low. Once a critical mass of crimes tips the balance and subverts the equilibrium, police face a dilemma: they modernize, gain significant strength, and confront the new challenges, or they slowly deteriorate, producing in the process even more crime.

Prevailing Theories

Different hypotheses have been formulated to account for the inability of police departments to meet the challenges of rising crime, among them:

1) *Path dependence.* Police departments have always been weak and they have been very difficult to reform. They performed somewhat adequately in containing the spread of crime when the threat was small.

2) *Lack of good human and material resources.* Scholars have repeatedly blamed subpar recruitment of officers, inadequate equipment, insufficient funding, and low wages.

3) *Politicians benefiting from bad police departments, or avoiding action (for-bearance).* Inaction might also bring short-term benefits to political bosses as corrupt policemen allow them to raise illegal resources and recruit forces for political purposes.

4) *The level of criminality increased substantially.* Police departments fail to live up to the task once crime spikes.

5) *Lack of professionalism.* Police have failed to modernize, that is to make radical changes in professional careers, training and recruitment, to eliminate chronic corruption, and so on.

6) *They are partners in crime.* Many scholars have argued that police officers not only benefit from kickbacks, they are full partners in crime, including membership in rackets, and/or fund-raising for political elites.

To a large extent these theories find substantial support in the scattered evidence available. This chapter will make passing remarks on several aspects raised by these interpretations that are well known in the specialized literature. However, I will focus on two understudied variables that inhibit deterrence and control of crime by police departments: a) their poor investigative capacities, and b) their inability to foster bonds of trust with the community.

The following pages evaluate to what extent the police have been able to maintain low levels of criminality or have failed to achieve peaceful solutions to emerging crime. The important questions of police reforms (Fruhling 2012; Dammert 2007; Beato 2004; Macaualey 2012; Neild 2002), police organization (Sain 2008; Carrión 2006; Llorente 2004; de Lima et al. 2014), police training (López Portillo 2003; Herrera and Tudela 2005; Frederic and Galvani 2013) and brutality (Brink 2003; Tiscornia 2004; Cruz 2015) are not the specific focus of this chapter, nor are the quality of life problems which police help to resolve. Although maintaining order, containing conflicts, and problem solving are the pillars of modern policing, I concentrate on its most basic function: the enhancement of public safety through crime fighting and violence reduction.

I argue that most police departments in the region were structurally ill prepared to develop effective strategies to contain the rapid rise of criminality. Organized crime has grown much faster than police capacities, exacerbating weak and corrupt policing traditions. Under HCE, police lose control and fail to perform their most standard functions, while under LCE they might keep crime under control because they can exert at least moderate deterrence. Police–community relations in Latin America have been historically weak, keeping police departments from building bonds of trust that help them serve the community (Fruhling and Beato 2004).

I begin with a historical summary of policing in Latin America and a brief overview of police structure and resources in the region. Original survey data are used to study arrest patterns and to show the inadequate criminal investigation capacities of the police. Information and intelligence is presented to highlight the shortcomings of police departments in their investigations of networks of crime. The problem of trust and legitimacy of police in the region is then analyzed, showing the importance of healthy police–community relations in improving public safety. Finally, the challenges underachieving police departments face under different types of equilibria are summarized.

Police in Latin America: Legacies and Current Structure
Police and Crime in the Twentieth Century

The historical decline of violence that began in Europe in the seventeenth century resulted from the emergence of modern states (Pinker 2011; Eisner 2003). The strengthening of the region's central authorities in the early twentieth century fostered the professionalization of law enforcement in the larger nations. The police, in the words of one author, became "the state in the street" (Hinton 2006).

Police forces in Latin America have traditionally served the interests of political patrons, caudillos, and local bosses. In the first half of the twentieth century, police remained very sensitive to political control, and they continued to serve rulers and occasionally repress political opposition groups during administrations in Mexico, Peru, Brazil, Argentina, and many others.[1] In several countries authorities and police developed an unwritten pact in which authorities allowed the police to earn dirty money in exchange for their loyalty and ability to repress mass revolts. The development of a professional cadre to serve and protect its citizens was rarely a top priority.

This implicit pact between police and ruling elites has had several negative externalities. Police became effective protectors of illicit activities in exchange for illegal earnings that became important sources of income for political bosses. Police made profits from two activities in demand: prostitution and gambling. As corruption and illegal protection increased, police got involved in other profitable black markets (such as street trading or *ambulantismo*, drugs, smuggling) and officers resisted reforms that would force them to relinquish such benefits (Caimari 2012; Vanderwood 1992; Piccato 2001; Andersen 2002).

Several scholars have underscored this perverse pact which continued until the late twentieth century (Alvarado and Silva 2011; Davis 2006; Sain 2002 2004; Binder 2004). There was low demand for police accountability as long as they either legally or illegally kept moderate levels of public safety. In turn, politicians turned a blind eye to the creation of a police "circuit of illegal self-financing" (Sain 2002, 86).

I argue that this implicit pact survived for several decades because the threat of criminality remained moderate (partly due to the repressive nature of this perverse system).[2] Rising crime and stronger demands for stricter adherence to the rule of law after democratization in the 1980s and 1990s ushered in significant changes in several countries. Police departments that had been moderately successful in containing crime during the 1940s–1980s suddenly faced the challenge of matured criminal organizations. "Old tricks" no longer worked to address new challenges.

Police Administration, Structure, and Resources

Police departments in the region vary greatly in terms of structure, organization, and resources. They can be unified in one large organization, or be decentralized in multiple autonomous departments.[3] The type of police governance is tied to political patronage, and ultimately produces different systems of accountabilities. Usually, large federal countries such as Argentina, Brazil, and Mexico have several police departments, whereas small countries such as those of Central America have unified organizations. But this is not always the case. Chile, Peru, and Colombia are relatively large countries but have a single command, and Venezuela has a federal system. Although there is no strong association between police governance, its structure, and the level of criminality, this topic has sparked extensive debate in many countries. In Mexico, for example, in addition to thirty-two state police departments every municipality (there are over 2,000) has its own police force, most of which are very weak and susceptible to falling under the control of powerful cartels.

Table 7.1 (columns 4 and 5) scores levels of effective political control and police efficacy (low, moderate, and high), and levels of threat produced by organized crime (criminal organizations' ability to capture police organization). Effectiveness and political control usually operate in equilibrium (high effectiveness–low threat, and vice versa). Police departments face serious limitations in places where criminal networks are solidly established and the earnings from crime are very high. Mexico is a case in point. After the 1940s, there was no serious threat to the regime, but the current level of earnings produced by drug-related crime poses formidable challenges for subpar police forces.[4]

A recently released index for 127 countries in the world measures the ability of security bodies to render security services (see footnote of Table 7.1). Column 6 of Table 7.1 presents each country´s index scores (between 0 and 1), and in parentheses its rank within the 127 countries for which there is information. The highest police indexes are for Uruguay and Chile, although they rank 35 and 37 respectively. Most Latin American countries are in the bottom half or last quartile of the ranking. Despite some methodological questions and incomplete information for these indicators, the poor state of police departments of the region is clearly evidenced by this independent index. Moreover, consistent with the equilibria proposition, most police departments that rank high are under LCE and those in the bottom are under HCE.[5][6]

There are different police structures, in terms of governance and functions, within the region. Judging by the levels of criminality that exist in different countries and the variance in outcomes, this functional and governance structure does not constitute a key variable to predict success in reducing crimes. Performances vary within both types of structures.

Resources are hard to measure since there are very few reports on police budgets or equipment, so here I use the number of officers as a proxy. The median number of police officers for Latin America and the Caribbean is 283.9 per 100,000, halfway between the highest of 435.5 officers for parts of Asia and the lowest of 187 for Oceania.[7] The rate of police officers per 100,000 is negatively correlated to the homicide rate (r: −0.371) but this association is not statistically significant. Negative but weak correlations are obtained also with other crimes such as robbery and car theft.[8] The number of officers appears to be weakly associated with criminality; however, it is not a key factor.[9] Finally, there are close to four million private security guards in Latin America, and the number is growing by 9 percent per year (Villalobos 2014).[10]

Table 7.1 Police in LATAM: Structure and basic performance indicators

	Police governance	Function: Prevention and/or Investigation	Effective Control and/or Efficacy	Level of current criminal threat	WISPI Index[a]	Officers (per 100,000)	Homicides (per 100,000)	Private officers (per 100,000)
Argentina	F	U	M	L–M	0.542 (77)	222	5.8	379.8[c]
Bolivia	C	U	M	L	0.403 (114)	363	10.1	5.8[c]
Brazil	F	S	M	L–M	0.478 (94)	178	15.5	872.7[c]
Chile	C	S	H	L	0.699 (43)	318	4.3	558.2[c]
Colombia	C	U	M–H	M	0.458 (96)	349	34	428.3[c]
Costa Rica	C	S	H	L	0.494 (87)	275[b]	11	452[b]
Ecuador	C	U	M	M	0.529 (79)	292[b]	21.0	309[c]
Dominican R	C	S			0.473 (95)	307	22.0	301.4[c]
El Salvador	C	U	L	H	0.496 (86)	343	64.5	349[b]
Guatemala	C	U	L	H	0.426 (107)	156	41.0	944[b]
Honduras	C	S	L–M	H	0.398 (116)	N/A	77.5	870[b]
Mexico	F	S	L–M	H	0.394 (118)	447	23.8	431.8[c]

Nicaragua	C	U	H	L	0.452 (99)	199	9.1	37[b]
Panama	C	S	M–H	L	0.551 (73)	498[b]	12.0	928[b]
Paraguay	C	U	L–M	L	0.495 (113)	331[b]	10.7	433.4[c]
Peru	C	C	M–H	L–M	0.434 (105)	323[b]	9.0	175.3[c]
Uruguay	C	U	H	L	0.718 (35)	876	6.1	N/A
Venezuela	F	S	L–M	M–H	0.381 (119)	297	39.0	N/A

Notes: Special thanks to Carlos Basombrío, Luis Enrique Anaya, Lucia Dammert, and Mark Ungar for providing information for this table.

[a] "WISPI . . . (is) an international index measuring the ability of police institutions worldwide to render security services that establish security within society and achieve safety of its members. WISPI focuses on both effective rendering, of security services and the outcome of rendered services." "WISPI . . . rank countries according to their ability to provide security services and boost security performance in general."

"WISPI adopts a wide range of qualitative and quantitative data in order to classify countries' levels of internal security. It measures the ability of security institutions to maintain security, the effectiveness of those services, the public's trust in rendered services, and police operations and activities." It includes an array of indicators such as capacity (police and other law enforcement personnel and resources), process (corruption and effectiveness), legitimacy (confidence in the police and due process) and outcomes (levels of criminality). See "World Internal Security and Police Index" at http://wispindex.org/#

[b] Private officers UNDP (2012).

[c] *Observatorio de Seguridad Ciudadana,* OEA at http://www.oas.org/dsp/Observatorio/database/indicatorsdetails.aspx?lang=es&indicator=44 and Harrendorf and Smit (2010, 136–138).

Control and Efficacy: Author elaboration based on consultation with experts.

Sources: Police rate: UNDP (2013) *Seguridad Ciudadana con Rostro Humano. Informe Regional de Desarrollo Humano 2013–2014.* p. 113. Homicide rate UNDP (2013) and Harrendorf et al. (2010).

Police administration, its functional structure and available resources, are important factors for effective crime control. Each country has its own historical, political, and geographical conditions that have shaped its police structure. What matters, however, is what the police do and how they perform within a flexible structure. In this book, I argue that one of the most important determinants for police success is the scope of the challenges they face. Resources, functionality, and structure, can have an incremental impact on outcomes.

Police and Crime
Police and Deterrence

Law enforcement alone cannot prevent crime (Skogan 2003; Sherman et al. 1997; Bayley and Perito 2010). Even in advanced democracies, police rarely solve the lion's share of criminal acts.[11] The standard model of policing, identified by a panel of experts as hiring more officers, increasing random patrols, targeting repeat offenders, non-focusing law enforcement, responding to calls, and so on, does not produce meaningful reductions in criminality (Skogan and Frydl 2004; Weisburd and Braga 2006). Police, however, might deter potential offenders from embarking upon criminal careers and prevent outlaws from engaging in multiple criminal acts. They can certainly contain crime and reduce its damaging effect.

Deterrence matters for crime control. To the extent that would-be delinquents are aware of the risk of being apprehended and sanctioned, many will avoid committing crime or at least reduce the frequency of their offenses. Although deterrence is subjectively perceived, it is grounded in close, objective probabilities of detection and punishment, and endogenously, it works better under LCE.[12] Under this paradigm, police investigate crimes, make arrests, and by bringing offenders to justice, make it more likely that laws will be enforced.

To enhance deterrence, good policing prioritizes cases, going after "the big, the bad and the heinous" in order to disband rackets and reduce collateral damage. Most police departments in Latin America instead adopted a strategy of mass detentions and incarcerations of less dangerous offenders These arrests and efforts at crime control have not proved successful because police: a) failed to introduce modern systems of intelligence for effective criminal investigations, b) underinvested in community service that would encourage community participation in solving crime, and c) were unable to make the transition from militarized hierarchies to state institutions governed by rule of law. The next section presents original data on the real "output" of police departments in the region to support these assumptions, paying particular attention to arrests, corruption, and the meager results of fighting organized crime.

Arrests

In 2010, police departments in the United States made 11,479,500 arrests (BJS 2012) from a total adult population of 235,205,700. If each arrestee was detained only once, this would yield a rate of 4.9 percent of adult arrest. However, since at least 80 percent of crimes are committed by men, and many arrestees are repeatedly detained, it could be safely assumed that the rate of male adult arrests ranges between 2 and 5 percent.[13] Is this arrest rate high or low? Are most delinquents being detained and punished? More importantly, what is the effect of arrests on deterrence?

Unfortunately, there is no equivalent data for countries in Latin American because most police departments never report the number of arrests they make.[14] But information for the United States helps to understand the scope of deterrence the police is capable of achieving. A large number of arrests signal lawbreakers that they are likely to be caught. Although this probability is perceived subjectively, information about friends, peers, and personal experience anchors these subjective perceptions in terms of objective probabilities of detention. Here, using inmate data on police arrests, I examine the poor investigative capacities of police forces in the region.

Flagrancy

A large number of offenders in Latin America do not plan their crimes because they do not take the police very seriously. An indirect indication for this assertion is obtained from inmate surveys that provide information on the universe of apprehended delinquents. Table 7.2 shows where arrests were made.

Half the inmates were arrested either at the crime scene or in its vicinity. Detention at the crime scene denotes that offenders probably did not plan their crimes well enough to avoid detention, since arrests do not result from a police investigation. Moreover, the arrests of recently admitted offenders detained for drug dealing and theft (representing 38 percent of the sample) derive from random patrolling.[15]

In addition, surveys show that most arrests were made shortly after the crime was committed. More than half of the detainees reported that they were apprehended less than three hours after committing the crimes they

Table 7.2 Where were you arrested for the crime you are charged with?

	Argentina	Brazil	Chile	El Salvador	Mexico	Peru
At the crime scene	30.4 (34.0)	24.9 (26.5)	21.4 (20.9)	12.5 (15.0)	19.7 (20.9)	27.9 (34.8)
In the vicinity of the crime scene	23.1 (25.4)	26.1 (27.2)	24.4 (26.2)	16.8 (15.9)	30.6 (36.3)	17.2 (17.8)
At home	15.3 (15.0)	20.3 (18.9)	15.6 (16.8)	31.5 (31.0)	12.5 (10.6)	12.5 (7.6)
Other	31.2 (25.7)	28.6 (27.4)	38.6 (36.1)	39.2 (38.0)	37.1 (32.2)	42.5 (39.8)

Total n: 6,145. In parentheses, the percentage of a restricted sample of 2,822 recently admitted inmates (i.e. arrested within the last two years).

Sources: Inmate Surveys 2013.

were charged for, denoting that detention probably did not result from a criminal investigation. Most detainees are less professional offenders, such as muggers, corner dealers, and amateur robbers (Kessler 2009).

In most countries, two out of three offenders sentenced to prison were arrested within twenty-four hours of committing the alleged crime, and this rate is even higher for property and drug crimes. The vast majorities of robberies that end in convictions were flagrant acts (Table 7.3). It can be safely assumed that when no arrests are made on the first day of a property crime, this crime is unlikely to be solved.

The majority of arrests by the police are of petty crooks. I claim that the inadequacy of police investigations produces this disproportionate number of petty crimes. Police focus on criminals who are easy to arrest to compensate for their deficient capacity of targeting the upper echelon of criminal networks. In short, police arrest the "small fish" because they are unable to solve more complex crimes.

Table 7.4 shows that approximately half of homicide arrests were made the same day the crime was committed. Very likely offenders were arrested at the scene or after a short chase. From this evidence, it can be concluded that if no arrest is made within twenty-four hours after a homicide, it is unlikely the crime will ever be solved. In effect, following Zepeda's work (2013) only one in seven homicides in Mexico results in a criminal conviction. Assuming this rate as a constant, there is only an 8 percent chance that an offender who commits homicide and successfully escapes detection the first day will ever be caught. In Argentina, just 46 percent of homicides are solved (SNIC 2008), and of the cases that are solved, 48 percent of the

Table 7.3 Time elapsed between committing a crime and being arrested

	Argentina	Brazil	Chile	Mexico	Peru
Less than 1hour	40.7	49.3	45.7	38.0	37.8
1–3 hs	13.8	10.7	13.0	16.8	11.2
3–24 hs	6	6.4	6.5	11	7.6
1–365 days	33.3	29.1	31.9	31.5	37.6
Doesn't know/declines to answer	6.4	4.5	2.9	2.7	5.8

Sources: Inmate Surveys 2013.

Table 7.4 Same-day arrest by type of crime (% of inmate within each category)

		Robbery	Homicide	Drug Crimes	Sexual Crimes
Argentina	Full sample	88.2	48.0	74.6	22.3
	Restricted (2010–2012)	84.9	46.6	72.6	21.5
Brazil	Full sample	82.5	55.8	88.1	26.7
	Restricted (2010–2012)	81.9	43.9	88.0	26.9
Chile	Full sample	80.2	42.9	71.9	17.9
	Restricted (2010–2012)	77.9	32.5	67.3	17.9
El Salvador	Full sample	74.7	29.6	82.1	34.9
	Restricted (2010–2012)	28.6	68.5	20.1	65.3
Mexico	Full sample	88.4	40.2	86,1	61.3
	Restricted (2010–2012)	84.0	41.2	89.8	52.0
Peru	Full sample	73.7	45,2	93.0	44.4
	Restricted (2010–2012)	83.8	41,9	88.3	51.6

Note: Due to sample restrictions, there is no arrest information for kidnapping and abductions. In Mexico, out of the estimated 105,000 abductions carried out in 2012 (ENVIPE 2012, reported by Menendez in *El Excelsior* October 2, 2013) just 137 were reported to the police and an initial investigation was only launched in 60 percent of these cases. Many people believe that officers are partners to criminal rings (a topic to be analyzed in following sections), and many of the few kidnappers arrested turn out to be police officers (see, for example, Mexico, where thirteen members of an eighteen-member kidnapping ring turned out to be federal police officers). http://www.noroeste.com.mx/publicaciones.php?id=901345&id_seccion=

Source: Inmate Surveys 2013.

offenders are detained the same day. It follows that when no arrests are made in the first 24 hours (76 percent of all homicides committed), there is only a 1 in 5 odd the case will ever be solved. Chapter 8 expands on these high impunity rates for the entire region.

Inmates were asked which police (patrolling and investigative units) made the arrest, and for the most part, arrests were handled by police patrols (Table 7.5). Chile is the only country where investigative units were significantly involved in arrests—because they target career criminals. Chile has the lowest crime rate in Latin America, signaling the important role arrests play in deterrence.

Corruption and Use of Force

Police in Latin America are perceived as corrupt and abusive. Data from the inmate surveys show the scope of this corruption and brutality. Inmates were asked whether they believe they could have paid someone off to avoid arrest and/or criminal prosecution, and whether they were asked for bribes. The first question measures perception, while the second provides a threshold of actual corruption (Table 7.6).

The data support the differences between LCE and HCE. Perceived corruption and actual bribe solicitation are lowest in Chile and highest in Mexico. More importantly, since most offenders in Mexico believe that money can buy freedom and impunity, this indirectly suggests that other offenders who had the means to bribe were probably able to avoid arrest. Very likely, delinquents who participated in lucrative robberies and drug trades simply bribed their way out of arrest in Mexico. This would not have been possible in Chile. Deterrence diminishes under HCE due to the pervasive effects of corruption.

Inmates were also asked if they were victims of violence at police stations before their arraignment.[16] When evidence for indictment is weak, testimonies and collateral information obtained from the suspects through coercion can help prosecution authorities and police to build cases. The data show that the use of violence is widespread across the

Table 7.5 Arresting officers

Who made the arrest?	Argentina	Brazil	Chile	Mexico	Peru
Patrols	92.1	65.8	34.2	56.5	91.2
Detectives (investigative unit)	N/A	24.0	45.8	37.2	N/A

Source: Inmate Surveys 2013.

Table 7.6 Perceived vs. actual police corruption and use of force

	Argentina	Brazil	Chile	El Salvador	Mexico	Peru
Perception of corruption[a]	55	43	40	53.8	78	42
Bribe solicitation[b]	28	21	14	N/A	45	37
Use of force[c]	39.7	44.4	31.9	37.1	46.4	N/A

Notes:

[a] percent of respondents who answered yes to the following question: "Do you believe that if you had had enough money you could have been freed by the police at the time of your detention?"

[b] percent of respondents who answered yes to the following question: "From the time you were arrested until your sentencing, did the police ask you for money or for personal belongings?"

[c] percent of respondents who answered yes to the following question: "Did someone (an officer) hit you or use physical force to oblige you to make a statement (or enter a plea) or to change your statement (or plea)?

Source: Inmate Surveys.

region but consistent with police professionalism: Chile has the lowest rates while Brazil and Mexico have the highest.

Organized Crime

Latin American police departments are mostly reactive and rarely develop strategies for dismantling rackets that commit crime for profits. While many countries have special units specializing in sophisticated criminality, they are not proactive, do not share information with other agencies, and often lack professional skills.[17]

The inmate surveys provide evidence on arrests of organized criminals, or rather the lack thereof. Excluding sexual crimes, 41.5 percent of respondents committed their crimes on their own. Among those who reported being part of a group, more than 15 percent were part of relatively large organizations (such as the PCC in San Pablo, Brazil, or Mara Salvatrucha or Calle 18 gangs in El Salvador). In addition, 64 percent teamed up with a partner or group to commit robbery and 53 percent to deal drugs.

Within the inmate population foot soldiers greatly outnumber crime organizers. Although this should be expected, there are very few inmates that could be considered as mid- to high-level operators in organized crime networks. For example, only 1.2 percent of the total inmate populations are white-collar offenders. Among offenders who were charged with crime for profit (robbery, drug crimes, kidnapping, and so on), just 4.1 percent committed crimes exceeding US$50,000 or more. In terms of these perpetrators, 62.4 percent were arrested in flagrance, showing that very likely they were detained randomly.

In short, the inmate survey data suggest that very few crime organizers are ever arrested, and their apprehension does not appear to result from criminal investigation.

Summary

Police officers make thousands of arrests every day, and most offenders are caught red-handed. Conversely, deterrence is enhanced when few but significant cases are solved and when the police have the ability to dismantle criminal organizations. This is important because, as I argue in this book, many crimes are interconnected and many property or drug-related crimes have a market dynamic. Arrested street dealers or thieves are rapidly replaced and thus the crime rate is hardly affected. However, a disbanded ring can lower criminality because this can reduce the supply of illegal goods.

Overall, the survey evidence provides indirect proof about the low investigative capacities of police departments throughout the region. Thousands of new entries arrive at prisons each year, but most detainees are petty thieves and street drug dealers while few high-profile offenders are ever arrested. Widespread corruption and the use of force reveal the shortcomings of police intelligence. Effective deterrence does not build on mass arrests or overwhelming force, but mainly on projecting an image of competent policing. An examination of the poor investigative capacities of police departments that result from the poor handling of information and intelligence follows.

Information, Intelligence, and Deterrence

Police departments in LCE countries can put limits on predatory crimes. Several homicides and other extreme crimes still happen, yet they remain somewhat under control. Police are capable to maintain a level of low criminality using a mix of strategies that always includes information and investigation systems adequate to the type of criminality they face. Here I examine the role of information and intelligence in policing, and how they help to enhance deterrence.

Police and Public Safety: How Rudimentary Information Systems "Worked" for Low Levels of Crime

The old police repertoire of crime control is inspired by the "corner cop," the man who usually knew the whereabouts of everyone in the neighborhood. According to this narrative, when a crime occurred, the street patrol already had in mind several potential suspects. In the old days, police officers usually had a pretty good idea as to who the "trouble makers" were—the muggers, the drunks, or the violent family beaters. These street policemen usually shared this information with higher ranked officers, and they used it strategically, whether to sanction law violators, to warn potential criminals, or to extract bribes from offenders in exchange for impunity.

This information system was vertically integrated. Street patrols collected data on criminality in the neighborhood and passed it up the chain of command to their superiors. Depending of the severity of threats, actions against delinquents were decided at the low, middle, or high level. A petty crime on the corner was dealt with by street patrols, a small-scale prostitution ring by mid-level officers and detectives, and a large carjacking operation by top officers and chief detectives. An array of "resolutions" was available, from the simple arrest of delinquents to cover-ups and protection of rackets. From the deterrence standpoint, "resolution" meant that police always had the upper hand. Even when they tolerated criminal rings, or partnered with delinquents, police had the final say, and imposed limits on the criminal behavior of these groups.

This old system, with its varying degrees of corruption and efficacy, was "normal" in most countries throughout the region for many decades—until the 1980s—with the exception of countries suffering from civil strife (such as Colombia and Guatemala). Crime remained under control. There were, of course, homicides, robberies, and other felonies, but their scope was limited. Homicides occurred mostly among acquaintances (family altercations, feuds over lands and money, disputes in cantinas, and so on). Under this equilibrium there were a significant number of robberies and snatchings. Occasionally, there was a bank robbery, a large-scale burglary, or a spectacular shoot-out between gangs and groups, but mostly crime was circumscribed to petty theft and interpersonal conflicts. Police effectively contained this criminality.

Sometimes crime got out of hand, either because a group committed a spectacular crime with tragic outcomes, or victims were well-known figures. In these cases, under LCE, the political leadership told the police to get the problem "solved." Police would then successfully identify the offenders and made arrests.[18] This mechanism has several implications. Since offenders and policemen knew that certain boundaries should not be crossed, a bargaining between police officers and offenders established the scope and depth of crime that would be tolerated (usually in exchange for sharing profits with the police). As explained above in this chapter in section "Police in Latin America: Legacies and Current Structure," the political elite mostly accepted these terms of agreement: the police were allowed to operate in the shadows in exchange for low criminality. That was the nature of LCE in most of the region during the twentieth century.

Deterrence worked moderately because delinquents were easily identified by officers. Crimes happened, arrests were made, and criminals were sent to prisons. However, there were few large-scale criminal operations, and only occasionally did criminal networks operate beyond the scope of police control. Police had the upper hand. Traditional information systems were adequate for moderate levels of criminality. Success relied on the personal engagement of officers working street patrols and rudimentary systems of information that effectively targeted a relatively small universe of delinquents.[19] However, this rudimentary police information system underperformed when criminal networks expanded, acquisitive crimes were fully developed, and HCE became a serious threat.

Adoption of Crime Control Strategies

Every good strategy to fight crime builds on good information systems. In the past few decades, three strategies were used to reduce complex criminality in the United States and elsewhere: zero tolerance, hot spot analysis, and program notification.[20] The first was based on the broken windows paradigm (Wilson and Kelling 1982) and further developed using the crime as opportunity paradigm (routine activity and rational choice theories). The second is a crime reduction strategy that targets areas where the concentration of crime is very high and police make strategic interventions and conduct heavy monitoring.[21] The third strategy, less known in Latin America, targets hard offenders and makes them fully accountable for crimes committed under their watch ("pulling levers").[22] This list is not exclusive as other strategies have been implemented, but they are the most important in terms of deterrence. These three strategies have yielded meaningful results while sparking public controversies and academic debates.

Different approaches toward police deterrence use intelligence collected from officers in order to maximize its capacity, enabling the police to signal to would-be delinquents its ability to identify and punish them. In traditional policing, efficiency is gained when police gather information about incidents and design an appropriate response based on the nature of the underlying conditions that cause the problems (Goldstein,

1990). These three strategies can be successful to the extent that police can effectively collect and use such information. This is precisely one of the shortcomings of Latin American police departments.

Zero tolerance is a well-known strategy that several Latin American countries have attempted to introduce (Davis 2007; Dammert and Salazar 2009).[23] In most cases this strategy has failed because it lacks an information management system, a key component for its favorable outcome. For zero tolerance to succeed, police officers require information about crime frequencies. The New York Police Department invested heavily in information gathering and processing to address the most serious crimes; officers analyze crime events daily and criminality is mapped in real time (using Compstat). Zero tolerance then focused on serious crimes that were addressed immediately and Compstat has been a key element in its success.

Hot-spot policing has also been emulated in the region.[24] However, few studies measure the real impact of these initiatives. Two well-known programs in Bogota and Santiago de Chile, both named *Plan Cuadrante*, were variations of hot-spot strategies in which neighborhoods were heavily patrolled. Initially, both were successful at reducing criminality (FIP 2012; Tudela et al. 2014).[25] This strategy reduces crime in part by assembling crime maps (identifying hot spots), which is rarely done in the region. Most crimes are never reported to the police; many police officers do not collect data while on duty; and coordination with other agencies that could provide useful data on crime concentration (such as schools and local agencies) is non-existent. But, in general, hot-spot strategies have had limited success.[26]

The third strategy (pulling levers) consists of informing offenders on the consequences of bad choices they might make, ensuring greater compliance with the law. In particular, repeat offenders, prison re-entries, and identified violent individuals receive credible messages that they are being watched and that no tolerance will be displayed if they are found to be involved in serious crimes. The key to these initiatives is precisely the ability of police to notify those at-risk individuals of the danger they face if they opt for crime.

All three crime reduction strategies are based on credible intelligence and police ability to act based on gathered information. This is deterrence at its best. Would-be offenders refrain from committing crimes because they trust that the police are watching, have valuable knowledge which is used strategically, and are capable of acting swiftly. Police are effective to the extent they convey that message.[27]

Zero tolerance, hot spot initiatives, or pulling levers can succeed only to the extent that intelligence is gathered, data are systematically collected, coordination with other agencies is displayed, and information is effectively processed and used. Several initiatives in Latin America to imitate these strategies failed because they emulated patrolling or training aspects, but failed to build the information systems.

Poor Intelligence: Alternative Explanations

Why have Latin American countries failed to develop strong information and intelligence-gathering systems for crime reduction? Based on the scant sources available and multiple interviews conducted with experts, specialists, and officers over the last ten years, I identify six variables that have reduced the capacity of police departments to build functional information systems to enhance deterrence and fight crime:[28]

a) *Reactivity.* In criminal law, institutions such as the police are built to react to a deviant event, however, under HCE crimes are not as deviant, and a large number of cases are never investigated. To reduce crime, police departments must take a proactive stance, intervene, and dismantle the crime rings that are ultimately responsible for the vast majority of crimes. Such intervention can test the constitutionality of police activity and is more in tune with military-style operations. It is no coincidence that proactive measures taken under HCE by the Colombian national police and those in Rio de Janeiro, Brazil and Ciudad Juarez, Mexico were led by military-style policing.

b) *Backlash to legacies of the authoritarian period.* The bloody legacies of police participation in repressive dictatorships during the 1970s and 1980s led to a new legal approach based on government restraint and the expansion of citizen rights, including police and justice reforms. An unintended consequence of this, however, was the restriction of police initiatives to gather information, which has affected the ability of police departments to build databases on criminal networks and track the activities of delinquents over time (Beato 2012). The very welcomed curtailment of executive abuses used under dictatorships to obtain information ended up paralyzing police intelligence in democracies.

c) *Centralization.* The mistrust of local police and patrols (sometimes due to legitimate concerns about corruption) has encumbered healthy police–community relations. Personnel, including local police chiefs, are often rotated. Local police often collect valuable non-criminal and non-reactive information (on alcohol consumption, intimidating groups, power relations within the community, truancy, and so on) that can later be used for intelligence (particularly as they relate to organized criminality). Central police departments in the region have failed to integrate first-hand street-level information that constitutes an important input for Compstat- or NIP (Notification Intervention Program)-type strategies, because residents tend to mistrust local units and personnel rotates very often.

d) *Technology and specialization.* Police reforms that sought to address the problem of information included two strategies: new technologies and specialized agencies. The incorporation of technology requires intensive training, supervision and analysis that have not been used successfully in Latin American police departments. Although ballistic tests, toxicology labs, and cameras have been introduced across the region, these are usually operated from the top down, serving only top officers and prosecutors. In addition, large-scale criminal activities that posed serious threats ushered in the development of special units (money laundering, human trafficking, anti-extortion, and so on). These highly specialized divisions build data centers but do not share information with other units.

e) *Lack of interagency coordination.* Multiple law enforcement agencies produce valuable information for crime control: customs, health departments, tax agencies, and money laundering surveillance offices. These departments lack channels for intelligence sharing, and they mostly operate autonomously. Once an investigation is under way, police can request data from other agencies but there are no familiar programs for sharing information on suspicious schemes or transactions. Although this is a problem worldwide, interagency and coordinating institutions function more effectively in Europe and the United States.

f) *Cultural resilience.* An important but not yet well-studied aspect of police underperformance is tied to cultural patterns of policing in the region. Training at police academies on human rights and strict adherence to the law have not managed to change the hierarchical, detached, and strongly repressive nature of the police. The inherent danger of the profession (Skolnick 1966) and the tradition of repression and corruption continue to impede more democratic policing (Ungar 2009). Since "old habits die hard," Latin American police departments face a great challenge when it comes to reversing legacies and cultural trends in which the community is rarely involved in the process of gathering information for effective crime control.

These six factors are typical weaknesses of Latin American states. Problems related to interagency coordination, overlap and competition, a lack of innovation, ineffective bureaucracies, and institutional mistrust all transcend law enforcement agencies. Most police reforms have failed to produce effective information schemes and the consolidation of intelligence systems that are necessary for HCE. Several departments have been moderately successful in working with data produced on their own (most department have crime maps based on reports from police precincts, cameras, and emergency calls stations) yet they fail to anticipate the moves of crime rings, to intervene in illegal markets, or to coordinate effectively with other law enforcement agencies. Future work should thoroughly examine the structural sources of this underperformance.

Police Trust: A Dukheimian Challenge

I have already described the limited capacities of police to solve cases and the unsuccessful use of intelligence to prevent and fight criminality, dealing mainly with a "Webberian" concern: How to foster a strong police organization that can effectively manage flows of information, hierarchies, structure, and so on. I will now turn to the flip side of the coin, to a Durkheimian perspective of the problem: How to build bonds of trust between citizens and police in order to improve policing. For the majority of Latin Americans, policemen are adversaries, hindering the emergence of cohesiveness, where both citizens and police fighting crime in tandem. Poor police legitimacy inhibits the sharing of information and the fostering of strong bonds between citizens and police, which in turn limits their ability to fight crime effectively. Here, I show that high criminality strongly contributes to such disconnect between police and community so that it takes "a life on its own." The equilibrium approach explains why some societies fail into the trap of low trust and high crime.

Levels of Police Trust

Confidence in the police is essential to cement the link between civilians and police officers and allow policemen to better "serve and protect" (Tyler 2005; Horowitz 2007). Without trust, police departments have a hard time eliciting cooperation from their citizens, which further increases public insecurity and undermines the chance of future collaboration. Poor police performance accounts for a large share of the mistrust.

As crime rises in Latin America, trust in the police remains low. Policemen are seen either as inefficient or as partners of criminals. Using data from the Barometer of the Americas, Cruz reports that in Latin America 44 percent of respondents believe that the police are in cahoots with offenders and only 38 percent say that police protect the citizens.[29] In a recent new wave, close to 50 percent of Latin Americans report that they believe that police partner with criminals.[30] Citizens rarely share their information with the police out of fear it may backfire and be transmitted to crooks (Arias 2006).

Trust appears to be causally related to police effectiveness at fighting crime. On the LAPOP survey, the correlation between police trust and police efficacy yields a very strong coefficient of −0.902.[31]

Several surveys address trust with standard questions about confidence in the police. Table 7.7 presents means or frequencies for several questions about confidence in police, their ability to fight crime, police abuse, and measures of victimizations. The correlation matrix that uses mean scores for each country (n = 18) is presented in Table 7.8.

Although the association between police efficacy and trust is predictable, the strength of these correlations stands out. Victimization in the region correlates with low trust (Bateson and Malone 2010; Perez 2003). The coefficients of Table 7.8 include only 18 cases (mean results for each country); they have the expected direction but are not statistically significant at standard levels (due to the low number of cases). A pooled sample of 10 countries (including more than 15,000 respondents) for these variables yielded a statistically significant coefficient of −0.305. It appears that police trust is moderately affected by one's personal experience with crime, particularly among those who have suffered severe victimization.[32]

Why is Trust so Low?

Many studies in the United States have compared low trust in police with socio-demographic correlates (Schuck and Rosenbaum 2005; Tyler 2001; Skogan 2005; Tyler and Huo 2003) and ecological and behavioral variables (Parks and Reisig 1998; Sampson and Bartusc 1998; Schafer et al. 2003). In Latin America, additional factors account for low trust in the police.[33] First, most Latin American police forces played a key role in the authoritarian regimes of the 1970s to 1990s.[34] Furthermore, many of the police's informal and illegal practices continued into the democratic period (Ragendorfer 2002; Davis 2006; Caldeira 2000). Latin American

Table 7.7 Law enforcement perception and public safety indicators

	Trust in the Police (1-7)	Police Efficacy (1-4)	Judicial Efficacy (1-4)	Victim. General (%)	Victim. Robbery (%)	Severity of Crime (1-4)	Police Abuse (8%)
Argentina	2.92	3.03	2.93	27	12	1.37	8.3
Belize	4.34	2.52	2.49	11	6	1.74	10
Bolivia	3.47	2.99	2.81	18	6	1.45	7.7
Brazil	3.74	2.85	2.85	16	7	1.3	6.2
Chile	5.03	2.62	2.92	22	9	1.52	3.7
Colombia	4.52	2.57	2.44	15	8	1.49	7.2
Costa Rica	3.51	2.86	3.03	16	5	1.34	3.1
Ecuador	3.26	2.85	2.79	21	14	1.48	4.4
El Salvador	3.91	2.78	2.72	19	11	1.24	8.3
Guatemala	3.41	2.97	2.85	17	11	1.34	3.6
Honduras	3.64	2.82	2.69	14	6	1.76	2.8
Mexico	3.63	2.94	2.85	16	6	1.65	5.8
Nicaragua	4.23	2.59	2.63	17	6	1.33	4.5
Panamá	3.91	2.69	2.62	8	4	1.46	2
Paraguay	2.75	3.23	3.27	17	6	1.25	2.7
Peru	3.32	3.01	3.00	25	7	1.47	7.0
Uruguay	4.29	2.54	2.69	22	4	1.52	4.2

	Trust in the Police	Police efficacy	Judicial System efficacy	Severity of the problem	Victimization—General	Victimization—Robbery	Police Abuse
Venezuela	3.09	2.99	2.88	21	14	1.31	3.5
USA	4.55	N/A	N/A	18	8	N/A	N/A
Mean	3.79	2.78	2.72	16	8	1.5	5.3

Trust in the Police: "To what extent do you trust the police department?" 1. Not at all, 7. Completely

Police efficacy (perception): "If you are a victim of a robbery or assault, how likely does you think it is that the police will apprehend the perpetrator?" (1) Very likely, (2) Somewhat likely, (3) Not very likely, (4) Not at all.

Judicial System efficacy (perception): "If you are a victim of a robbery or assault, how likely do you think it is that the judicial system will punish the perpetrator?" (1) Very likely, (2) Somewhat likely, (3) Not very likely, (4) Not at all.

Severity of the problem (perception): "Speaking of the country in general, to what extent do you think that the current level of crime represents a threat to our future well-being?" 1: Very much, 4: Not at all.

Victimization—General: "Have you been a victim of any crime in the past 12 months?"

Victimization—Robbery: "Have you been a victim of an armed property robbery (not including your vehicle) in the past 12 months?"

Police Abuse: "In the past 12 months, has any police officer mistreated you verbally or physically assaulted you?"

Source: Barometer of the Americas 2008.

Table 7.8 Police trust, performance, and victimization: Bivariate correlations

	Trust on the police	Police efficacy	Victimization general	Victimization armed robbery	Severity of crime	Police abuse
Police trust	1	−.902[a]	−.252	−.301	.380[c]	.113
Police efficacy	−.902[a]	1	.333	.287	−.407[c]	−.132
Victimization– General	−.252	.333	1	.516[b]	−.286	.183
Victimization– Armed robbery	−.301	.287	.516[b]	1	−.320	.128
Severity of crime	.380[c]	−.407[c]	−.286	−.320	1	.136
Police abuse	.113	−.132	.183	.128	.136	1

[a] Statistically significant at p 0.01 (bilateral).
[b] Statistically significant at p 0.05 (bilateral).
[c] Statistically significant at p 0.10 (bilateral).
Source: Author elaboration based on data presented in Table 7.7.

police officers frequently violate human rights and the rule of law, often engaging in torture and summary executions, which typically go un-punished by the judicial system (see Chevigny 1995; Brinks 2003; Davis 2007). This of course diminishes people's trust.

Second, Latin American police forces are regarded as highly ineffi-cient at controlling and preventing crime. They typically operate on low budgets, which mainly go to cover inadequate wages for police personnel, while investment in infrastructure, equipment, technology, and human resources is secondary (Bergman and Arango 2011). Professionals in law enforcement have very low social esteem (Azaola 2006).

Third, the police are perceived to be riddled with corruption, accepting bribes in an array of activities such as traffic violations, drug dealing, human trafficking, prostitution, illegal gambling, and kidnapping (Snyder and Durán Martinez 2009; Rios 2013; Sain 2004, 2008). Police departments have found it difficult to break away from these stigmas and gain the support and trust of citizens.

The Role of Police Performance

According to distributive justice models, the police earn approval and re-spect when people perceive that they effectively fight crime and punish rule breakers. Another model, procedural fairness, emphasizes that trust is earned to the extent that police treat people fairly and make the public's voice count (Sunshine and Tyler 2003; Huo 2003). Still, it remains unclear whether trust is earned from "process-oriented" policies (how officers behave) or from "outcome-oriented" results (whether they keep crime under control) (Hickman and Simpson 2003; Skogan and Frydl 2004; Patternoster et al. 1997). I will present a data analysis for Latin America that reveals that even in high-crime environments, both the process and the outcomes matter. Whether police departments listen to citizens and treat them fairly is often as important as preventing crime and arresting miscreants. Not surprisingly, predatory police practices such as corruption, extortion, and misconduct negatively affect trust (Gerber and Mendelson 2008; Sabet 2013).

In order to assess the effect of police performance on developing trust with the community the following pages present a study on the impact of the former upon the latter. This addresses two empirical questions: (1) what are the determinants of trust in the police, and (2) how does process and/or performance affect trust? The analysis of the data finds that trust in the police is largely explained by how people evaluate their performance.

Police Performance and Trust: A Multivariate Analysis

This study compares citizens' beliefs and attitudes toward police forces in the Mexican Federal District (MEX) and the City of Buenos Aires (BA), and analyses the effect of critical factors to explain the public's inclination (and hesitation) to trust in the police. These variables are measured through victimization surveys that include similar questions on police performance. It also examines the effects of police corruption and abuse, measures of criminality, and other socio-demographic factors Table 7.9.

The data are drawn from two surveys administered in 2007–2008 in Mexico City and its surroundings and in Buenos Aires.[35] Sample sizes are different. The Mexico City survey consists of one wave of a longitudinal victimization survey of 1,500 respondents. The Buenos Aires survey includes 18,000 respondents and was designed to capture samples for each of the fifteen communes (districts) within the city. Both surveys include similarly worded questions on police performance.[36]

Results

Police trust. In order to measure trust in Buenos Aires, people were asked if they would inform the police that they were leaving their home

to go on a trip.[37] This question reveals how much people will entrust police agents with private and sensitive information concerning the safety
of their home. Less than 15 percent of respondents reported they would
be willing to undertake such a concrete act of trust in the police. Lower-
income individuals, males, and victims are slightly more willing to inform
the police, while perceived crime in the neighborhood does not seem to
affect responses.[38]

Unfortunately, this dependent variable could not be replicated in Mexico
since in the pre-test more than 98 percent of respondents answered negatively. In the Mexican survey, trust in the police was measured using the
following question: "How much trust do you have in the police in your neighborhood?" Cases were coded 1 when respondents reported they felt "a lot of
trust" and 0 when they felt "some trust, little trust or no trust." Respondents
in Mexico reported a higher level of distrust: more than 62 percent expressed
that they have little or no trust while only 14 percent said they have "a lot" of
trust.[39] Trust determinants, however, are similar in both cases.

Police Performance. Perception of police performance uses four
parameters: 1) crime control and protection offered; 2) frequency of
patrols; 3) time elapsed in responding to crimes reported by phone; and
4) the manners and respect shown by the police.[40] Both surveys have anal-
ogous questions.[41] Table 7.9 presents responses for each question in both
countries. On average both police departments fare poorly. However, the
perceptions of Mexico City's police are considerably inferior to those for
the Buenos Aires police.

I used these measures to construct the main independent variable: the
Police Evaluation Index (PEI). Within this index, the scores of two questions
(crime protection and frequency of patrolling) were combined into an indicator that refers to the evaluation of *outcome* of police performance, and
the other two scores (response time, and manners and respect) into *process*. PEI index is a simple non-weighted average of the four grades, which
simplifies the interpretation of the coefficients.[42] The outcome and process variables reflect average scores of the respective questions. Table 7.10
reports two sample t tests with unequal variances for mean differences
between groups, comparing individuals who report to trust and those who
report not to trust the police. The results provide initial support for the
notion that citizens' perceptions of police performance have a significant
effect on their predisposition to trust the police.

Table 7.9 Scores for Police Satisfaction for BA and MEX (1 = very bad, 5 = very good)

Variable	Mexico City	Buenos Aires
Crime Protection	2.65 (1.05)	2.99 (1.02)
Frequency of Patrolling	2.67 (1.14)	3.06 (1.15)
Time of Response	2.43 (1.17)	3.25 (1.22)
Manners and Respect	3.02 (1.12)	3.78 (0.97)
Average	2.67 (0.94)	3.28 (0.93)
Number of Cases	1424	17482

Sources: Authors elaboration from Bergman et al., *Encuesta de Victimización y Eficacia Institucional* and UdeSA-GCBA, *Encuesta de Victimización de la Ciudad Autónoma de Buenos Aires*.

Regression Analysis

In order to estimate the effect of performance on trust, I present results from a logistic regression. The central hypothesis is that individuals' evaluation of the police—their perception of police performance—carries a crucial explicative weight in the willingness to trust them. To test for this effect, I constructed models that control for variables directly related to perceptions of safety and the objective insecurity that people feel, as well as other socio-demographic variables. Given the different measurement of the dependent variable for each country, I present separate models, although most independent variables are identical.

Dependent Variable: Police Trust

Trust in the police is measured with different questions for both countries. Nevertheless, the regression coefficients are similar. Approximately 15 percent of the samples exhibit significant trust. In the logistic regression models, trust is coded 1 if respondents were willing to inform the police they will be leaving their home for vacation (BA) or they have a lot of trust (MEX), and 0 otherwise.

Independent Variables

Police Evaluation Index (PEI). This independent variable evaluates police performance and also has two subcomponents to test for the effect of performance based on *outcome* or *process* on trust.[43]

Table 7.10 Difference in means between "trusting" and "not trusting"
individuals

	Argentina			Mexico		
	PEI	Process	Outcome	PEI	Process	Outcome
No trust	3.17	2.95	3.41	2.51	1.28	2.47
Trust	3.67	3.31	3.87	3.69	1.86	3.69
T-test	−25.01	−18.13	−22.46	−8.95	−8.36	−9.52

Source: Author elaboration based on data from Table 7.9.

The models include crime related variables, and socio-demographic controls.[44] Crime related variables are:

Victimization (VICTIM). A dummy variable for whether anyone in the respondent's household has been the victim of at least one crime during the last year.

Perception of Crime Frequency Index (PCFI). This index measures perception of crime in the neighborhood based on perceived frequency of criminal activities.[45] Respondents were asked, for a list of crimes or disorders, whether they perceived such behavior to happen very frequently, somewhat frequently, or not frequently at all. Responses were converted into dummies—1 = "very or somewhat frequent," 0 = "not frequent"—and all responses were added. PCFI ranges from 0 to 7, where 0 indicates that no crime has been observed in the neighborhood and 7 indicates that all crimes are perceived as frequent.[46]

Expectation of Being the Victim of Crime (Expectation). Perceived likelihood to be a victim of one of the following crimes: street robbery, aggression, car theft, sexual attack, burglary, or police abuse. Respondents were asked, "How likely do you expect that one of these crimes will happen to you?" Answers are ordinal, ranging from not likely at all to very likely. The index is an average of responses for each category.

Fear of Being the Victim of a Crime (Fear). Respondent were asked, "How much do you fear that one of these crimes will happen to you? Would you say that you feel no fear, little fear, neither little nor a lot, some fear or a lot of fear?" Crimes listed were the same as those for the expectation of being victimized. Higher values denote higher fear. I also control specifically for the fear of burglary: *Fear (home)*.

Police Abuse. A dummy variable of respondents that in Buenos Aires suffered or witnessed one of the following police misconducts: mistreatment, beating, unlawful detention, asking for or eliciting bribes, discrimination because of skin color, clothing, or gender. The survey for Mexico measures only whether the police informed an individual of the reasons for his or her arrest. Coded 1, if there was any report of misconduct and 0 otherwise. In BA 27 percent reported some form of police misconduct, while in Mexico one every five respondents have witnessed misconduct in the process of arrests.

Demographic Variables

Gender. Men are coded 1.

Socio-economic Level (BA) [47] *and Income (Mex).* Lower socio-economic strata grade the police higher than those from middle and higher levels.[48] In Argentina lower income in SEL methodology is coded higher. In Mexico, income is measured by the reported added numbers of minimum salaries each household has earned. Therefore, it is expected that coefficients in both models will have a different sign.

Age. For Buenos Aires, age was coded as responded, while in Mexico respondents had been already grouped into six categories.[49]

Communes (districts). For Buenos Aires, 15 districts were grouped into 5 segments according to their socio-economic status and their perceived levels of security in the commune.[50] High values denote neighborhoods with better social services, as well as low victimization rates.

Table 7.11 presents summary statistics of the variables.

Table 7.12 presents the results obtained from two specifications of the model: one measures perceived overall performance of the police and the other disaggregates this index into process-oriented and outcome-oriented performance. I report also the exponential of B to provide the magnitude of the effect for each variable in the equation.

"Pseudo" r squares are much larger in Mexico City than in Buenos Aires. On the other hand, some results are not significant in MEX given the smaller number of cases (455). Gender, fear, and fear of home victimization for MEX would probably pass the test of conventional statistical significance with a larger sample size.

The evaluation of police performance (PEI) is, by far, the factor with the greatest impact on trust in the police. The magnitude of this effect is significant and the results are very robust. Respondents in Buenos Aires that believe police officers do a good job, are roughly twice as likely to share important information with the police than those who believe the police do their jobs poorly. In Mexico, the likelihood of trusting the police increases approximately four times when they perceive the police do their job properly.

While in Buenos Aires *outcome* is the most important performance indicator for trusting the police, in Mexico City *process* is overwhelmingly the stronger predictor of trust. Clearly Mexicans are more concerned with how the police treat them, and they evaluate police performance accordingly. It is rather the arbitrariness and corruption of police, as well as the lack of a "voice" for Mexican citizens that greatly determine their poor evaluation of police.

Victimization is also a strong predictor in both cities. This suggests that if police treat the citizens respectfully after they have suffered a crime, police confidence might improve. Fear of crime, meanwhile, is not significant. Another strong finding is that, among those who have suffered or

Table 7.11 Summary of descriptive statistics

| Variable | Min-Max | Buenos Aires | | Mexico City | |
		Mean	Std. Dev.	Mean	Std. Dev.
PEI	1–5	3.28018	.9264664	2.617117	1.016399
Victim	0–1	.329658	.4701109	.4075521	.4916993
PCFI	0–7	2.056641	.9464766	3.83724	3.164473
Crime Expectation	0–5	2.769436	1.268938	2.811234	1.045462
Fear	0–5	2.954921	1.319189	3.041898	1.079118
Fear (Home)	1–5	3.300527	1.419637	2.894256	1.376001
Police Abuse	0–1	.2721842	.4450934	.5221354	.4998353
Gender	0–1	.4352394	.4957985	.4036458	.4909478
Age (BsAs)	15–99	45.62894	19.65306		
Age (Mex)	1–6			3.83442	1.474753
SEL (BsAs)	1–4	2.09986	.8132087		
Income (Mex)	1–4			2.414855	.8874996
Communes	1–20	3.243841	2.389068		

Empty cells denote no data available.

Source: Author elaboration from UdeSA-GCBA, *Encuesta de Victimización de la Ciudad Autónoma de Buenos Aires*, and Bergman et al., *Encuesta de Victimización y Eficacia Institucional*.

Table 7.12 Logistic regression models of police trust in Buenos Aires

	Buenos Aires				Mexico			
	(1)		(2)		(1)		(2)	
Variables	B	Exp (B)	B	Exp (B)	B	Exp (B)	B	Exp (B)
Police Evaluation Index	.678[a] (.054)	1.971	—	—	1.418[a] (.322)	4.131	—	—
Outcome	—	—	.202[a] (.029)	1.224	—	—	.344 (.299)	1.411
Process	—	—	.0306 (.023)	1.031	—	—	2.319[a] (.737)	10.118
Victimization	.297[a] (.089)	1.346	.315[a] (.074)	1.371	.590 (.583)	1.804	.619 (.589)	1.857
Crime Perception (PCFI)	.098[b] (.047)	1.103	.0369 (.034)	1.037	−.223[b] (.112)	.799	−.224[c] (.114)	.799
Crime Expectation	.0535 (.058)	1.055	−.040 (.044)	.959	3.688 (.351)	1.455	.365 (.353)	1.440
Fear	−.062 (.056)	.939	.022 (.044)	1.022	−.601 (.512)	.548	−.603 (.508)	.546
Fear (home)	−.016 (.043)	.983	−.073[b] (.036)	.929	.530 (.402)	1.699	.565 (.399)	1.759
Police Abuse	−.284[a] (.103)	.752	−.526[a] (.085)	.590	−1.9 [a] (.688)	.148	−1.9 [a] (.695)	.148
Gender	.196[b] (.086)	1.216	.190 [a] (.071)	1.209	.713 (.540)	2.041	.661 (.543)	1.937
Age	−.008[a] (.002)	.991	−.006[a] (.002)	.993	.239 (.207)	1.270	.224 (.211)	1.251
Socioeconomic Level	.161[a] (.061)	1.174	.185[a] (.051)	1.204	−.211 (.291)	.809	−.183 (.292)	.832
Commune	−.094[a] (.029)	.909	−.123[a] (.0247087)	.883				
Constant	−3.886[a] (.319)	.0205	−2.158[a] (.228)	.115	−6.14[a] (2.060)	.002	−6.5 [a](2.110)	.001
N	4938		7259		455		455	
Pseudo R-squared	.058		.0321		.42		.43	
-2loglikelihood	−1,923.873		−2,812.994		−57.272		−56.282	

Empty cells denote no data available.

Standard errors in parentheses; [a] p<.01, [b] p<.05, [c] p<.1.

Source: UdeSA-GCBA, *Encuesta de Victimización de la Ciudad Autónoma de Buenos Aires* and Bergman et al. (2009), *Encuesta de Victimización y Eficacia Institucional*.

witnessed police abuse, the odds of trusting the police are significantly lower than those that did not. (25–40 percent lower in BA, and up to 90 percent lower in MEX).[51]

Finally, the perception of the frequency of criminal activity (PCFI) has different results in each country. A moderate positive association in BA and a strong negative association in MEX signal that those who perceive high levels of crimes in their neighborhoods are less inclined to trust the police.

In terms of the demographic controls, as expected, the odds of males trusting the police are close to 20 percent higher than for females. Age is almost neutral in BA and a strong predictor in MEX (elderly people trust the police more), while people with lower income exhibit higher trust (high SEL actually denotes low income)

Results in both models show that police performance matters for gaining trust; that both outcome- and process-oriented evaluations are relevant, and that experiencing police abuse dramatically reduces trust in the police. Furthermore, the severe lack of trust of Mexican police is strongly affected by the poor levels of fairness in the process that it grants to citizens, while both police abuse and misconduct severely affects bonds of trust.

Summary

The empirical evidence indicates that a vast majority of the inhabitants of these cities judge the performance of their police forces as deficient and that low levels of trust are strongly associated with this assessment. Citizens' evaluation of police performance is what best explains their trust in the police. The magnitude of this effect is large and significant in both cities, despite their high rates of overall victimization. The robustness of these results across both cases is highly relevant, given the many differences (socio-economic, demographic, and criminological) that exist between these two metropolitan areas. The results of these models also shed light on the devastating effect that police abuse and misconduct have on the public's trust (see also Brinks 2003; Tiscornia 2004).[52] Future research should illuminate which aspects of police misconduct are more likely to impede the building of trust.

These models show some differences and similarities with findings from other countries in Europe and in the United States. First, people living in neighborhoods that are safer have the same or even less trust in the police. This finding differs from the United States and European cities, where trust is clearly higher in wealthier neighborhoods. This result stems from a cultural predisposition of wealthier individuals to mistrust the police in Latin America, probably due to legacies of police corruption and abuse during authoritarian regimes. Second, while women in Europe and the United States exhibit more trust in the police, the opposite was found in Mexico City and Buenos Aires.

These models yielded similar results for various factors that influence citizen trust in the police in two different cities and they have an important policy implication: despite differences, police departments will only enhance citizens' trust if they seriously devote their energies to improving the performance of their officers. Better policing enhances trust. Consistent with the overall argument of this chapter, this will improve cooperation, information sharing, and performance and can contribute to forging the virtuous circle of stronger deterrence and low crime.

The empirical findings have several broader implications. First, whether it is built through effective crime prevention or procedural fairness, the performance of police officers enhances public trust and lawful behavior even in high-crime environments. Second, rates of criminality and victimization do not necessarily have a negative impact on trust in the police, as long as individuals perceive that the police try to do a good job. Third, building trust in police departments battered by high criminality will take much more than improving methods and procedures. It will require some success in reducing crime levels, which is difficult to achieve in these circumstances.

In summary, trust appears to be causally related to police effectiveness in fighting crime. The data show that perceptions of adequate performance improve trust. Several police departments in Latin America are trapped in an equilibrium where they cannot gain the population's trust because they cannot serve and protect, creating a vicious cycle of growing crime and public distrust. This further reduces the police's ability to cooperate with the public in order to contain criminality. This under-examined catch-22 presents a challenge to police in Latin America (see also Bailey´s 2014 concept of "security trap"). How can poor policing and broken ties with the citizenry be reversed to improve public safety in environments of high criminality?

Crime under HCE is especially challenging because most police departments are clearly not doing a good job. As the models show, poor police performance inhibits the development of bonds and cooperation between police and citizens, further diminishing crime deterrence and creating a vicious cycle of growing crime and public distrust.

Summing-up: From Low to High Criminality

Transitions from low to high criminality produce serious deteriorations in crime deterrence. At a given point in time, delinquents consider they are less likely to get caught and that, even if they are, they might get away thanks to corruption. Several offenders in these high-crime environments completely disregard the punitive capacity of the criminal justice system. HCE requires that the primary objectives of policing be redefined.

The rudimentary information systems that effectively contained low-level crime prove fruitless for large-scale criminality. Law enforcement departments in the region failed to adapt when crime rates doubled or even tripled in just five to ten years. High rates of crime require aggressive, pro-active, and professional police departments. Strategies that once proved effective no longer work. As Braga and Weisburd (2006, 4) contend, "The police most easily adopt innovations that require the least radical departures from their hierarchical paramilitary organizational structures, continue incident-driven and reactive strategies, and maintain police sovereignty over crime issues." HCE poses challenges that police departments are not prepared to face.

Police departments are able to "tolerate" crime rings (as they did historically with gambling and prostitution) as long as these groups do not branch out into other crimes. Under this relative LCE, criminal bosses avoid violence and use it exclusively to retaliate against their rivals. Crime bosses still need to negotiate with police officers, they are even occasionally harassed by the police, and the threat of arrest remains high.

A typical example of such bargaining in many countries is the free zone or *zona liberada*, a territory (streets, neighborhoods, city squares) where police allow crime rings to commit crimes in exchange for a share of the proceeds. In a vacated free zone, police stop patrolling, ceding it to offenders for their criminal activities.[53] In most of these cases, police can re-enter the area and re-establish order, which often happens if crimes in the area make it onto the news. Such cases show that police can still impose deterrence, forcing crime rings to bargain with officers.

Organized crime succeeds when deterrence weakens. When criminal organizations operate successfully, crime deterrence collapses. To restore it, other forces (usually armed forces or foreign support) are necessary. In summary, previously corrupt police departments can impose deterrence when the scale of crime remains low. Once it reaches a high threshold, traditional law enforcement strategies cease to be effective and deterrence collapses.

8

Courts, Criminal Procedures, and Deterrence

THE DISTRICT OF Comayagua, just north of Honduras' capital Tegucigalpa, suffered 391 homicides between 2010 and 2012 (a rate of 75 per 100,000), though bodies were only recovered in 308 cases. Prosecutors successfully brought suspects to hearings in 32 cases, and 14 went to trial. The indictment rate for prosecutors was 85 percent (considering only the cases that went to court), with a 79 percent conviction rate. In short, they had impressive rates of success at hearings and trials, but suspects were only convicted in 11 out of 391 homicides (3 percent).[1]

This epitomizes a larger trend in the region: staggering impunity rates. Despite many important reforms and major investments in prosecutor offices[2] and courts, very few offenders are brought to justice. Criminal investigations are poor, the likelihood of punishment is very small, and criminal rings are rarely dismantled. This chapter studies the role of prosecutors and judges in containing criminality in Latin America and highlights their lack of effectiveness. The justice reforms implemented over the last few decades promoted transparency and reduced arbitrariness but failed to reduce crime, because poor criminal investigations had only limited impacts on public safety. This chapter analyzes the inability of courts to enhance deterrence.

In democracies, criminal courts play two important roles: first, they protect individual rights by granting due process to suspects, shielding them from state abuses. Second, they evaluate cases and determine responsibilities when crimes are committed, sanctioning those who violate the law. Both rights and sanctions are at the heart of judicial practice. Over the past two decades in Latin America, courts have moved to strengthen their role as the protectors of rights but have lagged severely in their ability to effectively punish serious offenders and dismantle criminal organizations. In the following pages, I study this double role and examine several reasons for the undermining of judicial and prosecutorial efficacy.

A central claim of this chapter is that impunity reduces deterrence, which is, of course, only effective when offenders are detected and sanctions are imposed. Prosecutors and judges have a limited role when it comes to detection but they are the cornerstone for the application of sanctions. This chapter shows that in countries with rising crime, impunity rates are also high. Deterrence has been weak because offenders, particularly crime organizers and leaders, have rarely been sanctioned. Impunity has thus reduced the ability of law enforcement agencies to deter potential criminals.

The distinction between LCE and HCE is crucial to analyzing the role of courts. In low-crime environments, balanced caseloads allow courts to punish a sizeable share of offenders, enhancing deterrence. However, when the density of offenders within a population is very large, this rate shrinks drastically, impunity rises, and deterrence diminishes. The normal impact of court sanctioning capacity under LCE does not work properly under HCE. In the following pages, I present evidence on the merits of this approach and on the radically different role courts fulfill in different crime equilibria. However, this approach should not overlook an additional problem of LCE in LATAM: many judges and prosecutors have downplayed their role as enforcers, producing high rates of impunity, and consequently criminality has also risen in countries with low crime.

In the next section, I briefly review the makeup of the judiciary, describe the salient features of criminal-law institutions, and present basic descriptive data for international comparison. This is followed by a study of the main penal justice reforms widely promoted in the region, which were, in part, directed at more effective crime fighting. I present some facts and evidence that support a cautiously pessimistic outlook on the role played by these institutions in helping to reduce crime in the region. Next, I examine the central argument on the role of sanctions and impunity within given equilibria, drawing on various data sources to show the high rates of impunity in homicides and other crimes. Under a classic Weberian approach, I contend that bureaucratic prerogatives of judges and prosecutors trumped the good intentions of reformers, and justice reforms did not deliver through on their promises.

Criminal Courts and Prosecutor Offices in Latin America

Resources, Structure, and Efficacy

Courts are broadly understood as the criminal justice institutions in charge of bringing people to justice. They encompass different organizations that may vary between countries. Here I present basic information on the administration of penal justice in the region. Since it cannot deal fully with the wide range of organizations, I concentrate on two pillars of justice: judges and prosecutors. In all Latin American countries, judges are constitutionally separated from the other two branches of government, although in practice the true level of autonomy is subject to debate (Helmke and Rios Figueroa 2011). To guarantee independence, most countries offer life tenure and salary protection for judges. In Table 8.1 the perceived level of judicial independence is assessed in column 2.

Judicial structures vary considerably between countries. For example, police detective units (*policía judicial*) could fall under the scope of the executive, prosecutor offices, or judicial branch. Similarly, several offices tied to the administration of justice could fall under different jurisdictions. For instance, morgues and forensic departments, special investigative units such as money laundering departments, environmental police, and public defense offices have different structures and organizations and report to different authorities. In terms of outcomes, structure does make a difference.

Prosecutor offices also vary. Some report to the executive while others are independent. Moreover, within offices, single prosecutors can enjoy high degrees of autonomy (including tenure and salary protection) or can be subject to dismissal by higher authorities. Prosecutors in Latin America are not elected, and therefore accountability is usually tied to institutions within the executives, the congress, or mixed commissions.

Table 8.1 summarizes the salient features of prosecution and the bench, with an evaluative dimension of autonomy and strength based on current literature and personal consultations with experts. Since the administration of justice follows the constitutional makeup of federal or centralized countries, the structure of the bench is similar to that depicted in chapter 7 for the police (Table 7.1).

Judicial efficacy depends on the courts' ability to handle cases and sentence offenders in a transparent, relatively quick, and effective way. To accomplish these goals, basic infrastructure designed to insure institutional

Table 8.1 Judges, prosecutors, and budgets in Latin America

Country	Gov. Fed or Centralized	Judges' autonomy (H, M, L)[a]	Judges (per 100,000)[b]	Judges (per 100,000)[c]	Prosecutors (per 100,000)[d]	Prosecutors (per 100,000)[e]	Cases per prosecutor[f]	Budget Variation Prosecutor (% increase)[g]	Budget (% GDP)[h]
Argentina	F	M	12.31	1.61 (06)		0.86 (06)	671	285	
Bolivia	C	L	8.45	10.3 (06)		4.08 (06)		51	1.51
Brazil	F	M–H	8.24	8.39 (09)		4.86 (04)			
Chile	C	H	7.46	50.41 (08)	3.9	3.29 (09)	2001		11.38
Colombia	C	H	9.97	9.8 (10)	7.93	8.43 (05)	231	123	5.61
Costa Rica	C	H	23.19	23.88 (11)	8.48	7.7 (07)	419	380	7.51
Ecuador	C	M–L	6.55	1.02 (04)	3.03		139	139	
El Salvador		M–L	10.53	5.36 (06)		4.78 (06)		99 (03–13)	7.11
Guatemala	C	L	4.97	0.67 (09)	8.99		277	130	5.82
Honduras	C	L	9.41					161	
Mexico	F	M	0.96	4.36 (10)			690	22 (07–09)	1.96
Nicaragua	C	M–L	7.23	1.17 (10)	4.58			N/A	
Panama	C	M	7.73	8.11 (09)	2.53		394	94	9.45
Paraguay	C	M–L	16.25			4.72 (06)		199	7.03
Peru	C	M–H	7.96	8.41 (09)	8.77	9.4 (08)	245	206	7.51

Dominican Republic	C	M–L		5.93 (09)	9.22		44	192	7.73
Uruguay	C	H		14.23	3.8				
Venezuela	F	L	6.58	6.86 (05)	2.47 (10)		277		3.83

Note: a Empty cells denote no data available. Year of the original data in parentheses. Guatemala data includes both prosecutors and assistant prosecutors. Chilean data on prosecutors updated through 2010.

Source: a Authors estimation and peer consultations.

b COMJIB: Conference of Latin American Ministers of Justice (COMJIB, 2012). *Estadísticas e Indicadores Armonizados de los Sistemas de Justicia: América Latina*, 37.

c OAS. "Judges or magistrates" mean both full-time and part-time professionals as of December 31 of a given year, authorized to rule on civil, criminal, and other cases, including appeal courts, and to establish precedence in a court of law. It also includes authorized associate judges and magistrates. Some countries with less than 100,000 inhabitants have their rates presented for comparison purposes. The rate is estimated similarly to the prosecutor rate. http://www.oas.org/dsp/Observatorio/database/indicatorsdetails.aspx?lang=es&indicator=48

d CEJA: Reporte sobre Justicias de las Américas 2008-2009, CEJA.

e OAS. A prosecutor is a government official who conducts criminal prosecutions on behalf of the state in countries with either the common law adversarial system or the civil law inquisitorial system. Rate is estimated as $PR = (TnP/TP) * 100,00$; PR = Prosecutor rate, TnP = Total number of prosecutors, TP = total population. http://www.oas.org/dsp/Observatorio/database/indicatorsdetails.aspx?lang=es&indicator=46

f CEJA (2010) Persecución de Delitos Complejos: Capacidades de los Sistemas Penales en América Latina. CEJA-JSCA. www.cejamericas.org

g CEJA (2010, 33) for all cases excluding Mexico. For Mexico, see Bergman and Cafferata (2013, 16). Period for Argentina, Bolivia, Colombia, D.R., Ecuador, Paraguay, and Peru: 2002–2008. For Costa Rica, El Salvador, Guatemala, Honduras, Nicaragua and Panama, 2005–2012.

h *Reporte sobre Justicias de la Américas 2008–2009*, CEJA.

performance is needed. Although it is hard to effectively assess this capacity (judges, prosecutors, budgets, and so on), it is clear that there is a threshold that guarantees basic performance; otherwise judicial institutions will be perceived as paper tigers. Once this threshold has been met, the question remains as to whether additional resources improve performance.

There are no good comparative data on justice officers in the region. Table 8.1 summarizes the salient features of prosecution and the bench. This data has been collected from different sources to provide the reader with descriptive information for each country. I present information on the number of prosecutors and criminal law judges per 100,000 inhabitants (a "rate" estimate) as well as budgets, however no clear pattern emerges.[3] In terms of performance, however, there is considerable variance. For example, the numbers of prosecutors and judges (per 100,000 inhabitants) in Chile are among the lowest in Latin America. Yet, Chile's judicial system has one of the best reputations in the region. On the other hand, El Salvador has a relatively high number of judges but crime rates are still very high (and presumably deterrence is low).

Analysis of this data does offer some insights. The number of reported thefts per country (drawn from Table 2.8) and the number of judges yield a correlation coefficient of 0.32, while the association for auto-thefts (Table 4.8) and numbers of judges yields a Pearson r of 0.18. Both coefficients suggest a weak positive association between caseloads and the number of judges, denoting that more judges weakly correlate with more thefts. However, the coefficients turn negative when measured by more reliable rates of criminality such as homicides (−0.20) and victimization surveys (−0.15), (crime data taken from chapter 2). Similarly, the r coefficient between judicial budgets as a percentage of total expenses and reported theft is 0.21, but it turns negative (−0.42) for victimization rate (i.e., more budgets, less victimization).[4] In short, despite the limited number of cases and incomplete information, there is no indication of a strong relationship between the allocation of resources to the judiciary and the level of criminality.

Initial indications show that countries that allocate relatively larger budgets to the judiciary and hire more officers also have lower crime rates. As Table 8.1 shows, Argentina, Paraguay, Uruguay, Costa Rica, and Nicaragua have more judges/prosecutors and/or larger budgets compared to other nations, and they also boast the lowest crime rates in the region (in this case, including Chile) lending some support to a central hypothesis of this book, that crime and the criminal justice system operate in equilibrium. Low criminality means that resources are invested more effectively, which in turn reduces crime. Conversely, countries with more crime cannot easily reverse course, suggesting that more judges and budgets will not necessarily reduce crime when criminality is very high. In short, and this is a critical first indication, it appears that the same quantity of resources has a different effect in LCE than in HCE countries. The link between resources and crime, however, is weak and probably mediated by the type of crime environment.

An International Perspective

How does the administration of penal justice in Latin America compare to other regions? Are courts and prosecutors elsewhere more effective in deterring crime? This section briefly presents comparative data on basic international performance indicators.

Individual judges and prosecutors should be evaluated by the quality of their decisions rather than the quantity of indictments and sentences. However, the productivity of the system as a whole is tied to the overall level of judicial performance. Evidence shows that countries where prosecutors press more charges and judges issue more sentences also have lower crime rates. Far from a spurious association, it appears that such intensive supervision of the criminal justice system correlates with lower the level of criminality.

Two tables of descriptive information are used to back this assertion. Data assembled by the UNODC survey (CTS), despite its numerous problems (see appendix 8.A at the end of this chapter), yield some tentative yet very intriguing results that are consistent with the hypothesis of this chapter, namely, that institutional strength does affect rates of crime, though this effect varies according to the equilibrium of each country.

Using available information, Table 8.2 depicts the number of people arrested detained or processed for suspected involvement in crimes in various regions, estimating a median rate per 100,000 (the number of countries for each region is in parenthesis). The data do not refer, strictly speaking, to individuals indicted and/or sentenced by the courts but to those who were subjected to intensive police surveillance. They reflect ". . . the total number of persons brought into contact with the police or otherwise contacted by the criminal justice system—persons

Table 8.2 **Suspects per 100,000 inhabitants (median)**

Intensive supervision		Non-intensive supervision	
North America (2)	3,300	Latin America and Caribbean (18)	700
Southern Africa (3)	2,600	Near and Middle East/South West Asia (11)	650
Oceania (2)	2,500	South Asia (5)	550
Western & Central Europe (27)	2,200	Eastern Europe (4)	500
North Africa (3)	1,000	East and Southeast Asia (9)	450
Southeast Europe (9)	800	Central Asia and Transcaucasian countries (7)	200
		East Africa (3)	180

Note: Number of countries within region in parentheses.

Source: Harrenford, Heiskannen, and Malby (2010, 32). Processed from the last available year of UNODC-CTS.

suspected, arrested or cautioned . . . excluding minor traffic offenses and other petty offences" (Harrenford, Heiskannen, and Malby 2010, 32).

Regions whose countries have a median high number of people targeted by police, indicted, and/or processed and sentenced are referred to as having intensive supervision and are placed on the left hand of the table.[5] These are also the countries with low criminality. With the exception of South Africa (where crime has been brought under control), all other regions of this group have moderate to low criminality. Regions on the right side have two different outcomes. Those that recently evolved from stable traditionalist societies (the Middle East, Southeast Asia) do not rely on strong supervision to control crime (presumably other informal social control mechanisms such as religion and social ties are at work). On the other hand, regions with low-intensity supervision have higher criminality (Latin America, Africa, and others). Medians, of course, hide significant variance within regions; they indicate, however, that active law enforcement tends to be associated with low criminality.

The Latin American median is one-fifth of the United States and Canada median, close to one-fourth that of Oceania, and one-third that of Western Europe. I underscore that Latin America is comparable to countries with very strong democracies. Some of the differences may be explained by recording disparities (Latin America departments could be underreporting) but the differences are still very significant. This supports the general assumption that low crime and effective CJSs supplement one another and operate in a virtuous circle.

A better measure of judicial activity is obtained from data on convictions. In order to compare Latin American nations with other democracies, I use CTS data on conviction rates for several countries over eight years (2003–2010).[6] Table 8.3 presents the means for each country with at least two observation years.

Latin American countries have approximately half the rate of convictions of East Asian countries. Eastern European nations have about four times the conviction rate of LATAM, and Western European countries between four to ten times the Latin American rates. In short, the number of convictions in developed countries denotes very active courts that are generally associated with low criminality. Although no clear causality is established, the data point to a strong correlation between court convictions and levels of criminality.

Ultimately, the international comparison appears to suggest that institutions and states matter. When countries are hit by crime waves, those that have strong judicial institutions have stronger resources to keep crime under control, whereas those with poor or inefficient judiciaries usually fail to contain or reduce the impact of crime.

Administration of Justice and Criminality
Criminal Procedure and Organized Crime

Justice institutions face severe challenges when they are asked to curtail criminality. Courts cannot adequately deal with large crime waves, thus yielding large impunity rates. This section introduces this conceptual dilemma.

Courts are naturally reactive institutions. Judges and prosecutors enter the scene once crimes have been committed. The goal is to identify offenders, prove their involvement, and apply the measures that seem appropriate—letting the punishment fit the crime. By its very nature, criminal law deals with individuals and not with organizations or networks. When crimes are committed, criminal law determines individual responsibilities and dictates corrective measures.

Table 8.3 Mean number of convictions per 100,000, 2003–2010

LATAM		Asia and East Europe		West Europe and Oceania	
Bolivia	31.3	Republic of Korea	574.2	Denmark	1,514.7
Chile	126.2	Malaysia	369.4	Norway	351.4
Colombia	253.9	Philippines	10.7	Finland	4,974.2
Costa Rica	141.0	Thailand	1,231.5	Sweden	1,372.3
Dominican Republic	50.9				
Ecuador	28.8	Albania	297.0	Austria	587.1
Guatemala	27.8	Belarus	842.9	France	1,266.7
Mexico	207.8	Bosnia-Herzegovina	565.2	Germany	1,100.6
Nicaragua	198.2	Bulgaria	476.4	Italy	447.2
Panama	221.6	Croatia	2,670.0	Netherlands	839.9
		Czech Republic	820.6	Portugal	773.8
		Estonia	737.9	Spain	1,389.7
		Hungary	1054.2	Switzerland	726.8
		Latvia	533.6	UK (England and Wales)	3,212.8
		Lithuania	470.6	UK (Scotland)	1,106.1
		Poland	1,474.0		
		Republic of Moldova	369.6	Australia	1,652.2
		Romania	285.8	New Zealand	2,683.7
		Russian Federation	693.5		
		Serbia	482.0		
		Slovakia	609.4		
		Slovenia	483.3		
		Ukraine	411.3		

Note: Countries with at least two yearly observations.
Source: Author estimation based on CTS 10.

Organized crime operates under a different logic. Businesses and networks that rely on threats or explicit use of violence and that generate profits by infringing the law create incentives for their members to continue breaking the law. More importantly, even though some individuals within those organizations avoid the criminal path, others are very likely to choose it. Take, for example, illegal drugs: profits are high enough to attract people to deal drugs. These dealers could be called "deviants," but the greater the potential profits, the more people will get involved. Taken to the extreme, in very large illegal markets, law breakers are not deviants but part of the norm.

The large demand-side increase of crime in Latin America, described in the first part of this book, has posed a challenge to judges and prosecutors. Courts and police were asked to contain a crime threat that has vastly exceeded their traditional scale. What worked before for a few, "deviant" cases, ceased to be effective when waves of crime, produced by the demand for illicit goods, have exploded.

Criminal law is not well-suited to dealing with large waves of criminality. Criminal law scholars will argue that crime policy, and not the courts, must effectively deal with illegal markets and the conditions that breed criminality. However, criminology in Latin America has been studied at law schools for generations, and the courts and prosecutor offices are staffed by legal specialists who are now better trained for the protection of individual rights and due process, and are not trained to fight the rising waves of crime (Zaffaroni 2005; Binder and Obando 2004).

Until very recently, organized crime was never considered a major concern.[7] During the return to democracy in the 1980s and 1990s, judges and prosecutors focused on controlling the police and keeping their abuses in check and on deterring complacency regarding crime. As a result, little effort has been made to investigate the leaders of organized crime. Executive offices entrusted with drafting crime policies were staffed by judges and prosecutors with little training or knowledge on the logistics and economic issues that are specific to organized crime. Moreover, judges and prosecutors have a natural tendency to mistrust intelligence and surveillance, usually associated with infringements on individual rights but also keys to fighting sophisticated crime networks.

In summary, the criminal law tradition in the region, along with the dominant role of lawyers and legal scholars in law enforcement agencies, has hampered the development of professional offices to fight organized crime. To face the challenges of public insecurity, the new legal establishment promoted reforms in criminal procedures. A brief review of justice reforms follows and then an assessment of their effect on controlling crime.

The New Legal Approach: Judges, Prosecutors, and Crime

Major justice reforms have been introduced across the region over the last two decades (Pasara 2014; Hammergren 1999, 2007; CEJA 2006), promising greater public security in return for social and political support. Reformers tacitly tied the need for reforms to the surge in crime assuming that criminal investigations in the hands of corrupt police departments and unaccountable executive branch offices were at the heart of the problem. They shifted the burden of criminal investigations from judges to independent prosecutors, and introduced other major reforms to further insure the protection of individual rights. After two decades, they have made significant strides in strengthening due process of law, but mostly failed in reducing criminality. Tying criminal procedure reforms to the fight against crime has been a critical mistake because it implied that the success of such reforms would be gauged by the level of public security attained.[8]

The new legislation mostly centered on empowering the prominent role of prosecutors (*fiscales*); modernizing the bench by increasing court resources; and strengthening the role of judicial investigation.[9] Strong prosecutors in adversarial rather than inquisitorial penal processes became the standard in most countries. Crime, however, does not appear to have been curtailed by these reforms. Do new courts and prosecutors make a difference?

Reforms were influenced by the political precedents in the region. The harsh legacies of authoritarianism and violations of human rights during Latin American dictatorships have refocused the role of the judiciary (Hilbnik 2007; Helmke and Rios-Figueroa 2011; Guinsburg and Moustafa 2008; Domingo and Sieder 2001). Judges, prosecutors, lawyers, and scholars questioned the passive and even permissive role of the legal establishments during military rules in which dictators had ordered killings, disappearances, and incarcerations without trials, among the many blatant violations of due process.

A critical revision of the role of justice in the protection of basic rights began soon after transitions to democracy. According to this new legal approach, judges and prosecutors were no longer seen as technical assistants to the executive but as the active protectors of individual rights (Binder and Obando 2004; Duce and Perdomo 2003; CEJA 2003). Standards of proof for conviction were raised, and sentences became more lenient.[10] While this inner revision has a welcome human-centered approach to criminal procedure, other CJS institutions have not been able to adapt. These changes increased the number of structural dysfunctions that have hindered courts' ability to stem criminality.

The financial costs of these reforms have been significant. In loans and grants from IADB (Inter American Development Bank) and the World Bank alone, the region has received US$1.5 billion dollars in aid (Pasara 2012). Foundations and foreign countries have contributed additional resources, although data on these is not available. The lion's share of these costs, however, came from national budgets, which have risen sharply since the 1990s (Bergman and Cafferata 2013; CEJA 2010). Independent prosecutorial offices, new benches, and thousands of newly hired officers have all dramatically increased budgets. For example, column nine of Table 8.1 indicates that national budgets have doubled for prosecutor offices alone, or even tripled or quadrupled in a span of six to eight years. As this chapter shows, however, the state of public security does not yet fully reflect the amount of resources invested.

Penal Justice Reforms

Reforms to justice administration have been encompassing and diverse.[11,12] They have included significant shifts in allocations of resources, changes in procedures, and new institutional designs. Each country adapted these reforms to fit their own structures and therefore outcomes varied. The following are the salient reforms that were introduced in most countries:[13]

1) *Shift from an inquisitorial to an accusatorial (adversarial) system.*[14] This reform eliminated the "instructional judge" (*juez de instrucción*) and disposed of judges' investigation duties, which were transferred to prosecutors (*fiscales*). Reforms sought a new clear division between prosecution and adjudication.[15]

2) *Oral proceedings.* Public hearings were thought to be an effective mechanism to reduce corruption and arbitrariness and to enhance transparency.

3) *Public prosecution office (Ministerio Publico Fiscal-MPF).* This became the most important institution in terms of criminal investigation and prosecution.[16]

4) *Pre-trial detention (PTD).* Reformers sought to reduce the incarceration of suspects awaiting trial.

5) *Case selection.* Prosecutors were allowed to dismiss cases and strategically concentrate on the most harmful criminals.[17] This is a critical instrument for deterrence.
6) *Alternative resolutions.* More flexible, alternative methods for solving cases, such as mediation and conciliation between the parties, were introduced.
7) *Summary judgments (speedy trials).* Different formats, sometimes including plea bargaining.
8) *Victim's role in support of prosecution (querella).* The new codes will allow victims to have a more active role in the prosecution of cases. Under the old penal procedure, only the state could prosecute suspected felons.
9) *New management offices.* It was expected that a new powerful department will introduce new managerial systems to make processes more efficient.

These reforms resulted in five major promises (goals):

1) *Reduce lapse* of time *from arrest to conviction.* To be achieved through the introduction of: a) a less formal and more flexible criminal procedure; b) new selection criteria (*criterio de oportunidad*); c) new mechanisms for solving cases through simplified procedures.
2) *Improve the quality of criminal investigations.* This should be achieved by strengthening prosecutor offices (MPF) and by concentrating on the most important cases.
3) *Reduce pre-trial detentions (PTD) and the number of inmates imprisoned without a conviction.* New regulations imposed shorter time frames for dispositions of cases. This will expected to reduce the number of people waiting for trials.
4) *Improve due process.* This would be achieved by better criminal investigations combined with stronger defense in an oral, public, and adversarial trial in front of an impartial tribunal.
5) *Augment transparency of CJS.* Public and oral hearings at the preliminary and trial phases would make the whole process more transparent, improve scrutiny of the judiciary, and reduce corruption.

To improve public safety, the most important reform was entrusting the public prosecution office (MPF—*Ministerio Publico Fiscal*) with criminal investigation—an attempt by reformers to take power away from regular police and put it under the direct supervision of prosecutors.[18]

In short, reformers sought to improve the fight against crime by introducing reforms that targeted at least three stated goals: a) By providing prosecutors with more legal discretion to decide which cases to pursue, reformers hoped to *improve case selection* and concentrate on cases with a social impact. b) By allowing prosecutors to accept plea bargaining and other settlements, a process designed to *unclog a congested system* while also concentrating on high-impact criminality. c) By empowering the prosecution offices and increasing their budgets, *criminal investigations will be better coordinated and executed.* In short, reformers clearly intended to provide prosecutors with more power and make them the central figure of crime policy.

Have Reforms Reduced Criminality?

Findings from several studies are presented here to ascertain the impact of justice reforms on crime. The evidence is rather indirect, because no studies have independently assessed the effect such reforms had on public safety in the region. The scant evidence from existing research indicates that reforms have had only a minor impact on impunity, a topic that will be examined in the following pages.

Recent research on the topic. Only a handful of studies have empirically evaluated whether justice reforms have met their goals. One study by Pasara (2014), based on a review of caseloads from Chile, Ecuador, Peru, and Costa Rica, concludes that reforms have actually kept courts from dealing with the type of cases that never got through the system anyway. Prosecutors now have the power to dismiss cases that previously slept in archives for years until their statute of limitation expired.[19] In most cases (96 percent in Ecuador) prosecutors never launched an active judicial investigation.

Case selection has not produced the desired transformations. According to Pasara, the rate of judicial resolution of crimes that resulted from active prosecution in Chile was 80 percent for homicides, 58 percent for drug offenses, and 30 percent for sexual crimes (2013, 10). Similar rates were found in Ecuador (2013, 11). Based on personal interviews with prosecutors in Chile and Costa Rica, Pasara concludes that case selection was not based on the severity of crime but on perceived likelihood of conviction, which depends on access to good evidence.

Other investigations have echoed these findings. A comprehensive study in Chile (Alacino Arellano 2013), perhaps the leading country in justice reform, examines the prosecution of complex crimes, particularly large-scale violent thefts, and is indicative of the power of inertia. In 2011, out of 110,000 robbery cases, 11,900 (10.8 percent) yielded guilty verdicts, and 1,200 not guilty (the conviction ratio for theft was 9 to 1). Most other cases (88 percent) went to the provisional archives, where they will most likely expire. There were 11,750 cases admitted to courts with alleged offenders, but 82,500 cases in which no suspects were charged. More importantly, the aggregate data indicates that in 10,200 cases, arrests were made in flagrance. In short, prosecutors processed a large number of cases of complex and violent robberies, but concentrated on those in which alleged offenders were arrested at the scene.

Through visits and in-depth interviews, Arellano shows that the overwhelming majority of serious crime investigations consist of written requests for information from prosecutors to police and responses returned without additional information. These cases lack serious forensic or expert evidence and depict very poor crime analysis. The study concludes that: 1) The prosecutor's office (MPF) does not have an effective policy or programs for pressing charges in robberies. The work of prosecutors, who mainly "push paperwork," is routine but there is no real effort to prosecute offenders. 2) There is no effective policy for caseloads. 3) There is a lack of coordination between the MPF and police departments.

In Colombia, an in-depth study of homicides, reviewing hundreds of cases in four cities (La Rota and Bernal 2014), indicates that even in the case of homicide, prosecution offices showed structural deficiencies. Between 2005 and 2012 more than 202,000 homicides were recorded but charges were only pressed in 10.4 percent of the cases, half of which ended in a guilty verdict. As in the Comayagua example given at the beginning of this chapter, there were convictions in around 5 percent of all homicides—this rate has remained stable throughout the seven years of the study. As in Chile, the authors noted such problems as a lack of institutional coordination with police and other investigative agencies, a scarcity of human and logistic resources, and a lack of incentives to solve cases other than those of special interest (media attention and political importance).

In short, although the stated goal of prosecutorial discretion was designed by reformers to minimize social harm, analysis indicates that prosecutors selected cases based on the availability of evidence (testimonies, available documentation, witnesses, and so on). There is no proof that reforms led to a better selection of crime prosecution.

Pre-trial detention. Another important goal for enhancing due process and improving the quality of criminal investigation was to abandon the practice of locking up suspects for years without a trial. Reformers lobbied heavily for the reduction of pre-trial detentions (PTD). Summary judgment (speedy trials), plea bargaining, and similar arrangements have allowed for a greater number of adjudications and have reduced timeframes (Pasara 2014; Baytelman and Duce 2003).

The goal of reducing PTD has had mixed results to date. Although there seems to have been some progress (CEJA 2011; Lorenzo et al. 2011)), I call for a more nuanced approach. Table 8.4 presents data especially assembled on PTD rates and absolute numbers for most countries before the reforms were in place and ten to fifteen years afterwards.[20] The data are mostly drawn from CEJA (2011) for the first measure, and the CIDH (*Comisión Interamericana de Derechos Humanos*, 2013) for the later measure, and completed from several other sources. Before the reforms, an average of approximately 57 percent of inmates were incarcerated as a result of PTD. Several years after the implementation of reforms, this average dropped to 47 percent. In several countries—Chile, Ecuador, Honduras, and Argentina—the reduction has been remarkable.[21] This suggests that reforms were very successful, as PTD has reduced significantly.

With the exception of Honduras, however, all countries had many more PTD inmates at the last tally. Most countries have reduced the share of PTD within the total inmate population over the past ten to fifteen years, yet there has been a significant increase in the absolute number of inmates detained without sentencing. This difference can be explained by the dramatic upswing in incarceration throughout Latin America in the past decades. The CJS is processing many more suspects yet producing lower rates of PTD because they adjudicate large number of cases faster.

This analysis confirms other studies and suggests that indeed recently there is an increasing number of inmates who are rapidly convicted. This explains why the PTD rate is declining, despite the fact that in absolute terms there are more inmates serving time without conviction due to the rise in incarceration (De la Jara et al. 2013; Pasara 2014; Vintimilla and Vallacis 2013; Duce et al. 2009; Duce 2013). PTD did not become *ultima ratio*, a last resort, but rather became the norm, an almost mechanical decision by judges. PTD has been impacted by other mechanisms promoted

Table 8.4 Pre-trial detention, before and after reforms

	Reform year	PTD numbers before reform	% on PTD	PTD numbers after reform	% on PTD	Difference in # on PTD
Buenos Aires	1997	8,164	84	16,681	59	8,517
Bolivia	1999	3,050	64	11,196	82	8,146
Brazil				193,176	38	
Chile	1999	7,994	51	11,166	21	3,172
Colombia	2004	12,256	42	35,304	31	23,048
Costa Rica	1995	326	28	3,254	25	2,928
Ecuador	1999	3,982	70	9,397	49	5,415
D.R.	2002	7,430	67	8,803	44	1,373
El Salvador	1998	4,776	72	6,452	24	1,675
Guatemala	1993	N/A	N/A	7,464	51	N/A
Honduras	1999	8,421	88	6,079	49	−2,341
Mexico	2008	6,038	38	7,584	33	1,547
Nicaragua	1999	687	31	1,192	13	505
Panama				9,439	65	
Paraguay	1996	3,192	95	5,768	73	2,576
Peru*	2004	24,798	68	34,622	59	9,824
Uruguay				6,065	65	
Venezuela	1997	12,176	69	18,843[a]	52	6,666

Notes: Empty cells denote no data available.

Numbers before reform are number of inmates one year before or during the year the reform entered into force.

The last year of inmate counts is 2012 for most countries except for the Dominican Republic (last year 2011) and El Salvador, Honduras, and Buenos Aires (last year 2013).

[a] The number and rate of inmates under PTD for last year only includes those assisted by public defense offices. Unfortunately, no other reliable information could be found. Therefore, differences with the period before reforms are far from accurate and changes between periods are underestimated.

* Data on 2006. In Peru, the reforms were implemented in phases and 21 districts had their reforms in place by 2010 when this process stopped. Four districts (Callao, Lima, Loreto and Ucalli) operate under the old penal system. Therefore, approximately 35% of inmates in 2012 were subjected to the old criminal procedure.

Source: Reform year and PTD numbers before reform: http://www.cejamericas.org/Documentos/librosvirtuales/librovirtualprisionpreventivaenamericalatina/index.html, 45–48. Inmates today and % on PTD at: CIDH at http://www.oas.org/es/cidh/ppl/informes/pdfs/Informe-PP-2013-es.pdf pp. 21–22. Mexico, 2006, Azaola and Bergman (2007,75), and Azaola, Bergman, and Magaloni (2006). Current data on Buenos Aires, SNEEP 2013. Dominican Republic, FINJUS 2012.

by reformers, namely abbreviated trials, plea bargaining, oral proceedings, and other, faster methods of adjudication. The CJS still overuses prison as a preliminary punishment. Strong proof for this claim is seen in the inmate surveys: out of the 4,500 respondents who were processed by the new adversarial proceedings, 98 percent of them were already in prison when their verdicts were secured.[22]

The impact of reforms on individuals. The inmate survey in Argentina allows for a quasi-natural experiment on the impact of reforms (Bergman and Langer 2015). Half the sample was drawn from the province of Buenos Aires, which shifted to new criminal procedures in 1998; the other half was drawn from the city of Buenos Aires and a federal jurisdiction where inmates were processed and tried under the traditional inquisitorial system.[23] In short, Argentina has two samples from otherwise very similar populations which were "treated" by different systems and criminal procedures.

The aggregated results for each jurisdiction are similar. The arrests of flagrant offenders and police abuse are slightly better for the Buenos Aires province (the reformed system), indicating that reforms may be making a slight dent, yet differences are small and not statistically significant. Nonetheless, the study indicates that prosecutors do not seem able to eradicate abuse and corruption in the police, nor has crime investigation improved qualitatively (half of all arrests are still in flagrance). In short, a natural experiment of similar populations treated by different penal procedures does not show significant differences in terms of criminal investigation, due process, corruption, and case selection for prosecution.

The special case of Mexico. Mexico presents an interesting contrast for criminal law reformers because it historically had a solid prosecutorial institution established in its 1917 constitution. Such strong prosecution offices resemble the ones Latin American penal reform sought to create, although the reform movement sought greater autonomy for the MPF than provided in Mexico. In Mexico (weak) police patrols depend directly on mayors while police investigations are carried out by (strong) detective units that report directly to prosecutors (MP) and indirectly to governors and the president. Under democracy, this system has clearly failed to protect individual rights and to impose deterrence.

Other countries do not appear to have learned from the lesson of Mexico. The MPF was the strongest institution (and within it, the judicial police), and judges usually rubber stamped accusatorial documentation (including alphabetical errors) without much scrutiny (see Pasara 2004). The system became a "sentencing machine" of (poor) people who had limited access to good legal defense. Detectives would coerce and threaten suspects to get bribes. Today, MPs in Mexico have close to 40,000 employees; 33 percent are detectives or police investigators (known as *judiciales*).[24] There are no indications that the system has changed significantly, although there is hope for the phased introduction of the 2008 constitutional justice reforms.

Summary. The penal and justice reforms pursued five main goals: 1) reducing the time of proceedings; 2) improving the quality of criminal investigation; 3) decreasing PTD; 4) enhancing due process of law; and 5) augmenting CJS transparency . The few empirical studies and the little available information, including data presented here, show mixed results. Due process has improved slightly. PTD rates have fallen due to expedited adjudication. However, no significant advances have been made in the quality and quantity of criminal investigations and control of the police. This is the critical dimension for deterrence, and so far, the available evidence indicates that reforms in this regard have failed. It remains to be seen whether these goals can be attained in the future.

Summary: The Effect of Reforms on Crime

Prosecutors and judges have not made significant advances in enhancing deterrence in Latin America. It was hoped that new penal reforms would, over the last two decades, have ushered in more effective prosecution and adjudication of crimes. However, those hopes have yet to translate into concrete measures indicating a more effective CJS. Crime is high or on the rise in most countries of the region. As we will see, impunity rates are astonishing, and offenders do not appear to be deterred by the region's justice systems. Safeguards of individual rights have indeed helped protect people from blatant abuses, but strong signs of corruption and brutality persist and inequalities in the administration of justice have not been erased. There are no good answers yet as to why all the efforts and budgets devoted to these reforms have not yielded measurable success.

This is an important question that transcends the scope of this book. It appears that several forces thwarted improvements to deterrence. First, reforms are always easier to design than to implement. Prosecutors, judges, and the large establishment that worked effectively for decades in the old system have not adapted smoothly to drastic changes. Secondly, bureaucratic inertia appears to have played a role; larger budgets that were funneled into the judicial systems to fund these reforms were absorbed by "judicial machines" shielded from public accountability. Third, a much-welcomed attention on human rights and due process inadvertently mitigated the circumstances and reversed the burden of proof on public institutions. Weak institutions (from police to forensic teams and auditing bodies) consistently failed to provide evidence for pressing charges and securing convictions. Fourth, the judicial establishment does not see itself as part of a deterrent apparatus. Although it "oversold" penal reforms as instrumental to fighting crime in order to gain public support, it has rarely considered fighting crime one of its goals. Fifth and perhaps more importantly, an inherent contradiction has developed. On the one hand, as shown by the international comparisons, the judicial surveillance of suspects and offenders requires intensive action on the part of officers of the court. On the other hand, the need to remedy past abuses has raised the standards of proof to effectively protect individual rights. This tension has produced high rates of impunity among the rich and powerful and systemic punishment of the poor and marginalized. This will be further elaborated in the rest of this chapter.

In short, the legacy of dictatorships on the one hand, and the inertial and unaccountable growing judicial establishment on the other, has inhibited the development of a powerful judicial sanctioning body that could have deterred many potential offenders. Prosecutor offices and courts have done little to reduce crime in the region.

Courts, Prosecution, and Deterrence: The Problem of Impunity

Impunity and Crime Equilibrium

The weak sanctioning capacity of criminal justice and the limited effect of penal reforms in Latin America have produced more impunity. I argue that the administration of justice in Latin America has had a low impact on states' capacities to deter offenders. Courts and prosecutors, for the most part, have failed to adjust or were not up to meeting the current challenge of high criminality.

The following pages deal with impunity and its effect on criminality. When there is a perception that large numbers of offenders go unpunished, two perverse social processes are put into motion. First, citizens are discouraged from reporting crimes to authorities because they believe that offenders, even if arrested, will enter a "revolving-door" system and be quickly freed.[25] Second, potential offenders are encouraged to follow in the footsteps of other delinquents who have already committed crimes since they perceive that the CJS dog might be "all bark but no bite." Impunity enhances contagion. Once rates of crimes in Latin America reach a critical level, the efficacy of the penal system severely diminishes and a larger sense of impunity spreads, endogenously nourishing a vicious and perverse equilibrium of high criminality.

Homicides and impunity. Unsolved homicides in Comayagua, Honduras and in Colombia epitomize a trend throughout the region. Very large rates of impunity persist even for the most serious crimes, with relentless prosecution in the few cases that produced arrests. With the exception of Chile, where 1,245 cases out of 1,545 homicides resulted in conviction (80 percent) in 2009,[26] all other countries in LATAM had a homicide conviction rate of 50 percent or less.

Several studies in the region confirm this pattern. In Argentina, a study by the supreme court has found that only 46 percent of homicides end with at least one conviction (SNIC 2008). As mentioned before, in Colombia less than 12 percent of homicides have resulted in a criminal conviction over a six-year period (La Rota and Bernal 2014). In Mexico, Zepeda estimates that less than 16 percent of homicides committed in 2010 have been solved (Zepeda 2013).[27] In Venezuela, the *Observatorio Venezolano de la Violencia* estimated that just 9 percent of homicides resulted in at least one arraignment (OVV 2014).[28] In Guatemala, between 2005 and 2013, there was an average of 5,500 victims of homicides per year, and 3.1 percent of cases, on average annually, reach convictions.[29]

Imperfect data from prison entries in Peru and Brazil yield similar results. In Peru, I estimate that less than 35 percent of those who commit homicide were sanctioned.[30] For Brazil, although I could not find any official rate on impunity, prison data allow me to estimate an impunity rate of over 80 percent for homicides.[31] Although it is very likely that there are significant variations among states within Brazil, the actual rate cannot be estimated from the available public records. In summary, most countries in the region cannot bring to justice the vast majority of murderers, who commit the most serious crime of all.

Available data at the state level in Mexico shows another very important pattern: the greater the number of homicides, the higher the rate of impunity. The five states in Mexico which had the highest impunity rates for homicide in 2010 (Durango 0.75 percent, 66 per 100,000; Chihuahua 1.1 percent, 182 per 100,000; Sinaloa 1.7 percent, 85per 100,000; Morelos

1.9 percent, 27 per 100,000; Guerrero 2.1 percent, 45 per 100,000) are also among the seven Mexican states with the highest rates of homicides.[32] I correlated state homicides rates and impunity rates for the thirty-two states of Mexico and reached a strong Pearson r of −0.65, implying that the higher the homicide rate, the lower the conviction rate.

Other available data for Mexico supports a hypothesis raised in this book: enforcement is tied to the crime equilibrium. For the whole country, I tracked the number of homicides and the number of convictions for homicides over fifteen years (Fig. 8.1), showing that as the number of homicides rose the number of convictions either stayed the same or even decreased. (The scale of the chart might obscure the real magnitude of this very important trend.) In 2005 there were 9,921 homicides and 6,372 convictions, and in 2011 there were 27,213 homicides and 5,487 convictions. While homicides increased by 174 percent, convictions decreased by 15 percent. In short, as the theory predicts, in high-crime environments the courts' ability to sanction offenders decreases. This diminishes deterrence and furthers a vicious cycle of high criminality and less punishment.

In sum, impunity rates are closely associated with homicides. The rate of sanctions appears to correlate with this lethal crime.

Crimes for profit. Impunity in property crime is much higher than in homicides. Original data from surveys and other sources is presented here to show that the CJS in the region has been very effective at convicting easy-to-detect felons but has lagged in its capacity to punish serious

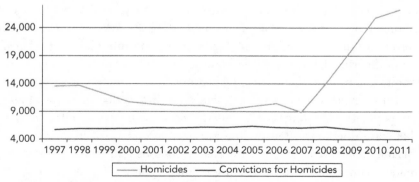

FIGURE 8.1 Homicides and convictions in Mexico.
Source: Inegi (see footnote 34).

offenders, indirectly producing high impunity rates. Take, for example, Chile, where a 2011 study estimated that 85 percent of violent theft convictions were flagrant offenses. The penal courts have processed 14,778 cases of violent thefts with at least one identifiable perpetrator, which represent less than 5 percent of all violent theft (Alcaino Arellano 2013, 48). Prosecutors and courts are mostly reactive, as indicated, they sanction easily identifiable offenders.

Most cases that are prosecuted are selected based on the collected evidence, and many are thrown out of court because they are considered *delitos de bagatela* or trifling (thefts of cell phones, bicycles, and so on). Considered separately, they are indeed trifling, but as I have argued throughout this book, thefts like these supply large secondary markets. There are no indications of any serious efforts to indict repeat offenders over occasional thieves, and more importantly, there are no indications that arrests of larceny offenders serve as a springboard to investigate the middle- or high-ranking organizers that supply these markets.[33] In short, prosecutors apparently do not use these weak links of the chain to go after crime-ring leaders.

In the following pages, I use data from the inmate surveys to show the ineffectiveness of arrests and the prosecution of inmates who committed for-profit crimes, and then analyze how this might have affected deterrence. I present data on current convictions along with self-reports of past involvement in crime.

Past criminal involvement. Offenders in the region feel relatively "safe" when they commit crimes. This sense of impunity is especially noteworthy in property offenses. The inmate surveys show that arrested offenders committed a large number of crimes before they were apprehended.[34] Approximately 50 percent of respondents acknowledge previous involvement in similar offenses.[35] Delinquents commit a large number of for-profit crimes, but more importantly, this number indicates a high impunity rate prior to their current detention.[36]

Initial evidence presented in Table 8.5 indicates that there are at least two populations among those arrested: 1) occasional thieves or drug dealers that committed few offenses, and 2) repeat offenders, or in the words of Pasara, the *habituales*, who committed numerous crimes and presumably made a career out of drug dealing or theft. These rates, as footnote 36 explains, should be thought of as a threshold or a baseline.

Table 8.5 Crimes committed before current arrest

	Argentina	Brazil	Chile	El Salvador	Mexico	Peru
Average number of thefts six months prior to arrest (median in parentheses)	21 (7)	17 (6)	44 (14)	10 (2)	47 (5)	17 (5)
Drugs: % of inmates who sell or transported drugs more than once a week (% per day in parentheses)	54 (32)	73 (55)	54 (32)	N/A	83 (0)	44 (20)
Average monthly sales per person (in US$)	1,273	6,435	5,110	69	1,4626	402

Question (author translation): "Approximately how many times have you been involved in thefts (or drug sales/transport) during the six months prior to your arrest?"

Source: Inmate Surveys 2013.

Drug dealers report heavily engaging in drug trafficking before their arrest. More than half profited from drug deals at least once a week, and in Argentina, Chile, and San Pablo, Brazil, at least a third did so daily. Average monthly proceeds are very large but the more accurate median value denotes that, excluding a handful of large drug traffickers, the small or medium-size dealers are the ones who get arrested.[37] Similarly, among those who report previous engagement in property crimes, the average for the six months prior to arrest suggests heavy involvement (I insist, this should be seen as baseline). Interestingly, in countries or states with low crime rates (Chile, Argentina, Sao Paulo, and Peru) the ratio between mean and median is about three; for El Salvador, it is five; and for Mexico, it is almost ten. It is probably more difficult to arrest habitual offenders in HCE than in countries with lower crime rates. In other words, the CJS can more effectively target high-frequency offenders under LCE.

Current crime. An indirect measure of judicial performance is the convictions that prosecutors seek and the verdicts judges render. The inmate surveys provide novel information on the crimes that led to guilty sentences. The data confirms that most offenders committed crimes of little value. Although the averages are somewhat high, the median clearly suggests that the overwhelming majority of property and drug crime offenders are not leaders of crime organizations. For the whole sample, a crime for profit that was valued at US$10,000 represents the 79th percentile for property crime offenders, and the 86th percentile for drug crime offenders.[38]

Only 113 individuals (1.8 percent of the sample) committed crimes worth US$100,000 or more. Analyzed by type of crimes, less than 1 percent of property-crime offenders, 6 percent of drug dealers, and 12 percent of kidnappers have committed crimes with proceeds greater than US$100,000. As Tables 8.6 and 8.7 show, Chile has a higher share of inmates who committed crimes of high economic value, while this share is much lower in Peru and Mexico. Chile appears to concentrate on slightly more serious offenders while the other two have a larger share of low-end delinquents.

High-value crimes (HVC) usually result in harsher sentences. The mean length of sentences for HVC in this sample was 14.2 years (median 10 years), while the average length for crimes valued at less than US$100,000 was 9.8 (median of 7.1).[39] Since this is an estimate based on stock and not on flow, the number of HVC processed by the CJS during a given year is even lower. In effect, this sample includes 952 individuals who were arrested in 2011 and 990 in 2010. Only 21 (2.2 percent) in 2011, and 14 (1.5 percent) in 2010 were convicted for crimes whose value exceeded US$100,000.[40] In short, this evidence suggest that judges and prosecutors seek convictions of delinquents whose crimes exceed US$100,000 in less than 3 percent of the total number of cases they process in a given year.

In summary, the survey data show that the judges and prosecutors do not target HVC or even moderate offenders. Although more than half of the inmates serve time for crimes for profit, they usually have committed crimes with a relatively low market value. It is at least puzzling how countries facing grand larceny, major drug crimes, and kidnappings are managing to capture only the small fish.

Table 8.6 Value of offense that resulted in conviction (in US$)

		Theft value	Drug value	Ransom value (kidnapping)
Argentina	Mean	12,912.76	39,585.95	55,290.59
	Median	2,546.74	1,320.53	10,823.65
	N	341	38	14
Chile	Mean	23,532.08	40,919.17	86,058.21
	Median	2,107.55	3,512.58	86,058.21
	N	388	102	2
Brazil	Mean	30,601.56	40,429.60	38,876.68
	Median	2,889.69	343.24	22,203.65
	N	236	141	7
El Salvador	Mean	466.42	863.99	2,075.35
	Median	34.95	16.69	959.96
	N	113	98	19
Mexico	Mean	14,681.28	137,768.67	267,757.59
	Median	878.95	311.67	18,926.63
	N	724	22	58
Peru	Mean	36,131.43	328,040.49	3,888.30
	Median	692.78	1,800.00	1,800.00
	N	387	109	8
Total	Mean	20,746.13	103,897.37	153,983.64
	Median	1,273.37	429.06	7,570.65
	N	2,189	482	110

Question: What is the amount (in today's currency) the authorities claim you made (from robbery, drug sale or kidnapping) or attempted to make? (Amounts were converted to US dollars at the current exchange rate of year of arrest.)

Source: Author elaboration from Inmate Surveys.

Table 8.7 Share of inmates committing high-value crimes within each country

	Argentina	Chile	Brazil	Mexico	Peru
% more than 10K	23.2	29.7	24.8	21.5	15.5
% more than 100K	4.1	6.9	6.5	3.4	3.2

Source: Author elaboration from inmate surveys.

Corruption. Another factor that enhances impunity is corruption, which also helps delinquents to escape sanctions. Miscreants that frequently engage in crime believe that they can get away with if they are willing to bribe police and/or court officers. As Table 7.6 in chapter 7 showed, 28 percent of inmates in Argentina, 45 percent in Mexico and 37 percent in Peru reported having been asked for a bribe from law enforcement agents. In contrast, that rate is much lower in Chile, only 13 percent. Given these rates of corruption, it is plausible that countless offenders have escaped arrest and punishment because they were able to bribe authorities, particularly those who commit HVC and had the means to escape prosecution and conviction. In short, corruption contributes to high levels of impunity.

Summary. Impunity in Latin America is very high, and is associated with high levels of criminality. Prosecutors and judges bring to justice relatively few offenders, and mostly those who are easily arrested. It appears that little progress has been made in effectively disbanding criminal networks. Deterrence is weak because few offenders are detected and sanctioned, and those who are, are easily replaced by new cadres of offenders, while leaders and organizers of crime networks have been able to dodge the CJS. The evidence presented here supports the hypothesis that poor deterrence is associated with CJS underperformance.

Conclusion

Latin American justice systems face a critical dilemma: how to improve public safety when the scale of crime continues to grow. The double equilibrium approach taken in this book provides a partial response. The reactive nature of the CJS produces inertia and low productivity. It is moderately suited for LCE but collapses entirely under HCE. In a few exemplary cases, successful prosecution can enhance deterrence when the scale of crime is low, but contagion and diminishing law enforcement capacities yield poor results in high-crime environments. In short, the traditional role of judges and prosecutors suits environments when delinquents can be considered deviants—a few outliers in an otherwise broadly compliant citizenry.

HCE poses a difficult challenge. When the number of offenders is very large and growing, a reactive approach to crime ceases to be effective. Law enforcement must be aggressively pursued, forcing judges and prosecutors to undertake measures that sometimes jeopardize the protection of individual rights. They have been trained to react, to evaluate a case, and to make judgments based on individual responsibilities. Organized crime, large-scale criminality, and corrupted institutions operate under a different logic, whereby illegal markets, established rackets of offenders, and powerful organizations consolidate before judges and prosecutors can get a case to court. That is why the poor—or the last link of the chain—bear the brunt of prosecution. These are the cases that clog the courts but do not address the challenge posed by criminal networks. Organized crime easily takes advantage of these ineffective judicial systems.

The few situations in which crime has significantly diminished (Bogota and Medellín, Colombia; Rio de Janeiro and San Pablo, Brazil; Ciudad Juarez, Mexico) can be explained by either a natural decrease from an abnormal epidemic crime rate (Medellin's homicide rate of 300 per 100,000 in the mid-1990s is so abnormal that some initial pacification measures will naturally lead to an astonishing reduction, in a process similar to what happened in some states of Mexico), or by aggressive and active law enforcement (combined with other social policies) where not only police but judges and prosecutors actively intervene.

Finally, this chapter has shown clearly that prosecutors and judges have indicted and sentenced overwhelmingly underpriviledged and poor offenders. This "conviction machine" mostly targets the underclass and has failed to strike any serious blows to crime organizers, large predatory offenders, or powerful culprits. Why do they continue with such a weak policy? Why no changes have been made to this "conviction machine" in spite of its meager achievements? Why does deterrence matter so little? These might be subjects for another study. I suggest an answer that lies within a Weberian framework. Criminal prosecution offices and tribunals formed a strong judicial bureaucracy that received significant resources, especially after returns to democracy, and tenured well-paid positions that required very little in terms of productivity. In the name of individual rights, countries opted not to make judges or prosecutors accountable for their decisions. In short, power and resources were handed over without much accountability. A typical failure of Latin American states.

Appendix 8.A Adults convicted of crime (per 100,000)

	2003	2004	2005	2006	2007	2008	2009	2010
Dominican Republic			42.4	59.3				
Costa Rica	135.5	149.9	127.7	122.7	124.3	124.9	156.9	186.1
Guatemala		13.1	24.7	24.6	26.6	37.0	40.5	
Mexico	216.9	218.9	218.1	208.0	208.7	2,03.0	196.0	192.9
Nicaragua								198.2
Panama			184.3	194.7			285.8	
Bolivia			29.0	33.6				
Chile	232.2		47.8	95.9	122.0	129.5	129.2	127.0
Colombia		335.1	243.7		277.5	238.8	217.1	210.9
Ecuador	28.5	29.0						
Republic of Korea	544.1	585.7	544.3	503.9	551.5	603.8	686.2	
Malaysia			348.7	390.0				
Philippines			10.7	10.6				
Thailand			1,202.6	1,260.4				
Belarus	760.8	874.9	925.4	924.4	839.9	816.7	758.0	583.0
Bulgaria	390.0	410.9	427.0	433.8	439.2	525.7	601.4	816.7
Czech Republic		790.0	764.7	798.5	888.3	858.7	827.2	
Hungary	1,075.7	1,129.2	1,120.7	1,109.1	997.8	959.3	987.9	

Poland	1,399.7	1,713.8	1,670.6	1,522.5	1,392.6	1,365.2	1,339.3	1,388.3
Republic of Moldova	547.5	388.0	432.7	394.1	322.6	245.4	257.1	
Romania	406.5	364.9	339.2	289.5	234.4	188.8	177.5	
Russian Federation		608.5	677.7	715.3	726.4	729.7	714.6	682.3
Slovakia	593.8	589.9	608.5	565.4	582.7	610.0	659.1	665.6
Ukraine	474.2	482.3	420.2	387.8	374.4	362.7	366.8	421.9
Estonia	566.9	908.9						
Finland	4,688.9	5,040.8	5,099.6	5,008.6	5,490.3	5,364.7	4,568.6	4,532.3
Iceland	1,135.8	1,141.3						
Latvia	634.0	616.0	534.5	471.6	490.2	524.8	522.2	475.3
Lithuania	574.8	515.7	471.7	438.1	422.1	429.7	436.2	476.3
Denmark	1,517.1	1,618.7	1,703.9	1,609.5	1,311.6	1,354.0	1,488.0	
Norway	357.6	332.9	404.1	372.4	350.9	330.2	308.1	355.0
Finland	4,688.9	5,040.8	5,099.6	5,008.6	5,490.3	5,364.7	4,568.6	4,532.3
Sweden	1,294.9	1,286.9	1,289.6	1,319.7	1,357.7	1,448.2	1,516.9	1,464.2
United Kingdom (England and Wales)	3,402.9	3,515.7	3,340.0	3,178.6	3,134.8	3,009.4	3,109.4	3,011.3
United Kingdom (Scotland)	1,007.5	1,099.8	1,077.7	1,159.0	1,165.5	1,152.7	1,100.8	1,085.6
Albania	280.0	304.9	297.1	304.7	256.9	338.4		
Bosnia and Herzegovina				604.3	588.2	532.7	558.1	542.7

(Continued)

Appendix 8.A Continued

	2003	2004	2005	2006	2007	2008	2009	2010
Croatia	643.8	668.2	608.2	676.4	682.0	674.0	707.0	680.3
Italy	451.5	489.8	448.8	398.7				
Portugal	724.4	712.8	683.2	709.8	853.7	902.6	802.2	802.0
Serbia			484.6	543.5	505.9	548.4	529.7	280.0
Slovenia	417.2	488.1	469.4	490.4	521.6	522.2	478.1	479.7
Spain				460.0	479.3	603.9	632.8	603.3
Austria	592.6	637.3	645.3	607.6	596.5	520.7	509.4	
France	1,117.0	1,172.4	1,226.1	1,303.0	1,338.0	1,333.2	1,325.4	1,318.1
Germany	1,016.0	1,063.7	1,064.8	1,017.0	1,217.6	1,183.8	1,140.1	1,101.9
Netherlands	906.9	919.8	872.4	870.8	904.7	794.9	796.1	653.6
Switzerland	1,361.6	643.8	641.6	643.1	583.6	624.1	649.7	666.8
Australia	1,443.9	1,443.9	1,484.0	1,505.9	1,795.6	1,818.1	1,790.8	1,727.2
New Zealand	2,567.2	2,587.4	2,483.9	2,543.8	2,705.3	2,686.1	2,989.7	2,906.1

Empty cells denote no data available.

Source: https://www.unodc.org/unodc/en/data-and-analysis/statistics/data.html

9

The Sad Story of Prisons

A BALANCE OF FAILURES

Introduction

The Latin American inmate population has tripled over the last twenty-five years, but despite mass incarceration in every country in the region, crime has continued to grow. This chapter examines the role of prisons in Latin America and their limited effectiveness at containing crime and deterring would-be offenders. It describes the failure of rehabilitation, deterrence, and incapacitation, and argues that prisons have been subverted by the use of a "just desert" policy that backfires when inmates are released out onto the streets and return to crime. I use survey data to depict the high rates of turnover at Latin American prisons and to show the link between inmates and outside crimes, the high rates of recidivism, and many other indicators of poor correction policies.

Analyses and narratives of life inside prisons in the region have been the focus of many excellent pieces and reports (Carranza 2012; Economist 2012; Macauley 2006, 2013; Antillano et al. 2015; CELS 2011; Salla et al. 2009; IBA 2010; Ungar 2003). Prison conditions, the protection of prisoner rights, rehabilitation policies, re-entry, and stigma, as well as many other important features of prisons in the region are very important research topics that have analyzed elsewhere (Bergman et al.2015). This chapter will instead focus on three distinctive features. First, the particular makeup of the prison population in the region and how it has affected the type of criminality that developed in Latin America. Second, the role played by corrections as a key component of the criminal justice systems in the region. Finally, the impact prison has on suppressing crime and whether or not prisons in the region have reached the goals of imprisonment, particularly in terms of deterrence and incapacitation. In summary, I survey both the role of prisons in society and how they have affected crime in Latin America.

Ultimately, I argue that in contexts of high criminality, corrections increasingly fail society in terms of deterrence and incapacitation. In other words, corrections might be more effective as an instrument for deterrence when the scale of crime is low and when the number of deviants is small. Conversely, when crime is systemic, when the incentives for crime grow, the marginal effect of rising incarceration decreases. This is because offenders are easily replaced by a new cadre of delinquents, and prison exits (after the initial wave of incarceration) put inmates back on streets who are now more dangerous, making social integration more difficult. In this chapter I argue that high rotation of inmates and the replacement of newly incarcerated low-level offenders by a new cadre of robbers, muggers, and dealers have prevented incapacitation policies from reducing criminality. Rather than controlling crime, corrections appear to solidify crime networks, forming an army of ex-offenders ready to re-offend once they are released. Instead of rehabilitating offenders, prisons seem to be merely transit zones between active delinquency periods.

The following section provides an overview of the growth in prisons in the region and several features of Latin American inmate populations. The third section uses survey findings and official statistics to evaluate the rehabilitation, deterrence, and incapacitation effect on crime in the region. The fourth section summarizes the arguments, presents an overall explanation for the shortcomings of recent correction policies in the region, and highlights the main thesis to account for the failure of mass incarceration to deter crime.

Mass Incarcerations and the Makeup of Prison Populations in Latin America

The rise in violence and drug trafficking in the region was met by a harsh response. As waves of thefts and violence overtook the region, the CJS responded by putting more people behind bars.

Incarceration—A Growing Trend

In 1992 there were 408,154 inmates (95.7 per 100,000) of Latin American prisons. By 2013, this number had risen steadily at a yearly average of

11.3 percent to 1,311,823 (227 per 100,000). If the pace of growth continues at a similar rate, more than 4,000,000 individuals are expected to be behind bars in the region by 2025.[1]

As Table 9.1 shows, most countries in the region experienced a noticeable boost in the number of people behind bars in just a few years. With the exception of two countries (Bolivia and Nicaragua), all others have reached rates of more than 150 inmates per 100,000, with most exceeding 200 per 100,000.

Approximately half of the inmates are in PTD (Pre trial Detention), that is, awaiting sentence or trial, and these inmates are usually housed in the same facilities as those who have already been sentenced. The PTD rate varies, with high rates in Paraguay (75 percent) and Venezuela (68 percent) contrasting with that of Costa Rica (17 percent) or Brazil (38 percent).[2] The percentage of people detained without firm sentences is very high in Latin America, although the rate is declining, a feature that will be further analyzed later.

Table 9.1 Changes in prison population

Countries	Circa 2002	Circa 2012	Dif (% increase)
Argentina	41,008	61,192	49
Bolivia	6,065	14,771	144
Brazil	239,345	5480,03	129
Chile	36,416	45,960	26
Columbia	52,936	113,884	115
Costa Rica	6,571	14,830	126
Ecuador	8,723	23,178	166
El Salvador	11,055	26,486	140
Guatemala	8,100	16,877	108
Honduras	11,502	12,263	7
Mexico	165,637	230,943	39
Nicaragua	5,109	8,846	73
Panama	10,423	14,990	44
Paraguay	4,519	9,332	107
Peru	27,417	61,390	124
Dominican Republic.	8,723	24,744	184
Uruguay	5,630	9,829	75
Venezuela	19,368	48,262	149

Source: Author elaboration based on Alertamerica.org.

Table 9.2 Prison populations in LATAM

Countries	% PTD	Juveniles (% total population)[a]	Females (% total population)	Rate per 100,000	Occupancy level (%, based on official capacity)
Argentina	50.9		4.4	160	103
Bolivia	85.4	12.9[b]	14.7	122	269
Brazil	38.3		6.4	301	154
Chile	29.6	0.4[c]	7.6	247	111
Columbia	35.6		6.9	244	155
Costa Rica	17.2	1.6	5.8	352	139
Ecuador	48.8	3.1	7.7	162	115
El Salvador	26.2		9.7	492	325
Guatemala	48.6	4.6	9.1	121	270
Honduras	51.8		4.3	196	189
Mexico	42.1	14.0	5.2	212	126
Nicaragua	12.3	0.6	5.4	171	128 (2010)
Panama	62.5		6.9	392	112
Paraguay	75.1	3.1	7.2	158	163
Peru	50.5	1.4[b]	5.9	242	226
Dominican Republic.	56.5	2.3	2.5	233	286
Uruguay	69.4	6.8[d]	5.8	291	109
Venezuela	68.4		5.9	178	270

Empty cells denote no data available.

[a] Minors are usually confined in separate facilities under a different legal authority. In many countries, the corrections authority does not have data on juvenile offenders and as a result, these rates are probably inaccurate.

[b] Under 21.

[c] In closed prisons.

[d] estimated rate of juveniles detained under other authority as a share of total number of arrestees. 2014: Argentina, Bolivia, Brazil, CR, Dominican Republic, Ecuador, Honduras, Paraguay, Venezuela. 2015: Chile, Colombia, El Salvador, Guatemala, Panama, Peru, Mexico, Bolivia, Uruguay.

Source: Author elaboration based on ICPS (2015), UNDP (2013).

The following are several features of prison populations in the region:

Gender. As in many countries worldwide, females account for approximately 5 percent of the inmate population (see Table 9.2). Most women are serving time for one of two felonies: homicide and non-violent drug crimes such as transporting or selling drugs from their homes. Over the last few years, the number of women arrested for property crimes has also increased. In several countries, women are allowed to live in prisons with children aged three and under; in a few correction facilities, children can live with their mothers until the age of five or six.

Distribution by type of felony. Males serving time for theft account for approximately 40 percent of the inmate population in the region. Drug-crime offenders account for 20 percent; murderers, for less than 20 percent.[3] Homicide and rape usually carry longer sentences, while thieves and drug offenders serve shorter sentences.[4] This creates two different populations within the same correctional facility: those who rotate rapidly and are mostly low-risk offenders, and another more stable population, usually very violent and high-risk offenders, that organize in gangs and sometimes exert coercive power over other inmates within the facilities, particularly on those whose day of release approaches, but also on gang and rackets members outside prison. As I will explain later, this has profound implications for criminality in the region.

Overcrowding. Prison conditions are very poor in Latin America. Many studies have documented problems of overcrowding and the lack of basic services such as drinking water, sheets, and adequate sleeping conditions, as well as material deprivations (Azaola and Bergman 2009; Antillano et al. 2015; Bergman et al. 2015; Carranza 2012). According to ICPS (2015), the official capacity of prison systems in the majority of the countries has reached critical levels. Table 9.2 shows that except for Argentina and perhaps Chile, Panama, and Uruguay, Latin American prisons are severely overcrowded. Most penitentiary systems have very precarious types of rehabilitation, including inadequate programs for education, prison work, and vocational training. Most countries have implemented policies of mass incarceration without making any significant investments in infrastructure or rehabilitation in order to provide adequate quarters and conditions for large numbers of incoming offenders. This has resulted in a total collapse of prison systems in some countries (Honduras, Guatemala, and Venezuela) where services have deteriorated and gangs have significant control over daily life inside prisons. In other countries, prisons are still functional but in very poor condition (Chile, Argentina, or Uruguay). This chapter will provide tentative explanations for such disparities.

Length of sentences. Prison sentences in Latin America are relatively lenient when compared to those in developed countries or Asian nations. Capital punishment has been entirely abolished, and even inmates who have committed first degree murder rarely serve more than twenty years in prison. The inmate survey provides data on sentencing—though covering just six countries, given its diversity, these distributions can be considered representative for the entire region. The average sentence for inmates convicted for homicide was nineteen years; for rape, thirteen; for theft, eight; and for drug crimes, seven.[5] Most inmates do not serve their entire sentence and a large majority are released after serving half to two-thirds of their sentence.[6] In short, after several years in correctional facilities, most inmates will re-enter society, some at a very young age, and even after committing violent crimes (Table 9.3).

Pretrial Detention

Many inmates in Latin America are locked in prisons awaiting trial. Constitutionally, individuals indicted for crimes are innocent until proven otherwise in court. Two considerations can lead judges to decide otherwise: first, the presumption that the suspect could tamper with evidence and witnesses, and second, the risk that the defendant will not show up for trial. Judges very often decide that perceived dangerous offenders who might sabotage the collection of evidence should await trial in prison. This practice has created controversy in judicial circles throughout the region because PTD has been the norm rather than the exception for years.

In most countries in LATAM, between 35 and 65 percent of prison inmates are in PTD (Table 9.2), although this rate has been declining.[7]

Table 9.3 Median length of sentence (years) grouped by type of crime

Crime	Argentina	Brazil	Chile	El Salvador	México	Peru	Mean
Theft	6	6	5	8	7	8	6
Homicide	12	20	10	30	32	13	21
Drug Trafficking/ Possession	4	5	5	7	6	9	6
Sexual Crimes	10	12	10	14	10	10	12
All	7	7	6	14	10	10	9

Source: Inmate Surveys.

As Table 8.8 in chapter 8 shows, this reduction is due to the accelerated proceedings introduced by recent justice reforms in the region over the past two decades, which facilitated plea bargaining and other speedy trial arrangements. More importantly, as the share of inmates awaiting trials has declined, the total number of individuals remanded in custody has grown, because of the massive increase in incarceration, and the number of new entries into the correction system has outpaced the number of cases adjudicated.

The share of PTD in the region also results from a high turnover of inmates. Ceteris paribus, longer sentences produce larger stocks of inmates. Therefore, prisons with a high turnover of inmates will naturally house a proportionally high share of inmates awaiting trial compared to those that house a larger share of permanent offenders serving longer sentences. Based on this assumption, the larger rotation of inmates in the region will endogenously produce higher rates of inmates under PTD.

In many countries around the world, detainees awaiting trial are locked up in special remand facilities, such as local jails, and specially designed confinement centers to avoid mixing them with convicted felons. This has rarely been the case in Latin America. The overwhelming number of prison facilities in the region house pretrial detainees and sentenced offenders together. This has accelerated the integration of new entries with established organized groups and gangs. As the newcomers outpaced those exiting the systems, most prison facilities have rapidly become overcrowded. Although new prisons have been built and new personnel hired, these processes have not kept up with the number of prison entries. As a result, not only are most prison systems in the region over capacity, dozens of prisons across LATAM house several thousands of inmates,[8] including a large share of inmates awaiting trials. This has led to deteriorating prison conditions, reduced the effectiveness of correctional officers, and exacerbated the criminogenic trends of corrections in the region. In short, housing pretrial detainees with sentenced inmates has had a number of negative external effects on crime and human rights in the region.

Flow or Stock?

The median age for the entire inmate sample of the six survey countries is thirty-three. The median age in US correctional facilities is thirty-seven (BJS 2014). While 34.7 percent of the inmates were under twenty-nine in the Latin American sample, only 27.3 percent of the inmate population is under that age in the United States (BJS 2014). The four-year difference in the median age and the larger share of inmates under thirty years means that in Latin America the inmate population is significantly younger than in the United States. Age is known to be a strong predictor of active criminality since involvement in crime is highly age dependent. These differences have important implications and reveal distinctive patterns of Latin American prison growth.

Age is one of many indications that the Latin American prison increase is related to a larger flow of inmates into the system. In effect, admissions arising from new commitments by US courts represented 24 percent of the total inmate population last year. There is no comparable data for Latin American countries, though 29 percent of the inmates from the survey sample have been sentenced within the last twelve months. Therefore, it is very likely that the rate of new admissions as a share of the inmate population is larger in Latin American than in the United States.

Over the past two decades, offenders have faced tougher sentences due to new laws and harsher judges. Latin American authorities became receptive to the "tough on crime" claims from the median voter. Despite this move to impose more time behind bars, sentences are still shorter than in the United States. The median length of sentences for the six countries where the surveys were conducted is nine years. Moreover, actual time served is usually two-thirds of the sentence (six years). On the other hand, the local prison systems in the region have relatively few prisoners serving extremely long sentences. This contrasts with US states such as California, where 55.3 percent of state prisoners are serving enhanced mandatory sentences and even life or death sentences (convicted for two and three strikes, serving life with or without parole, and even awaiting death sentences) (BJS 2014).

In summary, Latin American corrections have a significant share of very young inmates. Sentences lengths are moderate and inmates are conditionally released from prisons after serving just a fraction of their sentences. But the ratio of admissions to total prison population appears to be high. Thus, the evidence indicates that Latin American corrections have a high turnover of inmates. As many are released, more young people are admitted for the first time. Prison growth thus results from a large number of admissions and releases rather than from fewer admissions and longer sentences. In summary, the rise of the Latin American inmate population is derived from flow rather than from stock growth, particularly when compared to the US incarceration trend. As this chapter will show, high turnover has very important implications for the rise in crime in the region.[9]

Prison Growth and Crime

Prison growth has not produced the intended goal of reducing crime in Latin America. Initial evidence shows that countries whose inmate population rose significantly have also experienced high crime rates. Causality, however, is hard to establish with aggregate data. More crime naturally produces larger prison populations and it is thus necessary to isolate the effect of imprisonment rates on crime rates. There are no good studies with standard aggregate data that can estimate to what degree imprisonment actually prevents crime.[10]

Criminologists have addressed the question of whether prisons have any impact on crime (see next section "Corrections and Crime"). Current evidence from Latin America shows that a rapid rise in imprisonment rates positively correlates with more violent thefts and drug violations. Despite the absence of data to effectively test for counterfactuals, there is a clear association between prison growth and crime. Supporters of mass incarceration might argue that without it, crime would have increased even more. Although it is difficult to test this argument, this chapter will provide enough evidence to support the claim that crime appears to increase in the region when more people are incarcerated. Imprisonment, in other words, appears to be criminogenic.

In examining the impact of prison on crime in the region, I start by providing a brief overview of the goals of corrections, and then evaluate, using data from the region, whether corrections have attained, at least partially, their stated goals.

Corrections and Crime

Prisons can serve different goals. The literature (Blumstein 1995; Tonry and Petersilia 1999) recognizes four basic purposes of imprisonment: retribution, deterrence, rehabilitation, and incapacitation. Retribution refers to people's sense of "justice" and/or closure. It seeks to send a message to would-be offenders that crime will not be tolerated and delinquents will pay a price proportional to the crime committed (an eye for an eye). Deterrence signals to potential offenders that they will be severely punished if they are found committing a crime. Prisons, in this sense, reinforce the severity of sanctions as a dimension of deterrence. According to this claim, the threat of confinement for an extended period should deter offenders from committing crimes.[11] Rehabilitation refers to the constitutional mandate in most countries in the region whereby prisons should serve to re-educate or re-adapt offenders for their re-entry into society, and thus corrections should offer an array of rehabilitating programs. Incapacitation seeks to reduce crime by confining frequent offenders; prison in this scheme prevents them from committing more felonies and overall public safety is increased by the fact that serious offenders are locked up. From the theoretical perspective, all four prison objectives have their merits and shortcomings. Empirically, however, the evidence shows that each of them has failed in Latin America.

Prisons have not apparently deterred people's willingness to embark in a "criminal career"—at least, not significantly. Some argue that sentences are not harsh enough; others claim that most offenders go undetected or avoid arrest, and therefore sanctions fall on the most "catchable" but not necessarily the most dangerous offenders. In any case, millions of delinquents appear to be unfazed by long sentences and the prospect of severe punishment. The next section on Deterrence will show that prisons have actually been counterproductive. Many inmates reported that before the arrests, they expected to be incarcerated at some point.

Worldwide, corrections rarely rehabilitate criminals (Petersilia 2003; Travis and Visher 2005; Seiter and Kadela 2003), and they certainly fail in this regard in Latin America. Later, I will show that most countries have very ineffectual welfare programs for re-entry, and the penitentiary systems lack the resources and the institutional strength to foster effective initiatives.

Incapacitation policies in the region have thus far been unsuccessful.[12] In this chapter, I show that the waves of new offenders have outnumbered new entries to the correction systems. Despite the fact that thousands of people are sentenced daily for property crime or drug felonies, there has not been a significant reduction in thefts or in the illegal drug supply. Offenders are easily replaced by newcomers to crime rings who are ready to take their spots in the crime networks.

Finally, the retribution or just dessert policy is popular among those in favor of *mano dura* in spite of bringing closure to only a handful of victims and families, since most offenders are never arrested or prosecuted.[13] As Chapters 7 and 8 have shown, the CJS in the region is very weak and the likelihood of apprehension and sanction is very low. Therefore, retribution policies fall short because the overwhelming majority of offenders are never punished. In short, prisons in Latin America do not appear to be meeting any of their conventional goals. The following pages further analyze the shortcomings of deterrence, rehabilitation, and incapacitation effects in the region.

Deterrence

Criminologists distinguish between general and specific deterrence when considering the dissuasive effect of prisons. General deterrence refers to crimes prevented due to the subjectively perceived likelihood of sanctions. Prisons might deter potential offenders from committing crimes through the threat of confinement behind bars, which is perceived as harsh punishment. Specific deterrence implies the aversion of future crimes by people who have already been in prison. The perceived threat of re-incarceration prevents people from committing crimes anew. Both general and specific deterrence appear to produce little results in Latin America.

The Normalization of Prisons (General Deterrence)

Prisons are conceived of as an exceptional punishment. In the public imagination, correctional facilities are very undesirable places and incarceration is perceived as a true nightmare. Prisons can deter people from future criminal behavior because an individual views his or her removal from the community as a traumatic experience. Yet evidence shows that the actual deterrence effect of prison varies from none to very large depending on the perceived subjective cost of imprisonment (Nagin 1998, 2013; Paternoster 2010). Moreover, as this book has emphasized, the risk of apprehension (and, to a much lesser degree, the severity of the sanctions) is the key determinant for an individual's risk assessment.

Many individuals in Latin America have simply assimilated prison as a part of life. A number of inmates report that they expected to be incarcerated at some point; youngster brag to peers about family members being locked up; and visits to the facilities make prisons feel like a regular place, not desirable but not nightmarish either. Moreover, many inmates are arrested again within a year after their release, which suggests that for a large number of people, having been imprisoned before is no deterrent to committing new felonies. For many offenders, prison is perceived as a stage in life, and in some cases a rite of passage.

The inmate survey provides strong support for the diminished deterrence effect of prisons. Most inmates of the six countries have been previously convicted and incarcerated, or had family members in prisons. In addition, most inmates also report frequent visits from relatives, including their children. Between a quarter and half of the prison population also had a family member in prison when growing up (Table 9.4). Based on the survey, 23 percent of inmates have children under fifteen who have visited them in jail. If we extrapolate this estimate for the entire region, more than half a million children visit parents, siblings, or cousins in prisons each year. This, of course, does not imply that these youngsters will grow up to be miscreants, but it does suggest that they are somewhat familiar with prison facilities.

Several qualitative studies provide evidence on the role prisons play among youngsters growing up in disadvantaged communities.[14] Auyero and Berti (2013), Lessing (forthcoming), Jones and Rodgers (2009), Azaola (2015), and many others tell stories of children and adolescents who expect to be incarcerated one day. Some even take pride at being arrested and sent to prison, a prestigious coming of age that renders them status and power among their peers. This defiant culture has many shapes, ranging from the *mara* or other gang counter-culture in Central America, to the violent anti-police stance among youngsters in the *villas* of Buenos Aires and the *favelas* or Rio de Janeiro.

Table 9.4 **Inmates with a family member in prison**

	Argentina	Brazil	Chile	El Salvador	Mexico	Peru
Inmate with family member in prison (%)	41.5	48.3	56.4	26.6	32.5	31.2
Relationship						
Father	19.3	14.6	35.4	18.6	18.4	14.2
Mother	5.2	4.7	12.3	3.3	2.1	4.3
Uncle/Aunt	30.1	27.5	30.5	36.8	41.9	34.6
Cousins	25.7	39.7	30.3	18.1	28.5	23.5
Siblings or half siblings	57.7	51.7	50.0	32.0	38.5	43.8

Note: Family relationship do not add up to 100% because each inmate could have multiple relatives who have been prison. The family relationship percentage indicates the share among those who reported having had a family member in prison.

Source: Inmate Surveys.

Over the last decade, more than five million young people in Latin America have been incarcerated and released from prisons. The likelihood of having acquaintances who were confined in correctional facilities and later released is very large, particularly in specific communities. Thus, I hypothesize that high rotation has made prisons seem normal, a possible stage in a criminal career, and weakened prison's general deterrence effect.

Reoffending: Specific Deterrence

The effect of imprisonment on future offending has been the subject of academic debate (Nagin et al. 2009). Corrections might reduce an inmate's post-incarceration incentives to reoffend, because the experience of punishment could have been perceived as more detrimental than anticipated. However, the future proclivity to recidivate might increase if the incarceration experience is not perceived as adverse. Imprisonment might also encourage re-offending, because of new crime skills learned in prisons (schools of crime), the adoption of a deviant culture that provides inmates with an identity, and the stigma corrections can produce.[15] The evidence that incarceration reduces the individual's proclivity to commit crime is weak. Several randomized studies have neither supported nor rejected this hypothesis (Green and Winik 2010; Loeffler 2011; Nagin and Snodgrass 2012), but there is no strong evidence that incarceration deters future criminality. People recidivate for different reasons. Here, I present one possible explanation: that familiarity with prisons might reduce deterrence.

With a large number of individuals serving time behind bars, a larger number of people become acquainted with prison. Table 9.5

Table 9.5 Prior institutionalization (as % of the total population)

	Argentina	Brazil	Chile	El Salvador	Mexico	Peru
Prior detention (juvenile)	26.0	19.8	39.6	12.7	10.0	7.5
Prior detention (adult)	43.4	48.0	49.8	20.1	N/A	N/A.
Average months between release and re-arrest	28	24	24	18	N/A.	N/A.

Source: Inmate Surveys.

shows the share of inmates who have been locked up in a juvenile institution or in correction facilities, and the average time that passed between
their release and re-arrest leading to the sentence they are currently serving.

Nearly half of the inmate population in the region served time before
their current incarceration or were detained in a juvenile facility at some
point. A large share of respondents was re-arrested within one year.[16] As
Table 9.6 clearly shows, the rate of re-offending is very high, particularly
among those who committed acquisitive crimes at a very young age. This
high rate of recidivism is comparable to that of other countries around the
world.[17] Latin American inmate populations, however, are distinguished
by the short span between release and re-arrest and the high turnover of
inmates, meaning that a great number of individuals pass through the
corrections system in any given year.

Most re-offenders were apprehended for committing theft or drug
crimes. This is a strong indication that for-profit crime is the dominant
motive for recidivism. In fact, 85 percent of the sample was re-incarcerated
for an illegal attempt to boost their income. Half of those who were re-
arrested for theft were apprehended within six months of their previous
release, and most of these offenders were age thirty or younger. The age of
re-apprehension among drug offenders appears to be significantly higher,
but this is driven by gender. The median age of re-arrest is thirty-three for
males but forty-five for females. Women who re-offend with drug crimes
are usually poor and work as carriers or deal from their homes to support
their children and elders. In summary, over half of re-offenders who are
apprehended commit property and drug crimes, are young (except for
women in drug crimes), and tend to recidivate very early in their post-
incarceration period.

Table 9.6 Age of release and time to re-arrest per type of crime

	Median age at time of last re-entry (years)	Lapse time between release and re-arrest (months)	Percentage of re-offenders
Theft	29	6	64.0
Homicide	32	7.5	7.9
Drugs	38	20	21.5
Sexual	46	33	3.3
Other	32	7	3.3

Source: Inmate Surveys.

Turnover of Inmates: General and Specific Deterrence

A high rotation of offenders passing through prisons is another indicator of the shortcomings of general deterrence. More than one-third of inmates are serving time for theft and non-violent drug offenses that carry shorter sentences, producing a high rotation of inmates.[18] Moreover, even very serious crimes such as homicide and rape carry lower sentences on average (in the survey samples nineteen and thirteen years, respectively), and a large share of inmates do not serve the full sentence, making rotation even faster. This understudied feature of Latin American prisons has three very important implications: a) it has helped boost the crime rates in the region (to be examined in the next section); b) it has produced a strong link between offenders who live outside prison and the organized rings inside prisons; and c) it has reduced deterrence.

While countries such as Russia, the United States, and many European nations have imposed harsher sentences to keep inmates in prison longer, in Latin America, an increasing number of offenders are serving on average shorter sentences. A large number of people within a given population have developed ties to prisons either because they passed through the system or have acquaintances who have served time in custody. As seen earlier, greater familiarity with prison reduces its deterrence effect.

The rapid growth of prison populations in the region has produced several unintended consequences. The assimilation of prisons into society has reduced their ability to serve as a threat to selected populations. Just as being young, black, and male dramatically increases one's odds of being in prison at least once in a lifetime in the United States, being a young male from a disadvantaged neighborhood who is probably dark-skinned and has dropped out of school increases the likelihood of serving time in Latin American prisons. All have higher odds of being targeted by the CJS and ultimately serving time behind bars. Many recognize this vulnerability and come to terms with how likely it is they will be incarcerated at some point.

Re-entry and Recidivism (Specific Deterrence and Rehabilitation)

More than 300,000 individuals are released from Latin American prisons every year. The stated goal of prisons is to prepare inmates for re-entry and the expectation is that they will desist from crime. To achieve this goal, corrections are called on to provide job training, schooling, and other programs to help inmates complete their education and assist them if necessary with counseling, substance abuse therapy, and mental health support. According to legal statutes, offenders should be rehabilitated for life in society and therefore many penitentiary systems are named social re-adaptation centers. As Table 9.7 shows, most programs are usually unattended, they are vastly underfunded and poorly run with limited coverage, thus falling short of this goal.

Prisons in the region have failed to rehabilitate inmates. Although stronger state capacities and civil and human rights organizations in Argentina and Chile have pressured state institutions for services inside prisons better than those in countries like El Salvador and Mexico, overall preparation for re-entry has yielded only modest success throughout the region. The high rates of recidivism are testimony of prisons' limited capacity to prepare individuals for social reintegration. As in many countries worldwide, the success rate of effective re-entry among inmates has been limited (MacKenzie 1997).

In Latin America, only a handful of weak institutions are available to help former offenders towards successful transitions. There are no equivalents to US parole boards. While in prison or under probation-type arrangements, inmates are under the supervision of a special judge that oversees sanctions (*juez de ejecución penal*). However, after a sentence has been served, inmates exit prisons and are not required to keep in contact with authorities. Those who have been granted an early release report regularly to local police stations or other offices, but little more is done for them. There are no targeted social programs; very little help with job searches; and a lack of family support or other interventions. A few NGOs have programs to help former offenders in need of special support, but overall there is an alarming lack of initiatives in the region.

Table 9.7 Inmates who attended prison programs over the last year (%)

	Argentina	Brazil	Chile	El Salvador	Mexico	Peru
School programs	70.0	16.0	55.5	68.3	68.2	55.9
Work in prisons	74.2	48.3	63.6	46.1	37.6	71.8

Source: Inmate Surveys 2013.

Prison time strains relationships with partners and children, and many men often do not move back in with their families after they leave correction facilities. They may move frequently and have problems finding employment. Their return to crime thus comes as no surprise (Petersilia 2003; Travis and Visher 2005). They return to the communities where they used to live, rekindling relationships with other offenders, often after establishing criminal networks inside prisons facilities. Re-offending is very common, particularly among recently released youngsters.

Prisons in Latin America have done very little to reduce recidivism, and this has very likely contributed to the crime spike over the past decades.[19] Moreover, the rise in violence in the region is to some extent associated with the vicious violence witnessed in prisons. The homicide rate in Latin American prisons is estimated at a very high 57 per 100,000, compared to 1 per 100,000 in southeastern Europe and 3 per 100,000 in northwestern Europe (UNODC 2014, 99). The growth of the inmate population has strained offenders' ties to their non-criminal peers and reinforced their bonds with violent crime rings after their release. I hypothesize that massive incarceration over the last two decades has backfired, partly because as large numbers of released inmates have returned to broken down communities, they face new hardships and stress (Western et al. 2015), after having experienced or witnessed high levels of violence in prisons.

The surveys provide strong evidence on re-entry and re-offending (Table 9.8). Several questions on the survey were directed at the 40 percent of the sample that served time before their current sentence (n: 2,450). Although no firm conclusion can be drawn regarding the effect of rehabilitation programs on future recidivism, the data clearly shows the limitations of such programs.[20]

With the exception of the respondents in El Salvador, approximately half of the sample has served time in prison or in juvenile centers before, and among them only half had worked during the previous incarceration. The data shows one of the most critical failures of social policies: less than 20 percent of previously released inmates received support from or had contact with state or social organizations to help them in their transition period. This underinvestment in social interventions to support re-entry is puzzling and perhaps to some extent accounts for the high rates of recidivism.

In these six countries (and presumably throughout the region), most inmates return to live with their families after release. The data from this group indicates that they had trouble finding jobs; struggled to

Table 9.8 Prior institutionalization and time between imprisonments (%)

	Argentina	Brazil	Chile	El Salvador	Mexico	Peru
Not including the crime for which you are currently serving time, had you been previously convicted of any other crime?	46.5	49.2	69.9	11.5	33.3	18.2
Before turning eighteen, did you ever participate in a property crime or a drug sale?	48.3	37.7	61.2	13.3	13.5	16.9
Have you ever been detained in a juvenile institution?	26.0	19.8	39.6	12.7	10.0	7.5
Have you ever been in prison before?	43.4	48.0	49.8	20.1	(NIC)	(NIC)
The last time you were in prison, did you learn any trade?(% among those who were in prison before)	45.8	59.7	39.1	56.9	(NIC)	(NIC)
During the period between your last release from prison and your current detention, were you in contact with any organization that provides support or control for released detainees?	16.8	7.1	11.9	4.1	(NIC)	(NIC)

NIC: Questions not included for these countries.

Source: Inmate Surveys 2013.

support themselves and their families; and went back to old friends and communities. The data show several features of this population. First, prison does not appear to help inmates desist from crime when they are released. Second, after spending years in penal confinement characterized by poor conditions and material deprivation, inmates exit prisons poorly equipped for a successful transition back into community life.

In summary, this subsample of inmates previously released and rearrested indicates that they have returned to criminal activity relatively quickly; that education and work training during their previous time behind bars did not sufficiently prepare them for re-entry; and that there are few rehabilitation and support programs for the post-incarceration period. Worldwide, the success rate for such interventions is not high, yet in Latin America, they are remarkably low. This has a direct effect on the incarceration crisis in the region. If the rate of recidivism remains constant at least 40 percent, a yearly growth of 10 percent in the prison population includes 4 percent of previously arrested felons who are re-admitted to the penitentiary system. Part of the growth in prison population appears to be endogenous.

Incapacitation I: Crime from Prisons

Incapacitation is considered to be instrumental for reducing crime. Several studies have identified that the bulk of felonies, particularly violent crimes, are committed by just a few criminals. The physical isolation of these frequent offenders, it is believed, averts or at least reduces crime on the streets. There is some evidence to support this assumption (Levitt 1998; Liedka et al. 2006; Raphael and Stoll 2009), and particularly in the United States, a small fraction of the drop in crime in the 1990s and 2000s has been attributed to the massive wave of incarceration. (Blumstein and Wallman 2006; Zimring 2006.)

Although many gang members participate in criminal activities, gang leaders and high-risk offenders also account for the lion's share of crimes in a given community, while others commit far fewer offenses. Braga et al. (2014) distinguish in a typical gang between the truly dangerous (20 percent) and the situationally dangerous (80 percent). Prevention and re-entry programs have higher success rates among the latter, and incapacitation would yield low criminality if it targeted the truly dangerous offenders. If this assumption is correct, the evidence presented throughout this book shows that incarceration policies in the region have done exactly the opposite. Low-risk offenders have been the main target of the criminal justice system, while most criminal ring leaders and high-risk delinquents remain unpunished.

The prison growth story in the region is explained by the large number of offenders from disadvantaged communities who initiated their criminal careers by stealing goods and selling drugs, perceived as the best career option. Some grew up to be violent felons, committing serious crimes such as murder and rape, but most remained low-level offenders. Prisons have produced two negative externalities. First, by locking up these relatively low-risk offenders, prisons have enabled them to climb the criminal career ladder through networking with incarcerated high-risk offenders. Second, the incarceration of "replaceable" offenders has not reduced crime because other low-risk offenders took their places and may have contributed to more violence as new rivals fought for control of the vacancies. In short, incarceration policies clogged the prisons without doing much to reduce crime.

In addition, prison growth has subtly pushed crime higher in the last decade because it helped enhance the role of gangs and crime networks.[21] Besides the many criminal activities conducted from prisons, such as extortion and kidnapping, gangs and leaders were able to establish ties with cronies outside prisons through coercive power and by leading crime networks from the inside. (Sharbek 2011; Lessing forthcoming) Such leverage is achieved because offenders anticipate that one day they will be arrested and therefore they have strong incentives to be on good terms with imprisoned gang leaders. Massive incarceration in many countries of LATAM has fostered organized rackets within prison facilities (Amorim 2011; Biondi 2010). This has been noticeable in San Pablo and Rio de Janeiro in Brazil, as well as in Honduras, El Salvador, Colombia, Venezuela, and other countries. In addition, overcrowded prisons have produced another negative effect: the lack of resources in prisons has forced wardens to cede internal control to gangs and groups, which has granted de facto coercive power to criminal rings.[22] Crime is partly orchestrated from within prisons because gang leaders have been able to put in place cruel enforcement mechanisms to ensure the compliance by offenders on the outside.

Table 9.9 reveals the extent of criminal activity orchestrated from prison—respondents probably underreported the actual scope out of fear that affirmative responses could incriminate them. However, it is well known in Latin America that extortions or false kidnappings are often conducted from prisons by inmates with access to cell phones and partnering with networks outside prisons. In particular, among those

Table 9.9 Crimes committed while in prison and gangs

		Argentina	Brazil	Chile	El Salvador	Peru
Crime committed while in prison[a]		20.7	12.9	30.6	8.4	29.7
Type of crime[b]	Kidnapping	62.2	15.6	10.0	21.7	38.1
	Extortion	43.0	8.8	12.2	81.1	79.9
	Trafficking	39.7	45.2	59.2	9.1	15.5
	Theft	45.0	35.2	34.1	5.2	25.1

		Arg	Bra	Chi	El Sal	Mex	Per
The crime you have been convicted for was ordered by a gang or group?		7.0	4.7	5.0	6.8	(NIC)	(NIC)
Status of the leaders(Was the leader who asked you to commit that offense in jail or free at the time?)	In prison	9.2	39.2	17.8	35.2	(NIC)	(NIC)
	Free	82.1	34.0	37.8	50.5	(NIC)	(NIC)
	NS/NC DK/DA	8.7	26.8	43.4	14.3	(NIC)	(NIC)

NS/NC: Doesn't know, doesn't answer.

[a] Question: Do you know or have you heard about crimes being organized or planned from within this prison facility? (% of affirmative responses).

[b] Percentage of those who responded yes to the previous question. Multiple responses allowed. *Note*: This question was not asked in Mexico.

Source: Inmate Surveys.

who acknowledged committing crimes ordered by gangs, half of the respondents in El Salvador and Brazil reported to leaders inside prisons. In short, bosses might be incapacitated but their capacity to commit crimes and lead criminal rings from prisons is not.[23]

Incapacitation II: Prison and Rising Crime

Here I test one of the assertions of this chapter: massive rates of incarceration in Latin America have not contributed to reducing the crime rate. I present data on the association between the rising crime trends in the region and the soaring incarceration rates for several countries where data is available to demonstrate that far from preventing crime, mass imprisonment is instead correlated with more crime. I do not prove causality since, as mentioned, the data is not comprehensive enough to control for the possible "taming effects" this wave of incarcerations could have on crime rates. Supporters might argue that without policies of massive incarceration, crime could have climbed even higher, but this counterfactual is also hard to prove. However, it is safe to affirm that crime rates did not even diminish while incarceration was rising; just the opposite occurred, as these two variables positively correlate. I hypothesize that crime increased partly as a result of correctional policies which inadvertently augmented crime through two mechanisms: offender substitution in criminal networks and a high turnover of inmates.

To shed light on this argument, I use incarceration data over the past ten to fifteen years (depending on availability for each country) and examine data on three types of crimes: homicides, car thefts, and illegal drugs. Homicide rates are the most reliable crime data, but murders are considered rare events, and more importantly, the threat of prison does little to prevent or deter homicide (Paternoster 2010). On the other hand, theft and larceny are significantly underreported, making official records inadequate measures of real crime trends. Therefore, the best proxy for property crime is car theft, where there are at least five-year observations for several countries. In addition, I provide an indirect estimate on the evolution of illegal networks based on prevalence rates for marihuana and cocaine for all countries. Since incarceration policies have been a popular way to crack down on drug availability, I test the possible effect of such policies.[24] In this case the hypothesis is that incarceration policies might be effective to the extent they reduce the availability of drugs.

The data is scattered and collection has been in some cases discontinued, making conclusions only tentative. For most crimes, there are few observations for each country and the validity of the data could be questioned at times. For homicides, I use three different measures for countries where the data is publicly available. Unfortunately, the publicly available inmate data does not discriminate offenders by the type of felony they committed, and therefore no correlation could be established between the types of crime and the rate of offenders. Yet the evidence indicates that the total level of incarceration does not appear to have an impact on reducing these crimes.

Table 9.10 depicts correlation coefficients between changes in incarceration rates for each country, and different measures of crimes or availability of drugs (as a proxy to supply of illegal drugs). Since in almost all countries

Table 9.10 Correlation matrix of rates of incarceration (per 100,000) and rates of homicides, car thefts, and drug prevalence (HCE in italics)

Country	Homicide Rates	Hom. Rate from legal departments	Hom. rates from health departments	Rates of car thefts	Marijuana prevalence	Cocaine Prevalence
Argentina	−0.32		−0.43	−0.43	0.85 (es)	−0.47
Bolivia		0.89		0.26		0.51
Brazil		−0.50	−0.04	−0.72	0.95	0.88
Chile		0.35	−0.79	0.97	0.20	−0.27
Colombia	−0.72		−0.82	0.89		0.83
Costa Rica	0.59		0.40	0.12 (11)	0.59	0.02
Ecuador	0.88	0.60		0.22		
El Salvador	0.31		0.72	0.25		
Guatemala		0.41	−0.54	0.82		
Honduras	−0.31			0.25		
Mexico			0.51	0.60	−0.33	−0.08
Nicaragua		0.54	−0.38	−0.45		
Panamá		0.36	−0.07	0.23		
Paraguay		−0.61	−0.42	0.29		
Peru	0.78		0.83	0.90	−0.33	−0.12
Dominican Republic	0.81		0.89	0.87		−0.79
Uruguay		0.37	−0.38		0.99	0.94
Venezuela		0.75	0.94	0.39	−0.17	−0.34

Empty cells denote no data available.

Sources: Author elaboration based on: homicides (chapter 2, car thefts (UNDP 2013 and chapter 4) and illegal drugs prevalence rates (OAS-Alertamerica).

incarceration rates increased, a positive coefficient means that crime or drug availability also increased. If there is an effect of incarceration on reducing crime, strong negative correlation coefficients should be expected.

The correlation coefficients of Table 9.10 depict several interesting trends. First, car theft in most countries positively correlates with prison growth. Only three cases have negative associations, and these can mainly be attributed to problems with data.[25] Many others have strong correlations which signal that the rapid rise of the prison population in most countries was accompanied by an increase in the number of car thefts.

For drug crimes, I use prevalence rates, which are the best data available for several countries, to indirectly measure the availability of drugs on the street.[26] Most countries have positive coefficients for marihuana (the few negative coefficients are not statistically significant) and mixed coefficients for cocaine. In none of these countries has prison growth had a statistically significant association with a reduction in cocaine prevalence.

The most intriguing results derive from the homicide correlations. With the exception of Colombia, most countries with the expected negative association (more inmates, fewer homicides) are countries with LCE.[27] In contrast, strong positive correlations suggest that homicide rates have not fallen in countries with rapid prison growth under HCE.[28] This exploratory homicide analysis signals that deterrence or incapacitation associated with prison growth could have an effect on homicides when the scale of crime is relatively low, but it does not reduce crime when homicide rates are very high. This is consistent with the general hypothesis of this book. Crime equilibria should be distinguished since deterrence is usually effective only under LCE but fails under HCE. The case of Colombia also confirms the assumption that violence in HCE only declines when overwhelming force and determined strong-arm policies are used, yet crime cannot easily be brought down to LCE levels. This is what happened in Colombia, where homicide rates have dropped from approximately 80 to 25 per 100,000 in a fifteen-year period.

A second important lesson from these correlations is that there is no evidence that prison growth has reduced property crime or drug availability. The correlation between car theft and imprisonment rates indicates that there is no negative association, and car thieves probably remain undeterred. At the least, it suggests that those who have been apprehended were "replaced" by other offenders, since car thefts continued to rise even as more people went to prison. Similarly, the illegal drug supply remained steady, though the data here are not as strong. Additional studies on the reduction of street drug prices indicate that supply has continued to grow despite the rise in incarceration.[29] Most likely, there is also a "substitution effect" at work here as well.

Deterrence and Incapacitation: Shortcomings

Several findings developed throughout this chapter support two basic arguments: a) the idea of corrections as protection for the community is a myth that needs to be revised and b) prisons are criminogenic, therefore, under HCE, they not only fail to deter but even accelerate criminality. The following pages summarize these conclusions.

The Fallacy of the Prison Divide

Prisons are thought of as places of isolation where inmates are disconnected from the outside world. In the public's mind, locking up offenders offers a sense of security since criminals are separated from the general population. "Lock them up and throw away the keys" epitomizes the perception that people are safer if criminals are secluded. Prisons become the great divide between dangerous crooks and peaceful citizens.

This argument is ill-conceived, particularly as it relates to Latin American prisons. This chapter has shown that this imagined divide is blurry for several reasons. First, with the exception of those who die in prison, all inmates will eventually be released and about half will serve less than three years. They will return to communities where they have failed before—with the added disadvantage of a prison record. Second, many inmates receive temporary stays or probation, and judges regularly grant temporary releases for low-risk inmates. Third, most inmates receive frequent visits from family members who provide the material support prisoners need to purchase basic goods (food, clothing, medicines) due to severe shortages of prison resources. Inmates need assistance from the outside world, and family members are often "locked up" along with them. Fourth, as recent research and strong evidence has shown, crimes are arranged and even committed from within prison facilities. As a result, public safety is not enhanced by overcrowded prisons. Fifth, mass incarceration has helped consolidate the strength and power of gangs. This, in turn, has enabled more fluid contacts between inmates and offenders outside prisons, contributing to more criminality. Sixth, and last, the steep rates of recidivism and the high rotation of inmates in Latin American prisons indicate that many people and their families have come and gone from prisons. It is likely that over five million people have passed through the correctional systems of the region during the last decade (most are already free), without even considering the countless family members who have come into contact with jails and prison facilities on a regular basis.

In summary, this chapter has shown that the great divide is a fallacy, and more importantly, that mass incarceration has endogenously contributed to more criminality. The idea that a few outlaws are locked up to protect ordinary citizens from crime has become a colossal myth. Far from enhancing public safety, prisons in the region have become criminogenic. This is the topic of the last part of this chapter.

Prisons and Crime Equilibrium

Mass incarceration could become a self-defeating form of punishment. There is no evidence that Latin American prison growth over the last two decades has prevented crime from growing. Despite the fragmented data, in this chapter I have shown that there is little support for the assertion that harsher punishments and more offenders behind bars have deterred or incapacitated offenders. In Europe and particularly in the United States, the rapid rise in the prison population in the 1990s and 2000s coincided with a downward trend in crime. In Latin America, inmate population and crime are both rising. Here, I explore alternative explanations for these converging, regional trends.

The subjective perception of threat of punishment has only a meager effect on criminal activity, and as several authors have suggested, there is broad variance between individuals in their perception of risk, cost, and reward from crime (Loughran et al. 2009; Fagan and Piquero 2007; Pogarsky et al. 2004). As the literature has noted, deterrence is effective particularly as it relates to the certainty of sanctions (risk of detection). Incarceration is usually perceived as a high cost, and offenders will shy away from crime if they perceive the risks and the toll to be very high. However, perceptual deterrence among active offenders differs greatly, and this variance implies that deterrence could be differential, that some individuals are more "deterrable" than others (Loughran et al. 2009). Some will view serving time in prison as too costly while others assign a different weight to this cost. Variables such as age, background, context, and self-control could play a key role in explaining such heterogeneity (Nagin 2013).[30]

In this chapter, I presented data to argue that the perceived "cost" of prison might have diminished for many offenders. Undoubtedly, nobody wants to go to prison, but for some individuals such cost might not have a severe weight vis-à-vis the perceived rewards of crime. The toll of imprisonment is perceived as lower, at least in part, because prison has become a familiar institution, and one that is not always as unpleasant as anticipated. Half of the inmates in the region were locked up in a juvenile or correction facility before serving their current sentence. Many offenders have a close family member who has been imprisoned; several report visiting family and friends in prison when they were young. Others have friends and partners who are locked up, and some anticipated prison as a normal stage in their criminal career. The unintended consequence of mass incarceration is that it has brought prisons closer to a greater number of youngsters. Since deterrence theory teaches that offenders constantly adjust their perceptions of the threat of sanctions based on experience, familiarity with prison has probably diminished the perceived cost of corrections, adding a negative externality to the tough-on-crime policy. A tentative assertion from the mass incarceration policy in LATAM is that in high-crime environments, corrections have a diminishing social utility as a deterrent to crime.

The second goal of prison is its incapacitation effect. Several factors determine the role corrections plays in avoiding crimes by removing frequent offenders from communities. The initial evidence for Latin America indicates that this goal has not been achieved. If incapacitation indeed reduces criminality, what level of custodial sanctions maximizes public safety? Crime reduction through incapacitation may result from "stochastic selectivity" (Canela-Cacho et al. 1997) whereby frequent offenders are naturally more likely to be arrested and to serve more time behind bars. According to this assumption, a higher rate of imprisonment implies that there will be fewer high-rate offenders at large, and therefore crime will decrease. In the United States, this was the argument used to account for the marginal returns associated with incapacitation (Cohen and Canela-Cacho 1994; Johnson and Raphael 2012; Levitt 1996; Blumstein and Beck 2005). It might be argued that incapacitation is effective for crime prevention once a tipping point is reached and a critical mass of frequent offenders is apprehended. For Latin America, however, these assumptions have not held true. As shown throughout this book, mainly low-level offenders have been targeted while a stubbornly high rate of frequent offenders finds ways to remain "untargeted" by the CJS. In addition, illegal economies have thrived, providing ample opportunities for new offenders.

It could be argued that a tipping point for the region has not been reached, that is, the threshold at which a marginal increase in the incarceration rate produces a marginal reduction in criminality; most countries in the region, however, share similar trends despite having vastly different rates. For example, although Argentina and Ecuador have relatively low incarceration rates and Costa Rica and Brazil have relatively high ones, all four have seen their crime rates rise. Despite the variance in prison rates, and with the exception of Colombia, no country had crime rates correlate negatively with prison growth. There is no good evidence in the region that the sweeping incapacitation policies undertaken over the last two decades have contributed to reducing or containing criminality.[31]

In this book, I provide a plausible hypothesis to account for the shortcomings of incapacitation: inmate turnover and replacement. As mentioned in the flow or stock section in this chapter, prison growth in the region results from a large number of admissions rather than longer sentences, generating high rotation in the inmate populations. This reduces deterrence because, as mentioned earlier, prison becomes a familiar institution for a great number of offenders. More importantly, high turnover has yielded an even higher number of unsupervised re-entries, which in turned produced large recidivism.

Rotation, however, is more important for the criminal network analysis. Offenders who are arrested and locked up are rapidly replaced by new offenders who take over their role in the criminal ring. In the illegal drug market, for example, carriers, mules, and dealers who are apprehended are substituted by acquaintances or rivals who take over their street corners. A similar turnover is observed in theft circuits and even in extortion rings. From mobile phone robbers to carjackers and thieves, youngsters in Latin America, who constitute a large army of unskilled labor, have found a source of income and identity in petty or serious crime. This, of course, does not call for extending the length of sentences to reduce rotation, because as long as there is a large supply of undeterred entry-level potential offenders this policy may not succeed. My claim is that the low levels of criminal prosecution of bosses and leaders, and the lack of attention to systems of organized criminality, have enabled these illegal markets to prosper. Incarceration of the low-level rank and file did not disrupt these illegal economies that had fueled criminality.

The vigorous demand for stolen and illegal goods, combined with weak institutional capacity has unwittingly helped to consolidate this process. The CJS has concentrated its efforts on the final link of the crime chain (the muggers, the street dealers, and so on) but made little effort to dismantle the criminal networks that thrived in the midst of the consumer boom. Prisons were mostly filled by these offenders. Some were non-violent and many were repeat offenders, but few were leaders or organizers. Removing these offenders from the community did not disrupt the supply of illicit goods, and therefore opportunities for crime persisted.

Incapacitation policies were unable to make an impact on this structural makeup of criminality, and the transformation of labor markets in the region since the 1990s has contributed to boosting crime. The incarceration of muggers, thieves, street dealers, and carriers en masse has allowed a few newcomers to enter these "emerging crime industries." For criminal networks, the labor cost has been low, as inmate turnover and the unskilled labor supply have facilitated the recruitment of potential offenders.

In addition to the minor effect mass incarceration has had on the supply of drugs and stolen goods, it may have also enhanced highly predatory criminal rings. As shown in Table 9.9, crime is planned from prisons; offenders establish contacts with other criminals in prisons; and links with offenders on the inside and the outside have deepened. A well-known phrase in the region, "prisons are schools (or universities) of crime" is well founded, since many inmates commit serious crimes from prison facilities (orchestrating kidnappings, running extortion rings, controlling the drug supply, and so on) and more importantly, once released, many re-offend as members of established criminal networks. Mass incarceration in the region has helped to forge or consolidate rings of criminality in El Salvador, Guatemala, Honduras, Mexico, Brazil, Venezuela, and to a lesser degree in other countries as well.

Overall, massive confinement of low-level offenders in the region has produced two externalities: replacement and diversification. Law enforcement agents rarely reach the ring leaders, and when they do, other groups rapidly fill the void. As a result, secondary markets continue to thrive and street offenders continue to be recruited. This turnover has had a negative effect because the "old" offenders return to crime after their release as leaders, organizers, or "soldiers" in more sophisticated criminal rings. The evidence in the region shows that the diversification of serious crime has links to prison networks. Once released, these offenders rarely return to "entry level" street crime; instead, they serve the middle ranks and get involved in more sophisticated and predatory networks.

It can be concluded that the current wave of mass incarceration has not prevented crime from growing and in fact may be causally related to its increase. Latin America is a case where corrections may have endogenously accelerated the crime rate.

10

Concluding Remarks

EVEN THOUGH CRIME has increased sharply over the past thirty years in Latin America, there are no satisfactory responses to three critical questions: 1) Why has crime risen in every country in the region? 2) Why have new democracies failed to address what has become the most important concern for citizens in the region? 3) Why have local law enforcement institutions (police, courts, and prisons) underperformed? Despite an outpouring of recent literature on criminality in the region, no comprehensive theories have adequately addressed these questions. Some studies point to state weaknesses, corrupted institutions, failed politicians, and spiraling social problems. These efforts however, do not account for the encompassing patterns of crime across the region, particularly the surge of violence, at a time when Latin America has enjoyed relative prosperity.

By undertaking an ambitious comparative analysis, this book has shed light on understudied topics that underlie the crime problem in Latin America: the enduring stability of criminality in the region, the ineffectiveness of government actions to fight crime, and the mechanism of contagion and spillover. I have stressed the need to transcend the mostly journalistic and anecdotal outlook on crime and a narrow domestic approach to the problem in order to provide a solid empirical examination of facts and theory. Based on the best available information and on new data collected especially for this project, I have established the foundations for a new perspective on crime and violence in the region.

This book has shown that crime has been a region-wide problem over the past twenty-five years. All the countries in Latin America have higher crime rates today than they had in the 1970s and 1980s. Despite differences in rates and intensities, the region shares certain traits, such as rising violence, a growing perception of fear and insecurity among the population, and failed criminal justice systems. Despite improvements to social and economic indicators as well as several criminal justice reforms, crime continues to plague Latin America. This work has attempted to shed light on what has happened.

This book makes a critical contribution by explaining how the hike in acquisitive crime has contributed more broadly to a general rise in crime across the region. I show that the most dramatic rise is precisely in property crimes (thefts), which constitute the bulk of cases that have sparked people's fears and which have major public and social implications. Since most studies rely exclusively on homicide data, they have failed to address this important type of crime, which represents the vast majority of criminal victimization in the region.

Domestic and international actors driven by profits have turned crime into a "business," contributing to vibrant illegal markets. Well-developed criminal networks profit from the rising demand for cheap stolen and illegal goods. As crime rackets develop, authorities and state institutions fail from the outset to address the challenge of rising insecurity.

Intensities and criminal threats vary among countries, from low violence and contained crime to out-of-control criminal behavior and catastrophic homicide rates. I have argued that in each country, a generally stable equilibrium of high or low crime developed based on local opportunities for crime and each state's deterrence capacity, and this helps to explain why outcomes have diverged greatly from country to country. In short, despite rising crime across the region, very high criminality developed in countries where crime was most profitable and where state institutions were unable to address the challenge crime posed. Insecurity rapidly exacerbated in these scenarios and it became nearly impossible for the state to reestablish stable public security.

This book provides four important contributions for the study of crime in Latin America:

a. It develops a theoretical approach to study different crime trends in the region.
b. It undertakes a systematic comparison of governmental and institutional performance in each country.
c. It presents a very promising research design that is capable of answering the questions which other studies on crime in the region have not been able to address. By developing an innovative approach on the nature of crime equilibrium and the change and intensity of crime, this

book has addressed subtle and nuanced differences between the countries of Latin America.

d. It establishes the connection and causal mechanisms between crime in the region and other economic, social, and political processes. Beyond their usefulness in the Latin American context, these findings could be both relevant and applicable in other contexts.

In the following paragraphs, I briefly summarize the core argument and the innovative theoretical approach taken in the search for practical policy recommendations. Rather than providing a script for measures, I propose guidelines to better address the problem of criminality, taking into account current processes of democratization, decentralization, and state building in the region.

Findings

a. Crime has grown all across Latin America in the past thirty years. With the exception of Colombia, the crime rates in the past few years are higher than they were at the end of the 1980s or during the 1990s. Even Colombia has witnessed a rise in crime in comparison to the 1970s.

b. This region-wide growth of crime has been unique during this period. In all other world regions since the 1990s, crime rates have remained steady or dropped in the past few years. In other words, the rise in crime over the last two decades has been a very Latin American phenomenon.

c. Conceptually it is necessary to distinguish between the trend, intensity, and speed of changes in crime rates. While the trend has been the same in all Latin America, crime has grown more in certain countries. In addition, although the basic trend has been an upswing, the intensity of crime varies greatly between nations, with homicide rates in some countries so high that they resemble civil war casualty rates.

d. This conceptual distinction provides insight as to why countries with low violent-crime rates (Chile or Uruguay) have marked levels of social panic (original levels were very low, hence the rate of change has been high). In addition, the differences in intensity allow the region to be segmented into areas of high, medium, and low criminality. Thus, countries or cities whose crime rates have stayed relatively steady (Colombia, El Salvador, Venezuela) but with very high levels of criminal violence must be conceptually differentiated from countries or cities where crime is rising but is not as intense (Costa Rica, Peru).

e. Although homicide has also risen, acquisitive crimes have grown the most. While the data here is less linear, it is clear that robbery—though less dramatic than homicide—has become a daily event in the lives of millions. At least one in four Latin Americans has been robbed over the past twelve months.

f. Property or economic crimes have fostered other violent crimes associated with criminals vying for profits on new markets. Thus the spike in insecurity can be largely explained by the growth of organized crime, which has diversified the "portfolio" of criminal ventures.

g. The vast majority of traditional, structural socio-economic factors fail to explain the growth in crime across the region, and variables such as poverty, unemployment, and inequality do not affect crime as expected. In fact, the opposite of what is expected occurs in Latin America: crime grows in places where poverty has been reduced and unemployment and inequality are low.

h. The rise in crime is positively associated with general economic growth over the past few decades, and thus seems to result not from rising poverty but from greater prosperity. Crime in the region is closely tied to the opportunities that have accompanied the spike in economic activity, the intensified circulation of goods and more broadly, consumerism.

i. The increase in criminality is also the result of institutional failure. Law enforcement organizations and the criminal justice systems in the region have had limited success in containing the rise in crime. There has been, however, considerable variance, as many countries under LCE prevented out-of-control criminality. The war against crime has been waged by police, prosecutors, and courtrooms (judges and lawyers). There has been little creativity in the search for solutions beyond law-enforcement strategies, and particularly there have been meager efforts and resources allocated to social prevention programs. Poor institutional coordination among government agencies, such as those responsible for the economy or public health, inhibited the development of successful strategies against crime. Beyond public policies and effective coordination among institutions, the political leadership in the region has delegated the task to professionals and institutions that were unprepared for the threats posed by the new organized crime markets.

j. Impunity rates for serious crimes in the region are staggering. Convictions for homicides, abductions, and extortions are very low in most countries. High-crime equilibria are structurally ill prepared to significantly reduce impunity rates.

k. The massive incarceration policies over the last decade fell short in containing criminality. Incapacitation and deterrence failed because drug dealers and property crime felons were rapidly replaced by new cadres of offenders ready to take their places, leaving almost intact the business structure of these criminal enterprises.

Criminal law and decade-old policies in Latin America were designed to handle low or medium-crime equilibria (the problem of the "deviant" who needs rehabilitation, the policeman who deals with a gang of thieves in the neighborhood/colony, the criminal system that by nature *reacts* to crime but is unable to *act* beforehand to avoid it). The exogenous shock of criminality that has taken place over the past few decades has revealed the limits of these institutions, which nonetheless retain a veto power which they exercise to preserve their own power and privileges. Institutional paralysis is another term for this state of affairs, which is accompanied by a dramatic reduction in the state's ability to deter would-be offenders.

Implications

Following on from the analysis of the data and the aforementioned findings, a few general implications need to be understood before any policy recommendations can be made.

I. Low and high-crime equilibria are adequate constructs to distinguish the level of criminality in different countries. They have strong predictive power to account for aggregate patterns of criminal behavior. Once high equilibrium is reached, it becomes costly and very difficult to move back to low equilibrium.

II. Offenders rely on shared beliefs, values, and predispositions to determine their best decisions in a context of low information; past experience is the best predictor of future decisions. Hence, individual cumulative offenses reveal a path-dependent explanation, making radical changes almost impossible.

III. Rational imitation and socialization are the two mechanisms that best explain a would-be offender's proclivity to engage in crime. In an environment of severely limited information, such as the one in which offenders make decisions about crime, these individuals evaluate the behavior of others to guide them as they try to make the safest, most strategic decisions possible according to the crime equilibrium in which they live. Offenders commit crimes to a great extent because they see others succeeding at crime.

IV. Enforcement strategies are effective to the extent that they account for crime equilibria, mobilizing enforcement resources to create a low-crime environment where imitation and contagion create incentives for people to abstain from crime.

Policy Guidelines

Finally, I present a road map to address the challenges of rising crime that derives from the theoretical perspective developed in this book. These are not measures aimed at enhancing public security, but rather policy guidelines. The task of policymakers is to formulate measures that have the best chance of succeeding, and if my hypotheses are correct, there is a set of practical implications to be considered in this process.

1. The first and most obvious principle is that effective policies must account for the crime environment. Policy prescriptions cannot be simply replicated if the initial crime equilibria differ between countries. "Copy and paste" rarely works in law enforcement. Effective enforcement measures for LCE might not work under HCE and vice-versa.

2. Given that these crimes are ultimately economically driven, varied regulation instruments—not only those associated with the CJS—are the most effective. The markets for illegal products have hierarchies, resources and supply, and sale outlets; they are frequented by citizens whose actions and transactions generally take place within a legal framework. Therefore, price and tax policies and institutions entrusted with financial, tax, and municipal regulations (among others) are at least as important as police or judges—if not more important. In short, effective policies must consider both the state and markets.

3. There is no magic bullet, but rather a combination of factors working in concert to enhance public security. Reducing the crime rate does not require fundamental social or structural changes but rather a complex and coherent set of policies that take into account economic, social, political, and administrative measures. Even when they are successful, single disparate measures have a very limited impact, particularly under HCE, and are usually short lived.

4. The goal of enforcement is to reach broad compliance with norms, or, in other words, to enable such norms to run on "auto pilot." Policies that prescribe continuous and stringent enforcement face insurmountable costs and contribute to creating an unstable equilibrium.

5. Government should use a wide range of initiatives to reduce the powerful effect of contagion among potential offenders. Punishment may be less severe, but the likelihood of being caught and held accountable must remain high.

6. In countries with weak state capacities, it is necessary to re-evaluate the laws most frequently disobeyed and consider solutions outside the scope of the law. For example, the prohibition of goods in high demand generates very profitable black markets, and weak governments can be overwhelmed by the powerful rackets that emerge in such a context. In short, before passing any new laws, it is essential to consider the environment in which these rules operate.

7. It is crucial to take individual incentives and contextual environments into account if new policies are to work. Although this appears self-evident, most legal provisions are introduced in conditions that are adverse to resolving collective problems. For example, tough-on-crime laws are enacted when crime is on the rise, yet these laws usually accelerate the replacement of arrested felons with new miscreants on the street, the fight for spots, and more violent encounters with the police and among gangs, thus fostering even more crime. When state capacities are weak, policymakers should refrain from popular tough-on-crime policies if they truly want to reduce criminality.

8. Police departments and courts are extremely complex institutions and resistant to change. Although reforms are sometimes necessary, policymakers should be careful not to grant these institutions sweeping power and large budgets that later become difficult to eliminate. Reforms in these organizations should be incremental and tied to results and performance to avoid the typical principal-agent trap widely present in most countries.

9. Enforcement strategies should be used to implement simple enforceable laws that make it relatively easy to detect those who are in violation of the penal laws, and the strategies should insure punishment for offenders. At the enactment stage of legal norms, legislators must be assured of coordination between enforcement agencies (police, detectives, other government agencies, offices at the subnational levels, and courts) so that the probability of sanctions is very high. LCE can only be established when impunity is low.

10. Impunity should be very low, especially for ring leaders, crime entrepreneurs, policymakers who are in cahoots with criminals, and law enforcement officers. Since crime rackets usually operate with a degree of protection from state agents and otherwise non-violent business, law enforcement should be particularly stringent when it comes to the powerful links that enable crime rings to operate.

11. Epidemic levels of violence require overwhelming force to reverse and to bring crime under control. The most critical stage involves coordinating enforcement agencies at subnational levels and keeping up this co-operation over time. Scattered and spotty measures usually result in poor outcomes. Overwhelming force can be implemented when there is strong and capable political leadership that can overcome numerous obstacles and widespread corruption.

12. Social intervention is crucial. Effective crime strategies can only work when states allocate resources and effective programs for youth at risk. These are interventions that target children and adolescents, to alleviate poverty and provide effective schooling, housing, and family support.

13. Avoid mass incarceration and develop alternatives to prisons. The strong replacement effect and the low deterrence and incapacitation effect of today's prison systems could be highly criminogenic in relatively high-crime environments.

14. Finally, and perhaps most importantly, states should legislate only what can be enforced. A high violent-crime equilibrium will deteriorate further if it is impossible to enforce newly enacted laws. The perverse path-dependency of high crime can only be mitigated with minimal and strictly necessary rules. Reasonably successful enforcement of these rules will enhance deterrence while also generating a sense of equity, fairness, and renewed trust in institutions.

Data Collection and Databases

This appendix succinctly describes several data collections used in this book. First the data collections developed by the author through many years and which are used in most chapters are described: inmate surveys, victimization surveys, and penal judicial files. Second, several annotated notes on official records assembled from different sources are given, with brief remarks on the most important collections.

Author-Initiated Data Collections

Inmate Surveys

The first inmate survey was conducted in 2002 under the author's direction in prisons of Mexico City and the State of Mexico. New waves of the surveys were conducted in 2006 (2), 2009 (3), and 2013 (4) with the cooperation of other scholars: Elena Azaola (1, 2, and 3); Ana Laura Magaloni (1 and 2); Gustavo Fondevila (3 and 4); and Carlos Vilalta (4).

Each of these surveys replicated 95 percent of the questions originally drafted for the first and second wave. Questionnaires included close to 250 questions and 400 variables distributed in four large modules: a) sociodemographic questions for each interviewee, including family history, education, jobs and social networks; b) crime committed, including characteristics of the offenses such as substance, weapons, criminal career; c) due process of law, reviewing all the steps from arrest to conviction, including police behavior, evidence in trial, corruption, and actors such as attorneys and judges; and d) prison conditions, including services, programs, rehabilitation, and family ties.

Surveys were conducted only on a representative sample of convicted inmates, which represent approximately half of the prison population.

Throughout the decade the federal district and the state of Mexico housed 26 percent of Mexico's total inmate population, including those charged with federal felonies. In the last wave, due to the construction of new federal facilities, the proportion of federal convicted felons in these facilities shrank by 12 percent.

All samples were randomly selected and are representative for the state entity but not for the prison unit. Based on total convicted population, estimation of sample size was determined (usually approximately 1,200 cases) distributed in 75 percent of all prison facilities for the state. Quotas per prison unit were assigned based on their proportion to the total targeted universe. Case selection was randomly determined on the day of interview from daily registrars at each prison.

All interviews were personal, face-to-face, in a relatively quiet space where inmates could be seen but not heard by guards and/or officers. Interviews were run in classrooms, chapels, or multipurpose rooms within the units. They usually lasted 35 to 40 minutes (only 60–70 percent of questions were asked, depending on the type of felony committed and other considerations). Although women represent approximately 5 percent of the total population, they were oversampled, and constitute on average 16 percent of respondents in each wave. In this book, all results are weighted to account for this factor, unless otherwise specified.

Response rate was very high, averaging 81 percent. Reason for non-response varied, from unwillingness to participate (participation was strictly voluntary) to unavailability due to illness, court appearance, discipline measures, and so on. A randomly selected replacement list allowed for substitutions.

Basic information for the surveys in Mexico is presented in Table A.1.

Funding for these surveys was initially provided by the Hewlett Foundation, and later the MacArthur Foundation, Open Society, and the institutional support of CIDE in Mexico.

Table A.1 Inmate surveys in Mexico (Federal District and the state of Mexico)

Year	Universe of Convicted inmates	Sample size	Number of prison facilities	Date of administration (month/year)
2002	21,753	1,643	21	5–6/2002
2006	24,697	1,264	18	8–9/2006
2009	32,578	1,312	15	6–7/2009
2013	34,125	1,185	16	12/2012–01/2013

For additional information on the surveys see each wave report:

Delito, Marginalidad y Desempeño Institucional: Resultados de la Encuesta de Internos en Reclusión. CIDE, Mexico City. Data sets can be downloaded from CIDE repository data bases at www.cide.edu/ or can be requested from the author.

Inmate Surveys for Countries other than Mexico. In 2012 and 2013 thanks to different funding support and interest in several countries, this survey was replicated with minor adjustments in another five countries. The leading organization that supported the initiative was UNDP, which wanted to include some of the findings in the 2013 report *Citizen Security with a Human Face: Evidence and Proposals for Latin America.* Under my direction and with the collaboration of Gustavo Fondevila and Carlos Vilalta, four studies were conducted (funded by UNDP): national surveys in Peru and El Salvador and regional surveys in the state of Sao Paulo, Brazil, and central Chile. I conducted similar surveys in Argentina, sponsored by the Universidad Nacional de Tres de Febrero. These six country surveys were used to provide initial findings for the UNDP report.

Table A.2 provides basic information for the six country surveys.

All surveys followed similar sampling and other methodological steps as explained for the Mexico surveys. Minor adjustments were made to the questionnaires to accommodate other languages, laws, and penitentiary systems. Each country authority was allowed to add specific questions,

Table A.2 Inmate surveys in six countries

	Coverage	Universe of Convicted inmates	Sample size	Date of administration (month/year)
Argentina		23,340	1,033	06–07/2013
	Federal prisons, City and Province of Buenos Aires.			
Brazil	State of Sao Paulo	102,234	711	06–07/2013
Chile		10,173	871	07–08/2013
	Metropolitan area & Regions V and VIII			
El Salvador	National	19,988	1,126	04–06/2013
Mexico		64,125	1,215	
	Federal District State of Mexico			12/2012– 01/2013
Peru	National	26,048	1,185	02–03/2013

answers for which were not used in the analysis of this book. Further explanation and data bases for these surveys can be found at the UNDP site, which also includes a descriptive report for each country and methodology:

http://www.latinamerica.undp.org/content/rblac/en/home/library/ human_development/informe-regionalde-desarrollo-humano2013-2014- .html

The full reports for each country are available at www.untref.edu.ar/ celiv

Victimization Surveys

Mexico. I have led victimization surveys in Argentina and in Mexico; some of the descriptive data from those surveys was used in the analysis presented in several chapters.

In Mexico, with Rodolfo Sarsfield, we developed and conducted a longitudinally designed victimization survey for Mexico City and the state of Mexico (with approximately 25 percent of the country´s population). Bounding, i.e. the time reference for individual's victimization was six months, the unit of analysis was the household, and the respondent was an adult member of the household.

There were a total of eight waves, two every year between 2005 and 2008. Survey administration was conducted in early August and early February of each year. Samples were 1,500 units for each wave, 750 in Mexico City and 750 in the state of Mexico. Personal interviews were conducted at the house of each respondent.

The questionnaire included victimization as well as institutional performance questions. Non-response rate was 27 percent, and substitutions were randomly selected. Stratified samples were based on census tracks. Field work was conducted by IPSOS Mexico. Funding for these studies were generously provided by the Hewlett Foundation and the MacArthur Foundation

By 2010 INEGI (the central statistics and census agency in Mexico) decided to run a similar survey nationwide with a much larger sample of close to 95,000 respondents. They incorporated many of the questions and structure of this survey, which has now been run yearly since 2011.

Data and yearly reports (Encuesta de Victimización y Eficacia Institucional 2005, 2006, 2007 and 2008 by Marcelo Bergman and Rodolfo Sarsfield) can be downloaded from the repository on public security at the CIDE library at www.cide.edu.

Argentina. In 2007 together with Gabriel Kessler and Alberto Fohrig of San Andres University, we led a large victimization survey in the city of Buenos Aires. The sample was 22,500 respondents (out of a total population of 3,000,000) and included 1,500 cases for each of the 15 city communes (districts).

The questionnaire was very similar to that used in Mexico, but the unit of analysis was the single respondent. Fieldwork was conducted by students and groups associated with the university under professional supervision from a group especially assembled for this project. The survey was funded by the city of Buenos Aires and data is used here with the permission of the city authorities. Further information is available on request.

Penal Judicial Files

This is an underway project of collecting data from randomly selected criminal cases adjudicated in the courts of Argentina and Mexico, initiated in 2011 and completed over the last five years. Under the direction of Gustavo Fondevila, Maximo Langer, and myself, a sample of 1,100 cases in the state of Mexico and 480 cases in the city of Buenos Aires, Argentina were selected. Each file was reviewed to capture characteristics of the cases, of the victims and offenders, and particularly of the process, including information on evidence, role of attorneys and judges, nature of disposition and adjudication, etc. There are 480 variables that center on the judicial process. In this book, brief notes and initial data from this study are mentioned a few times. A full report, including databases, is to be released in 2018.

Other Data Sets

Other sources of data can be grouped in three categories: a) official records, b) victimization, drug prevalence, and general surveys, and c) other sources of information. In what follows I present brief descriptions of the most important collections used in the book

Official Records

Most countries collect data on criminal events, procedures, judicial activities, inmates, and other records as they relate to crime through courts, police, departments of health and other offices. Over the last twenty years, several initiatives headed by multilateral organizations have pursued the standardization and centralization of several data collections.

UNDP 2013. As one of the team of researchers that drafted UNDP's Citizen Security in 2013, I have contributed to an initiative that resulted in new data being collected. The Latin American office of UNDP officially requested that countries of the region provide official information on crime and criminal justice institutions over several years up to 2012. All countries provided new information with the exception of Argentina. Some of the new data that was thus obtained was included in this book.

United Nations. UNODC-CTS. These collections come from self-reports by countries to the UN of surveys conducted every three to four years since the 1970s. These surveys include questions about homicides and other crimes, as well as on criminal justice topics such as police, courts, prosecution, and prisons. Some of this data is found in the historic archives of UNODC at https://www.unodc.org/unodc/en/data-and-analysis/statistics/historic-data.html. Part of the data is processed in different publications. CTS has changed often over time and since 2000 its data is richer. But it is based only on national reports, and the validity of responses is uneven, particularly for the first few waves.

OAS-Alertamerica. Under the initiative of the Organization of American States the crime observatory has assembled official records on crime and drug topics for each Latin America and Caribbean country since turn of the century. Collections are assembled from official records produced by each country and validity is uneven. Some countries consistently produce data, while others have very poor collections. OAS has compounded more than 20 indicators of crime and criminal justice. See http://www.oas.org/dsp/espanol/cpo_observatorio.asp

Country collections. For the UNDP 2013 report I searched historical data on crime and criminal justice in official records and webpages from the eighteen countries under study. Sources varied as well as definitions of crimes and organizational structures. Nonetheless, this effort provides long term analysis for several trends, and has also allowed the filling in of specific missing observations.

General assessment of official records. This topic has been discussed by many scholars in the literature. As all Latin American researchers have noticed, the data is very poor, its quality questionable, and series are very difficult to keep. Records are uneven, particularly because reports from subnational units are very poor. Very rarely is data audited, and therefore the validity of records is at times questionable. This is particularly true in small countries that have not developed strong statistical departments— for the most part, those who suffer high rates of criminality. There is a particularly severe problem regarding the depth of information. Even if countries keep elemental records of events and measures, there is no rich or additional information on the characteristics of the events, on its geographical distribution, on concurrent processes, etc. In short, even if there are accounts of events and processes, there is limited information around them to allow for in-depth analysis, and only very limited studies with statistical controls can therefore be performed.

Surveys

No true victimization surveys have been assembled for comparative purposes. Most countries run different victimization surveys (varying in terms of questions, units of analysis, scope, depth, target population, etc.). Therefore, it is methodologically ill advised to make in-depth comparisons based on structurally different surveys. Two surveys however with similar methodologies apply to the eighteen countries under study.

Latinobarometro. This is not a victimization survey, but a general survey on social, economic, and political issues that has a few questions on victimization as well as police and court performance, fear of crime, and perceptions on issues related to public security. It is conducted yearly, starting in 1995 in several countries, and after several years other countries were added, but questions on crime-related issues were asked infrequently in the first waves. More information on samples and method can be obtained from www.latinobarometro.org.

LAPOP (Latin American Public Opinion Project). This is also a general survey that asks several questions on crime and criminal justice issues as well as public opinions related to public security in each country. It is conducted every two years, begining in 2004, and the 2012 wave included a special module on crime and citizen security issues funded by the UNDP. Some of its results were included in the 2013 report described earlier. In this book I use additional information from that wave and another one from 2014. For more information on method and sampling see http://www.vanderbilt.edu/lapop/.

CICAD (OAS-Alertamerica). The OAS led an observatory that also specialized in legal (including alcohol and tobacco) and illegal substances. This observatory has coordinated and promoted prevalence surveys of drug use in the region, both for the general population and for high-school aged adolescents. Scattered information for different years allow for restricted comparisons about drug use and abuse in the region. Other indicators of drug trafficking and seizures are developed, although their reliability is very poor.

Notes

1. There are several exceptions, most notably Colombia that went from an average of 62 homicides per 100,000 in the 1990s to 32.7 homicides per 100.000 in 2010. Also, several Central American nations such as El Salvador and Guatemala have for several years experienced drops in crime rates. Nonetheless, these countries still have catastrophic homicide rates—among the highest in the world. Declines have only been seen in countries where homicides had been out of control and later stabilized but remain very high.
2. Widely different lines of study in criminology like those of Robert Merton, Edward Sutherland, and Travis Hirschi share this focus on the individual who deviates.
3. The study of transactions in illicit goods has received more attention recently. See for example Naim 2006, Felbab-Brown 2010, Yashar 2012, Andreas 2015, Dewey 2015, and Jusionyte 2015.
4. These are the seventeen Spanish- or Portuguese-speaking countries in the continent and the Dominican Republic.
5. Crimes can be distinguished by their motivating factor: domestic crimes, settling of scores, personal revenge, and economic crimes.
6. Prohibition in the United States in the 1920s and 1930s is a good example of how an exogenous shock can decisively contribute to a rise in violence, even with strong levels of legal compliance. Also, during the crack epidemic of the 1980s several cities in the United States exhibited high crime environments similar to those of Prohibition.
7. There will always be a certain number of people who commit crimes. The question is whether such individuals constitute a large critical mass.
8. Other important differences between countries A and B are of course the pool of individuals sitting on the fence, that is, the number of people in each country (or in a city or society) who are willing to engage in crime. This topic has been

covered in the criminology literature, and in this book I give significant attention in recognition of its importance. Poverty, social inequality, upbringing, family, demography, and many other factors will impact the extent of such pool of potential criminals.

9. They might also invite politicians to take a cut, a subject I will examine in the section "Crime Equilibrium: Profits, Organized Crime, and Politics."

10. These are in addition to four other I listed in the "Law Enforcement," section as they relate to the effect of contagion and enforcement.

11. Of course, not all victimizations are property related. However, there is a lack of consistent measures on property crimes across time for most countries of the region. Since victimization survey rates include overwhelmingly stolen property from victims, I use these surveys many times as proxy to property crimes.

12. In addition, a cell phone thief in many countries is rarely incarcerated. The risk premium for such theft is small, therefore, and its cost is not transferred to buyers.

13. Car robbers who get arrested usually end up serving some time in prison.

14. As will be developed in chapter 6, authorities sometimes tolerate illegal trades in LCE as long as they do not produce violence. In HCE, authorities have lost their ability to deter crimes.

15. For instance, a guard unit working for a drug organization for the shipment of illegal substances might be replaced by another unit if its members are arrested.

16. I would like to thank the UNDP Latin American Office for allowing me to use part of the data (from Brazil, Chile, Peru, and El Salvador) the collection of which they have helped to fund. I directed these surveys as a member of the team that developed the 2013 public security report; "Human Development Report for Latin America 2013–2014: Citizen Security with a Human Face"

CHAPTER 2

1. A 2013 report by the NGO Consejo Ciudadano para la Seguridad Pública y la Justicia Penal the list of cities of over 300,000 inhabitants with the world's highest homicide rates is headed by San Pedro Sula (Honduras), Caracas (Venezuela), and Acapulco (Mexico). Another forty LATAM cities are among the top fifty in this list. See http://www.guiaeduca.com.mx/documentos/Seguridad_justicia_y_paz_50_ciudades_violentas_2013.pdf (accessed January 19, 2014).

2. WHO considers a homicide rate of more than 10 per 100,000 an epidemic. In 2011, twelve out of eighteen countries in the region exceeded that threshold.

3. In an international victimization survey of cities, Mexico, Brazil, and Argentina have among the highest victimization rates. See Van Dijk et al. (2007).

4. This might be one of the reasons for a lack of theories about or general explanation of this regional crime rise.

5. Data for each country is usually collected using the same methods each year. If there are errors in data collection, this error is probably systemic.

6. It is well beyond the scope of this book to debate the validity of this claim. Homicides could be the most "counted" crime, but homicide rates might not necessarily reflect real trends in criminality.

7. A drop in the homicide rate might not reflect a decrease in violence but instead a reduction in lethality. In effect, advances in urbanization, greater proximity to hospitals, and advances in medicines that became noticeable in the region over the past fifteen years have probably reduced the number of lethal outcomes from attacks.

8. Sources include police data, courts registrars, and health department records. No single source could be used for longer series for different countries.

9. A note on the homicide data: Most countries in the region have indeed improved the quality of criminal justice data over this period, and therefore, it could be argued that homicide counts are more reliable at the end of the series than at the beginning. Although data is to some extent more reliable at the end of the series, this effect is small because the rates of homicide rise were very significant, and this is a crime that has been generally well documented. Moreover, the series in Figure 2.1 come from the most developed countries in the region, which kept reliable homicide records for many decades. Additionally, as Martinez-Duran (2015) rightly shows, certain conditions make crime more visible (cohesion of the state security apparatus and levels of competition in the illegal market). Yet again, the growth in homicide is so large that greater visibility in later years (when traffickers decided to reveal executions) cannot obscure that growth. In sum, better counts and high visibility have a very small effect.

10. Colombia has a very small decrease because its rate peaked in the 1990s and has decreased since then, but it still has rates over 25 homicides per 100,000. In most other countries rates increased by 50, 100, and 200 percent over the period.

11. It is astonishing that countries with rates already above 20 homicides per 100,000 such as El Salvador, Honduras, Venezuela, and Colombia witnessed dramatic increases from these thresholds.

12. Studies on hot spots and crime as opportunity provide several hypotheses as to why this happens (see Weisburd et al. 2006, 2016; Eck 2002; Clarke 1997).

13. https://www.unodc.org/documents/gsh/pdfs/2014_GLOBAL_HOMICIDE_BOOK_web.pdf page 26.

14. In 2013, more than 40 percent of intentional homicides occurred in the states of Mexico, Guerrero, Chihuahua, Sinaloa Michoacán, and Jalisco (Henle et al. 2015, 17).

15. For an assessment of the classic Chicago school of criminology see Park et al. (1925) and Shaw and McKay (1942).

16. Notice that not every large city in the north has such a high growth rate. For example, Recife—one of the largest cities in Brazil and in the northeast—saw a dramatic reduction of close to 100 percent during the decade.

17. La Capital, daily newspaper of Rosario. See www.lacapital.com.ar, 9.1.2012 and 2.1.2015.

18. Converted to rates based on information by InSightCrime.org

19. Cities with high decay suffer from drug problems. What I claim here, however, is that there are several cities where the drug trafficking business is not the main driver in the rise in crime.

20. "Delincuencia y criminalidad en las estadísticas de Honduras, 1996-2000" (PDF) (in Spanish). Programa de las Naciones Unidas para el Desarrollo. See also https://en.wikipedia.org/wiki/Homicide_in_world_cities

21. Sources: Municipio Metropolitano de Quito INEe, Municipio Metropolitano de Quito (2005) at http://www.flacsoandes.edu.ec/biblio/catalog/resGet.php?resId=13002

22. There are many cases in which a rapid rise in homicide has been reversed (Ciudad Juarez, Medellin, San Pablo, and so on). These cases actually confirm the general argument. Only when massive, focused efforts and resources are applied to security issues is crime contained, though homicide in these cases rarely returns to "non-epidemic" levels.

23. This is a generalization with many exceptions. The most noticeable are civil wars and internal strife as occurred in rural Central America or Colombia. In the 1980s and 1990s internal conflicts, mainly politically in nature, have proven highly lethal.

24. Not coincidently, as will be shown, these countries have relatively low violent crime rates and offenders have a higher likelihood of punishment.

25. It covered Mexico City and urban populations of the state of Mexico, the largest state in the country. See Appendix.

26. For a complete explanation of the indexes and results, see Bergman and Sarsfield (2009).

27. These surveys also capture multiple victimizations for different household members. There is qualitative evidence indicating that many household members have been recently victimized and multiple times, but in the survey, someone who has been victimized on multiple occasions is only counted as a single observation.

28. In addition to victimization surveys, official records of criminality provide an approximation of the scale and depth of the problem. There are some caveats to these measurements. First, most crimes are never reported to the authorities, particularly low-value property crime, so that an increase of petty crime will not be properly captured by official records. Second, as is well known in the literature, official records in the region are generally regarded as unreliable and unvalidated. Authorities have never made serious efforts to collect data and

have not implemented good screening, categorization, and auditing procedures or other necessary systems to establish sound data collection systems. Third, throughout the region (see op-ed by Bratton in the *New York Times* February 17, 2010), officers tend to underreport crimes because the data they collect is being used to measure performance. Fourth, as authorities become less effective in resolving crime and providing public security, people become more reluctant to report crimes to the police. Despite these and several other pitfalls, official records do measure trends to some degree.

29. A word of caution is necessary. Cross-country comparisons of personal thefts are discouraged because the reporting rate and legal definitions vary. However, within country variations have better validity since it is reasonable to assume that measurements and definitions of felonies do not vary significantly over the years.

30. Express kidnapping is a serious crime in which a victim is abducted, usually in his or her own car or in a cab, and is taken to one or more ATM machines to withdraw cash for the abductors and is then released. No good data exists, but it appears that this practice is widespread in most major Latin American cities.

31. There has been some debate about these figures, yet the magnitudes are high regardless the precision of the estimates.

32. Obtained from Observatorio Nacional Ciudadano: Seguridad, Justicia, Legalidad. "Análisis de la Extorsión en México 1997-2003: Retos y Oportunidades," 37. Based on data from SESNSP up to January 17 2014 and from the National Population Council (CONAPO) the mexican demographic council. see https://www.gob.mx/conapo.

33. In the last years, due to alarms and other protections, many car thefts were carried out with the driver present, augmenting the level of violence.

34. Multiple press sources. See for example http://elmanana.com.mx/noticia/15086/Rompe-record-robo-de-combustible-a-Pemex.html

35. The estimate comes from Ecopetro (Colombia's national oil company). Since then, the amount has shrunk but is still estimated to be very high. See http://www.elnuevosiglo.com.co/articulos/4-2013-hurto-de-combustibles-derrame-econ percentC3 percentB3mico.html

36. A large amount of oil is also stolen from central agencies in Africa. In Nigeria (one of the largest oil producers), thieves reportedly steal an average of 100,000 barrels of oil per day (*New York Times*, September 20, 2013)

37. See http://www.las2orillas.co/los-nuevos-narco-tesoros-detras-de-la-mineria/

38. It is very hard to measure the scope and the monetary value of such extortions, but there are many reports. See http://riodoce.mx/narcotrafico-2/narcotrafico-controla-minas- en-cinco-estados-de-la-republica

39. See also http://revoluciontrespuntocero.com/pulsociudadano/mexico-y-el-infierno-de-la-trata-de-mujeres/ based on a report by the *Guardian*. Leaders of anti-trafficking groups estimate that Mexican cartels could be making over

US$10 billion. Although this estimate may be high, the value of the trade is nonetheless astounding.

40. See data presented on chapter 5.

41. Since rates are small, these surveys usually have a large number of respondents. Still done the estimates fluctuate within ample margins. Prevalence, however, does not clearly indicate the volume of drugs circulating. There is a large variation in quantity of use between users that most survey do not capture, nor the potency of each consumption. Therefore, prevalence is a proxy for trend in the number of users.

42. Since alcohol is legal, I will not devote much attention to its effects on criminality, but I do take into account the potential effect of intoxication on violence.

43. Most countries conducted similar surveys over the years and, therefore, changes in prevalence rates are more reliable indicators within country than across country variations.

44. Unfortunately, for some countries there is no data or just a single observation for the last decade.

45. Unless there happens to be a drastic drop in the number of young drug users. This does not appear to be the case in LATAM.

46. In addition, Mexico and to some extent Colombia are producers of opiates and heroin for the US market, yet the prevalence rates of these drugs in those countries is negligible.

47. Data from the national surveys is obtained from http://www.conadic.salud.gob. mx/pdfs/ena08/ENA08_NACIONAL.pdf

48. http://www.conace.cl/inicio/pdf/resumen_informe_VIII_estudio_drogas_ poblaciongeneral_junio2009.pdf

49. Most surveys do not include two population segments which usually have a high number of users that account for the lion share of the demand: drug addicts living on the street and prison populations.

50. Countries are often inconsistent in their yearly reports with omissions and double counting both common. Sources may also vary, from special agencies to police departments to courts and so on. Still, this is the best comparative data available and depicts the overall trends.

51. Nevertheless, marijuana still passes though the region as it moves between countries. For example, Chile has one of the highest prevalence rates of cannabis. Part of the marijuana consumed is produced in Paraguay and is transshipped through Argentina. Therefore, an unknown fraction of the marijuana seized in Argentina might actually be for the Chilean domestic market.

CHAPTER 3

1. Criminal justice enforcement agencies are not the focus here; chapters 7–9 are devoted to this subject.

2. Coefficients for the key variables were: Income inequality ratio measure, Mr = .416, Nstudies = 13; divorce rate, Mr = .277, Nstudies = 10; population growth, Mr = .251, Nstudies = 9; income inequality Gini Index, Mr = .224, Nstudies = 31, female labor force participation, Mr = .223, Nstudies = 13; infant mortality, Mr = .196, N = 8; ethnic heterogeneity, Mr = .163, N = 12.

3. For the negative correlation, the indicators are social welfare protection of the population, Mr = −.279, N = 4; ethnic homogeneity, Mr = −.247, N = 5; modernization as measured by the human development index, Mr = −.163, N = 14.

4. Income distribution in these studies is measured using Gini coefficients and/or the gap between opposite deciles and/or quintiles.

5. Similar trends are found with bank robberies and homicides. Because of the illegal drug crisis that has particularly impacted very hard in Columbia, I decided to not include homicides in this analysis and concentrate exclusively on property crime.

6. The property crime data for Ecuador should be viewed with caution. According to the data series, the theft rate for 2008, 2009, and 2010 dropped by 300 percent in comparison with the rest of the decade. That seems very unlikely, and there are most likely some problems with the reports.

7. Recent incomplete data for other countries show that as economies shrank, the homicide rates in some kept rising (Venezuela) while in others it decreased (Colombia). The main point is to show that at their peak, in Latin American's growing economies the rate of homicide increased rather than decreased.

8. For 2009, data for fifteen out of eighteen countries is available. For other years, data is available for six to fourteen countries and coefficients are all positive ranging from 0.3 to 0.7. Theft data comes from the OAS Alertamerica report (2015) and per capita GDP from WDI (2015).

9. Beltrán and Salcedo Albarán utilize data from 1976–1999 in Colombia to show that several types of crime and unemployment are not correlated. The exception is car theft, which is moderately correlated with higher urban unemployment. Their analysis does not control for male or youth unemployment. For a Spanish language study on the topic, see Beltrán and Salcedo-Albarán (2007).

10. Unemployment data are from 1990 to 1999, except for Colombia, which is 1991–1999.

11. Data has been processed from Cepalstat at http://estadisticas.cepal.org/cepalstat/WEB_CEPALSTAT/estadisticasIndicadores.asp?idioma=e   Tasa   de desempleo abierto y urbano según sexo y grupo de edad

12. Several large, panel studies by organizations such as the World Bank (2014) and UNODC (2014) found correlations between crime and urbanization, but Buhaug and Urdal (2013) and Urdal (2011) did not.

13. I only present data for the 1970s and 1990s; however, an analysis using the original databases show that the trend has been similar since the 1960s.

14. Hot-spot research faces methodological challenges that derive from endogeneity. Most studies use police or judicial data that comes from officer interventions which are not random but instead guided by their experience with crimes that occur regularly. In short, the data confirms the deployment of police and other agencies.

15. For a good summary, see Sampson and Laub (2005) and Farrington (2003).

16. Several factors are at work here. Large cohorts of youngsters suggest tougher competition for entry-level jobs and fewer resources per person for social programs, which can translate into more stress for young adults. Nevertheless, most youngsters will not turn to crime.

17. This can be attributed to out migration and the aging of the population.

18. The drop in fertility rates, rising age of first time mothers, and smaller household size are well documented in demographic trends in the region. For comprehensive data on these and other patterns see the CELADE website, the Latin American center for demography of ECLAC, at http://www.cepal.org/cgi-bin/getProd. asp?xml=/celade/agrupadores_xml/aes50.xml&base=/celade/tpl/top-bottom.xsl

19. The countries with an adolescent fertility rate above 100 circa 1990 were Ecuador, El Salvador, Guatemala, Honduras, the Dominican Republic, and Venezuela; the rate in Bolivia, Colombia, and Mexico was between 90 and 100; and in Argentina, Chile, Costa Rica, Panama, and Uruguay under 89 (Cepalstat 2015). (Adolescent fertility rate is births per 1,000 women ages 15–19.)

20. The data is processed from the raw percentages per country extracted from UNDP 2013 (see Figure 2.3).

21. It is important to consider that these are surveys of randomly selected convicted prison inmates. Although a similar survey was not conducted among non-offenders as a control, these indicators are still significantly different in the general population: less than 10 percent of youngsters have dropped out of elementary school; approximately a third has completed high school; and less than 20 percent probably left home before age fifteen. Clearly the offending population differs from the general population in these indicators.

22. This is an imperfect proxy, however, as we will see throughout this book. The criminal justice system detects and punishes a large number of non-violent or occasional offenders (street dealers, small time thieves, and so on) that could be clearly differentiated from professional crooks and very violent delinquents.

23. For a detailed explanation of each variable, see Bergman et al. (2014).

24. This upbringing presumably also affected formal education. Those who end up in crime have attended school for less time than first-time and nonviolent offenders.

25. See alertamerica.org (2012) For alcohol prevalence in the general population, see http://www.oas.org/dsp/observatorio/database/indicatorsdetails.aspx?lang=en&indicator=289

26. See alertamerica.org (2012). For alcohol prevalence in the school population, see http://www.oas.org/dsp/observatorio/database/indicatorsdetails.aspx?lang=en&indicator=281

27. Several data sources support this trend. See Bergman (2016, chapter 3) for rates of consumption by country. Data on the recent history of drug use in many countries of the region can be found at http://www.cicad.oas.org/Main/Template.asp?File=/oid/countriesprofile/default_spa.asp

28. Less than 1 out of 1,000 adults in the region have used opiates during the past twelve months.

29. Szabo et al. (2013) report that out of 16 million guns in Brazil, 7.6 million are not registered, and in Mexico, 85 percent of the 15 million weapons in circulation are illegally owned.

30. The GAO (The United States Government Accountability Office) has reported that 40 percent of arms that end up in the hands of Mexican cartels come originally from the state of Texas.

31. In Argentina the rate was 77.9 percent; in San Pablo, 70.5 percent; in Chile, 75.7 percent; in El Salvador, 49.8 percent; in Mexico, 42.3 percent; and in Peru, 39.7 percent.

32. In Argentina, 31 percent; Brazil, 18 percent; Chile, 23 percent; El Salvador, 22 percent; Mexico, 15 percent; Peru, 9 percent.

33. When guns are scarce and expensive guns, young people may not be able to acquire them, but easy availability suggests that the cost of guns on black markets is low.

34. The four Latin American countries where data for firearm homicides was unavailable were Bolivia, Chile, Peru, and Venezuela. For some countries, the reference year is 2009; see Table 2.10 of UNDP (2013).

CHAPTER 4

1. As mentioned in previous chapters secondary markets can be legal or can be black markets where goods (used or new) are resold, usually at low prices.

2. Colombia and some countries of Central America were exceptions to this. Faced with severe internal conflicts, these countries suffered extreme violence during the 1980s.

3. Even for those countries that had a positive growth during the 1980s, it was a very modest one. No country averaged more than 2 percent growth per capita during those years. In contrast, for the first decade of the twenty-first century, most countries averaged 25 percent growth.

4. These patterns can be interpreted in several ways, especially with regard to cash transfers and other government programs. For a comprehensive examination, see Lustig (2010, 2011, 2013) and Bourgignon and Platteau (2012).

5. Anthropologists and sociologists see consumption as a social process, not an economic activity. The motivation for consumption derives from social communication and symbolic action, rather than the drive to meet basic needs such as food, shelter, or clothing.

6. As Bourdieu brilliantly explained, consumerism brought changes in the social order in such a way that coercion was replaced by stimulation, command behavior by seduction, and normative regulation by new desires and needs (1984). For Bourdieu, patterns of consumer taste and choices are not givens, but they do reflect socioeconomic differences.

7. Most cities in the region have these marketplaces. For example, Tepito and Meabe in Mexico City, La Salada on the outskirts of Buenos Aires (with more than a thousand small stores), the *cachinas* of La Victoria in Lima, and the *bachaqueros* at the Coche or Quinta Crespo in Caracas. There are literally thousands of these small and medium-sized *ferias*. A 2016 report in Argentina estimates that these informal outlets sell 45 percent of total retail, approximately 56 billion dollars, and 10 percent of Argentina's GDP (*La Nación*, June 19, 2016) In addition, *ambulantismo* is widespread in the region. Many makeshift or moveable stores are active participants in illegal economies. Over the past few years, even Internet purchases and home deliveries of illegal goods have occurred.

8. In a recent study, Jusionyte (2015) insightfully examines these movements at the "triple frontera" border between Argentina, Paraguay, and Brazil, from an ethnographic perspective.

9. Bergman and Sarsfield (2009).

10. *Encuesta de Victimización Ciudad Autónoma de Buenos Aires, 2006–2007.* Universidad de San Andrés y Ciudad de Buenos Aires. Although the survey was conducted within the boundaries of the city of Buenos Aires (the federal district), a large number of those interviewed reported their residence was in the suburbs.

11. http://www.seguridadpublica.gov.cl/filesapp/Sintesis%20Delictual%20 ENUSC%20Pais%202013.pdf

12. More information is available at http://wsp.presidencia.gov.co/Seguridad-Ciudadana/estrategias-nacionales/Documents/Encuesta-Convivencia-Seguridad-Ciudadana-2013-DANE-comparativo.pdf.

13. By no means do I make an assessment of the value the owners assign to their belongings. For a day worker in Mexico whose weekly pay is 100$, any personal property probably represents a very valuable asset. Here I only make assessments of the monetary value of robberies as they relate to the overall market.

14. I will make introductory comments on the stolen car market later in this chapter.

15. Chapters 7 and 8 will develop these concepts further.

16. This is what is usually seen in the United States or Europe with highly coveted goods in the software, legal drugs, and apparel industries. Large firms force minor players to comply with market rules and to a large degree succeed in making customs agencies enforce protection from other countries' piracy.

17. Studies in Peru (Jaris Mujica 2008) show that the typical youngster who steals a high-end cell phone receives less than US$5 from the shop that will refurbish it. Given the low value of refurbished cell phones in the region, it is very likely that this will be a standard price.

18. More information is available at: http://www.iadb.org/wmsfiles/products/publications/documents/354774.pdf. In 1998, between a third and half of urban workers in Latin American countries were in the informal market (Table 1a, p. 37). For 2012, a report issued by the International Labor Organization established that 31.7 percent of the labor force in Latin America is in a state of "vulnerability," a category equivalent to the informal labor market. See Global Employment Trends 2014, Table A 12, p.98 in http://www.ilo.org/wcmsp5/groups/public/---dgreports/---dcomm/---publ/documents/publication/wcms_233953.pdf

19. Chapter 7 will expand on some of the corrupt police practices.

20. In a penetrating essay on Buenos Aires's poor suburbs, Auyero and Berti (2013) call this mechanism the *encadenamiento* (concatenation) of violence, whereby mundane daily disputes regularly devolve into violence. Violence engenders more violence without viable instruments to halt this cycle.

21. Even at these stages, agents will avoid violence if they can impose their will (selling drugs, stealing a cell phone) without using it.

22. http://www.sinembargo.mx/14-12-2013/844846

23. http://www.clarin.com/inseguridad/Argentina-roban-celulares-dia_0_818918287.html. Similar figures (5,000 phones stolen per day), were reported in 2015. See http://www.lanacion.com.ar/1886492-sebastian-cabello-las-operadoras-reportan-cinco-mil-robos-de-celulares-por-dia.

24. Mujica (2007).

25. http://testamarketing.blogspot.com.ar/2012/08/encuesta-sobre-sobre-robo-de-celulares.html#.U1jwwPldWHR.

26. http://www.rpp.com.pe/2013-08-28-latinoamerica-preocupada-por-aumento-de-robo-de-celulares-noticia_626182.html.

27. This 2012 city victimization survey estimated a total of 1.2 million victimizations, which means that half of the victimizations were cell-phone thefts. See http://www.noticiascaracol.com/nacion/video-305126-cada-minuto-del-ultimo-ano-han-robado-un-celular-bogota (accessed November 6, 2013).

28. If the denominator is only the population older than ten years, the most likely users of cell phones, the rate would be much higher.

29. http://www.eltiempo.com/archivo/documento/CMS-13009151 (accessed Nov 6, 2013). Total victimization for these cities was 2.8 million.

30. http://www.prensalibre.com/noticias/justicia/SIT-registra-triple-robos_0_653934675.html.

31. Dreyfuss et al. (2011b) present scattered data for Brazil that signals a growing private market in handguns.

32. http://www.ecopetrol.com.co/contenido.aspx?catID=200&conID=39423.

33. http://www.eltiempo.com/justicia/ARTICULO-WEB-NEW_NOTA_INTERIOR-12412701.html.

34. Refined petroleum, ready for commercial use, is of course much more expensive than crude oil. With prices exceeding $100 a barrel, thieves made at least $700,000 per day.

35. See the report from official sources at http://elmanana.com.mx/noticia/15086/Rompe-record-robo-de-combustible-a-Pemex.html.

36. IV Documento de Trabajo, Mesa Inter-empresarial de Piratería de Camiones. 1.8.2011-31.7.2012. See the report at http://www.pirateriadecamiones.com.ar (accessed December 1, 2013).

37. http://www.apoyovictimas.cl/noticias/ministerio-del-interior-puso-en-marcha-plan-intensivo-para-prevenir-robo-de-camiones/.

38. http://www.oem.com.mx/laprensa/notas/n3219759.htm. See also a similar report at http://contralinea.info/archivo-revista/index.php/2011/08/25/transporte-de-carga-blanco-del-crimen-organizado/.

39. Nee (1993) interviewed 100 offenders and concluded that most car thieves began to steal cars in their early to mid-teens, with the help of more experienced offenders. "The influence of friends, the excitement of stealing cars, and boredom were the primary reasons given for first becoming involved in car theft. Over time, the opportunity to make money from car theft apparently became increasingly important, and over one-third progressed to 'professional' car theft for financial gain." (Nee 1993, 4)

40. A study by Norza et al. (2013) reports that in Colombia between 2008 and 2012 two-thirds of car thefts took place not in front of the owner's house but "en la vía pública" (67) (on the street) and usually at gunpoint.

41. For an interesting case of a resilient type of organization that specialized in auto thefts for parts, see Herzog (2002).

42. The literature on the effect of trust and loyalty in mafia organizations (Gambetta 1996 and 2009; Tilly 1975; Schelling 1971) shows that when organizations can rely on keen and loyal membership, transaction costs diminish and the mafia can reap benefits from trades that might otherwise be too expensive.

43. Reported to the United Nations Surveys on Crime Trends and the Operations of Criminal Justice Systems (CTS), a compilation of crime data assembled by UNODC based on responses to questionnaires filled out by officials in each country.

44. Close to 40 percent of car owners in the greater-Mexico-City area do not carry car insurance, according to a longitudinal victimization survey (Bergman and Sarsfield 2009). In Argentina it is estimated that more than 20 percent of car owners do not have insurance policies.

45. Victimization surveys indicate that in Mexico over the last five years, 56 percent of car thefts were reported to the police.

46. An average stolen car could be sold for US$5,000. New luxury cars are high-ticket items, while auto parts are sold for less. At least 60,000 cars per year end up in the illegal market.

47. http://www3.inegi.org.mx/sistema(s/tabuladosbasicos/tabgeneral. aspx?c=31914&s=est table 1.4. These tallies appear to be very high, but even if inaccurate; they still show that the Mexico's stolen car industry is very big.

48. http://www.policia.gov.co/imagenes_ponal/dijin/revista_criminalidad/vol52_ 1/02Tablas.pdf (accessed February 8, 2014).

49. By 2010, 77 percent of the 10 million vehicles on the road were insured.

50. In 2010 the Security and Justice Minister of Buenos Aires Province said that approximately 10 percent of the cars produced in Argentina (some 65,000) are stolen each year. *La Nación* September 6, 2010.

51. http://www.ssn.gov.ar/storage/peacuadros/index.html (accessed November 12, 2013).

52. Alertamerica.org, OAS Hemispheric Security Observatory 2015, *Report on Security in the Americas*, 79. Rates of criminality in Argentina started to decline in 2004 after the country's deep crisis of 2001–2003 and stabilized at pre-crisis levels.

53. CESVI (*Centro de Experimentación y Seguridad Vial*) an Argentine umbrella organization of car insurance companies, deliberately does not report absolute numbers.

54. While CESVI does not report actual numbers, it is easy to work out that violent car thefts were more numerous in 2009 than in 2004. For 2004, the year taken as a base, 33 percent of cars were stolen by very violent means. In 2009 this rate was 27 percent, but the total number of cars stolen was 43 percent higher than in 2004.

55. These figures were provided by the UNDP by Chilean authorities and reported at UNDP 2013.

56. http://www.presidencia.gub.uy/_web/noticias/2009/06/observatorio.pdf page 7.

57. The expansion of credit is a by-product of relative macroeconomic stability gained through the 1990s and the early twenty-first century.

58. Reported by CESVI. See http://www.iprofesional.com/notas/148386-Por-freno-al-ingreso-de-bienes-importados-crece-el-robo-de-neumticos-y-precios-de-repuestos.

59. http://informe21.com/actualidad/andar-moto-asegurar-numero-loteria-muerte (accessed November 16, 2013).

60. For a twenty-first-century study on the relationship between crime and rising living standards, see Zehr (1976); a recently, very illuminating paper by Rosenfeld and Levin (2016); Cohen and Felson (1979); and van Dijk and Mahew (1992).

61. There is an array of instruments to reduce the price of legal goods. Lower taxes and import duties create incentives and legal venues for secondary markets. For car parts for example, insurance companies and other players can support and facilitate the development of junk yards for old and total-loss vehicles that can supply parts for a legal used-parts market.

62. States can reverse course and instill deterrence to regain social control. However, once the illegal markets mature, the resources and displayed capacities that are necessary to regain control must rely on an overwhelming force that states in the region can very rarely muster. An exception in its efforts to overturn the drug market and reduce homicides has been the case of Colombia.

CHAPTER 5

1. Over the last decade many countries have introduced legislation that has softened the penalties for illegal drug possession and personal consumption. For a summary of legislation in Latin America, see Carvalho (2009).
2. Medical marihuana legislation in California and more recently in the states of Washington and Colorado represented a crucial step in that direction.
3. The production and use of coca was legal in Peru until 1948 and in Bolivia until 1961. Only after strong pressure from the United States did these countries criminalize the production and use of the drug (Gootenberg 2009).
4. The amount of meth seized in Mexico rose from 341 kg in 2008 to 44 tons in 2012 (WDR 2014, 47).
5. It is generally believed that production data is more reliable than consumption statistics, though there are large discrepancies. For instance, as Piquet Carneiro (2009, 3) has shown, while UNODC estimated the quantity of hectares used for coca plantations at 159,600, the US National Drug Intelligence Center estimated this at 31 percent more (208,500 hectares) for the same year. However, when estimating production for that year, from coca leaves to pure cocaine, these agency results are reversed: while the US agency estimated total production at 780 tons, the UN agency estimated it at 980 tons.
6. Consumption in the United States appears to be the driver. See the *New York Times* article "New York Is a Hub in a Surging Heroin Trade," May 19, 2014.
7. In 2005 Argentina imported approximately 3 tons of ephedrine from the Far East. In 2006, imports doubled and then rose to 19 tons in 2007. Only a small fraction is believed to be used for the regular chemical industry. According to estimates, 80 percent is smuggled into Mexico, apparently to the Sinaloa Cartel. This case has already gone to court, with an indictment of the former head of Argentina's Drug Prevention Agency (SEDRONAR) and several suspicious homicides of people close to the case. For more on this case, see http://www.perfil.com/ediciones/elobservador/-20125-673-0001.html.
8. According to US estimates, 50 percent of cocaine consumed in America came through Mexico in 1991, while in 2005, 90 percent of cocaine and many other drugs the country consumed came from its southern neighbor (O'Neill 2009).

9. According to the Bureau of Transportation Statistics, 4.23 million trucks carrying 2.6 million loaded containers crossed the border in 2003 (Payan 2006).

10. See journalist Richard Marosi's account on the operation of the Sinaloa cartel smuggling schemes in a four-article series *Los Angeles Times*, July 24–28, 2011.

11. No serious study has ever confirmed these estimates, but the UNODC has estimated confiscation at 15 percent of all drug shipments. (WDR 2011).

12. Alcohol use, on the other hand, has been relatively high in most countries.

13. Colombia presents an interesting example. Despite an unmatched availability of cheap cocaine, with a gram costing just US$5 and a marijuana joint going for US$1.00 (COHA Report 2009), the rate of illegal drug consumption is no higher than the Latin American average. In other words, a high availability of drugs has not translated into a widespread consumer market.

14. Caulkins et al. (2015) and others argue that since there are disparities in the quantities consumed by different drug users, prevalence rates cannot accurately inform the amount consumers use per month or year, and this information is needed to adjust total market estimates.

15. Several excellent anthropological and sociological studies have considered the individual dimension, mostly for Hispanics in the United States or at the border. See for example Muehlmann (2013) and Burgois (2003).

16. There are several stages in the production of cocaine. Growers collect the coca leaves and grind them into coca paste, which is mixed with readily available chemicals to produce the cocaine paste (*pasta base*). This base is processed with expensive chemicals in clandestine laboratories to produce cocaine chlorohydrate. Large DTOs control some of these laboratories because they require heavy investments in equipment and chemicals.

17. These organizations, of course, hire large number of individuals to transport, secure, protect, and smuggle the drugs. But the number of organizations that control the trafficking remains relatively small.

18. Kilmer and Reuter (2009, 175) present similar figures using official sources.

19. A CAF study (2014, 146) reports that the value added for cocaine within Colombia is 29 percent for the growing and production stage and 71 percent for the traffic stage (from the laboratories to the Colombian borders).

20. Wages in the United States and Western Europe are among the highest in the world. Street dealer earnings must account for the cost of labor in each market.

21. In 2004, 282,590 people were arrested in the United States and 201,760 convicted for drug trafficking (BJS 2007).

22. See, for example Patrik Radden Keefe's profile of "El Chapo Guzmán" as an expert smuggler, *New Yorker*, May 5, 2014, http://www.newyorker.com/magazine/2014/05/05/the-hunt-for-el-chapo?currentPage=all

23. For more information, see http://www.cbp.gov/linkhandler/cgov/border_security/border_patrol/usbp_statistics/usbp_fy12_stats/staffing_1993_2012.ctt/staffing_1993_2012.pdf

24. During these years total cocaine consumption in the United States also began to decrease.

25. Various estimates suggest that approximately 40 percent of the cocaine produced in South America and sent north for the US market never reaches that country (NDIC 2010; Chalk 2011). UNODC estimates that in 2012 more than 500 tons of cocaine was seized in LATAM, although some seizures may have been double counted (WDR 2014, 34).

26. See Pacula et al. (2013) for a comprehensive review on the relationship between drugs and criminal violence.

27. The PCC allegedly enforced a "peace agreement" in 2016 between organized violent fans (*torcidas*) of soccer teams in Sao Paulo. See https://esportes.terra. com.br/corinthians/paz-entre-as-torcidas-em-sao-paulo-teria-relacao-com-ordem-do-pcc,8aaf3056c7a9e8090e49d79b7a3a427fa2wvxynp.html (accessed Dec 7, 2016).

28. Rosario is the most important city of Santa Fe province.

29. Inegi (Instituto Nacional de Estadistica y Geografía), www.inegi.org.mx. "Comunicación Social." *Boletín de Prensa* 301/14; July 23, 2014. Aguascalientes, AGS. Mexico.

30. Gangs fight also to protect transshipment routes for large DTOs in this Pacific state, where some of the South American cocaine lands before being moved northward and for the production of opiates for the US market.

31. Drug users are less likely to be imprisoned in Latin America, unless they also deal or transport drugs for an organization.

32. The total sample is not fully representative of the drug-related crimes of each country because in countries such as Mexico or Argentina drug-related offenses are federal crimes and in Mexico no inmates of federal penitentiaries were surveyed. Still, the number of observations and the countries covered provide an accurate description of the scope and breadth of the drug offenders in the region.

33. Some experts in personal interviews speculate that meth and ecstasy cater to a middle- and upper-middle-class consumer base which is supplied through channels of distribution that authorities do not fully pursue. The data from this survey do not allow this hypothesis to be tested.

34. Working as "mules" was quite common, particularly among women. The survey revealed that at least 20 percent of the people who were arrested for drug-related crimes were carrying only small quantities of drug.

35. This rate should be considered a baseline. Some inmates might not respond honestly to this question out of fear of additional sanctions.

36. This data does not lend support to the "Goldstein" hypothesis, whereby drug addicts commit crimes (among them drug dealing) in order to finance their own addictions (Goldstein 1985).

37. See inmate survey report on Argentina, Bergman et. al. (2014).

38. Retail sales are carried out by individuals autonomously because, as mentioned, the risk premium for apprehension is very high.

39. According to official reports from the National System of Public Security, in 2002 this state had 184 homicides, 4 kidnappings, 5 cases of extortions, and 2,650 car thefts. Ten years later (2012) there were 1,016 homicides, 123 kidnappings, 154 cases of extortions and a total of 8,960 car thefts. See http://www.secretariadoejecutivosnsp.gob.mx/work/models/SecretariadoEjecutivo/Resource/1/1/cifras_publicacion_junio14.pdf

40. The Sinaloa cartel has a long history and deeper roots, although their base operation has been traditionally Northwestern Mexico (which borders California and Arizona). The cartel failed to control Tamaulipas but was successful in controlling Ciudad Juarez years later.

41. See also Magaloni et al. (2015) who show that the large drop in homicides is due to a decrease in police killings.

42. For example, according to several reports, in a *favela* in the area of Nova Iguacu homicides almost doubled from 2008 to 2014, jumping from 177 to 310. See http://www.infolatam.com/2014/07/24/la-pacificacion-de-favelas-de-rio-traslada-la-violencia-hacia-la-periferia/?utm_source=Newsletter%20de%20Infolatam&utm_medium=email&utm_campaign=Newsletter_24_julio_2014_Infolatam:%20Ibope%20da%20a%20Rousseff%2038%20por%20ciento%20de%20apoyo%20y%20ganar%C3%ADa%20en%20segunda%20vuelta%20a%20Neves%20y%20Campos

43. It is worth mentioning that the PCC, originally from Sao Paulo, has tried since 2016 to penetrate also this market, creating more rivalries, particularly with Comando Vermelho. See Insight Crime http://es.insightcrime.org/analisis/mayor-pandilla-brasil-desafia-control-rival-rio

44. Bolivia, albeit different, also represents a case of low violence in the third largest producer of coca leaf and cocaine. As Bagley (2012, p.7) suggests, " . . . the presence of peasant cooperatives in the countryside since the . . . National Revolutionary Movement of 1952 produced coca growers' associations and generally inhibited the rise of either criminal organizations or guerrilla movements as intermediaries." A bottom up social foundation kept cartels and large-scale violence at bay in this country.

CHAPTER 6

1. As mentioned in chapter 1, Bailey (2014) also describes a similar process for Mexico he calls "security traps."

2. For illustrative purposes, a homicide rate of 20 per 100,000 can be considered a threshold for HCE

3. Conversely, data for the 1980s show an average of 1,700 homicides per year, a rate of 9 per 100,000 (Briceño-Leon et al. 2012, 55).

4. In chapter 1 I showed that unstable equilibriums are characterized by low crime but poor law enforcement is unable to cope with the challenge once major stressors unravel the crime equilibrium.

5. Many Latin American countries are cash-based societies and locals use cash even for major purchases such as homes and vehicles.

6. Another version of such robberies targets people who withdraw money from teller machines, though these generally involve smaller amounts of cash.

7. http://e-consulta.com/tags/robo-cuentahabiente?page=7

8. For more information, see http://www.iprofesional.com/notas/102924-Sepa-las-15-recomendaciones-para-evitar-ser-victima-de-una-salidera-bancaria

9. Eisner (2013) has studied cross-national variations in homicides and distinguishes between high- and low-violence countries. Using historical and UNODC data, he shows that in high-violence societies, the perpetrators and victims are predominantly males, are not marginalized, tend to victimize strangers, kill for instrumental reasons (strategic goals), and live in societies with a high circulation of weapons. Although I do not delve into these topics in this chapter, they are in line with my arguments here.

10. Kalyvas (2006) has developed a similar argument on the use violence in contexts of civil war.

11. The concept of organized crime has been contested. As Paoli and Vander Baken (2014) explain ". . . the understanding of organized crime has shifted back and forth between two rival notions: (1) a set of stable organizations illegal per se or whose members systematically engage in crime, and (2) a set of serious criminal activities mostly carried out for monetary gains" (p 14). The emphasis might be on the "who" or on the "what," although both perspectives recognize that they are deeply entrenched. In this book, I emphasize the criminal activities and opportunities as drivers for this type of criminality, recognizing that once groups and networks acquire autonomy of operation they diversify into other illegal trades. In short, they might start on the "what" (the crimes), but then the "who" (the criminals) can themselves drive crime up.

12. For example, between 2008 and 2010, sixty-eight border patrol and customs officers in the United States have been investigated (and many indicted) for corruption at the border (mostly for drug trafficking, bribery, or human smuggling). See report at http://bordercorruption.apps.cironline.org/

13. http://www.controlrisks.com/en/riskmap/kidnap

14. This also suggests that reporting rates are problematic. For instance, according to UNODC (2014), in 2009 Peru had one of the highest rates of kidnapping (2.5 per 100,000) while El Salvador has among the lowest (0.4), yet the incarceration rates in Peru were lower than in El Salvador.

15. In Chile and Argentina, some police involvement has been reported in robberies and drug dealing.

16. The ransom exceeded one million dollars in only a handful of cases.

17. Only a few of these cases are considered "express kidnappings," a form of abduction in which an individual is captured at random, forced to withdraw as much cash as possible from ATMs, and released soon afterwards.

18. Public Ministry of Guatemala, http://brujula.com.gt/trata-y-trafico-de-personas-en-cifras/

19. Public Ministry of Peru, http://www.mpfn.gob.pe/index.php/unidades/observatorio-de-criminalidad

20. Car theft is so common in many countries of the region that people often disregard red lights when driving at night out of fear of carjacking. See for example for Venezuela: https://www.osac.gov/pages/ContentReportDetails.aspx?cid=13038

21. Using data from the municipal level, Castillo, Mejía, and Restrepo (2012) show that the severe limitation of the cocaine supply from Colombia in 2007–2008 intensified the fight for traffic routes through Mexico.

22. http://justiceinmexico.files.wordpress.com/2014/04/140415-dvm-2014-releasered1.pdf

23. From 2007 until 2011, based on tabulations from INEGI data, four states accounted for more than 80 percent of criminal executions. Moreover, more than 70 percent of homicides are concentrated in 100 of the 2,450 Mexican municipalities.

24. Rios (2013) also highlights the shifting nature of extreme violence in Mexico. She claims that a self-reinforcing violent equilibrium caused by competition between gangs and the selective enforcement of government contributed to escalating violence in certain regions. High criminality also exists, but where there is no competition because consolidated gangs extort and terrorize populations.

25. Under HCE, regions can experience sharp declines in criminality in short periods of time, because many regions reduce crime from extremely high levels due to either some success at increasing law enforcement (e.g., in Medellin or Rio de Janeiro) or because conflicts that gave rise to high crime were resolved or settled (e.g., in Tijuana or Ciudad Juarez). But crime remains very high.

26. For excellent studies on historical patterns of crime in Mexico, see Picatto (2001) and Buffington and Piccato (2009).

27. Serious property crime was defined as crimes involving property worth at least US$200.

28. This is in addition to the familiar story of concentrated disadvantage, drugs, and poverty, depicted in the criminological literature in the United States and Europe. Here I concentrate on the macro consequences of the spread of organized crime on illegal drugs and illicit markets.

29. This is not to say that government authorities are absolutely blind. By several journalist accounts, in some violent encounters authorities refrain from participating in violent episodes, thus indirectly favoring one group over another.

30. As Andreas Schedler (2014) rightly states, "The rate of narco-executions that have led to judicial convictions is close to zero. The Mexican government has virtually consented to the privatization of the death penalty." (Author translation.)

31. The median ransom elucidated from the Mexican inmate survey was US$14,000. It must be assumed that even poor law enforcement selects cases for prosecution that are more noticeable and therefore this sample will naturally include the "high tickets." In addition, prisons naturally house a larger proportion of dangerous offenders who receive longer sentences. Presumably, the sample over-represents high-ransom kidnappers.

32. According to various estimations, approximately 40 percent of the cocaine produced in South America and sent northbound for the US market never reaches that country (Rand and others). This of course brings heavy losses that need to be taken in consideration.

33. Data from the national surveys is available at http://www.conadic.salud.gob.mx/pdfs/ena08/ENA08_NACIONAL.pdf.

34. In contrast, the number of US users and the share of the US market are both much larger. From the first survey in 1971 until 2000, cocaine use grew by 350 percent, heroin by 300 percent, and marihuana by 350 percent. However, drug consumption has appeared to be stabilizing over the last decade. In 2008, the national survey of drug use estimated that there are 20.1 million people ages 12 or older who use illegal drugs, or 8 percent of the adult population. Only 7 million of these people are considered dependent or addicts. For a good summary of these data, see "The Continued Standstill in Reducing Illicit Drug Use," Policy Brief de Carnevale Associates, September 2009 at www.carnevaleassociates.com/publications.html.

35. See the Mexican survey ENA (2011, 102–104) on drug use and addictions.

36. *Delito y Cárcel en México, deterioro social y desempeño institucional: Reporte histórico de la población carcelaria en el Distrito Federal y el Estado de México, 2002 a 2013: Indicadores clave.*

37. Of course, it must be assumed that there is considerable underreporting, though surveys provide rough approximations on the scale of drug use within prisons.

38. The data used here was obtained from www.observatorionacionalciudadano.org.mx, which builds an index of so-called "high-impact" crimes. Data sources are total reported crimes to DA offices (compiled by SNSP, *Sistema Nacional de Seguridad Pública*), which represent the standard venue for reporting crime.

39. Data from SESNSP shows a lower rate but as this official agency has recognized, it did not include cases in which federal agencies or the army and the navy had intervened. These adjusted figures include both. See Seguridad Paz y Justicia (2014).

40. Given that these estimates are derived from victimization surveys with samples of 90,000 households, the confidence intervals of such rare events are very large and it is therefore hard to establish a real trend. (For a debate on this topic, see

http://javier-marquez.com/2014/01/15/la-cifra-negra-de-secuestro-puede-estar-sobre-estimada/). While these numbers might be overestimated, these events are common enough in Mexico that the surveys reveal a significant number of cases.

41. From 2001 to 2008 the number of agents has doubled, and between 2002 and 2008 the number of Mexicans deported from the United States to Mexican border towns rose by 35 percent, increasing the availability of "soldiers" for DTOs (Aguilar Camin 2015).

CHAPTER 7

1. For Mexico, see Davies (2013), for Argentina, Kalmanowiecky (2000), and for Brazil, Holloway (1993).
2. This also indicates endogenously that stable LCE usually allows for bad police behavior.
3. Rather than a dichotomy, centralization–autonomy and crime prevention–investigation can be in practice conceptualized as a continuum. In centralized police, regional or local agencies have different levels of autonomy, while the difference between prevention and investigation can also become murky in practice.
4. Research on police reform in Mexico has shown that local police forces lack proper anti-corruption controls, professionalization programs, and adequate equipment to do their jobs (Bailey and Dammert 2006). In addition, policing strategies might change from administration to administration, in part due to the lack of a strong police career system and the reliance on informal rules and cronyism (Sabet 2012).
5. There is of course an endogenous effect. However, the index also includes resources, other agency support, and capacities which can be somewhat independent and compensate for the crime threat.
6. I also include homicide rates for each country to contrast the effect of this information on crime rates.
7. Note also that personnel rolls are an inexact measure of effectiveness as countries often do not differentiate between officers and administrative personnel in reporting.
8. Data for crime from chapter 2.
9. This lends support to the study of Schargrodsky and Di Tella (2004) on the role of police patrolling and crime.
10. Although the worldwide ratio of private to public officers is 2 to 1, it is much higher in Latin America: 4 to 1 in Brazil; 7 to 1 in Honduras; and 9 to 1 in Guatemala.
11. It has been estimated that only 10 percent of incidences are effectively solved when there is no direct witness or strong evidence (Skogan 2006).
12. For an excellent review on deterrence theory and crime, see Nagin (1998)

13. Over 1 percent of US adult males are in prison.

14. This in itself denotes a major weakness of police departments in the region in terms of data collection and management.

15. Worldwide, police mainly intervene in less serious incidents and infractions. Naturally, this produces large numbers of flagrant and random detentions. However, inmate surveys represent a different population of very serious offenders, those who committed crimes meriting long sentences. The overwhelming majority of cases resulting from random detention is puzzling and indirectly signals weak investigative capacities.

16. In most countries police officers and district attorneys have twenty-four to forty-eight hours to bring suspects before judges with initial charges.

17. For example, in Argentina, the official agency for fighting financial crimes (UIF) reported that in 2013 just ten individuals were arrested for money laundering. This official agency does not report whether these individuals were ultimately prosecuted or convicted for this crime. See http://www.uif.gov.ar/ section Informe de Gestión 2013/ Statistics

18. Sometimes, police were unable to identify perpetrators so they would produce one by planting evidence, changing testimonies, and so on, in order to bring at least one alleged perpetrator to justice.

19. See section "Police and Crime in the twentieth century" for references on police and crime throughout this period in several countries.

20. Naturally, other conceptual frameworks for policing such as community policing, crime watches, and others did prove important. These were community-based strategies and yielded at times meaningful results in terms of police–community relations and some crime reduction (for a good review on the implementation of these initiatives, see Maguire and Wells 2009). In this section, I concentrate exclusively on deterrence, which has not been the main goal of these policing strategies.

21. For hot-spot strategies see Weisburd and Braga (2003, 2006); Weisburd and Eck (2004); Braga et al. et al. (2012), Eck and Maguire (2006).

22. Examples of these initiatives include Boston's Operation Ceasefire (Braga, Piehl and Hureau 2009), Chicago's Project Safe Neighborhoods initiative (Papachristos, Meares and Fagan 2007, 2012), and North Carolina's Drug Market Initiative (Kennedy and Wond 2009).

23. Inspired by broken windows (Wilson and Kelling 1982), it builds on the basic assumption that serious crime develops because the police and citizens do not work together to prevent urban decay and social disorder.

24. Since crime is clustered in a few areas, hot-spot policing concentrates police efforts in these places.

25. *Plan Cuadrante* is a community police strategy, but includes the identification of crime hot spots as an important component.

26. An unpublished work by Jaitman (n.d.) shows somewhat initial encouraging results from experiments in Montevideo, Uruguay.

27. The current strategies of saturating the streets with uniformed officers—a practice widespread throughout the region—actually masks the inefficiencies of crime-fighting intelligence. The available research shows that unfocused community-oriented tactics such as foot patrols, storefront offices, newsletters, and community meetings do not reduce crime or disorder, though they do reduce people's fear of crime (Weisburd and Eck 2004; Skogan and Frydl 2004).

28. Special thanks to Mark Ungar for providing me with plenty of insight for this alternative explanation section.

29. "Some people say that the police in this neighborhood (town) protect the people from criminals, while others say that it is the police who are involved in crime: What is your opinion?" (Author translation). In 14 (out of 23) countries, including Brazil, Mexico, and Argentina, at least 40 percent of respondents believe that the police are involved in crime (Cruz 2010).

30. The variance between countries is noticeable: Chilean, Panamanian, and Nicaraguan police officers are perceived as less involved with criminals whereas in countries with high levels of criminality, such as Honduras, Guatemala, Venezuela and Mexico, there is equilibrium between crime and little trust in the police (LAPOP 2012).

31. Latin American Public Opinion Project (2008/2012) 'AmericasBarometer', www. LapopSurveys.org

32. Respondents were only asked about personal victimization experienced over the last twelve months, thus overlooking victims within a larger reference period (two to three years), and other household members (missing indirect victimization).

33. Latin American Public Opinion Project (2008/2012) 'Americas Barometer'. See also Dammert and Malone (2002).

34. As mentioned in section "Police in Latin America: Legacies and Current Structure", Latin American police forces have been geared toward maintaining order and protecting the state, whatever its political form, rather than safeguarding citizens and their rights (Andersen 2002; Waldmann 2003; Vallespir 2002; Davis 2010; Campesi 2010; Arias and Goldstein 2010).

35. I thank Hernan Flom for helping me to develop these ideas. Full explanation of survey data is found in Bergman and Flom (2012).

36. Both surveys were coordinated and directed by a team leading scholars in two prestigious universities: CIDE in Mexico and Universidad de San Andres in Argentina.

37. The question was: "In some countries people inform the police that they are going on vacation so that they will watch their house. If a similar system were implemented here, would you tell the police?"

38. For this analysis a perception of crime frequency index (PCFI) was elaborated and is explained along with the independent variables.

39. This rate of "a lot" of trust in Mexico is equivalent to the rate of people willing to trust the police to watch their homes in Buenos Aires while on vacation.

40. These parameters coincide with the three elements that Bayley (1994) identifies as pillars of police activity: patrols, rapid response to emergencies, and criminal investigation.

41. The question in both surveys is: "How do you evaluate/grade the form in which the police [protect from crime, patrol your neighborhood, respond to calls, and treat the people] in your neighborhood?" Responses were inverted. Original questions asked respondents to grade performance from very good (1) to very bad (5).

42. A principal component analysis using these four questions yielded one latent component with an eigenvalue of 2.8 and an explained variance of 56 percent. Using this factor in the logistic regressions has produced very similar results as the average index.

43. The extraction values for the PCA was similar across the four measures that compose this index: preventing crime 0.714, patrolling 0.712, response 0.688 and manners 0.694.

44. Prior tests for both countries reveal that the correlation between these variables is low.

45. Question: Close to your house/apartment, how frequently do the following take place: (a) armed robbery; (b) break-ins; (c) stolen cars; (d) rape; (e) homicide; (f) public alcohol or drug use; (g) assault among neighbors?

46. Ho & McKean (2004) have also found a negative relationship between the perceptions of personal risk and trust in the police.

47. This index derives from standard methodology used by the Argentine association of marketing. For a complete description see Bergman and Flom (2013).

48. Hidalgo López and Monsalve Briceño (2003) have found similar results for Caracas.

49. The following are the age groups (percent in the distribution): 15–19 (9.3 percent), 20–24 (8.8 percent), 25–34 (16.8 percent), 35–49 (23.3 percent), 50–64 (20.8 percent), and 65+ (21.1 percent).

50. Kessler and Bergman (2008) study the effect of Buenos Aires urban environment on perceptions of insecurity.

51. Several interaction effects were estimated but no important results were seen. The only modest evidence obtained is that female victims show more drastically reduced trust in the police compared to male victims.

52. Gerber and Mendelson (2008) found similar results in Russia. Skogan (2006) has also indicated that negative encounters with the police have a much larger impact than positive contacts.

53. There are variations. Typically, police avoid patrolling a chosen area at certain hours or given days. Sometimes crime gets out of hand, extreme violence or even homicides occur and a public outcry ensues (Lima et al. 2014; Binder 2004; Binder 2009; Sain 2004; Astorga 2000; Martinez 1999; Dewey 2015).

CHAPTER 8

1. "Combatiendo la Impunidad en Comayagua: Éxitos y Obstáculos." *Alianza por la Paz y La Justicia*. Tegucigalpa.

2. Prosecutor offices includes what it is known in Latin America to *fiscales* (prosecutors) and the *Ministerio Publico* (prosecution department).

3. This may be due to a lack of precision in the data, in terms of classification and processing of information in each country.

4. These data require careful interpretation since the percentage of expenses represents a share of total spending that varies significantly among countries.

5. The cutoff between intensive and non-intensive supervision is merely instrumental and for presentation purposes. In fact, as the data shows, this could easily be summarized as a continuous variable from high to low intensity. This table depicts the data in a way that allows Latin America to be compared to Western and Central Europe, Oceania, and North American.

6. CTS defines, *persons convicted* as "persons found guilty by any legal body authorized to pronounce a conviction under national criminal law whether or not the conviction was later upheld. The total number of persons convicted includes persons convicted of serious special law offences but excludes persons convicted of minor road traffic offenses." In addition, one important caveat: Most countries that do report to the UNODC's CTS are those that keep records and are more likely to have better institutional performance. In short, comparisons are made with LATAM countries that presumably have stronger law enforcement institutions.

7. Even today in most Latin American countries, drug trafficking violations are handled by judges who usually have to make decisions based on a poor investigation and limited information obtained by the police or another source. Judges oversee the proceedings from a legal standpoint but an investigation of the entire process is missing, as in the case of criminal networks where each particular crime is just one link in a long chain. Given the nature of organized crime, a "case" is part of a larger market and as such, it should be dealt with in coordination with multiple agencies. The goal should not be just to find who is guilty but to disband the market and more importantly, to deter potential agents from beginning a life of crime.

8. The new prominent role assigned to prosecutors was accompanied by a promise of a more effective fight against crime. The stated goal was to ". . . take charge and respond to important citizen demands . . . such as a reduction in crime rates" (Duce and Riego 2009) *Desafíos del Ministerio Público Fiscal en América Latina*, Santiago de Chile, p.14 (Author translation).

9. Most countries (with the exception of Brazil, Panama, and Uruguay) introduced constitutional and statutory reforms to overhaul penal procedures.

10. Abolitionism, critical criminology, and other brands of legal scholarship gained leverage among practitioners.

11. I am greatly indebted to Maximo Langer for many of the ideas presented in this section. In a paper we wrote together, I benefitted significantly from his contributions, which can be seen in the summaries and goals of the reform detailed in this section.

12. Several studies have been published on the subject; for summaries see Baytelman and Duce (2003), Langer (2011), Tiede (2012), and Pasara (2014).

13. For a thorough examination of different countries, see the publications of CEJA (Centro de Estudios de Justicia en las Américas) the think tank that promoted the penal reforms in Latin America since the 1990s, see www.cejamericas.org

14. Criminal procedure in Latin America inherited the continental inquisitorial process whereby an instructional judge conducts the criminal investigation and later passes the case to another court for trial if he or she finds sufficient evidence to indict a suspect. However, no LATAM judiciary was purely inquisitorial by the time reforms took place (Hammergren 2007).

15. For a good review of the inquisitorial vis-à-vis the accusatorial system in the Latin American context, see Langer (2007) and Meier (2003).

16. At the same time, a strong public defense office was to be created.

17. This *principio de oportunidad* (opportunity principle or criterion) allows the system to avoid routine overload.

18. In several countries, two different police departments were established (in some, such as in Mexico, they already existed), one for crime prevention (patrols), and a second, investigative unit under the supervision of the MPF.

19. The number of cases in which prosecutors decided not to pursue criminal investigation (approximately two out of three) was similar to the number of cases that never advanced through the system prior to the reforms, and where instructional judge never investigated or pressed charges (see Pasara 2013, 4–8).

20. I include only recent data for Brazil, Panama, and Uruguay because they have not yet made significant reforms to their criminal procedures. A similar study has been conducted by CEJA in a few countries but it only measured the effect of reforms two to three years after the reforms were enacted.

21. In Argentina, reforms at the federal levels were legislated in 2014, but some provinces, such as Buenos Aires, had passed reforms earlier.

22. The sample excluded two subsamples: inmates from San Pablo, Brazil and Buenos Aires, Argentina who were processed by the old inquisitorial systems.

23. Reforms introduced over the last decade allowed for public oral hearings and abbreviated trials.

24. INEGI 2014, *Boletín de Prensa* 552 (14): 6.

25. Countries with high levels of institutional trust also have relatively low rates of criminality. Citizens report more crimes, increasing the probability that offenders will be punished and improving the efficacy and trust in the system.

The opposite occurs with public mistrust, where police efficacy is reduced and criminality rises. Chapter 7 develops this argument for the police and provides abundant references from the literature on the relationship between trust and institutional performance.

26. See Fiscalías de Chile (2009); Boletín Estadístico del Ministerio Público (2009). http://www.fiscaliadechile.cl/Fiscalia/estadisticas/index.do?d1=30

27. http://www.mexicoevalua.org/wp-content/uploads/2013/02/IVVI-H-20126.pdf

28. OVV estimates that out of the at least 16,047 homicides committed in 2009, there were 1,497 arraignments in that year.

29. See https://www.plazapublica.com.gt/content/condenas-que-liberan, Graph 2.

30. This is, of course, an imperfect calculation, but it is the best estimate from the available data. I added the monthly report of prison entries for 2012 from the INPE (penitentiary office http://www.inpe.gob.pe/contenidos. php?id=532&np=1&direccion=1), a total of 1,002 entries between *homicidio calificado* and *homicidio simple* (these will closely resemble murder in the first and second degrees in the United States). Since there were 2,865 homicides in 2012 (http://www.datosmacro.com/demografia/homicidios/peru), the rate would be 34.9 percent. These are not convictions but prison entries for homicides, and of course many people could be indicted for the same homicide. The actual rate, therefore, is probably lower or close to this estimate.

31. In 2012 there were 52,198 homicides in Brazil (Waiselfisz 2014, 27). At the beginning of that year, there were 59,045 inmates imprisoned for homicide, while at the end of 2012 there were 63,066, a difference of 4,021 (Execusao Penal 2014). The same database indicates that less than 60 percent of the total inmate population had already been convicted, with half of them serving between 9 and 50 years. Those convicted for homicides are likely to serve between 15 to 50 years; therefore, turnover among this group is very small. It can be safely estimated that no more than 10 percent of the people convicted for homicide are released or die in prison each year, therefore, in 2012 they probably did not exceed 6,000 inmates. In short, from the release (6,000) and the increment in number of homicide inmates (4,021) it can be safely assumed that no more than 10,000 new entries for homicides were registered in Brazil's prisons in 2012. Assuming that each inmate accounts for one homicide (which is not always the case), that yields less than a 20 percent conviction rate (10,021/52,198). The impunity rate thus exceeds 80 percent. The difference with the estimates for Peru is that in that country, there is information on flows according to the type of crime committed while in Brazil, the information is only on stocks (number of inmates according to type of crime at the end of a given year).

32. Author estimation based on data obtained from www.inegi.org.mx consulta inteactiva de datos/estadísticas de mortalidad/defunciones por homicidio (year and state).

33. In his work based on interviews with prosecutors and case examinations, Pásara (2010) observes that these repeat robbers regularly benefit from alternative measures that allow them to avoid the sanctions of this accusatorial system (p. 13). The "opportunity criterion" that prosecutors often used to dismiss cases like these rarely involved any serious examination of previous contacts of offenders with the CJS. "The prosecutors appear to only see the case at hand and not the person involved, who generally was a repeat offender" (p. 13). (Author translation).

34. This sample cannot assess the level of criminality of those who have avoided detection. They were presumably more "professional" at carrying out crimes.

35. This underreported rate is difficult to estimate with precision, because many inmates refuse to respond.

36. Since the CJS very rarely sentences first time drug or property crime offenders to prison, it is likely that the overwhelming majority of inmates have indeed committed similar crimes before apprehension, though they may refuse to acknowledge it. The analysis is thus based on those who did report a number of crimes and the profits they made.

37. In Peru, a single very large case drives up the mean. Most are very small drug sales.

38. This means that for the sample, 79 percent of property crimes and 86 percent of drug crimes that led to convictions involved less than $10,000.

39. The actual time served by these inmates could be less since sentences are often reduced due to good behavior and other early releases venues. Most, however, serve between two-thirds and the entire sentence.

40. When the value is set at $10,000, the rate of conviction reaches 8.8 percent for 2011.

CHAPTER 9

1. These rates were calculated by Vilalta (2015).

2. For a comprehensive summary of the current prison population for each country, see ICPS (2015).

3. Between 5 and 20 percent of inmates are serving time for sex crimes.

4. Costa Rica represents a typical case where 40.5 percent of inmates serve time for property crime violations, 20.6 percent for drugs, 16.3 percent for sexual crimes, 14.8 percent for homicides, and less than 8 percent for all other felonies. See MJP (2014)

5. By country, the average sentence for the sample was nine years in Argentina, eleven years for Sao Paulo, Brazil, eight years for Chile, twenty years for El Salvador, eighteen years for Mexico, and thirteen years for Peru. These are country means that are different from country medians reported in Table 9.3.

6. Due to the recent upsurge in drug trafficking, countries have passed longer sentences for drug crimes, some of which violate the proportional criteria of retributive justice (the punishment must fit the crime). In some countries, homicide could mean twenty-five years behind bars but someone convicted of drug trafficking could receive a similar sentence. See CELS (2015) and WOLA (2010).

7. In developed countries, the rate of offenders detained without a firm sentence varies but it is usually lower. For example, the rate is 18 percent in Germany, 26 percent in France, 34 percent in Italy, 16 percent in Portugal, 25 percent in Sweden, 14 percent in England and Wales, 35 percent in Canada, and 21 percent in the United States.

8. Many prison facilities in the region house more than 5,000 inmates, and several such as in Mexico, house more than 10,000. These facilities are very difficult to run.

9. A topic that has yet to be adequately addressed in the region is the effect of incarceration at very young ages. The younger median age and shorter time served suggests that many more young people are re-entering the community at an age that represents a criminogenic risk. Although, there is no data to prove this assertion, future research should evaluate such an impact.

10. Levitt (1996) and Johnson and Raphael (2012) use instrumental variable regression models to identify the causal effects of imprisonment on crime, and they do lend some support for crime prevention. I will discuss these findings in the Latin American context in this chapter.

11. Lengthy sentences are justified in terms of deterrence. There is not enough evidence that the threat of extended rather than shorter sentences avert offenders' decision to commit crimes (Nagin 2013). Risk of apprehension, on the other hand, has a more powerful deterrent effect.

12. The measurable impact of incapacitation has been debated over the last decade. A comprehensive meta-study by Gendreau et al. (1996) reviews more than one hundred studies found little support to the claim that more and tougher sanctions prevent future crime.

13. *Mano dura* refers to tough-on-crime policies in the region, including some whose legality could be questionable.

14. The effect of social inequality and rise in incarceration has been studied by Wacquant (2000).

15. Conventional routes for social integration are blocked for most inmates as they return to their communities. See Steffensmeier and Ulmer (2005); Bernburg and Krohn (2003); Sampson and Laub (1997).

16. Although the average is one year, the median between prior release and current re-arrest is ten months. This means that for the sample of those re-arrested, half were apprehended no more than ten months after they exited prisons.

17. A study in the United States for inmates released between 2005 and 2010 in thirty states (BJS 2014) found that 68 percent were re-arrested within three years of their release.

18. Rare data on Argentina for 2007 lends proof to the high rotation hypothesis. At the end of that year, there were 50,980 inmates in jails, with data on the time of detention for 42,653 of them. Fifty percent of these inmates had been arrested within the last two years. On the other hand, only 961 of the entire inmate population were serving ten years or more and 4,900 inmates (just 11.5 percent) had been in prison for five years or more. See SNEEP (2008, 28) at http://www.jus. gob.ar/areas-tematicas/estadisticas-de-politica-criminal/mapa.aspx

    In Costa Rica, a 2014 report established that for those inmates for whom they have information, more than half will be released by 2017—in less than three years—and two-thirds by 2019. See MJP (2014, 54) at http://www.mjp. go.cr/Downloads/Estadistica/II percent20TRIMESTRE percent202014.pdf

19. Rates of recidivism are particularly high in gang-dominated systems. Lessing (2013) reports 70 percent in San Pablo and 90 percent among the *mara* populations in El Salvador.

20. It is important to note that the inmate surveys do not include a control group that did not recidivate, and therefore, there is no true comparison between independent groups. These data only reflect the offenders who were re-arrested.

21. My core claim is simple: the more likely a potential criminal is to go to prison and the longer he will stay, the more he is willing to "pay" for membership in a prison gang that can protect him on the inside.

22. A true story illustrates the frustration of prison sergeants and the question of who really runs prison facilities. I met with all the penitentiary system directors to ask for authorization to conduct the surveys. In one of these meetings, the head of the prison system of the country in question assented to the study with the following words: ". . . I grant you the permit to do the study. Now you have to ask *them* for authorization." I replied to him: "What do you mean by *them*?" Very naturally, he responded "The group leaders. If you don't negotiate with them, nobody will show up for the interviews. They must also approve this project . . ." Of course, my team and I talked to these inmate leaders and they also agreed to participate in the surveys.

23. In San Pablo, the removal of privileges for PCC leaders inside prisons triggered a crime wave on the outside, including the burning of buses and stores, the murder of police, and riots (Adorno and Salla 2007).

24. Some have argued that an effective crackdown affects retail prices and so harsh punishment could raise prices. Yet the available data indicate exactly the opposite: retail prices of drugs have been coming down in the region, signaling that there was not a short supply and availability is probably on the rise.

25. One noteworthy development in Argentina is the data on property crime, which has been underreported or discontinued entirely since 2008. In Brazil, two very

important states (Minas Gerais and Santa Catalina) are not included in the total car theft figures but are included in prison population (the figures could not be separated). If missing data for those two states are imputed from 2009 onwards, the r coefficient would have turned positive.

26. Higher prevalence does not necessarily mean a greater supply of illegal drugs. I base the argument on the assumption that higher prevalence indirectly suggests higher availability, particularly when street prices are lower.

27. The case of Honduras is puzzling and derived from data for the first decade. Although there was a dramatic increase in the homicide rate, the incarceration rate stagnated. Prison conditions in that country are terrible, but the number of inmates significantly increased only in recent years. For example, while in 2007 the homicide rate was 43 and the imprisonment rate was 171, four years later homicide increased to 82 while imprisonment was 162. In short, the increase in homicide was dramatic but incarceration rates did not grow (data for homicide and incarceration from alertamerica.org)

28. Colombia is an outlier in this matrix because it has succeeded in a dramatic reduction of homicide rates after a peak in the 1990s and early 2000s.

29. For a study on the retail prices in different countries and the relative low prices in Latin America, see a report by the UNODC (United Nations Office of Drugs and Crimes) at https://www.unodc.org/unodc/secured/wdr/Prices_Cocaine.pdf

30. In addition, the "discount rate," that is, how individuals discount the future and instead prioritize the present and immediate gratification, does affect people's propensity to consider the adverse consequences of crime, including the likelihood of getting caught and sent to prison. In short, some offenders may not even seriously consider incarceration as an outcome.

31. Because of type of data available I cannot estimate whether incapacitation might work for some crimes and not for others. For example, incapacitation for predatory sex offenders has been found to reduce the number of rapes. Yet for car thefts, homicides, and illegal drug supply there is no evidence that these crimes have been seriously curtailed in the region after an increase in incarceration rates.

References

CHAPTER 1

Adams, T. 2011. *Chronic Violence and Its Reproduction: Perverse Trends in Social Relations, Citizenship, and Democracy in Latin America.* Washington, DC: Woodrow Wilson Center for Scholars.

Amnesty International. 2016. *Amnesty International Report 2015/2016: The State of the World´s Human Rights*, http://www.amnesty.eu/content/assets/Docs_2016/ReportsBriefings/air201516-english.pdf

Andreas, P. 2015. "Illicit Americas: Historical Dynamics of Smuggling in U.S. Relations with Its Neighbors." In *American Crossings: Border Politics in the Western Hemisphere*, Maiah Jaskoski, Arturo C. Sotomayor, and Harold A. Trinkunas, eds. Baltimore, MD: Johns Hopkins University Press. 153–170.

Antillano, A., Pojomovsky, I., Zubillaga, V., Sepulveda, C., and Hanson, R. 2016. "The Venezuelan Prison: From Neoliberalism to the Bolivarian Revolution." *Crime Law and Social Change* 65: 195–211.

Arias, E. 2006. *Drugs and Democracy in Rio de Janeiro: Trafficking, Social Networks, and Public Security.* Chapel Hill: University of North Carolina Press.

Arias, E. 2017. *Criminal Politics: Illicit Activities and Governance in Latin American and the Caribbean.* New York: Cambridge University Press.

Arias, E., and Goldstein, D., eds. 2010. *Violent Democracy in Latin America: Toward an Interdisciplinary Reconceptualization.* Durham: Duke University Press.

Arias, E., and Ungar, M. 2009. "Community Policing and Policy Implementation: A Four-City Study of Police Reform in Brazil and Honduras." *Comparative Politics* 41 (4): 409–430.

Astorga, L. 2005. *El siglo de las drogas: el narcotráfico, del Porfiriato al nuevo milenio.* México City: Plaza y Janes.

Auyero, J., and Berti, M. 2013. *La Violencia en los Márgenes: Una maestra y un sociólogo en el conurbano bonaerense.* Buenos Aires: Katz Editores.

Azaola, E., and Ruiz, M. 2012. "El rol de la corrupción en la reproducción institucional de la Policía Judicial de la Ciudad de México." *Atlas de la Seguridad y la Defensa de México*. Mexico, DF: CASEDE/Open Society.

Bagley, B., and Rosen, J. 2015. *Drug Trafficking, Organized Crime, and Violence in the Americas Today*. Gainsville: University Press of Florida.

Bailey, J. 2014. *The Politics of Crime in Mexico: Democratic Governance in a Security Trap*. Boulder: Lynne Rienner Publisher.

Bateson, Regina. 2012. "Crime Victimization and Political Participation." *American Political Science Review* 106 (3): 570–587.

Beato, C. 2012. *Crime e Cidade*. UFMG, Cincias Humanas e Sociais.

Beltran, I. de L., and Salcedo, Albarán E. 2003. "¿Por qué no hay una relación entre crimen y distribución del ingreso en Colombia? Una explicación para el período 1976-1997 a partir de la evolución de la actividad criminal." *Borradores de Método Área de Crimen y Conflicto ISSN: 1692-9667*, http://www.esalbaran.com/oldocs/crimenydesigualdad.pdf

Bergman, M., Fondevila G., and Vilalta, C. 2014. *Delito, Marginalidad y Desempeño Institucional. Resultados de la Encuesta de Internos en Reclusión*. Buenos Aires: UNTREF.

Blumstein, A., and Wallman, J., eds. 2006. *The Crime Drop in America*. Cambridge: Cambridge University Press.

Braga, Anthony A., and Weisburd, David L. 2010. *Policing Problem Places: Crime Hot Spots and Effective Prevention*. New York: Oxford University Press.

Briceño, Leon R. 2008. *Sociologia de la Violencia en America Latina*. Quito: Facultad Latino americana de Ciencias Sociales, FLACSO.

Briceño, León R., Avila, O., and Camardiel, A. 2012. *Violencia e Institucionalidad: Informe del Observatorio Venezolano de Violencia 2012*. Caracas: Editorial Alfa.

Brinks, D. 2008. *The Judicial Response to Police Killings in Latin America. Inequality and the Rule of Law*. New York: Cambridge University Press.

Bruneau, T., Dammert, L., and Skinner E., eds. 2011. *Maras. Gang Violence and Security in Central America*. Austin: University of Texas Press.

CAF. 2014. *Por una América Latina más Segura: Una Nueva perséctiva para prevenir y controlar el delito*. Corporación Andina de Fomento, Reporte de Economía y Desarrollo.

Caimari, L. 2012. *Mientras la ciudad duerme: pistoleros, policías y periodistas en buenos aires, 1920–1945*. Buenos Aires: Siglo XXI.

Caldeira, T. 2001. *City of Walls: Crime, Segregation, and Citizenship in São Paulo*. Berkeley, CA: University of California Press.

Cano, I. 2012. 'OS DONOS DO MORRO': UMA AVALIAÇÃO EXPLORATÓRIA DO IMPACTO DAS UNIDADES DE POLÍCIA PACIFICADORA (UPPs) NO RIO DE JANEIRO. Foro Brasileiro da Seguranca Publica and o Laboratório de Análise da Violência—(LAV-UERJ), http://www.lav.uerj.br/docs/rel/2012/RelatUPP.pdf

Carrillo, A. 2009. "Internal Displacement in Colombia: Humanitarian, Economic, and Social Consequences in Urban Settings and Current Challenges." *International Review of the Red Cross* 91 (875): 527–546.

Casas-Zamora, K., ed. 2013. *Dangerous Liaisons: Organized Crime and Political Finance in Latin America and Beyond*. Washington, DC: Brookings Institution Press.

Clarke, R. 1997. *Situational Crime Prevention: Successful Case Studies*. Reprint [1992]. New York: Harrow and Heston.

Cornish, D., and Clarke, R. 1987. "Understanding Crime Displacement: An Application of Rational Choice Theory." *Criminology* 25 (4): 933–947.

Cruz, J. M. 2010. "Central American Maras: From Youth Gangs to Transnational Protection Rackets." *Global Crime* 11 (4): 379–398.

Cruz, J. M. 2011. "Criminal Violence and Democratization in Central America: The Survival of the Violent State." *Latin American Politics and Society* 53 (4): 1–33.

Dammert, L. 2012. *Fear of Crime. Redefying State-Society Relations*. London: Routledge.

Dammert, L., and Malone, M. F. T. 2006. "Does It Take a Village? Policing Strategies and Fear of Crime in Latin America." *Latin American Politics and Society* 48 (4): 27–51.

Davis, D. E. 2010. "The Political and Economic Origins of Violence and Insecurity in LatinAmerica. Past Trajectories and Future Prospects." In *Violent Democracies in Latin America*, E. D. Arias and D. M. Goldstein, eds. Durham: Duke University Press, 35–62.

Dewey, M. 2015. *El Orden Clandestino*. Buenos Aires: Katz Editores.

Di Tella, R., Edwards, S., and Schargrodsky, E. 2010. *The Economics of Crime: Lessons for and from Latin America*. Chicago: University of Chicago Press.

Duce, Mauricio, Fuentes, Carlos, and Riego, Cristian. 2009. *La Reforma Procesal Penal en América Latina y su Impacto en el Uso de la Prisión Preventiva*, en *Prisión Preventiva y Reforma Procesal Penal en América Latina*. Cristián Riego y Mauricio Duce, eds. Santiago de Chile: CEJA.

Dudley, S. 2012. *Transnational Crime in Mexico and Central America: Its Evolution and Role in International Migration*. Washington, DC: Woodrow Wilson Center-Migration Policy Institute.

Dudley, S. 2016. *Elites and Organized Crime: Conceptual Framework*. http://www.insightcrime.org/investigations/elites-and-organized-crime-conceptual-framework-organized-crime

ECLAC. 2016. *Social Panorama of Latin America*. Santiago de Chile: Economic Comission for Latin American and the Caribbean 2015.

Escobar, G. 2012. "El Uso de la Teoría de la Desorganización Social para Comprender la Distribución de Homicidios en Bogotá." *Revista INVI* 27: 21–85.

Fajnzylber, P., Lederman, D., and Loayza, N. 2002. "Inequality and Violent Crime." *Journal of Law and Economics* 45: 1–40.

Felbab-Brown, V. 2010. "Rules and Regulations in Ungoverned Spaces. Illicit Economies, Criminals and Belligerents." In *Ungoverned Spaces. Alternatives to*

State Authority in an Era of Softened Sovereignty, A. L. Clunan and H. Trinkunas, eds. Standord, CA: Stanford University Press, 175–192.

Felson, M. 1998. *Crime and Everyday Life*. Second Edition. Thousand Oaks, CA: Pine Forge Press.

Fruhling, H. 2009. "Recent police reform in Latin America." In *Policing Insecurity. Police Reform, Security, and Human Rights in Latin America*, Niels Uildriks, ed. Lanham: Lexington Books, 21–46.

Fruhling, H. 2012. "La eficacia de las politicas públicas de seguridad ciudadana en América Latina y el Caribe. Como medirla y como mejorarla." Documento para discusión N°245 (IDB-DP-245). Banco Interamericano de Desarrollo, Instituciones para el Desarrollo (IFD/IFD).

Garzon, J. C. 2008. *Mafia and Company*. Editorial Planeta Colombiana.

Gaviria, A., and Pagés, C. 2002. "Patterns of Crime Victimization in Latin American Cities." *Journal of Development Economics* 67: 181–203.

Hagopian, F., and Mainwaring, S., ed. 2005. *The Third Wave of Democratization in Latin America: Advances and Setbacks*. Cambridge: Cambridge University Press.

Hammergren, L. 1999. "Quince años de reforma judicial en América Latina: dónde estamos y por qué no hemos progresado más." In *Reforma judicial en América Latina Una tarea inconclusa*, Alfredo Fuentes Hernández, ed. Bogotá: Corporación Excelencia en la Justicia.

Hinton, M. 2006. *The State on the Streets: Police and Politics in Argentina and Brazil*. Boulder, CO: Lynne Rienner.

Holland, A. 2016. "Forbearance." *American Political Science Review* 110: 2.

Jusionyte, I. 2015. *Savage Frontier: Making News and Security on the Argentine Border*. California University Press.

Kessler, G. 2004. *Sociología del Delito Amateur*. Buenos Aires: Paidós.

Kessler, G. 2009. *El sentimiento de inseguridad: sociología del temor al delito*. Buenos Aires: Siglo XXI.

Koonings, K., and Krujit, D. 2015. *Violence and Resilience in Latin American Cities*. London: Zed Books.

Lessing, B. 2017. *Making Peace in Drug Wars: Crackdowns and Cartels in Latin America*. New York: Cambridge University Press.

Levitsky, Steven, and Murillo, María Victoria. 2009. "Variation in Institutional Strength." *Annual Review of Political Science* 12: 115–133.

Levitt, S. 2004. "Understanding Why Crime Fell in the 1990s: Four Factors that Explain the Decline and Six that Do Not." *Journal of Economic Perspectives* 18 (1): 163–190.

Lustig, N. 2015. "Income Redistribution and Poverty Reduction in Latin America: The Role of Social Spending and Taxation in Achieving Development Goals." *Development Journal—Society For International Development* 57: 3–4.

Lustig, N., Lopez-Calva, F., and Ortiz-Juarez, E. 2013. "Declining Inequality in Latin America in the 2000s: The Cases of Argentina, Brazil, and Mexico." *World Development* 44: 129–141.

Macaulay, F. 2013 "Modes of Prison Administration, Control, and Governmentality in Latin America: Adoption, Adaptation, and Hybridity." *Conflict, Security and Development* 13 (4): 361–392.

Maihold, G., and Jost, S. 2014. "Las Drogas, su combate, y regulación: Los retos Políticos." In *El Narcotráfico y su combate*, G. Maihold and S. Jost, eds. Mexico, DF: SITESA.

Mainwaring, S., and Perez Liñan, A. 2014. *Democracies and Dictatorships in Latin America Emergence, Survival, and Fall*. Cambridge: Cambridge University Press.

Misse, M. 2006. *Crime e violência no Brasil contemporâneo: estudos de sociologiado crime e da violência urbana*. Rio de Janeiro: Lumen Juris.

Moncada, E. 2016. *Cities, Business, and the Politics of Urban Violence in Latin America*. Redwood City: Stanford University Press.

Muggah, R. 2012. *Researching the Urban Dilemma: Urbanization, Poverty and Violence*. IDRC, https://www.idrc.ca/sites/default/files/sp/Images/Researching-the-Urban-Dilemma-Baseline-study.pdf

O'Donnell, G. 2004. "El desarrollo de la democracia en América Latina." Buenos Aires: Programa de la Naciones Unidas para el desarrollo-PNUD, 33–73.

Naim, M. 2006. *Illicit: How Smugglers, Traffickers, and Copycats are Hijacking the Global Economy*. New York: Anchor Publishing.

Naylor, R. 2009. "Violence and Illegal Economic Activity: A Deconstruction." *Crime Law and Social Change* 52: 231–242.

Park, Robert E., Burgess, Ernest W., and McKenzie, R. D. 1925. *The City: Suggestions for Investigation of Human Behavior in the Urban Environment*. Chicago: University of Chicago Press.

Pasara, L. 2014. *Una reforma imposible. La justicia latinoamericana en el banquillo*. Lima: Pontificia Universidad Católica del Perú.

Picatto, P. 2001. *City of Suspects: Crime in Mexico City, 1900–1931*. Durham: Duke University Press.

Reuter, P. 1985. *Disorganized Crime: Illegal Markets and the Mafia*. Cambridge, MA: MIT Press.

Rodgers, D. 2007. "Joining the Gang and Becoming a Broder: The Violence of Ethnography in Contemporary Nicaragua." *Bulletin of Latin American Research* 26 (4): 444–461.

Rodgers, D. 2009. "Slums Wars of the 21st Century: Mano Dura and the New Urban Geography of Conflict in Central America." *Development and Change* 50: 5.

Rosenfeld, R., and Messner, S. 2009. "The Crime Drop in Comparative Perspective: The Impact of the Economy and Imprisonment on American and European Burglary Rates." *British Journal of Sociology* 60: 445–471.

Sabet, D. 2012. *Police Reform in Mexico: Informal Politics and the Challenges of Institutional Change*. Redwood City: Stanford University Press.

Salla, F. 2007. "De Montoro a Lembo: as políticas penitenciárias de São Paulo." *Revista Brasileira de Segurança Pública, São Paulo* 1 (1): 72–90.

Schelling, T. 1978. *Micromotives and Macrobehavior*. New York: W. W. Norton and Company.

Shaw, C., and McKay, H. 1942. *Juvenile Delinquency in Urban Areas*. Chicago: University of Chicago Press.

Snyder, R., and Duran-Martinez, A. 2009. "Does Illegality Breed Violence? Drug Trafficking and State-sponsored Protection Rackets." *Crime, Law and Social Change* 52 (3): 253–273.

Sozzo, M. 2014. "Delito común, inseguridad y respuestas estatales. Inercia e innovación durante la década kirchnerista a nivel nacional." *Cuestiones de Sociología* 10: 23–38.

Trejo, G., and Ley, S. 2016. "Federalismo, drogas y violencia: Por qué el conflicto partididta intergubernamental estimuló la violencia del narcotráfico en México." *Política y Gobierno* 22 (1): 11–56.

UNDP. 2013. *Informe Regional de Desarrollo Humano 2013–2014. Seguridad ciudadana con rostro humano: diagnóstico y propuestas para América Latina*. Panama: Centro Regional de Servicios para América Latina y el Caribe, PNUD.

UNDP. 2015. *The Millenium Development Goals Report 2015*. United Nation Development Programme.

Ungar, M. 2011. *Policing Democracy: Overcoming Obstacles to Citizen Security in Latin America*. Baltimore, MD: Johns Hopkins University Press.

UNODC. 2014. *Global Study of Homicides 2014*, https://www.unodc.org/documents/gsh/pdfs/2014_GLOBAL_HOMICIDE_BOOK_web.pdf

Van Dijk, J., van Kasteren, J, and Smit, P. 2008. *Victimazación en la Perspectiva Internacional*. UNICRI-Tilburg University (Spanish translation by ICESI).

Van Dijk, J., Manchin, R., Van Kesteren, J., Nevala, S., and Hideg, G. 2005. *The Burden of Crime in the EU*. Research Report: A Comparative Analysis of the European Crime and Safety Survey (EU ICS).

Villalobos , J. 2014. "El Infierno al Sur de México." *Nexos*, http://www.nexos.com.mx/?p=22331

Weisburd, David, Wyckoff, Laura A., Ready, Justin, Eck, John E., Hinkle, Joshua C., and Gajewski, Frank. 2006. "Does Crime Just Move around the Corner? A Controlled Study of Spatial Displacement and Diffusion of Crime Control Benefits." *Criminology* 44: 549–591.

Whitehead, L. 2002. *Democratization: Theory and Experience*. New York: Oxford University Press.

World Bank. 2011. *Conflict, Security and Development*. Washington, DC: World Developmen Report.

Yashar, D. 2012. "The Illicit, Violence, and Citizenship." In *Shifting Frontiers of Citizenship in Latin America*, Mario Sznajder and Luis Roniger, eds. The Netherlands: Brill, 431–458.

Zimring, F. 2007. *The Great American Crime Decline*. New York: Oxford University Press.

CHAPTER 2

Beltran, I. de L., and Salcedo Albarán, E. 2003. "¿Por qué no hay una relación entre crimen y distribución del ingreso en Colombia? Una explicación para el período 1976-1997 a partir de la evolución de la actividad criminal." *Borradores de Método Área de Crimen y Conflicto ISSN: 1692-9667*, http://www.esalbaran.com/oldocs/crimenydesigualdad.pdf

Bergman, M. 2001. "Rising Crime in Urban Argentina: The Effects of Changes in Labor Markets and Community Breakdown." *International Journal of Comparative and Applied Criminal Justice* 25 (1): 71–91.

Bergman, M. 2016. *Drogas, Narcotráfico y Poder en América Latina*. Buenos Aires: Fondo de Cultura Económicas.

Bergman, M., and Sarsfield, R. 2009. *Encuesta de victimización y eficacia institucional informe anual 2008*. México City: CIDE.

Blumstein, A., and Rosenfeld, R. 2008. *Factors Contributing to U.S. Crime Trends Workshop Report*, chapter 2, http://www.nap.edu/read/12472/chapter/1

Clarke, Ronald V. 1997. *Situational Crime Prevention: Successful Case Studies*. Reprint [1992]. New York: Harrow and Heston.

Coscia, M., and Rios, V. 2012. "Knowing Where and How Criminal Organizations Operate using Web Content." Proceedings of the 21st ACM International Conference on Information and Knowledge Management. Harvard University, 1–10.

van Dijk, J., van Kesteren, J., and Smit, P. 2007. *Criminal Victimisation in International Perspective. Key Findings from the 2004–2005 ICVS and EU*. UNICRI-UNODC, http://www.unicri.it/services/library_documentation/publications/icvs/publications/ICVS2004_05report.pdf

Duran-Martinez, A. 2015. "To Kill and Tell? State Power, Criminal Competition, and Drug Violence." *Journal of Conflict Resolution* 59 (8): 1348–1376.

Eck, John E. 2002. "Preventing Crime at Places." In *Evidence-Based Crime Prevention*, Lawrence Sherman, David Farrington, Brandon Welsh, and Doris MacKenzie, eds. New York: Routledge, 241–294.

Eisner, M. 2003. "Long-Term Historical Trends in Violent Crime." *Crime and Justice* 30: 83–142.

Escalante, F. 2009. *El Homicidio en México entre 1990 y 2007*. Mexico City: El Colegio de México.

Fleitas Ortiz de Rosas, D. 2015. *Homicidios en Argentina en el año 2013. Informe Estadístico*. Buenos Aires: Asociación de Políticas Públicas.

Godberger, A., and Rosenfeld, R. 2008. *Introduction to Understanding Crime Trends*. Workshop Report, http://www.nap.edu/read/12472/chapter/1

GSH. 2013. *Global Study of Homicides*. Vienna: UNODC, https://www.unodc.org/documents/gsh/pdfs/2014_GLOBAL_HOMICIDE_BOOK_web.pdf

Heinle, K., Molzahn, C., and Shirk, D. 2015. *Drug Violence in Mexico, Data and Analysis through 2014: Special Report*. Justice in Mexico Project University of San

Diego,   https://justiceinmexico.org/wp-content/uploads/2015/04/2015-Drug-Violence-in-Mexico-final.pdf

Hofmann, Susanne. 2015. "Borderline Slavery: Mexico, United States, and the Human Trade—Edited by Tiano, Susan and Murphy-Aguilar, Moira." *Bulletin of Latin American Research* 34 (2): 279–281. doi:10.1111.

Holland, A. 2016. "Forbearance." *American Political Science Review* 110 (2): 232–246.

Idobro, N., Mejía, D., and Tribin, A. 2014. "Illegal Gold Mining and Violence in Colombia." *Peace Economics, Peace Science and Public Policy* 20 (1): 83–111.

IGARAPE. 2015. "Tendencias y proyecciones globales en la violencia homicida: 2000 a 2030 by Carlos Vilalta." https://igarape.org.br/notas-de-homicidios-2-pt/

Luckembill, D. 1977. "Criminal Homicide as a Situated Transaction." *Social Problems* 25: 176–186.

Park, Robert E., Burgess, Ernest W., and McKenzie, R. D. 1925. *The City: Suggestions for Investigation of Human Behavior in the Urban Environment.* Chicago: University of Chicago Press.

Rydell, C., Caulkins, J., and Everigham, S. 1996. "Enforcement or Treatment: Modeling the Relative Efficacy of Alternative to Controlling Cocaine." *Operations Research* 44 (5): 687–695.

Shaw, C., and McKay, H. 1942. *Juvenile Delinquency in Urban Areas.* Chicago: University of Chicago Press.

Small Arms Survey. 2012. *A Fatal Relationship: Guns and Deaths in Latin America and the Caribbean.* Cambridge, UK: Cambridge University Press.

Ugarte, Marisa B., Zarate, Laura, and Farley, Melissa. 2004. "Prostitution and Trafficking of Women and Children from Mexico to the United States." *Journal of Trauma Practice* 2 (3/4): 147–165.

UNDP. 2013. *Citizen Security with a Human Face: Evidence and Proposals for Latin America.* New York: Regional Human Development Report 2013–2014.

UNDP-Annex. 2013. *Citizen Security with a Human Face: Evidence and Proposals for Latin America.* Methodological-Statistical Anne, http://www.aecid.es/Centro-Documentacion/Documentos/Publicaciones%20coeditadas%20por%20AECID/IDH-ALAnexoEstadisticoMetodologico.pdf

UNODC. 2014. *Global Studies on Homicides Statistical Annex,* https://www.unodc.org/documents/gsh/pdfs/2014_GLOBAL_HOMICIDE_BOOK_web.pdf

UNODC-CTS. *Homicide Statistics.* Historic data at https://www.unodc.org/unodc/en/data-and-analysis/statistics/historic-data.html

Waiselfisz, J. 2012. *Mapa da violencia 2012. Os novos padroes da violencia homicida no Brazil.* Instituto Sangari, http://mapadaviolencia.org.br/pdf2012/mapa2012_web.pdf

Weisburd, David, Wyckoff, Laura A., Ready, Justin., Eck, John E., Hinkle, Joshua C., and Gajewski, Frank. 2006. "Does Crime Just Move around the Corner? A Controlled Study of Spatial Displacement and Diffusion of Crime Control Benefits." *Criminology* 44: 549–591.

Weisburd, David, et al. 2016. *Place Matters: Criminology for the 21st Century.* Cambridge, UK: Cambridge University Press.

World Drug Report. 2011. UNODC, Viena. At https://www.unodc.org/unodc/en/data-and-analysis/WDR-2011.html

World Bank. 2011. *Conflict Security and Development.* World Development Report. Washington, DC: The World Bank.

Yashar, D. 2012. "The Illicit, Violence, and Citizenship." In *Shifting Frontiers of Citizenship in Latin America*, Mario Sznajder and Luis Roniger, eds. Leiden, The Netherlands: Brill, 431–458.

CHAPTER 3

Adams, T. 2016. *How Chronic Violence Affects Human Development, Social Relations, and the Practice of Citizenship: A Systemic Framework for Action.* Washington, DC: Woodrow Wilson Center Reports on the Americas #36.

Alaniz, M. L., Cartmill, R. S., and Parker, R. N. 2000. "Community-Identified Alcohol Issues in the Mexican American Community." Special Issue: Community Action and the Prevention of Alcohol-Related Problems at the Local Level. *Substance Use and Misuse* 35 (157): 69.

Alves da Silva, B. 2014. "Social Disorganization and Crime: Searching for Determinants of Crime at the Community Level." *Latin American Research Review* 49 (3): 218–230.

Arnson, C., Bosworth, J., Dudley, S., Farah, D., Lopez, J., and Olson, E. 2014. *Organized Crime in Central America: The Northern Triangle.* Washington, DC: Woodrow Wilson Center Reports in the Americas #29.

Auyero, J., and Berti, F. 2013. *La violencia en los márgenes.* Buenos Aires: Katz Editores.

Ayres, Ian, and Donohue, J. 2003. "Shooting Down the 'More Guns, Less Crime' Hypothesis." *Stanford Law Review* 55: 1193–1214.

Azaola, E. 2008. *Crimen, Castigo y Violencias en México.* Flacso: Ecuador.

Bailey, J. 2014. *The Politics of Crime in Mexico: Democratic Governance in a Security Trap.* Boulder: Lynne Rienner Publishers.

Bailey, J., and Dammert, L. 2005. *Public Security and Police Reform in the Americas.* Pittsburgh: Pittsburgh University Press.

Bagley, B. 2009. "La conexión Colombia-México-Estados Unidos." In *Atlas de la Seguridad y la Defensa de México*, Raúl Benítez Manaut, Abelardo Rodríguez Sumano, and Armando Rodríguez Luna, eds. Mexico City, Mexico: CASADE.

Beato, C. 2012. *Crimes a Cidades.* Belo Horizonte: UFMG.

Beltrán, I., and Salcedo-Albarán, E. 2007. *El Crimen Como Oficio: Ensayos sobre economía del crimen en Colombia.* Bogota: Universidad Externado de Colombia.

Bergman, M. 2002. "Changes in Labor Markets and Community Breakdown: The Rapid Increase in Urban Criminality in Buenos Aires." *International Criminal Justice Review* 11 (1): 25–43.

Bergman, M. 2013. "Delito Patrimonial e Inserción Laboral: La Naturaleza de la Relación entre Crimen y Empleo en México." *Estudios Sociológicos* 91: 27–58.

Bergman, M. 2016. *Drogas Narcotráfico y Poder en América Latina.* Buenos Aires: Fondo de Cultura Economica.

Bergman, M., Masello, D., Arias, C., and Peralta Agüero, G. 2014. "Condiciones de Socialización, entorno y trayectoria asociada a la reincidencia ene le delito." *Revista Argentina de Estadística Aplicada* 2: 2.

Binder, Alberto. 2004. *Justicia penal y estado de derecho.* Buenos Aires: Ed. Ad-Hoc.

Blumstein, A., Piquero, A., and Farrington, D. 2007. *Key Issues in Criminal Career Research.* Cambridge: Cambridge University Press.

Braga, A., and Clarke, R. 2014. "Explaining High Risk Concentrations of Crime in the City: Social Disorganization, Crime Opportunities, and Important Next Steps." *Journal of Research in Crime and Delinquency* 514: 480–498.

Briceño-Leon, R. 2008. *Sociologia de la Violencia en America Latina.* Quito: Facultad Latino Americana de Ciencias Sociales, FLACSO.

Bruneau, T., Dammert, L., and Skinner, E. 2011. *Maras: Gang Violence and Security in Central America.* Austin: University of Texas Press.

Buhaug, H., and Urdal, H. 2013. "An Urbanization Bomb? Population Growth and Social Disorder in Cities." *Global Environmental Change* 23: 1–10.

CAF. 2014. *Por una América Latina más Segura: Una Nueva perspectiva para prevenir y controlar el delito.* Corporación Andina de Fomento, Reporte de Economía y Desarrollo.

Caldeira, T. 2001. *City of Walls: Crime, Segregation, and Citizenship in Sao Paulo.* Berkeley: University of California.

Carrion, F., ed. 2002. *Seguridad ciudadana, ¿espejismo o realidad?* Quito: Flacso Ecuador.

Cepalstat. 2015. *Panorama Social de America Latina 2012,* http://www.cepal.org/es/publicaciones/1247-panorama-social-de-america-latina-2012

Cook, P., and Moore, M. 1995. "Gun Control." In *Crime,* J. Wilson and J. Petersilia, eds. San Francisco: ICS Press (Institute for Contemporary Studies), 267–294.

Cruz, J. M. 2010. "Central American Maras: From Youuth Grangs to Transnational Protection Rackets." *Global Crime* 11 (4): 379–398.

Davis, D. 2007. "Urban Violence, Quality of Life, and the Future of Latin American Cities." In *Global Urban Poverty: Setting the Agenda,* A. Garland, M. Massoumi, and B. Ruble, eds. Washington, DC: Woodrow Wilson International Center for Scholars, 57–87.

De Lima, R., Ratton, J. L., and de Azevedo, R. 2014. *Crime, Polícia e Justiça no Brasil.* Ciencias Humanas e Sociais edition. São Paulo: CONTEXTO.

Dingwall, G. 2006. *Alcohol and Crime.* London: Willan Publishing.

Di Tella, R., Edwards, S., and Schargrodsky, E. 2012. *The Economics of Crime: Lessons for and from Latin America.* Chicago: University of Chicago Press.

Eisner, M. 2003. "Long Term Historical Trends in Criminal Violence." *Crime and Justice* 30: 83–142.

Eisner, M. 2013. "What Causes Large-scale Variation in Homicide Rates?" In *Aggression in Humans and Other Primates: Biology, Psychology, Sociology*, Hans-Henning Kortum and Jurgen Heinze, eds. Berlin: de Gruyter, 83–142. http://www.crim.cam.ac.uk/people/academic_research/manuel_eisner/large_scale-variation.pdf

Eisner M., and Nivette, A. 2014. "Does Low Legitimacy Cause Crime?: A Review of the Evidence." In *Legitimacy and Criminal Justice: An International Exploration*, J. Tankebe and A. Liebling, eds. Oxford: Oxford University Press. 308–325.

Escalante, F. 2009. "¿Puede México ser Colombia? Narcotráfico, violencia y Estado." *Nueva Sociedad* 220 (Marzo-Abril): 84–96.

Fagan, Jeffrey, and Freeman, Richard B. 1999. "Crime and Work." *Crime and Justice* 25: 225–290.

Fajnzylber, P., Lederman, D., and Loayza, N. 2002. "Inequality and Violent Crime." *Journal of Law and Economics* 45 (1): 1–39.

Farrington, D. P. 2003. "Key Results from the First Forty Years of the Cambridge Study in Delinquent Development." In *Taking Stock of Delinquency: An Overview of Findings from Contemporary Longitudinal Studies*, T. P. Thornberry and M. D. Krohn, eds. New York: Kluwer/Plenum, 137–183.

Felson, M. 2002. *Crime and Everyday Life*. Thousand Oaks: Sage, and Pine Forage Press.

Fleitas, D. 2016. "Fire Fighters: Latin America Battles to Stem Illegal Arms Flows." *IHS Jane's Intelligence Review*, http://sehlac.org/analisis-sobre-el-trafico-de-armas-y-politicas-de-control-en-america-latina-por-diego-fleitas-para-ihs-janes-intelligence-review/

Freeman, R. 1995. "The Labor Market." In *Crime: Public Policies for Crime Control*, James Wilson and Joan Petersilia, eds. San Francisco, CA: ICS Press, 171–192.

Freeman, R. 1996. "Why Do So Many Young American Men Commit Crimes and What Might We Do About It?" *Journal of Economic Perspectives* 10: 25–42.

Frühling, Hugo. 2009. *Violencia y organización policial en América Latina*. Quito, Ecuador: FLACSO.

Garcia, J., Mejia, D., and Ortega, D. 2013. "Police Reform, Training and Crime: Experimental Evidence from Colombia's Plan Cuadrantes." *CAF Working Papers*, https://www.caf.com/media/4243/police_reform_training_crime_experimental_evidence_colombia.pdf

Garzón, J. C. 2010. *Mafia & Co: The Criminal Networks in Mexico, Brazil and Colombia*. Washington, DC: Woodrow Wilson International Center for Scholars, Latin American Program.

Gaviria, A., and Pagés, C. 2002. "Patterns of Crime Victimization in Latin American Cities." *Journal of Development Economics* 67: 181–203.

Goldstein, D., and Arias, D. 2010. *Violent Democracies in Latin America.* Durham, NC: Duke University Press.

Gorman, D. M., Speer, P. W., Gruenewald, P. J., and Labouvie, E. W. 2001. "Spatial Dynamics of Alcohol Availability, Neighborhood Structure and Violent Crime." *Journal of Studies on Alcohol* 62 (5): 628–636.

Gottfredson, M., and Hirschi, T. 1990. *A General Theory of Crime.* Stanford: Stanford University Press.

Gouvis, C., Reid, H., Bhati, A., and Tereshchenko, B. 2008. "Alcohol Outlets as Attractors of Violence and Disorder: A Closer Look at the Neighborhood Environment." URBAN INSTITUTE, Justice Policy Center, https://www.ncjrs.gov/pdffiles1/nij/grants/227646.pdf

Greenfeld, L. 1998. *Alcohol and Crime: An Analysis of National Data on the Prevalence of Alcohol Involvement in Crime.* National Symposium on Alcohol Abuse and Crime. Washington, DC: US Department of Justice, Bureau of Justice Statistics.

Grogger, Jeff. 1995. "The Effect of Arrests on the Employment and Earnings of Young Men." *Quarterly Journal of Economics* 110 (1): 51–72.

Guerrero, E. 2011. "La Raíz de la Violencia." *Nexos,* June 1. https://www.nexos.com.mx/?p=14318

Hagan, J. 1993. "The Social Embeddedness of Crime and Unemployment." *Criminology* 31 (4): 465–491.

Hinton, M. 2006. *The State on the Streets: Police and Politics in Argentina and Brazil.* Boulder: Lynne Riener Publishers.

Jaitman, L., and Ajzenman, N. 2016. *Crime Patterns and Hotspots Dynamics in Latin America.* IDB Working Paper Series N° IDB-WP-699. Washington DC.

Kellerman, A., Rivara, F., Rushforth, N., Banton, J., Reary, D., Francisco, J., Loccio, A., Prodzinski, J., Hackman, B., and Somes, G. 1993. "Gun Ownership as a Risk Factor for Homicides in the Home." *New England Journal of Medicine* 329: 1084–1091.

Kessler, G. 2004. *Sociología del Delito Amateur.* Buenos Aires: Paidós.

Kessler, G. 2014. *Controversias sobre la Desigualdad Argentina 2003–2013.* Buenos Aires: Fondo de Cultura Economica.

Koonings, K., and Krujit, D. 2007. *Fractured Cities: Social Exclusion, Urban Violence and Contested Spaces in Latin America.* London: Zed Books.

Krujit, D., and Koonings, K. 1999. "Introduction: Violence and Fear in Latin America." In *Societies of Fear: The Legacy of Civil War, Violence and Terror in Latin America,* K. Koonings and D. Kruijt, eds. London: Zed Books, 1–30.

LaFree, G.1999. "A Summary and Review of Comparative Cross-National Studies of Homicide." In *Homicide: A Sourcebook of Social Research,* M. D. Smith and M. A. Zahn, eds. Beverly Hills: Sage, 125–145.

Lessing, B. 2017. *Making Peace in Drug Wars: Crackdowns and Cartels in Latin America.* Cambridge: Cambridge University Press.

Levitt, Steven D. 2001. "Alternative Strategies for Identifying the Link Between Unemployment and Crime." *Journal of Quantitative Criminology* 17 (4): 377–390.

Llorente M., Escobedo, R., Echandía, C., and Rubio, M. 2002. "Violencia Homicida y Estructuras Criminales en Bogotá." *Sociologias* 8: 172–205.

Lott, J. 2010. *More Guns, Less Crime: Understanding Crime and Gun Control Laws.* Chicago: Chicago University Press.

Lustig, N., Lopez-Calva, and Ortiz-Juarez, E. 2013. "Declining Inequality in Latin America in the 2000s: The Cases of Argentina, Brazil, and Mexico." *World Development* 44: 129–141.

Magaloni, B., Franco, E., and Melo, V. 2016. Killing in the Slums: An Impact Evaluation of Police Reform in Rio de Janeiro. Typscrypt, http://scid.stanford.edu/sites/default/files/publications/556wp.pdf

Mazzitelli, A. 2012. "Influencia de los cárteles mexicanos en Centroamérica." In *Atlas de la Seguridad y la Defensa de México 2012*, S. Aguayo and Manaut R. Benitez, eds. Mexico DF: CASEDE, 15–24.

McIlwaine, C., and Moser, C. 2003. "Poverty, Violence and Livelihood Security in Urban Colombia and Guatemala." *Progress in Development Studies* 3 (3): 113–130.

Mejia, D., and Restrepo, P. 2016. "The Economics of the War on Illegal Drug Production and Trafficking." *Journal of Economic Behavior & Organization* 126: 255–275.

Misse, M. 2006. *Crime e violência no Brasil contemporâneo: estudos de sociologiado crime e da violência urbana.* Rio de Janeiro: Lumen Juris.

Moncada, E. 2016. *Cities, Business and the Politics of Urban Violence in Latin America.* Redwood City: Stanford University Press.

Muggah, R. 2012. *Researching the Urban Dilemma: Urbanization, Poverty and Violence.* Ottawa: IDRC.

Neumayer, E. 2005. "Inequality and Violent Crime: Evidence from Data on Robbery and Violent Theft." *Journal of Peace Research* 421: 101–112.

Nivette, A. 2011. "Cross-National Predictors of Homicide: A Meta-Analysis." *Homicide Studies* 15 (2): 103–131.

Nivette, Amy, and Manuel, Eisner. 2014. "Political Legitimacy and Homicide: A Crossnational Analysis." *Homicide Studies.* 17:1 pp 3–26.

O'Brien, Robert, and Stockard, J. 2002. "Variations in Age-Specific Homicide Death Rates: A Cohort Explanation for Changes in the Age Distribution of Homicide Rates." *Social Science Research* 31:124–150.

Park, Robert E., Burgess, Ernest W., and McKenzie, R. D. 1925. *The City: Suggestions for Investigation of Human Behavior in the Urban Environment.* Chicago: University of Chicago Press.

Pásara L. 2014. "Una Reforma Imposible: La justicia latinoamericana en el banquillo." Lima: Fondo Editorial PUCP.

Piehl, A. 1998. "Economic Conditions, Work, and Crime." In *Handbook of Crime and Punishment*, Michel Thorny, ed. New York: Oxford University Press, 302–319.

Pinker, S. 2011. *The Better Angels of Our Nature: Why Violence Has Declined.* London: Penguin Books.

Riego, R., and Duce, M. 2009. *Prisión Preventiva y Reforma Procesal Penal en América Latinas.* Santiago de Chile: CEJA.

Rosenfeld, Richard, and Messner, Steven. 1991. "The Social Sources of Homicide in Different Types of Societies." *Sociological Forum* 6 (1): 58–70.

Rosenfeld, Richard, and Levin, Aaron. 2016. "Acquisitive Crime and Inflation in the United States: 1960–2012." *Journal of Quantitative Criminology* 32: 427–447.

Sain, M. 2008. *El leviatán azul: policía y política en la Argentina.* Buenos Aires: Siglo Veintiuno.

Sampson, R. 2013. *Great American City: Chicago and the Enduring Neighborhood Effect.* Chicago: University of Chicago Press.

Sampson, R., and Laub, J. 2005. "A Life-Course View of the Development of Crime." *ANNALS of the American Academy of Political and Social Science* 602: 12–45; 73–79.

Scribner, R.A., Cohen, D. A., Kaplan, S., and Allen, S. H. 1999. "Alcohol Availability and Homicide in New Orleans: Conceptual Considerations for Small Area Analysis of the Effect of Alcohol Outlet Density." *Journal of Studies on Alcohol* 60: 310–316.

Shaw, C., and MacKay, H. 1942. *Juvenile Delinquency and Urban Areas.* Chicago, IL: University of Chicago Press.

Siegel, M., Ross, C., and King, C. 2013. "The Relationship Between Gun Ownership and Firearms Homicide Rates in the United States 1981–2010." *American Journal of Public Health* 103: 2098–2105.

Simone, L. 2013. "El desafío del tráfico de armas en México y Centroamérica." In *Atlas de la seguridad y la defensa de México*, S. Aguayo and R. Benítez, eds. Mexico City: Colectivo de Análisis de la Seguridad con Democracia. 47–63.

Small Arms Survey. 2012. *Moving Targets.* Cambridge: Cambridge University Press.

Snyder, R., and Duran, Martinez A. 2009. "Does Illegality Breed Violence? Drug Trafficking and State-Sponsored Protection Rackets." *Crime Law and Social Change* 52: 253–273.

Soares, R., and Naritomi, J. 2010. "Understanding High Crime Rates in Latin America: The Role of Social and Policy Factors." In *The Economics of Crime: Lessons for and from Latin America*, R. Di Tella, S. Edwards, and E. Schargrodsky, eds. Chicago: University of Chicago Press, 19–55.

Stohl, R., and Tuttle, D. 2008. *The Small Arms Trade in Latin America.* New York: NACLA.

Szabó, I., Garzón, J., and Muggah, R. 2013. *Citizen Security Rising: New Approaches to Addressing Drugs, Guns, and Violence in Latin America.* The Norwegian Peacebuilding Resource Centre: NOREF Report July 2013.

Thoumi, F. 2003. *Illegal Drugs, Economy, and Society in the Andes.* Washington, DC: Woodrow Wilson Center for Scholars.

Trent, C., and Pridemore, W. 2012. "A Review of the Cross-National Empirical Literature on Social Structure and Homicide." In *Handbook of European Homicide Research*, M. C. A. Liem and W. A. Pridemore, eds. New York: Springer, 111–135.

Trejo, G., and Ley, S. 2016. "Federalismo, drogas y violencia: Por qué el conflicto partididta intergubernamental estimuló la violencia del narcotráfico en México." *Política y Gobierno* 22 (1): 11–56.

Tokatlian, J. ed. 2010. *Drogas y prohibición: Una vieja guerra, un nuevo debate.* Buenos Aires: Libros del Zorzal.

Tudela, P., Schwaderer, Z., Varela, F., and Palacios, A. 2012. *Plan Cuadrante: Informe final principales resultados y recomendaciones.* Santiago de Chile: Fundación Paz Ciudadana.

UNDP. 2013. *Informe Regional de Desarrollo Humano 2013-2014. Seguridad ciudadana con rostro humano: diagnóstico y propuestas para América Latina.* Panama: Centro Regional de Servicios para América Latina y el Caribe, PNUD.

Urdal, H. 2011. *Demography and Armed Conflict: Assessing the Role of Population Growth and Youth Bulges.* Centre for Research on Peace and Development CRPD: Working Paper 2.

Ungar, M. 2011. *Policing Democracy: Overcoming Obstacles to Citizen Security in Latin America.* Baltimore, MD: Johns Hopkins University Press.

UNODC. 2014. *Global Studies on Homicides Statistical Annex,* https://www.unodc.org/documents/gsh/pdfs/2014_GLOBAL_HOMICIDE_BOOK_web.pdf

Villarreal, A., and Bráulio, F. A. Silva. 2006. "Social Cohesion, Criminal Victimization and Perceived Risk of Crime in Brazilian Neighborhoods." *Social Forces* 84: 1725–1753.

Weisburd, S., Groff, E., and Sue-Ming, Yang. 2012. *The Criminology of Place: Street Segments and Our Understanding of the Crime Problem.* New York: Oxford University Press.

Wolf, S. 2013. "The *Maras*: The Making of a Transnational Issue." In *The Criminalization of Immigration: Contexts and Consequences,* Alissa R. Ackerman and Rich Furman, eds. Durham, NC: Carolina Academic Press, 175–191.

World Bank. 2011. *Conflict, Security and Development.* Washington, DC: World Development Report.

WDI. 2015. World Development Indicators, http://data.worldbank.org/data-catalog/world-development-indicators

Yashar, D. 2012. "The Illicit, Violence, and Citizenship." In *Shifting Frontiers of Citizenship in Latin America,* Mario Sznajder and Luis Roniger, eds. Leiden, The Netherlands: Brill, 431–458.

Zepeda, G. 2004. *Crimen sin Castigo: Procuración de Justicia Penal y Ministerio Publico en Mexico.* Mexico DF: FCE.

Zimring, F. 1991. "Firearms, Violence and Public Policy." *Scientific American* 265: 48–54.

CHAPTER 4

Andreas, P. 2013. *Smuggler Nation: How Illicit Trade Made America*. Oxford: Oxford University Press.

Auyero, J., and Berti, M. F. 2013. *La violencia en los márgenes. Una maestra y un sociólogo en el conurbano bonaerense*. Ciudad Autónoma de Buenos Aires: Katz Editores.

Baker, A. 2009. *The Market and the Masses in Latin America: Policy Reform and Consumption in Liberalizing Economies*. Cambridge Studies in Comparative Politics. New York: Cambridge University Press.

Bauman, Z. 2007. *Consuming Life*. Oxford: Polity Press.

Bergman, M., and Sarsfield, R. 2009. *Encuesta de victimización y eficacia institucional informe anual 2008*. México City: CIDE.

Bourdieu, Pierre. 1984. *Distinction: A Social Critique of the Judgement of Taste*. Cambridge: Harvard University Press.

Bourdieu, P. 1999. *Meditaciones Pascalinas*. Barcelona: Anagrama.

Bourgignon, F., and Platteau, J. P. 2012. "Does Aid Availability Affect Effectiveness in Reducing Poverty?" *Working Paper Series UNU-WIDER*, Helsinki, Finland: World Institute for Development Economic Research (UNU-WIDER).

Casas, P., Rivas, A., Gonzalez, P., and Acero, H. 2005. *Seguridad Urbana y Policía en Colombia: Ensayos de Seguridad y Democracia*. Bogotá: Fundación Seguridad y Democracia.

CESVI. 2014. *Centro de Experimentación y Seguridad Vial Esatadísticas de Robos*, https://www.cesvi.com.ar/MundoAutomotriz/Estadisticas/EstadisticasAutomotriz.aspx

Chicoine, L. 2011. *Exporting the Second Amendment: U.S. Assault Weapons and the Homicide Rate in Mexico*. South Bend, IN: University of Notre Dame, Department of Economics.

Clarke, R. V. 2002. "Thefts of and from Cars in Parking Facilities." *Problem-Oriented Guides for Police*. Washington, DC: US Department of Justice, Office of Community Oriented Policing Services, www.popcenter.org

Cohen, L., and Felson, M. 1979. "Social Change and Crime Rate Trends: A Routine Activity Approach." *American Sociological Review* 44: 588–608.

Dreyfus, P., Lessing, B., de Sousa Nascimento, M., and Purcena, J. C. 2011. "Small Arms in Brazil: Production, Trade, and Holdings." In *Cross-Border Spillover: U.S. Gun Laws and Violence in Mexico*, A. Dube, O. Dube, and O. García-Ponce, eds. New York: New York University.

Dube A, Dube O, and Garcia Pone, O. 2013. "Cross-Border Spillover: U.S. Gun Laws and Violence in Mexico." *American Political Science Review* 107 (3): 397–417.

ENUSC. 2016. *Encuesta Nacional Urbana de Victimización*. Santiago de Chile. http://datos.gob.cl/dataset/9926

ENVIPE. 2016. *Encuesta Nacional de Victimización y Percepción sobre Seguridad Pública*, INEGI, México DF. http://www.beta.inegi.org.mx/proyectos/enchogares/regulares/envipe/2016/

Fleitas D. ed. 2010. *El Control de las Transferencias de Armas: Problemas y Desafíos a la Seguridad, Derechos Humanos y Desarrollo. Hacia un tratado de Comercio de Armas.* Buenos Aires: APP.

Gambetta, D. 1996. *The Sicilian Mafia: The Business of Private Protection.* Cambridge, MA: Harvard University Press.

Gambetta, D. 2009. *Codes of the Underworld: How Criminals Communicate.* Princeton: Princeton University Press.

García Canclini, N. 2001. *Consumers and Citizens: Globalization and Multicultural Conflicts.* Minneapolis: University of Minnesota Press.

Herzog, S. 2002. "Does Proactive Policing Make a Difference in Crime? An Implementation of Problem-Solving Policing in Israel." *International Journal of Comparative & Applied Criminal Justice* 26 (1): 29–52.

Jusionyte, I. 2015. *Savage Frontier: Making News and Security on the Argentine Border.* Oakland: California University Press.

Kalyvas, S. 2006. *The Logic of Violence in Civil War.* New York: Cambridge University Press.

Lauritsen, J., and Rezey, M. 2013. *Measuring the Prevalence of Crime with the National Crime Victimization Survey.* Technical Report NCJ 241656. Washington, DC: Bureau of Justice Statistics, http://www.bjs.gov/content/pub/pdf/mpcncvs.pdf

Lustig, N. 2010. *Declining Inequality in Latin America. A Decade of Progress?* Washington, DC: Brookings Institution.

Lustig, N. 2011. "Multidimensional Indices of Achievements and Poverty: What Do We Gain and What Do We Lose?" *Journal of Economic Inequality* 9: 227–234.

Lustig, N. 2013. "Declining Inequality in Latin America in the 2000s: The Cases of Argentina, Brazil, and Mexico." *World Development* 44: 129–141.

Malone M. F., and Malone Rowe C. 2013. "Transnational Organized Crime in Latin America." In *The Handbook of Transnational Crime and Justice*, Philip L. Reichel and Jay Albanese, eds. Thousand Oaks: SAGE.

McDougal T., Shirk, D., Muggah R., and Patterson, J. 2013. *The Way of the Gun: Estimating Firearms Traffic Across the U.S.–Mexico Border.* San Diego, CA: Trans-Border Institute.

Ministerio del Interior de Perú. 2013. *Oficina de Planificación, UNDP.* New York.

Mujica, J. 2007. *Estrategias locales de acceso a la telefonía móvil. Funciones y estructuras del mercado informal en un espacio de escasos recursos.* Lima: DIRSI. http://www.dirsi.net/sites/default/files/dirsi_07_CJ3_es_0.pdf

Mujica, J. 2008. "El mercado negro y las estrategias informales de acceso a la telefonía móvil." *Sur Casa de Estudios del Socialismo* 61: 43–61.

Naim, M. 2006. *Illicit: How Smugglers, Traffickers and Copycats are Hijacking the Global Economy.* New York: Doubleday.

Nee, C. 1993. *Car Theft: The Offender's Perspective.* Great Britain Home Office Source, https://www.ncjrs.gov/App/Publications/abstract.aspx?ID=142220

Norza C. E., Duarte V. Y., Castillo R. L., and Torres G. G. 2013. "Hurtos de Automotores y Estrategias contra el Delito: Una Mirada desde la Academia, el Victimario y la Policía." *Revista Criminalidad* 55 (2): 49–78.

Report of the US National Commission on the Causes and Prevention of Violence. 1969. https://www.ncjrs.gov/pdffiles1/Digitization/275NCJRS.pdf

Reuter, P. 1985. *Disorganized Crime: Ilegal Markets and the Mafia.* Cambridge: MIT Press.

Rosenfeld, R., and Levin, A. 2016. "Acquisitive Crime and Inflation in the United States: 1960–2012." *Journal of Quantitative Criminology:* 1–21.

Rujano, Raima R. "El Secuestro en el Zuila: Estadísticas y Tendencias." In *Violencia e Institucionalidad*, R. Briceño-León, O. Avila, and A. Camardiel, eds. Caracas: Editorial Alfa, 217–228.

Salcedo, Albaran E., and Garay, y Salamanca L. 2016. *Macro-Criminalidad: Complejidad Y Resiliencia De Las Redes Criminales.* Bloomington: IUniverse, Kindle Edition.

Schelling, T. C. 1971. "What is the Business of Organized Crime?" *Journal of Public Law* 20: 71–84.

SEDLAC. 2013. *Socio-Economic Database for Latin America and the Caribbean.* Washington: CEDLAS and the World Bank.

Soares, R., and Chimeli, A. 2017. "The Use of Violence in Illegal Markets: Evidence from Mahogany Trade in the Brazilian Amazon." *American Economic Journal: Applied Economics* 9 (4): 30–57.

Szabo de Carvalho, I., Garzón, J. C., and Mugah, R. 2013. *Citizen Security Rising: New Approaches to Addressing Drugs, Guns and Violence in Latin America.* NOREF, Norwegian Peace Building Resource Center, http://www.peacebuilding.no/var/ezflow_site/storage/original/application/061bc30adffa795e6a5e43bf664c8666.pdf

Tilly, C. 1975. "Food Supply and Public Order in Modern Europe." In *The Formation of National States in Europe*, C. Tilly and G. Ardan, eds. Princenton: Princeton University Press, 380–456.

UNDP. 2013. *Citizen Security with a Human Face: Evidence and Proposal for Latin America.* Regional Human Development Report 2013–2014. New York: United Nations Development Program.

UNODC. 2012. *United Nation Office for Drugs and Crime.* Crime Data. http://www.unodc.org/unodc/en/data-and-analysis/statistics/data.html

Varese, Federico. 2011. *Mafias on the Move: How Organized Crime Conquers New Territories.* Princenton: Princeton University Press.

Varese, F. 2012. "The Structure and the Content of Criminal Connections: The Russian Mafia in Italy." *European Sociological Review* 29 (5): 899–909.

Villalobos, Joaquín. 2014. *Niños Inocentes y Oligarcas Voraces.* El País Internacional. July 12. https://elpais.com/internacional/

Zehr, H. 1976. *Crime and the Development of Modern Society: Patterns of Criminality in Nineteenth Century Germany and France.* Rowman & Littlefield.

CHAPTER 5

Angrist, J., and Kugler, A. 2008. "Rural Windfall or a New Resource Curse? Coca, Income, and Civil Strife Conflict in Colombia." *Review of Economics and Statistics* 90 (2): 191–215.

Arias, Enrique Desmond. 2006. *Drugs and Democracy in Rio de Janeiro: Trafficking, Social Networks, and Public Security*. Chapel Hill: University of North Carolina Press.

Arias, Enrique Desmond. 2017. *Criminal, Enterprises and Governance in Latin America and the Caribbean*. New York: Cambridge University Press.

Astorga, L. 2005. *El siglo de las drogas: el narcotráfico, del Porfiriato al nuevo milenio*. México City: Plaza y Janés.

Bagley, B. 2012. *Drug Trafficking and Organized Crime in the Americas: Major Trends in the Twenty-First Century*. Washington, DC: Woodrow Wilson Center for Scholars, https://www.wilsoncenter.org/sites/default/files/BB%20Final.pdf

Becker, G., Murphy, K., and Grossman, M. 2004. *The Economic Theory of Illegal Goods: The Case of Drugs*. NBER Working Paper No. 10976. Cambridge: National Bureau of Economic Research.

Bergman, M., Masello, D., and Arias, C. 2014. *Delito, Marginalidad y Desempeño Institucional en la Argentina: Resultados de la encuesta de presos condenados*. Buenos Aires: UNTREF.

BJS (Bureau of Justice Statistics). 2007. *State Court Sentencing of Convicted Felons, 2004, Statistical Tables*, NCJ 217995, http://www.bjs.gov/content/dcf/ptrpa.cfm

Blumstein, A., and Rosenfeld, R. 1998. "Explaining Recent Trends in U.S. Homicide Rates." *Journal of Criminal Law and Criminology* 88 (4): 1175–216.

Blumstein, A., and Wallman, J. 2005. *The Crime Drop in America*. 2nd ed. New York: Cambridge University Press.

Bruce, B. 2012. *Drug Trafficking and Organized Crime in the Americas: Major Trends in the Twenty-First Century*. New York: Woodrow Wilson Center Updates for the Americas.

Bourgois, P. 2003. *In Search of Respect: Selling Crack in El Barrio*. 2nd ed. Cambridge: Cambridge University Press.

Cano, Ignacio. 2012. *Os Donos do Morro: Uma avaliacao exploratoria do impacto das UPP*. São Paulo: Forum Brasiliero de Seguranca Publica.

Carvalho, F. 2009. ¿Existe envejecimiento precoz entre los consumidores de drogas de abuso? *Adicciones: Revista de socidrogalcohol* 21 (2): 99–104.

Carvalho, L., and Soares, R. 2013. *Living on the Edge: Youth Entry, Career and Exit in Drug Selling Gangs*. IZA Discussion Paper N 7189. Bonn: Institute for the Study of Labor.

Castillo, J. C., Mejía, D., and Restrepo, P. 2013. *Illegal Drug Markets and Violence in Mexico: The Causes Beyond Calderón*, http://cie. itam. mx/SEMINARIOS/Marzo Mayo_2013/Mejia. pdf

Castillo, J. C., Mejía, D., and Restrepo, P. 2014. *Scarcity without Leviathan: The Violent Effect of Cocaine Supply Shortages in the Mexican Drug War.* Center for the Global Development Working Paper 356. Washington DC: Center for Global Development.

Caulkins, J., Kilmer, B., Reuter P., and Midgette, G. 2015. "Beyond Prevalence: Importance of Estimating Drug Consumption and Expenditures." *Addiction* 5 (110): 6.

Chalk, P. 2011. *The Latin American Drug Trade: Scope, Dimensions, Impact, and Response.* Santa Mónica, CA: Rand Corporation.

COHA Report. 2009. *Talking about Legalization.* Part I: The Legalization Debate and Drug Consumption in Colombia, http://www.coha.org/talking-about-legalization-part-i-the-legalization-debate-and-drug-consumption-in-colombia/

Comisión Andina de Fomento (CAF). 2014. *Por Una América Latina más Segura: Una Nueva Perspectiva para Prevenir y Controlar el Delito.* Bogotá: CAF.

Drucker, Dr. Ernest. 1998. "Drug Prohibition and Public Health." Public Health Reports. U.S. Public HealthService. 114 (Jan./Feb.1998): 24.

Gambetta, D. 2010. "Codes of the Underworld: How Criminals Communicate." *Rationality, Markets and Morals* 1 (36): 9–11.

Goldstein, P. 1985. "The Drugs/Violence Nexus: A Tripartite Conceptual Framework." *Journal of Drug Issues* 15: 493–506.

Gootenberg, P. 2009. *Andean Cocaine: The Making of a Global Drug.* Chapel Hill: University of North Carolina Press.

Gootenberg, P. 2009. "Talking About the Flow: Drugs, Borders, and the Discourse of Drug Control." *Cultural Critique* 71 (1): 13–46.

Guerrero, E. 2014. "El Estallido de Iguala." *Nexos,* http://www.nexos.com.mx/?p=23086

Hendee, T. 2013. *The Health of Pacification: A Review of the Pacifying Police Unit Program in Rio de Janeiro, Brazil.* Center for Democracy, Development, and the Rule of Law Stanford University, http://fsi.stanford.edu/sites/default/files/Thomas_Hendee.pdf

Kilmer, B., and Reuter, P. 2009. "Doped: How Two Plants Wreak Havoc on the Countries that Produce Them and Everyone in Between." *Foreign Policy* 175: 34–35.

Kleiman, M. 2009. *When Brute Force Fails: How to Have Less Crime and Less Punishment.* Princeton: Princeton University Press.

Laffiteau, C. 2011. *The Balloon Effect: The Failure of Supply Side Strategies in the War on Drugs,* https://www.academia.edu/889972/The_Balloon_Effect_The_Failure_of_Supply_Side_Strategies_in_the_War_on_Drugs

Levitt, S. 2004. "Understanding Why Crime Fell in the 1990s: Four Factors that Explain the Decline and Six that Do Not." *Journal of Economic Perspective* 18 (1): 163–190.

Levitt, S., and Venkatesh. 2000. "An Economic Analysis of a Drug-Selling Gang's Finances." *Quarterly Journal of Economics* 115 (3): 755–789.

Lessing, B. 2013. "When Business Gets Bloody: State Policy and Drug Violence." In *Small Arms Survey*. New York: Cambridge University Press, 41–72.

MacCoun, R., and Reuter, P. 2001. *Drug War Heresies: Learning from Other Vices, Times, and Places*. RAND Studies in Policy Analysis. New York: Cambridge University Press.

Maihold, G., and Jost, S. 2014. *El Narcotráfico y Su Combate: Sus Efectos Sobre las Relaciones Internacionales*. Mexico DF: Sitesa Editores.

Magaloni, B., Franco, E., and Melo, V. 2015. Killing in the Slums: An Impact Evaluation of Police Reform in Rio de Janeiro. Typscrypt, http://scid.stanford.edu/sites/default/files/publications/556wp.pdf

Mejia, D., and Restrepo, P. 2013. *The Economics of the War on Illegal Drug Production and Trafficking*. Documentos Cede 011935. Universidad De Los Andes-Cede.

Misse, M. 2007. *Crime e Violência no Brasil contemporâneo. Estudos de sociologia do crime e da violência urbana*. Rio de Janeiro: Editora Lúmen Juris.

Muehlmann, S. 2013. *When I Wear My Alligator Boots: Narco-Culture in the U.S. Mexico Borderlands*. Oakland: California University Press.

National Drug Intelligence Center. 2010. *National Drug Threat Assessment 2010*, Washington, DC.

OEA-CICAD 2011. *Informe del Uso de Drogas en Las Américas 2011*, http://www.cicad.oas.org/oid/pubs/Uso_de_Drogas_en_Americas2011_Esp.pdf

OEA (Organización de los Estados Americanos). 2013. *El Problema de las Drogas en las Américas*. Washington DC: OEA.

Nunes Dias, C. 2013. *PCC: Hegemonia nas prisões e monopólio da violencia*. Sao Paulo: Saraiva.

O'Neill, S. 2009. "The Real War in Mexico." *Foreign Affairs* 88 (4): 63–77.

Payan, T. 2006. *The Three U.S.-Mexico Border Wars: Drugs, Immigration, and Homeland Security*. Santa Barbara: Praeger Security International.

Pacula, R. Lundberg, J. Caulkins, B. Kilmer, S. Greathouse, T. Fain, & P. Steinberg. (2013). "Improving the measurement of drug-related crime. Prepared for the Office of National Drug Control Policy". Washington, DC: Executive Office of the President. Rand Corporation.

Piquet, Carneiro L. 2009. *A Economia das Drogas na América Latina: magnitude, conceitos e políticas de controle SSRN*, http://papers.ssrn.com/sol3/papers.cfm?abstract_id=1472428

RAND. 2014. *What America's Users Spend on Illegal Drugs: 2000–2010*. Prepared for the Office of National Drug Control Policy Office of Research and Data Analysis, by Kilmer, B., Everingham, S., Caulkins, J., Midgette, G., Pacula, R., Reuter, P., Burns, R., Han, B., Lundberg, R., http://www.whitehouse.gov/sites/default/files/ondcp/policy-and-research/wausid_results_report.pdf

Reuter, P., and Caulkins, J. 2011. "Purity, Price and Production: Are Drug Markets Different?" In *Illicit Trade and Globalization*, C. Costa Storti and P. De Grauwe, eds. Cambridge, MA: MIT Press. 7–30.

Saviano, R. 2013. *Zero Zero Zero*. London: Penguin Books.

Schelling, T. 1980. *The Strategy of Conflict*. Cambridge, MA: Harvard University Press.

Thoumi, F. E. 2003. *Illegal Drugs, Economy, and Society in the Andes*. New York: Woodrow Wilson Center Press.

Thoumi, F. E. 1994. *Economía política y narcotráfico*. Bogota: TM Editores.

Tilly, C. 2003. *The Politics of Collective Violence*. New York: Cambridge University Press.

Tokatlian, J., ed. 2009. *La Guerra contra las Drogas en el mundo Andino*. Buenos Aires: Libros del Zorzal.

UNODC. 2011. *Cocaine and Heroin Retail Prices*, http://www.unodc.org/unodc/secured/wdr/Cocaine_Heroin_Prices.pdf

UNODC. 2012. *Delincuencia Organizada Internacional en Centroamérica y el Caribe*. Vienna: Oficina de las Naciones Unidas contra la Droga y el Delito.

Valdés, Guillermo. 2013. *La historia del narcotráfico en México*. México DF: Editorial Aguilar.

Waiselfiesz, J. 2014. *Mapa da Violencia 2014: Homicídios e Juventude no Brazil*. Brasilia: Secretaria-Geral da Presidência da República, www.juventude.gov.br/juventudeviva

WOLA and TNI. 2011. *Systems Overload: Drug Laws and Prisons in Latin America*. Washington, DC: WOLA and TNI.

World Drug Report 2011. United Nations Office on Drugs and Crime. Vienna.

World Drug Report 2014. United Nations Office on Drugs and Crime. Vienna.

CHAPTER 6

Aguilar Camin, Hector. 2015. "La Captura Criminal del Estado." *Nexos* 37: 19–31.

Astorga, L. 2005. *El siglo de las drogas: el narcotráfico, del Porfiriato al nuevo milenio*. México City: Plaza y Janes.

Bailey, J. 2014. *The Politics of Crime in Mexico: Democratic Governance in a Security Trap*. Boulder: Lynne Rienner Publisher.

Bateson, Regina. 2012. "Crime Victimization and Political Participation." *American Political Science Review* 106 (3): 570–587.

Baumer, Eric P., Lauritsen, Janet L., Rosenfeld, Richard, and Wright, Richard. 1998. "The Influence of Crack Cocaine on Robbery, Burglary, and Homicide Rates: A Cross-City, Longitudinal Analysis." *Journal of Research in Crime and Delinquency* 35: 316–340.

Bergman, M., and Sarsfied, R. 2009. *Encuesta de Victimización y Eficacia Institucional: Informe Anual 2008*. Méxcio DF: CIDE.

Bergman, M., and Whitehead, L., eds. 2009. *Criminality, Public Policy and the Challenge to Democracy in Latin America*. South Bend, IN: Notre Dame University Press.

Briceño León, R., Avila, O., and Camardiel, A. 2012. *Violencia e Institucionalidad: Informe del Observatorio Venezolano de Violencia 2012*. Caracas: Editorial Alfa.

Buffington, R., and Piccato, P., eds. 2009. *True Stories of Crime in Modern Mexico*. Albuquerque: University of New Mexico Press.

Calderon, G., Robles, G., Díaz Calleros, A., and Magaloni, B. 2015. "The Beheading of Criminal Organizations and the Dynamics of Violence in Mexico." *Journal of Conflict Resolution* 59: 1348–1376.

Castillo, Juan Camilo, Mejía, Daniel, and Restrepo, Pascual. 2012. *Illegal Drug Markets and Violence in Mexico: The Causes Beyond Calderón*. Mimeo: Universidad de los Andes.

CIDE. 2014. *Delito y Cárcel en México, deterioro social y desempeño institucional: Reporte histórico de la población carcelaria en el Distrito Federal y el Estado de México, 2002 a 2013: Indicadores clave*. Mexico City.

Eisner, M. 2003. "Long-Term Historical Trends in Violent Crime." *Crime and Justice: A Review of Research* 30: 83–142.

Eisner, M. 2013. "What Causes Large-scale Variation in Homicide Rates?" In *Aggression in Humans and Other Primates: Biology, Psychology, Sociology*, Hans-Henning Kortum and Jurgen Heinze, eds. Berlin: de Gruyter, 83–142.

ENA. 2008. Encuesta Nacional de Adicciones Report. http://www.conadic.salud.gob.mx/pdfs/ena08/ENA08_NACIONAL.pdf

ENA. 2011. Encuesta Nacional de Adicciones Report, http://encuestas.insp.mx/ena/ena2011/ENA2011_drogas_con_anexo.pdf

Escalante Gonzalbo F. 2011. "Homicidios 2008–2009: La muerte tiene permiso." *Nexos* 397 (January): 43–44.

Finckenauer, J. 2005. "Problems of Definition: What Is Organized Crime?" *Trends in Organized Crime* 8 (3): 63–83.

Grayson, G., and Logan, S. 2012. *The Executioner's Men: Los Zetas, Rogue Soldiers, Criminal Entrepreneurs, and the Shadow State They Created.* Piscataway: Transaction Publishers.

Guerrero, Eduardo. 2011. "La Raíz de la Violencia." *Nexos* 34 (402): 31–38.

Heinle, K., Rodríguez, Ferreira O., and Shirk, D. 2014. *Drug Violence in Mexico: Data and Analysis through 2013*. San Diego: Justice in Mexico Project.

Hope, A. 2013. "Violencia 2007–2011: La Tormenta Perfecta." *Nexos* 35 (431): 36–41.

Human Rights Watch Report. 2011. "Neither Rights Nor Security: Killings, Torture, and Disappearances in Mexico's 'War on Drugs.'" New York: Human Rights Watch.

INEGI. 2014. *Boletín de Prensa n.* 301/14 23.7.2014 AGS, Instituto Nacional de Estadísticas Geografía y Censos, México.

Kalyvas, S. 2006. *The Logic of Violence in Civil War*. New York: Cambridge University Press.

LaFree, G. 1998. *Losing Legitimacy: Street Crime and Decline of Social Institutions*. Boulder, CO: Westview Press.

Longmire, S. 2013. *Cartel: The Coming Invasion of Mexico's Drug Wars.* New York: Palgrave Macmillan.

Martínez, Ramiro Jr., Rosenfeld, Richard, and Mares, Dennis. 2008. "Social Disorganization, Drug Market Activity, and Neighborhood Violent Crime." *Urban Affairs Review* 43 (6): 846–874.

Mazzitelli, A. 2012. "Influencia de los cárteles mexicanos en Centroamérica." In *Atlas de la Seguridad y la Defensa de México 2012,* S. Agauayo and R. Manaut Benitez, eds. Mexico DF: Colectivo de Análisis de la Seguridad con Democracia (CASEDE), 15–24.

Nivette, Amy. 2011. "Cross-National Predictors of Homicide: A Meta-Analysis." *Homicide Studies* 15 (2): 103–131.

O'Donnell, Guillermo, Iazzeta, Osvaldo, and Quiroga, Hugo. 2011. *Democracia Delegativa.* Buenos Aires: Prometeo.

ONC. 2014. Observatorio Nacional Ciudadano Análisis Integral de Secuestro en México: Cómo Entender su Problemática, http://onc.org.mx/wp-content/uploads/2014/08/Secuestro2014.pdf

Osorio, Javier. 2014. "Democratization and Drug Violence in Mexico." Unpublished paper, http://media.wix.com/ugd/76b255_739f78db4c024414bf6c92a152cca668.pdf

Ousey, Graham C., and Lee, Matthew R. 2002. "Examining the Conditional Nature of the Illicit Drug Market–Homicide Relationship: A Partial Test of the Theory of Contingent Causation." *Criminology* 40: 73–102.

Paoli, L., and Vander Beken, T. 2014. "Organized Crime: A Contested Concept." In *The Oxford Handbook of Organized Crime,* L. Paoli, ed. New York: Oxford University Press.

Picatto, P. 2001. *City of Suspects: Crime in Mexico City, 1900–1931.* Durham: Duke University Press.

Picatto, P. 2003. *Estadísticas del crimen en México: Series históricas, 1901–2001,* http://www.columbia.edu/~pp143/estadisticascrimen/EstadisticasSigloXX.htm

Rios, V. 2103. "Why Did Mexico Become so Violent? A Self-reinforcing Violent Equilibrium Caused by Competition and Enforcement." *Trends in Organized Crime* 16 (2): 138–155.

Rosenfeld, R. 2011. "Changing Crime Rates." In *Crime and Public Policy,* James Q. Wilson and Joan Petersilia, eds. New York: Oxford University Press.

Roth R., Eckberg, D., and Maltz, M. 2011. "Homicide Rates in the Nineteenth-Century West." *Western Historical Quarterly* 42: 173–196.

Rujano, Raima R. "El Secuestro en el Zuila: Estadísticas y Tendencias." In *Violencia e Institucionalidad,* R. Briceño-León, O. Avila, and A. Camardiel, eds. Caracas: Editorial Alfa, 217–228.

Salcedo-Albaran, E., and Garay-Salamanca, L. 2016. Macro-Criminalidad: Complejidad y Resiliencia de las Redes Criminales. iUniverse, Bloomington, Indiana.

Schedler, A. 2014." La llama de la indignación." *Reforma,* November 15.

Schelling, Thomas. 1978. *Micromotives and Macrobehavior*. New York: W.W. Norton.

Seguridad Paz y Justicia. 2014. *Radiografía del Secuestro 2013—Tendencias al 2014*, http://www.seguridadjusticiaypaz.org.mx/biblioteca/analisis-estadistico/finish/4-analisis-estadistico/182-radiografia-del-secuestro-2013-tendencias-al-2014/0

Trejo, G. 2014. "La industria criminal en México." *El País* October 16.

Trejo, G., and Ley, S. 2016. "Federalismo, drogas y violencia: Por qué el conflicto partididta intergubernamental estimuló la violencia del narcotráfico en México." *Política y Gobierno* 22 (1): 11–56.

UNDP- 2013. *Citizen Security with a Human Face: Evidence and Proposals for Latin America*. Methodological-Statistical Annex, http://www.aecid.es/Centro-Documentacion/Documentos/Publicaciones%20coeditadas%20por%20AECID/IDH-ALAnexoEstadisticoMetodologico.pdf

UNODC. 2014. *Crime and Criminal Justice Statistics*, http://www.unodc.org/unodc/en/data-and-analysis/statistics/crime.html

Valdés, G. 2013. *La historia del narcotráfico en México*. México DF: Editorial Aguilar.

Villalobos, J. 2014. "El Infierno al Sur de México." *Nexos*, http://www.nexos.com.mx/?p=22331

CHAPTER 7

Alvarado, A., and Silva, C. 2011. "Relaciones de Autoridad y Abuso Policial." *Revista Mexicana de Sociología* 73 (3): 445–473.

Andersen, Martin E. 2002. *La Policía. Pasado, Presente y Propuestas para el Futuro*. España: Sudamericana.

Arias, Enrique Desmond. 2006. *Drugs and Democracy in Rio de Janeiro: Trafficking, Social Networks, and Public Security*. Chapel Hill: University of North Carolina Press.

Arias, Enrique, and Goldstein, Daniel, eds. 2010. *Violent Democracies in Latin America: Toward an Interdisciplinary Reconceptualization*. Durham: Duke University Press.

Astorga, L. 2000. "Crimen Organizado y Organización del Crimen." In *Crimen Organizado y Gobernabilidad Democrática: México y la Zona Fronteriza*, Bailey John and Godson Roy, eds. México: Grijalbo, 85–106.

Azaola Garrido, Elena. 2006. *Imagen y Autoimagen de la Policía de la Ciudad de México*. Mexico DF: Ediciones Coyoacán.

Bailey, J. 2014. *The Politics of Crime in Mexico: Democratic Governance in a Security Trap*. Boulder: Lynne Rienner Publisher.

Bailey, J., and Dammert, L. 2006. "Public Security and Police Reform in the Americas." In *Public Security and Police Reform in the Americas*, J. Bailey and L. Dammert, eds. Pittsburg: University of Pittsburg Press, 1–25.

Barometer of the Americas. 2008. LAPOP (Latin America Public opinion Program), Vanderbilt. https://www.vanderbilt.edu/lapop/ab2008.php

Bateson, R., Malone, M. 2010. "Does Crime Undermine Public Support for Democracy? Evidence from Central America and Mexico." SSRN, September 4, http://ssrn.com/abstract=1668789 or http://dx.doi.org/10.2139/ssrn.1668789

Bayley, David. 1994. Police for the Future. Oxford: Oxford University Press.

Bayley, D. H. 2006. Changing the Guard: Developing Democratic Police Abroad. Vol. 10. Oxford: Oxford University Press.

Bayley, D. H., and Perito, R. 2010. The Police in War: Fighting Insurgency, Terrorism, and Violent Crime. Boulder, CO: Lynne Rienner Publishers.

Beato, Claudio. 2004. "Reinventar la policía: la experiencia de Belo Horizonte." In Calles más seguras ed, Vol. 1. M. Loreto, ed. Washington: Inter American Development Bank, 2004, 100–134.

Beato, Claudio. 2012. Crimes e Cidades. Belo Horizonte: Editora, UFMG.

Bergman, M., and Flom, H. 2012. "Determinantes de la confianza en la policía: una comparación entre Argentina y México." Perfiles latinoamericanos, 20 (40): 97–122.

Bergman, Marcelo, and Durán, Arturo Arango. 2011. Mucho Gasto y Resultados Inciertos. El Creciente Costo de Nuestra Policía Federal. Centro de Investigación y Docencia Económica Cuadernos de Debate 11, Mexico.

Bergman, M, Sarsfield R and Miller A, Encuesta de Victimización y Eficacia Institucional (ENVEI)-2008 (Primer semestre): 1 Base general, México, Programa de Estudios para la Seguridad Pública y Estado de Derecho, Centro de Investigación y Docencia Económicas (CIDE) en http://biiacs-dspace.cide.edu/handle/10089/3714

Binder, Alberto. 2004. Policías y Ladrones: La Inseguridad en Cuestión. Buenos Aires: Editorial Cecoopal.

Binder, Alberto. 2009 "El control de la criminalidad en una sociedad democrática. Ideas para una discusión conceptual." En Seguridad y ciudadanía. Nuevos paradigmas y políticas públicas. Foros del bicentenario, ponencias, Gabriel Kessler, coord. Buenos Aires: Edhasa, Secretaría de Cultura de la Nación y PNUD Argentina.

BJS. 2012. "Patterns & Trends October 2012." NCJ 239423 Arrest in the United States, 1990–2010, Table 1, http://www.bjs.gov/content/pub/pdf/aus9010.pdf

Braga, A. A., and Weisbord, D. 2006. "Police Innovation and Crime Prevention: Lessons Learned from Police Research over the Past 20 Years." Paper presented at the National Institute of Justice (NIJ) Policing Research Workshop: Planning for the Future, Washington, DC, November 28–29, https://www.ncjrs.gov/pdffiles1/nij/grants/218585.pdf

Braga, A., Papachristos, A., and Hureau, D. 2012. "Hot Spots Policing Effects on Crime." Campbell Systematic Reviews 8: 1–96.

Braga, A. A., Piehl, A. M., and Hureau, D. 2009. "Controlling Violent Offenders Released to the Community: An Evaluation of the Boston Reentry Initiative." Journal of Research in Crime and Delinquency 46 (4): 411–436.

Brinks, Daniel. 2003. "Informal Institutions and The Rule Of Law: The Judicial Response to State Killings in Buenos Aires and Sao Paulo in the 1990s." *Comparative Politics* 36 (1): 1–19.

Brinks, Daniel. 2007. *The Judicial Response to Police Killings in Latin America: Inequality and the Rule of Law.* New York: Cambridge University Press.

Caimari, L. 2012. *Cuando la Ciudad Duerme: Pistoleros, Policías y Periodistas en Buenos Aires 1920-1945.* Buenos Aires: Siglo veintiuno editores.

Caldeira, Teresa. 2000. *City of Walls: Crime, Segregation and Citizenship in São Paulo.* Berkeley: California University Press.

Campesi, Giuseppe. 2010. "Policing, Urban Poverty and Insecurity in Latin America: The Case of Mexico City and Buenos Aires." *Theoretical Criminology* 14 (November): 447–471.

Carrión, Mena, F. 2006. "Reforma policial." *Boletín Ciudad Segura. Reforma policial.* 4: 1, http://works.bepress.com/fernando_carrion/254

Chevigny, Paul. 1995. *Edge of the Knife: Police Violence in the Americas.* New York: The New Press.

Cruz, José M. 2010. *Police Misconduct and Democracy in Latin America.* Latin American Public Opinion Project, Insights Series #33, http://www.vanderbilt. edu/lapop/insights/I0833en.pdf

Cruz, José M. 2015. "Police Misconduct and Political Legitimacy in Central America." *Journal of Latin American Studies* 47 (2): 251–283.

Dammert, L. 2007. "Dilemas de la reforma policial en América Latina." In *Policía, Estado y Sociedad: Prácticas y Saberes Latino-Americanos*, Hayde´e Caruso, Jacqueline Muniz, and Antonio Carlos Carballo Blanco, eds. Rio de Janeiro: Publit, 145–164.

Dammert, L. 2014. "La relación entre confianza e inseguridad: el caso de Chile." *Criminalidad* 56 (1): 189–207.

Dammert, Lucía, and Malone, Fran T. 2002. "Inseguridad y Temor en la Argentina: El Impacto de la Confianza en la Policía y la Corrupción sobre la Percepción Ciudadana del Crimen." *Desarrollo Económico* 42 (July–September): 285–301.

Dammert, L., and Salazar, F. 2009. *¿Duros con el Delito?: Populismo e Inseguridad en América Latina.* Santiago de Chile: FLACSO.

Davis, D. 2007. *The Political and Economic Origins of Violence and Insecurity in Contemporary Latin America*, http://www.princeton.edu/~piirs/projects/Democracy percent26Development/papers/Panelpercent20Ipercent20percent20 Davis.pdf

Davis, D.. 2007. "El Factor Giuliani: delincuencia, la 'cero tolerancia' en el trabajo policiaco y la transformación de la esfera pública en el centro de la ciudad de México." *Estudios Sociológicos* 25 (75): 639–683.

Davis, D. 2013. "Policing and Mexican Regime Change: From Post-Authoritarianism to Populism to Neo-Liberalism." In *Violence and the State in Mexico*, Wil Pansters, ed. Redwood City: Stanford University Press.

Davis, Diane. 2006. "Undermining the Rule of Law: Democratization and the Dark Side of Police Reform in Mexico." *Latin American Politics and Society* 48 (1): 55–86.

Davis, Diane. 2010. "The Political and Economic Origins of Violence and Insecurity in Contemporary Latin America: Past Trajectories and Future Prospects." In *Violent Democracies in Latin America: Toward an Interdisciplinary Reconceptualization*, Enrique Desmond Arias and Daniel Goldstein, eds. Durham: Duke University Press. 35–62.

De Lima, R., Ratton, J. L, and Ghiringhelli de Azevedo, R. 2014. *Crime, Polícia e Justiça no Brasil*. São Paulo: Editora Contexto.

Dewey, M. 2015. *El Orden Clandestino*. Buenos Aires: Katz Editores.

Eck, John E., and Maguire, Edward R. 2006. "Have Changes in Policing Reduced Violent Crime? An Assessment of the Evidence." In *The Crime Drop in America*, Alfred Blumstein and Joel Wallman, eds. New York: Cambridge University Press, 207–265.

Eisner, M. 2003. "The Long-Term Development of Violence: Empirical Findings and Theoretical Approaches to Interpretation." In *International Handbook of Violence Research*, J Hagan and Heitmeyer W eds. Dordrecht: Springer Netherlands, 41–59.

ENVIPE 2012 reported by Menendez in El Excelsior Oct 2, 2013.

FIP (Fundación Ideas para la Paz). 2012. *Evaluación de impacto del Plan Nacional de Vigilancia Comunitaria por Cuadrantes*. Metropolitanas de Bogotá, Medellín, Cali, Barranquilla, Cúcuta, Bucaramanga, Pereira y Cartagena. Serie Informes #18, http://www.oas.org/es/sap/dgpe/innovacion/banco/ANEXO percent20II. percent20PNVCC.pdf

Frederic, S., and Galvani, M. 2013. "De la desmilitarización a la profesionalización policial: estudio etnográfico de la formación policial básica." *La reforma educativa de las fuerzas policiales y de seguridad. El caso de la Policía Federal Argentina*, Cuadernos de Seguridad, Investigación y Análisis. Buenos Aires: Ministerio de Seguridad de la Nación.

Fruhling, H. E., and Beato, C. C. 2004. *Calles más seguras: estudios de policía comunitaria en América Latina*. Washington, DC: IDB.

Frühling, Hugo. 2012. "A Realistic Look at Latin American Community Policing Programmes." *Policing and Society* 22 (1): 76–88.

Gerber, Theodore P., and Mendelson, Sarah E. 2008. "Public Experiences of Police Violence and Corruption in Contemporary Russia: A Case of Predatory Policing?" *Law & Society Review* 42 (March): 1–44.

Goldstein, H. 1990. *Problem-Oriented Policing*. Philadelphia, PA: Temple University Press.

Harrendorf, Stefan, and Smit, Paul. 2010. "Attributes of Criminal Justice Systems—Resources, Performance Punitivity." In *International Statistics on Crime and Criminal Justice*, Stefan Harrendorf, Markku Heiskanen, and Steven Malby, ed. Helsinki: European Institute for Crime Prevention and Control, 113–52, http://www.unodc.org/documents/data-and-analysis/Crime-statistics/International_Statistics_on_Crime_and_Justice.pdf

Herrera, A., and Tudela, P. 2005. "Modernización policial: La relación de la policía con la comunidad como campo de gestión y referente de cambio en la Policía de Investigaciones de Chile." *Persona y Sociedad* 19 (1): 157–178.

Hickman, Laura J., and Simpson, Sally S. 2003. "Fair Treatment or Preferred Outcome? The Impact of Police Behavior on Victim Reports of Domestic Violence Incidents." *Law & Society Review* 37 (September): 607–634.

Hidalgo López, Reynaldo and Briceño, Yoana Monsalve. 2003. "Percepción del Policía de su Rol en la Comunidad." *Capítulo Criminológico* 31 (April–June): 79–100.

Hinton, Mercedes. 2006. *The State on the Streets: Police and Politics In Argentina and Brazil.* Boulder: Lynne Rienner.

Holloway, T. 1993. *Policing Rio de Janeiro: Resistance and Repression in a XIX century City.* Stanford: Stanford University Press.

Horowitz, Jake. 2007. "Making Every Encounter Count: Building Trust and Confidence in the Police." *National Institute of Justice.* https://www.nij.gov/journals/256/Pages/building-trust.aspx

Huggins, M. K. 1998. *Political Policing: The United States and Latin America.* Durham: Duke University Press, 177.

Jaitman L. n. d. *Predictive Policing in Latin America: Evidence from Policing Experiments in Uruguay.* IDB Unpublished Working paper.

Kalmanowiecki, L. 2000. "Police, People and Repression in Modern Argentina." In *Reconstructing Criminality in Latin America*, C. Aguirre and R. Buffington, eds. Wilmington, DE: Scholarly Resources.

Kennedy, D. M., and Wond, S. L. 2009. *The High Point Drug Market Intervention Strategy.* Washington, DC: US Department of Justice, Office of Community Oriented Policing Services.

Kessler, Gabriel. 2009. *El sentimiento de inseguridad: sociología del temor al delito.* Buenos Aires: Siglo XXI.

Kessler, Gabriel, and Bergman, Marcelo. 2008. "Vulnerabilidad al Delito y Sentimiento de Inseguridad en Buenos Aires: Determinantes y Consecuencias." *Desarrollo Económico* 48 (July–September/October–December): 209–234.

LAPOP. 2012. Latin American Public Opinion Project. 2008/2012. "AmericasBarometer," www.LapopSurveys.org.

Llorente, M. V. 2004. "La Experiencia de la Policía Comunitaria de Bogotá. Contexto y Balance." In *Calles más seguras: Estudios de la Policía Comunitaria en América Latina*, H. Fruhling, ed. Washington DC: IADB.

López Portillo Vargas, E. 2003. *Educación y Entrenamiento Policial para la Democracia.* Center for US–Mexican Studies. Project on Reforming the Administration of Justice in Mexico, http://repositories.cdlib.org/usmex/prajm/lopez_portillo

Macaulay, F. 2012. "Cycles of Police Reform in Latin America." In *Policing in Africa*, David J. Francis, ed. London: Palgrave Macmillan, 165–190.

Maguire, Edwards, and Wells, William. 2009. *Implementing Community Policing: Lessons from Twelve Agencies*. Washington DC: US Department of Justice, Office of Community Oriented Policing Services.

Martinez, B. 1999. *La Policía en México: Orden Social o Criminalidad?* México: Planeta.

Nagin, D. S. 1998. "Criminal Deterrence Research at the Outset of the Twenty-first Century." In *Crime and Justice: A Review of Research*, M. Tonry, ed. Chicago: University of Chicago Press, 1–42.

Neild, R. 2002. *Sustaining Reform: Democratic Policing in Central America*. Washington, DC: WOLA.

Papachristos, A. V., Meares, T. L., and Fagan, J. 2007. "Attention Felons: Evaluating Project Safe Neighborhoods in Chicago." *Journal of Empirical Legal Studies* 4 (2): 223–272.

Papachritos, A. V., Meares, T. L., and Fagan, J. 2012. "Why do Criminals Obey the Law: The Influence of Legitimacy and Social Networks on Active Gun Offenders." *Journal of Criminal Law & Criminology* 102: 397.

Parks, Roger B., and Reisig, Michael D. 1998. "Community Policing and Perceived Safety: Psychological and Ecological Effects." 50th Annual Meeting of the American Society of Criminology, Washington, DC.

Paternoster, Raymond, Brame, Robert, Bachman, Ronet, and Sherman, Lawrence W. 1997. "Do Fair Procedures Matter? The Effect of Procedural Justice on Spouse Assault." *Law & Society Review* 31 (1): 163–204.

Perez, Orlando. 2003. "Democratic Legitimacy and Public Insecurity: The Impact of Crime Victimization on Support for Democracy in El Salvador and Guatemala." *Political Science Quarterly* 118 (4): 627–644.

Piccato, P. 2001. *City of Suspects: Crime in Mexico City 1900–1931*. Durham: Duke University Press.

Pinker, Steven. 2011. *The Better Angels of Our Nature: Why Violence Has Declined*. New York: Penguin.

Ragendorfer, Ricardo. 2002. *La Secta del Gatillo. Historia Sucia de la Policía Bonaerense*. Buenos Aires: Planeta.

Rios, Viridiana. 2013. "Why Did Mexico Become So Violent? A Self-reinforcing Violent Equilibrium Caused by Competition and Enforcement." *Trends in Organized Crime* 16 (2): 138–155.

Sabet, Daniel. 2012. *Police Reform in Mexico: Informal Politics and the Challenge of Institutional Change*. Redwood City: Stanford University Press.

Sabet, Daniel. 2013. "Corruption or Insecurity? Understanding Dissatisfaction with Mexico's Police." *Latin American Politics and Society* 55: 22–45.

Saín, Marcelo. 2004. *Política, Policía y Delito: La Red Bonaerense*. Buenos Aires: Capital Intelectual.

Sain, Marcelo. 2008. *El leviatán azul. Policía y política en la Argentina*. Buenos Aires: Siglo XXI.

Sain, M. F. 2002. *Seguridad, democracia y reforma del sistema policial en la Argentina*. Buenos Aires: Fondo de Cultura Económica.

Sampson, Robert J., and Bartusch, D. 1998. "Legal Cynicism and Subcultural? Tolerance of Deviance: The Neighborhood Context of Racial Differences." *Law & Society Review* 32: 777–804.

Schafer, Joseph A., Huebner, Beth M., and Bynum, Timothy S. 2003. "Citizen Perceptions of Police Services: Race, Neighborhood Context, and Community Policing." *Police Quarterly* 6 (December): 440–468.

Schargrodsky, E., and Di Tella, R. 2004. "Do Police Reduce Crime? Estimates Using the Allocation of Police Forces after a Terrorist Attack." *American Economic Review* 94 (1): 115–133.

Schuck, Amie M., and Rosenbaum, Dennis P. 2005. "Global and Neighborhood Attitudes Toward the Police: Differentiation by Race, Ethnicity and Type of Contact." *Journal of Quantitative Criminology* 21 (4): 391–418.

Seri, G. 2013. *Seguridad: Crime, Police Power, and Democracy in Argentina*. New York: Bloomsbury.

Sherman, Lawrence W., Gottfredson, Denise, Mackenzie, Doris, and Eck, John. 1997. *Preventing Crime: What Works, What Doesn't, What's Promising*. Collingdale: Diane Pub Co.

Skogan, W. 2003. *Community Policing: Can It Work?* The Wadsworth Professionalism in Policing Series. Boston: Cengage Learning.

Skogan, W., and Frydl, K. eds. 2004. *Fairness and Effectiveness in Policing: The Evidence*. National Research Council: Committee to Review Research on Police Policy and Practices. Washington, DC: The National Academies Press.

Skogan, Wesley. 2005. "Citizen Satisfaction with Police Encounters." *Police Quarterly* 8 (September): 298–321.

Skogan, Wesley. 2006. "Asymmetry in the Impact of Encounters with Police." *Policing & Society* 16 (2): 99–126.

Skolnick, J. H. 1966. *Justice Without Trial*. New York: John Wiley and Sons.

SNIC-(Argentina) Sistema Nacional de Informacion Criminal. 2008. Cantidad de sentencias condenatorias*: distribución de hechos delictuosos y sentencias condenatorias por tipo de delito, 35 http://www.jus.gob.ar/media/1125632/SnicARGENTINA2008.pdf

Snyder, Richard, and Duran-Martinez, Angelica. 2009. "Does Illegality Breed Violence? Drug Trafficking and State-Sponsored Protection Rackets." *Crime, Law and Social Change* 52: 253–273.

Sunshine, Jason, and Tyler, Tom R. 2003. "The Role of Procedural Justice and Legitimacy in Shaping Public Support for Policing." *Law & Society Review* 37 (3): 513–548.

Tiscornia, S. 2004. "Seguridad ciudadana y policía en Argentina. Entre el imperio del estado de policía y los límites del derecho." *Revista Nueva Sociedad* 191 (Mayo—junio): 78–90. Venezuela ISSN 0251-3552.

Tudela, T., Schwaderer, S., Varela, F., and Palacios, A. 2014. *Análisis del Plan Cuadrante de Seguridad Preventiva de Carabineros de Chile en comunas de la Región Metropolitana de Santiago*. Santiago de Chile: Fundación Paz Ciudadana.

Tyler, Tom R. 2001. *Examining Minority Trust and Confidence in the Police*. Washington, DC: National Institute of Justice, Office of Justice Programs, US Department of Justice.

Tyler, Tom R. 2005. "Policing in Black and White: Ethnic Group Differences in Trust and Confidence in the Police." *Police Quarterly* 8 (3): 322–342.

Tyler, Tom R., and Huo, Yuen J. 2003. *Trust in the Law: Encouraging Public Cooperation with Police and Courts*. New York: Russell Sage Foundation.

UNDP. 2013. *Seguridad Ciudadana con Rostro Humano. Informe Regional de Desarrollo Humano 2013–2014*, 113.

Ungar, M. 2009. "Police Reform in Argentina: Public Security versus Human Rights." In *Policing Insecurity: Police Reform, Security, and Human Rights in Latin America*, Uildriks N, ed. New York: Lexington Books, 169–196.

Ungar, M. 2011. *Policing Democracy: Overcoming Obstacles to Citizen Security in Latin America*. Baltimore: John Hopkins University Press.

Vallespir, Alejandra. 2002. *La Policía que Supimos Conseguir*. Buenos Aires: Ed Planeta.

Vanderwood, P. 1992. *Disrder and Progress: Bandits, Police and Mexican Development*. Wilmington, DE: Scolarly Resources.

Villalobos, J. 2014. "El Infierno al Sur de México" *Nexos*, http://www.nexos.com.mx/?p=22331

Waldmann, Peter. 2003. *El Estado Anómico: Derecho, Seguridad Pública y Vida Cotidiana en América Latina*. Caracas: Nuevas Sociedad.

Weisburd, D., and Braga, A. 2003. "Hot Spots Policing." In *Crime Prevention: New Approaches*, H. Kury and J. ObergfellFuchs, eds. Mainz, Germany: Weisser Ring, 337–354.

Weisburd, D., and Braga, A. A. 2006. "Introduction: Understanding Police Innovation." In *Police Innovation. Contrasting Perspectives*, D. Weisburd and A. A. Braga, eds. Cambridge: Cambridge University Press, 123.

Weisburd, D., and Eck, J. E. 2004. "What Can Police Do to Reduce Crime, Disorder, and Fear?" *The Annals of the American Academy of Political and Social Science* 593 (1): 42–65.

Wilson, J. Q., and Kelling, G. L. 1982. "Broken Windows." *Atlantic Monthly* 249 (3): 29–38.

Zepeda G. 2013. *Seguridad y Justicia Penal en los estados: 25 indicadores de nuestra debilidad institucional*. A report of *Mexico Evalua* at http://www.mexicoevalua.org/wp-content/uploads/2013/02/MEX-EVA_INDX_SJPE-LOW.pdf

CHAPTER 8

Azaola, E., Bergman, M., and Magaloni A. 2006. *Delito, Marginalidad, y Eficacia Institucional: Resultados de la Segunda Encuesta de Internos en Reclusión*. Mexico City: CIDE.

Azaola, E., and Bergman, M. 2007. "Cárceles en México: Cuadros de una Crisis." *URVIO Revista Latinoamericana de Seguridad Ciudadana* 1: 74–87.

Baytelman, A., and Duce, M. 2003. *Evaluación de la Reforma Procesal Penal: Estado de Una Reforma en Marcha.* Santiago de Chile: CEJA.

Bergman, M., and Cafferata, F. 2013. "Procuración de Justicia en las Entidades federativas: Gasto Fiscal y Eficacia de las Procuradurías Estatales." *Gestión y Política Pública* XXII: 157–194.

Bergman M., and Langer M. 2015. "El Nuevo Código Procesal Penal Nacional Acusatorio: Aportes Empíricos para la Discusión en Base a la Experiencia en Provincia de Buenos Aires." *Revista de Derecho Procesal Penal* 2015–1 pp. 51–80.

Binder, A. M., and Obando, J. 2004. *De las "Repúblicas aéreas" al Estado de derecho. Debate sobre la marcha de la reforma judicial en América Latina.* Buenos Aires: Ad-Hoc.

CEJA Centro de Estudios de las Américas. 2003. *Justicia y Gobernabilidad Democrática.* Santiago de Chile: CEJA, www.cejamericas.org

CEJA. 2006. *La Reforma Procesal Penal en Colombia.* Santiago de Chile: CEJA, www.cejamericas.org

CEJA. 2010. *Persecución de Delitos Complejos: Capacidades de los Sistemas Penales en América Latina.* Santiago de Chile: CEJA-JSCA, www.cejamericas.org

CEJA. 2011. *Prisión Preventiva y Reforma Procesal Penal en América Latina: Evaluación y Perspectivas- Volume 2. Santiago.* Santiago de Chile: CEJA, www.cejamericas.org

Comjib. 2012. *Estadísticas e Indicadores Armonizados de los Sistemas de Justicia América Latina.* Conferencia de Ministros de Justicia de los Países Iberoamericanos. COMJIB. http://www2.congreso.gob.pe/sicr/cendocbib/con4_uibd.nsf/DC2359 ED340786A605257CB7006CAFE1/$FILE/INFORME_2012.pdf

De la Jara, E., Chávez-Tafur, G., Ravelo, A., Grández, A. Del Valle, O., and Sánchez, L. 2013. *La prisión preventiva en el Perú: ¿medida cautelar o pena anticipada?* Lima. Perú: Instituto de Defensa Legal, file:///C:/Users/marcelo/Downloads/Prision%20Preventiva%20Per%C3%83%C2%BA%20IDL.pdf

Domingo, P., and Sieder, R., eds. 2001. *Rule of Law in Latin America: The International Promotion of Judicial Reform.* London: Institute of Latin American Studies, University of London.

Duce, Mauricio, Fuentes, Carlos, and Riego Cristian. 2009. *La Reforma Procesal Penal en América Latina y su Impacto en el Uso de la Prisión Preventiva,* en *Prisión Preventiva y Reforma Procesal Penal en América Latina,* Cristián Riego y Mauricio Duce, compiladores. Santiago de Chile: CEJA, 13.

Duce, M., and Pérez Perdomo, R. 2003. "Citizen Security and Reform of the Criminal Justice System in Latin America." In *Crime and Violence in Latin America: Citizen Security, Democracy, and the State,* H. Frühling and J. Tulchin, eds. Baltimore: John Hopkins University Press.

Duce, M. 2013. "Visión Panorámica sobre el uso de la prisión preventiva en América Latina en el contexto de los sistemas procesales reformados." In *Prisión*

Preventiva en América Latina: Enfoques para Profundizar el Debate. Santiago de Chile: CEJA, 13–62.

Execusao Penal. 2014. *Relatórios Estatísticos / Analíticos do Sistema Prisional Brasileiro*, Estadisticas do Sistema Prisional. Ministerio da Segurnca Publica.

FINJUS. 2012. *Segundo Censo Penitenciario*, Fundación Institucionalidad y Justicia. Santo Domingo. http://www.finjus.org.do/

Guinsburg, T., and Moustafa, T. 2008. *Rule by Law: The Politics of Courts in Authoritarian Regimes*. New York: Cambridge University Press.

Hammergren, L. 1999. "Quince años de reforma judicial en América Latina: dónde estamos y por qué no hemos progresado más." In *Reforma judicial en América Latina. Una tarea inconclusa*, Alfredo Fuentes Hernández, ed. Bogotá: Corporación Excelencia en la Justicia, 3–33.

Hammergren, L. 2007. *Envisioning Reform: Improving Judicial Performance in Latin America*. University Park, PA: The Pennsylvania State University Press.

Harrenford S., Heiskannen M., and Malby, S. 2010. International Statistics on Crime and Justice, European Institute for United Nations Office on Drugs and Crime (UNODC). Crime Prevention and Control, Helsinki Finland. https://www.unodc.org/documents/data-and-analysis/Crime-statistics/International_Statistics_on_Crime_and_Justice.pdf

Helmke, G., and Ríos-Figueroa, R. 2011. *Courts in Latin America*. New York: Cambridge University Press.

Hilbnik, L. 2007. *Judges beyond Politics in Democracy and Dictatorship: Lessons from Chile*. New York: Cambridge University Press.

Langer, M. 2011. "Revolution in Latin American Criminal Procedure: Diffusion of Legal Ideas from the Periphery." *American Journal of Comparative Law* 55 (5): 656.

La Rota E., and Bernal C. 2014. Esfuerzos irracionales: Investigación penal del homicidio y otros delitos complejos. Colección DeJusticia, Bogotá. https://www.dejusticia.org/wp-content/uploads/2017/04/fi_name_recurso_588.pdf

Lorenzo, L., Riego, C., and Duce, M. eds. 2011. *Prisión preventiva y reforma procesal penal en América Latina. Evaluación y Perspectivas*. Vol. 2. Santiago: CEJA.

Meier, J. 2003. *Derecho Procesal Penal. Sujetos Procesales*. Buenos Aires: Editorial Del Puerto.

OVV. 2014. *Observatrio Venezolano de la Violencia*, http://observatoriodeviolencia.org.ve/ws/impunidad-cero/

Pásara, L. 2004 "Como Sentencian los Jueces en México D.F. en Materia Penal." *Revista Penal* 14: 141–173. http://www.uhu.es/revistapenal/index.php/penal/article/view/221/212

Pásara, L. 2010. "El impacto de la reforma procesal penal en la seguridad ciudadana." *Derecho PUCP* 65: 55–67.

Pasara, L. 2012. International Support for Justice Reform in Latin America: Worthwhile or Worthless? Washington, DC: Woodrow Wilson Center, http://www.wilsoncenter.org/publication/justice-reform

Pasara, L. 2014. *Una reforma imposible. La justicia latinoamericana en el banquillo.* Lima: Fondo Editorial de la Universidad Católica del Perú.

SNEEP. 2013. *Sistema Nacional De Estadísticas Sobre Ejecución De La Pena* Informe Annual, http://www.jus.gob.ar/media/2736750/Informe%20SNEEP%20ARGENTINA%202013.pdf

SNIC (Argentina) Sistema Nacional de Informacion Criminal. 2008. *Cantidad de sentencias condenatorias*: distribución de hechos delictuosos y sentencias condenatorias por tipo de delito,* 35, http://www.jus.gob.ar/media/1125632/SnicARGENTINA2008.pdf

Tiede, L. 2012. "Chile's Criminal Law Reform: Enhancing Defendants' Rights and Citizen Security." *Latin American Politics and Society* 54 (3): 65–93.

Vintimilla, J., and Vallacís, G. 2013. "Independencia judicial insuficiente, prisión preventiva deformada: Informe Ecuador." En *Independencia judicial insuficiente, prisión preventiva deformada.* Washington DC: Due Process of Law Foundation, 115–146.

Waiselfisz, J. J. 2014. *Homicidios e Juventude no Brazil. Mapa da Violencia 2014. Brasilia,* www.juventude.gov.br/juventudeviva

Zaffaroni, E. 2005. *En Torno de la Cuestión Penal.* Buenos Aires: Editorial B de F.

Zepeda, G. 2013. *Seguridad y Justicia Penal en los estados: 25 indicadores de nuestra debilidad institucional.* A report of *Mexico Evalua* at http://www.mexicoevalua.org/wp-content/uploads/2013/02/MEX-EVA_INDX_SJPE-LOW.pdf

CHAPTER 9

Adorno, S., and Salla, F. 2007. "Criminalidade organizada nas prisões e os ataques do PCC." *Revista Estudos Avançados* 21 (61): 7–29.

Amorim, C. 2011. *Comando Vermelho: A Historia do Crime Organizado.* São Paulo: Bestbolso.

Antillano, A., Pojomovsky, I., Zubillaga, V., Sepúlveda C., and Hanson, R. 2015. "The Venezuelan Prison: From Neoliberalism to the Bolivarian Revolution." *Crime Law and Social Change* 64 (1): 1–17.

Auyero, J., and Berti, M. F. 2013. *La Violencia en los Márgenes: Una Maestra y un Sociologo en el Conurbano Bonaerense.* Buenos Aires: Katz editores.

Azaola, E. 2015. *Diagnóstico de las y los adolescentes que cometen delitos graves en México.* UNICEF-Mexico, http://www.unicef.org/mexico/spanish/Diagnostico_adolescentes_web.pdf

Azaola, E., and Bergman, M. 2009. *Delincuencia, Marginalidad y Desempeño Institucional; Resultados de la Tercera encuesta de internos en reclusión de México.* México: CIDE.

Bergman, M., Fondevila, G., and Vilalta, C. 2015 *Delito y Desempeño Institucional en la Argentina: Resultados de la encuesta de presos Condenados.* Buenos Aires: UNTREF.

Bernburg, Jon Gunnar, and Krohn, Marvin D. 2003. "Labeling, Life Chances, and Adult Crime: The Direct and Indirect Effects of Official Intervention in Adolescence on Crime in Early Adulthood." *Criminology* 41: 1287–1318.

Biondi, C. 2010. *Junto e Misturado: Uma Etnografia do Pcc*. Sao Paulo: Terceiro Nome.

BJS. 2014. *Recidivism of Prisoners Released in 30 States in 2005: Patterns from 2005 to 2010*. NCJ 244205. Washington, DC: Bureau of Justice Statistics, http://www.bjs.gov/

Blumstein, A. 1995. "Prisons." In *Crime*, J. Q. Wilson and J. Petersilia, eds. San Francisco: Institute for Contemporary Studies, 91–117.

Blumstein, A., and Beck, A. J. 2005. "Reentry as a Transient State between Liberty and Recommitment." In *Prisoner reentry and Crime in America*, J. Travis and C. Visher, eds. Cambridge, UK: Cambridge University Press, 50–79.

Blumstein, A., and Wallman, J., eds. 2006. *Crime Drop in America*. 2nd Ed. New York: Cambridge Studies in Criminology.

Braga, Anthony A., Hureau, David M., and Papachristos, Andrew V. 2014. "Deterring Gang-Involved Gun Violence: Measuring the Impact of Boston's Operation Ceasefire on Street Gang Behavior." *Journal of Quantitative Criminology* 30 (1): 113–139.

Bureau of Justice Statistics. 2014 *Prisoners in 2013*, NCJ 247282, http://www.bjs.gov/content/pub/pdf/p13.pdf

Canela-Cacho, Jose A., Blumstein, Alfred, and Cohen, Jacqueline. 1997. "Relationship between the Offending Frequency (λ) of Imprisoned and Free Offenders." *Criminology* 35 (1): 133–176.

Carranza, E. 2012. "Situación penitenciaria en América Latina y el Caribe: Qué hacer?" *Anuario de los Derechos Humanos* 8: 31–66. http://www.anuariocdh.uchile.cl/index.php/ADH/issue/view/1970

CELS. 2011. *Mujeres en prisión: Los alcances del castigo*. Buenos Aires: Editorial.

CELS. 2015. *El Impacto de la Política de Drogas en los Derechos Humanos: La Experiencia del Continente Americano*. Buenos Aires: CELS https://www.cels.org.ar/web/publicacion-tipo/libros/page/2/

Cohen, J., and Canela Cacho, J. 1994 "Incarceration and Violent Crime 1965–1988." In *Understanding and Preventing Violence*. Vol. 4. *Consequences and Control*, A. Reiss and J. Roth, eds. Washington, DC: National Academy Press, 296–388.

The Economist. 2012. "Prisons in Latin America. A Journey into Hell." Sept. 2012. http://www.economist.com/node/21563288

Fagan, J., and Piquero, A. 2007. "Rational Choice and Developmental Influences on Recidivism among Adolescent Felony Offenders." *Journal of Empirical Legal Studies* 4 (4): 715–748.

Gendreau, Paul, Tracy, Little, and Claire, Goggin. 1996. "A Meta-analysis of the Predictors of Adult Offender Recidivism: What Works!" *Criminology* 34 (4): 575–607.

Green, D., and Winik, D. 2010. "Using Random Judge Assignment to Estimate the Effect of Incarceration and Probation on Recidivism Among Drug Offenders." *Criminology* 48 (2): 357–387.

IBA. 2010. *One in Five: The Crisis in Brazil's Prisons and Criminal Justice System.* International Bar Association Human Rights Institute Report, supported by the Open Society Institute.

ICPS. 2015. *World Prison Briefs Data.* International Center for Prison Studies, London. http://www.prisonstudies.org/world-prison-brief-data

Johnson, R., and Raphael, S. 2012. "How Much Crime Reduction Does the Marginal Prisoner Buy?" *Journal of Law and Economics* 55 (2): 275–310.

Jones, G., and Rodgers, D., eds. 2009. *Youth Violence in Latin America: Gangs and Juvenile Justice in Perspective.* London: Palgrave MacMillian.

Loughran, T., Mulvey, E., Schubert, J., Fagan, F., Piquero, A., and Losoya, H. 2009. "Estimating a Dose-Response Relationship between Length of Stay and Future Recidivism in Serious Juvenile Offenders." *Criminology* 47 (3): 699–740.

Lessing, B. 2013. *A Hole at the Center of the State: Prison Gangs and the Limits to Punitive Power.* CDDRL Working Papers, Vol. 143. Stanford University, Center on Democracy Development and the Rule of Law.

Lessing, B. Forthcoming. *Making Peace in Drug Wars: Crackdowns and Cartels in Latin America.* New York: Cambridge University Press.

Levitt, S. 1996. "The Effect of Prison Population Size on Crime Rates: Evidence from Prison Overcrowding Legislation." *Quarterly Journal of Economics* 111: 319–352.

Levitt, S. 1998. "Why do Increased Arrest Rates Appear to Reduce Crime: Deterrence, Incapacitation, or Measurement Error?" *Economic Inquiry* 36 (3): 353–372.

Liedka R., Piehl, A. M., and Useem, B. 2006. "The Crime Control Effect of Incarceration: Does Scale Matter?" *Criminology and Public Policy* 5 (2): 245–276.

Loeffler, C. 2011. *Estimating the Effects of Imprisonment on the Life-course.* PhD diss., Harvard University, Cambridge, MA.

Macauley, F. 2006. "Política carcerária e prisões." In *Segurança pública e violência,* Liana de Paula and Renato Sérgio de Lima, eds. São Paulo, Brazil: Editora Contexto, 15–29.

Macauley, F. 2013. "Modes of Prison Administration, Control and Governmentality in Latin America: Adoption, Adaptation, and Hybridity." *Conflict, Security and Development* 13 (4): 361–392.

MacKenzie, D. L. 1997. "Criminal Justice and Crime Prevention." In *Preventing Crime: What Works, What Doesn't, What's Promising,* L. W. Sherman, D. Gottfredson, D. MacKenzie, J. Eck, P. Reuter, and S. Bushway, eds. Washington, DC: National Institute of Justice, Department of Justice, 9: 1–76.

MJP. 2014. "Anuario Estadístico." Departamento de Investigación y Estadística. Instituto Nacional de Criminología. Ministerio de Justia y Paz. San José, Costa Rica. http://www.mjp.go.cr/Documento/Catalogo_DOCU/64

Nagin, D. 1998. "Criminal Deterrence Research at the Outset of the Twenty-First Century." In *Crime and Justice: A Review of Research*, Vol 23, Michael Tonry, ed. Chicago: University of Chicago Press.

Nagin, D. 2013. "Deterrence in the 21st Century: A Review of the Evidence." In *Crime and Justice: An Annual Review of Research*. M. Tonry, ed. Chicago: University of Chicago Press, 2: 211–268.

Nagin, Daniel S., Cullen, Francis T., and Jonson, Cheryl Lero. 2009. "Imprisonment and Re-offending." In *Crime and Justice: A Review of Research*, Vol. 38. M. Tonry, ed. Chicago: University of Chicago Press, 115–200.

Nagin, D., and Snodgrass, G. 2012. The Effect of Incarceration on Re-offending: Evidence from a Natural Experiment in Pennsylvania. Working Paper, Heinz College, Carnegie Mellon University, Pittsburgh.

Paternoster, R. 2010. "How Much Do We Really Know about Criminal Deterrence." *Journal of Criminal Law and Criminology* 100 (3): 765–823.

Petersilia, J. 2003. *When Prisoners Come Home: Parole and Prisoner Reentry*. New York: Oxford University Press.

Pogarsky, G., Piquero, A., and Paternoster, R. 2004. "Modeling Change in Perceptions about Sanction Threats: The Neglected Linkage in Deterrence Theory." *Journal of Quantitative Criminology* 20: 343–369.

Raphael, S., and Stoll, M. eds. *Do Prisons Make Us Safer? The Benefits and Costs of the Prison Boom*. New York: Russell Sage Foundation.

Salla, F., Ballesteros, P. R., Espinoza, O., Martínez, F., Litvachky, P., and Museri, A. 2009. *Democracy, Human Rights and Prison Conditions in South America*. Núcleo de Estudos da Violência Center for the Study of Violence University of São Paulo NEV/USP. São Paulo—Brazil, http://www.nevusp.org/downloads/down249.pdf

Sampson, Robert J., and Laub, John H. 1997. "A Life-Course Theory of Cumulative Disadvantage and the Stability of Delinquency." In *Developmental Theories of Crime and Delinquency*, Terrence P. Thornberry, ed. New Brunswick, NJ: Transaction Publishers.

Seiter, R., and Kadela, K. 2003. "Prisoner Reentry: What Works, What Doesn't, and What's Promising." *Crime and Delinquency* 49: 360–368.

Sharbek, David. 2011. "Governance and Prison Gangs." *American Political Science Review* 105 (4): 702–716.

SNEEP. 2008. *Informe Anual 2008*. Sistema Nacional de Estadísticas sobre la Ejecución de la Pena. Ministerio de Justicia. Buenos Aires. http://www.jus.gob.ar/media/1125557/Informe%20SNEEP%20ARGENTINA%202008.pdf

Steffensmeier, Darrell, and Ulmer, Jeffery T. 2005. *Confessions of a Dying Thief*. New Brunswick, NJ: Aldine/Transaction Publishers.

Travis, J., and Visher, C. 2005. *Prisoner Reentry and Public Safety: Introduction*. In *Prisoner Reentry and Crime in America*, J. Travis and C. Visher, eds. New York: Cambridge University Press, 1–12.

Tonry, M., and Petersilia, J. 1999. "American Prisons at the Beginning of the Twenty-First Century." In *Crime and Justice: A Review of Research*, Vol. 26. Chicago: University of Chicago Press.

UNDP. 2013. *Citizen Security with a Human Face: Evidence and Proposals for Latin America*. Regional Human Development Report 2013–2014.

Ungar, M. 2003. "Prisons and Politics in Contemporary Latin America" *Human Rights Quarterly* 25 (4): 909–934.

UNODC. 2014. *Global Study of Homicide 2013*. Vienna: United Nations, https://www.unodc.org/documents/gsh/pdfs/2014_GLOBAL_HOMICIDE_BOOK_web.pdf

Vilalta, C. 2015. *Tendencias y proyecciones globales en la violencia homicida: 2000 a 2030*. Instituto Igarapé. Notas sobre Homicidios 2, https://igarape.org.br/outras-publicacoes/

Wacquant, L. 2000. *Las cárceles de la miseria*. Buenos Aires: Manantial.

Western, B., Braga, A., Davis, J., and Sirois, C. 2015. Stress and Hardship after Prison. *American Journal of Sociology* 120 (15): 1512–1547.

WOLA. 2010. "Sistemas sobrecargados: Leyes de drogas y cárceles en América Latina. Reformas a las Leyes de Drogas en América Latina." Washington, DC. www.wola.org/es/informes/sistemas_sobrecargados_leyes_de_drogas_y_carceles_en_america_latina

Zimring, F. 2006. *The Great American Crime Decline*. Oxford: Oxford University Press.

Index